FIRE FORCE

23

ATSUSHI OHKUBO

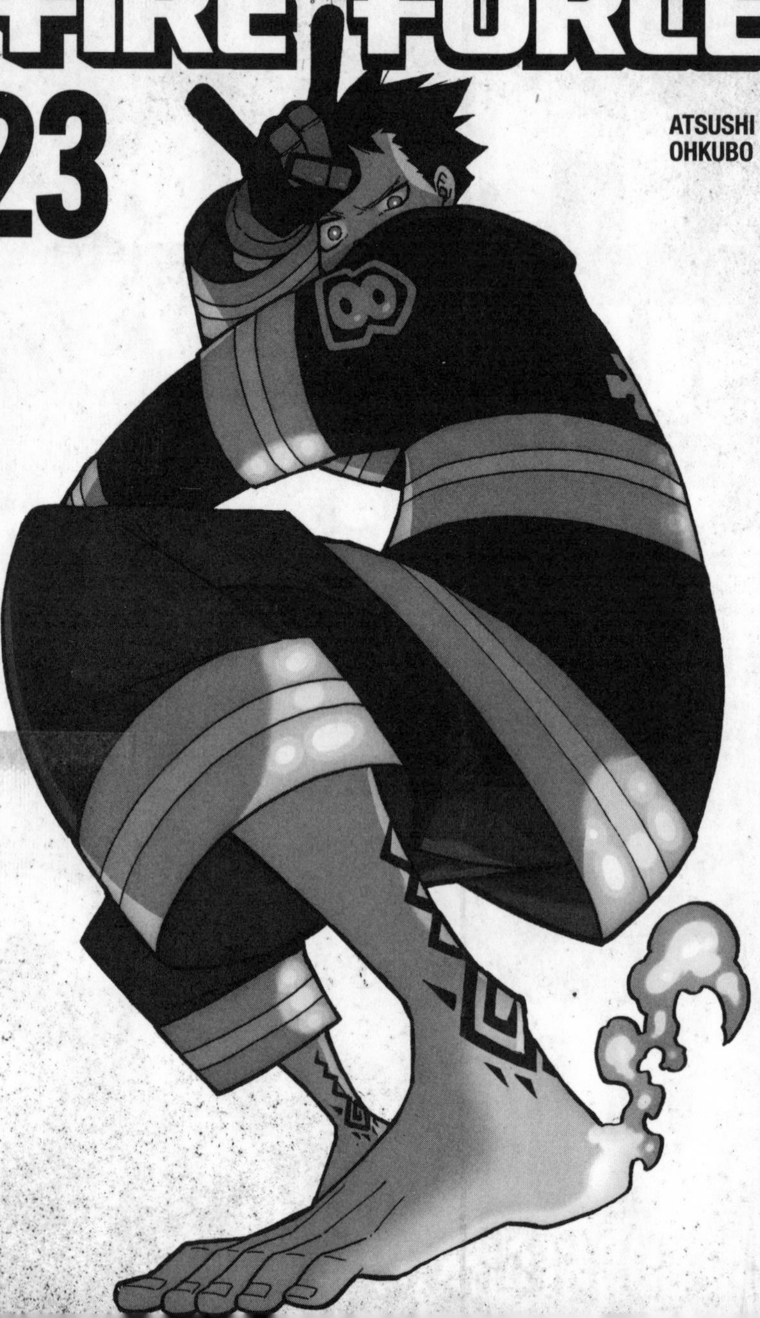

truth surely the light.

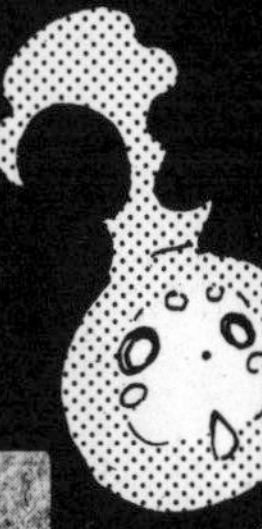

VOL. 23

ATSUSHI OHKUBO

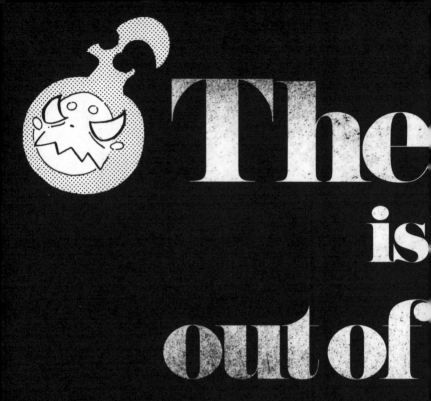

The
is
out of

FIRE FORCE

FIRE FORCE: SPECIAL FIRE FORCE ROSTER OF FIRE SOLDIERS

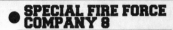

SPECIAL FIRE FORCE COMPANY 8

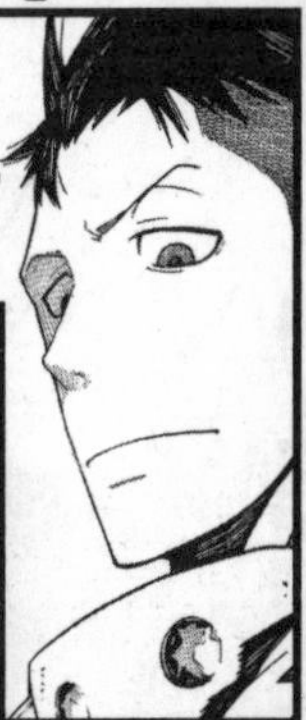

CAPTAIN (NON-POWERED)

AKITARU ŌBI

The caring leader of the newly established Company 8. He has no powers, but uses his finely honed muscles as a weapon in a battle style that makes him worthy of the Captain title. Currently he is being detained by the military.

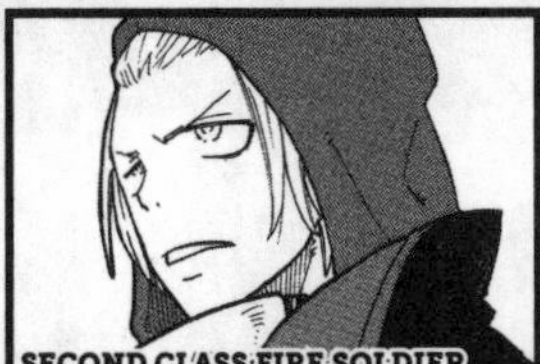

SECOND CLASS FIRE SOLDIER (THIRD GENERATION PYROKINETIC)

ARTHUR BOYLE

Trained at the academy with Shinra. He follows his own personal code of chivalry as the self-proclaimed Knight King. He's a blockhead who is bad at mental exercise. He's a weirdo who grows stronger the more delusional he gets. In Fuchū, he confronts the Destroyer Dragon and loses Excalibur.

WATCHES OUT FOR

TRUSTS

IDIOT!!

WATCHES OUT FOR

TRUSTS

STRONG BOND

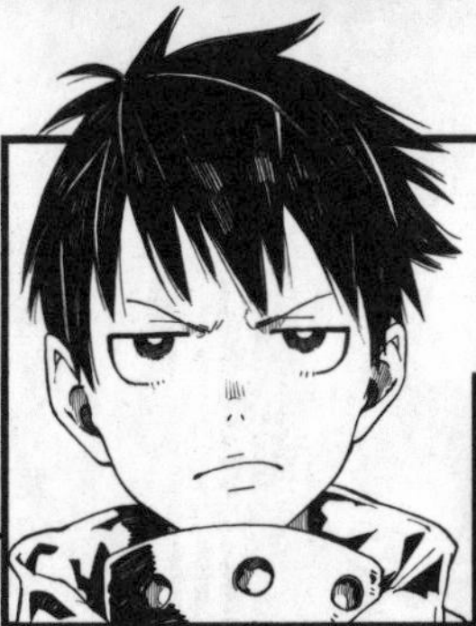

SECOND CLASS FIRE SOLDIER (THIRD GENERATION PYROKINETIC)

SHINRA KUSAKABE

Dreams of becoming a hero who saves people from spontaneous combustion! His weapon is a fiery kick. He wields a special flame called the Adolla Burst. In Fuchū, he fights an intense battle against Burns to save Captain Ōbi. What he sees at its end is...

A NICE GIRL

LOOKS AWESOME ON THE JOB

A TOUGH BUT WEIRD LADY

HANG IN THERE, ROOKIE!

TERRIFIED

STRICT DISCIPLINARIAN

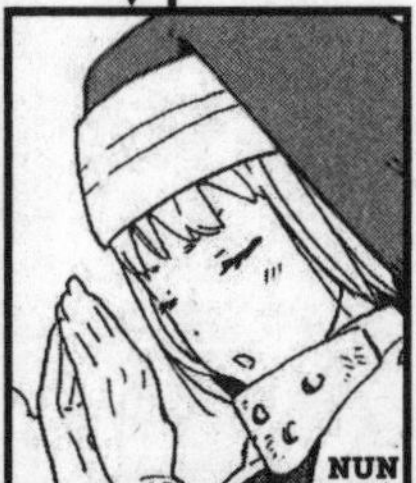

NUN (NON-POWERED)

IRIS

A sister of the Holy Sol Temple, her prayers are an indispensable part of extinguishing infernals. She has demonstrated incredible resilience in facing the infernal hordes.

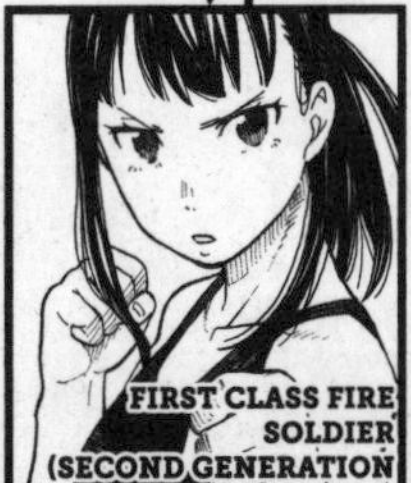

FIRST CLASS FIRE SOLDIER (SECOND GENERATION PYROKINETIC)

MAKI OZE

A former member of the military, she is an excellent fighter who controls fire. She's a cool lady, but is mad about love stories, and her beauty is overshadowed by her "head full of flowers and wedding bells."

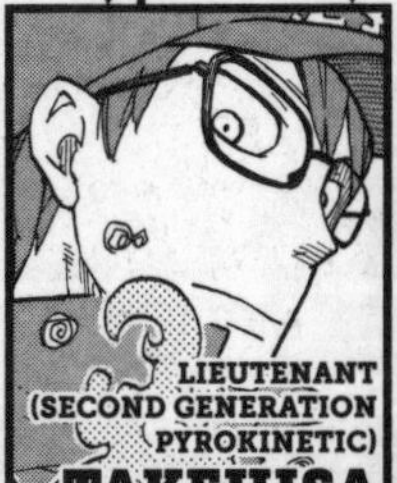

LIEUTENANT (SECOND GENERATION PYROKINETIC)

TAKEHISA HINAWA

A dry, unemotional ex-military man, whose stern discipline is feared among the new recruits. The gun he uses is a cherished memento from his friend who became an infernal.

THE GIRLS' CLUB

RESPECTS

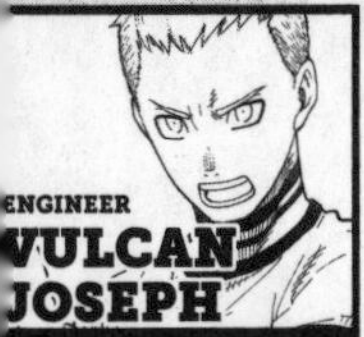

ENGINEER

VULCAN JOSEPH

The greatest engineer of the day, renowned as the God of Fire and the Forge. The weapons he created have increased Company 8's powers immensely.

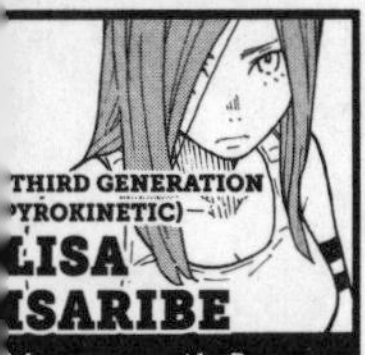

THIRD GENERATION PYROKINETIC

LISA ISARIBE

A former spy sent by Dr. Giovanni, she is now a member of Company 8. She controls tentacles of flame.

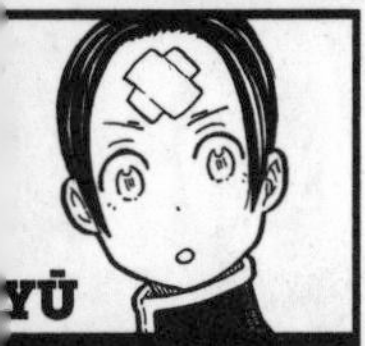

YŪ

A self-proclaimed apprentice of Vulcan's. Has now recovered from the injuries inflicted by Dr. Giovanni.

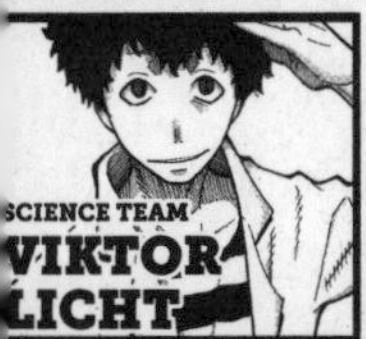

SCIENCE TEAM

VIKTOR LICHT

A genius deployed to Company 8 from Haijima industries. Has confessed to being a Haijima spy.

HAS HIM ON HER MIND

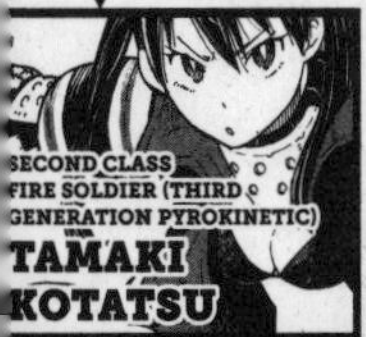

SECOND CLASS FIRE SOLDIER (THIRD GENERATION PYROKINETIC)

TAMAKI KOTATSU

A rookie from Company 1 currently in Company 8's care. She controls nekomata-like flames.

SPECIAL FIRE FORCE COMPANY 5

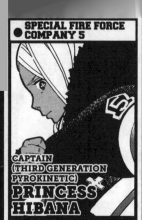

CAPTAIN (THIRD GENERATION PYROKINETIC)
PRINCESS HIBANA

An imperious former woman of the cloth. Has a crush on Shinra. Surmises that the key to finding the truth of SHC may be at the convent where she and iris grew up...

SPECIAL FIRE FORCE COMPANY 1

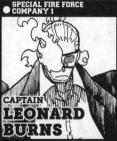

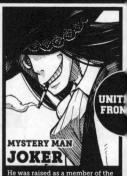

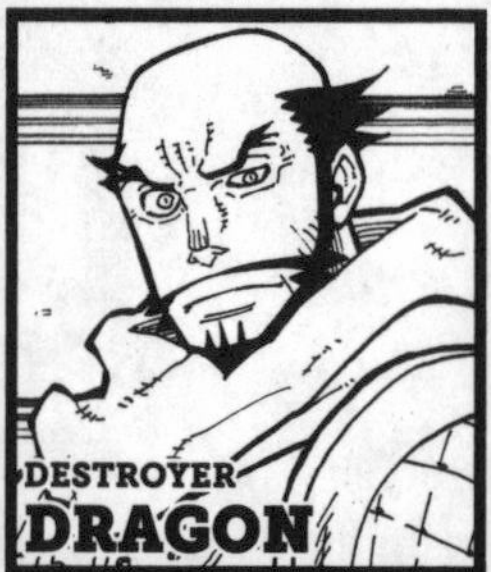

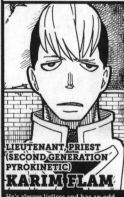

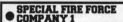

LIEUTENANT, PRIEST (SECOND GENERATION PYROKINETIC)
KARIM FLAM

He's always listless and has an odd speech pattern, but is an excellent fire soldier. He uses thermoacoustic cooling to freeze flames.

HOLY SOL TEMPLE + "EVANGELIST"

SPECIAL FIRE FORCE COMPANY 1

CAPTAIN
LEONARD BURNS

Following an intense battle with Shinra, he demonstrates his chosen way of life and becomes a martyr.

DESTROYER
DRAGON

Has subdued Arthur using dragonic powers befitting his name.

TRAITORS TO THE EMPIRE

VS.

CAPTORS OF THE CAPTAIN

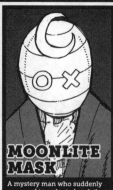

MOONLITE MASK

A mystery man who suddenly appeared in order to break the stalemate between Company 8 and their White Clad enemies! Who is he really?!

MYSTERY MAN
JOKER

He was raised as a member of the Holy Sol Temple's secret death squad, the Holy Sol's Shadow, but has left the organization. He searches for the world's truth.

UNIT
FRON

SUMMARY

The Holy Sol Temple has joined forces with the Evangelist. To rescue Captain Ōbi from their clutches, Company 8 teams up with Joker, and together they storm Fuchū Grand Penitentiary. Shinra fights through the press of death to gain the upper hand against Burns, only to see Burns impaled by a one-eyed Demon.

As the rest of Company 8 struggles against the attacks of the Destroyer Dragon, more White Clad enemies appear, and Haumea states that they will kill all but the Pillars. Company 8, Shinra, and Joker move to retreat. Then in the midst of the chaos, a mysterious personage calling himself Moonlite Mask suddenly enters the scene!

SPUTT

FIRE FORCE 23
CONTENTS

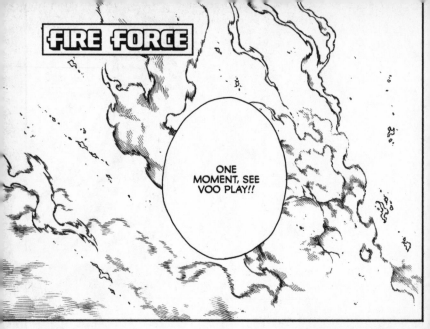

ONE
MOMENT, SEE
VOO PLAY!!

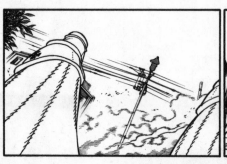

WHO
GOES
THERE?

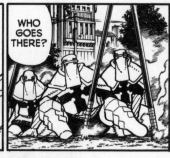

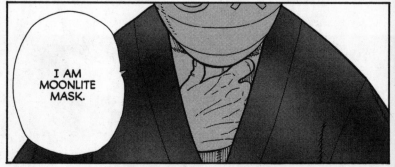

I AM
MOONLITE
MASK.

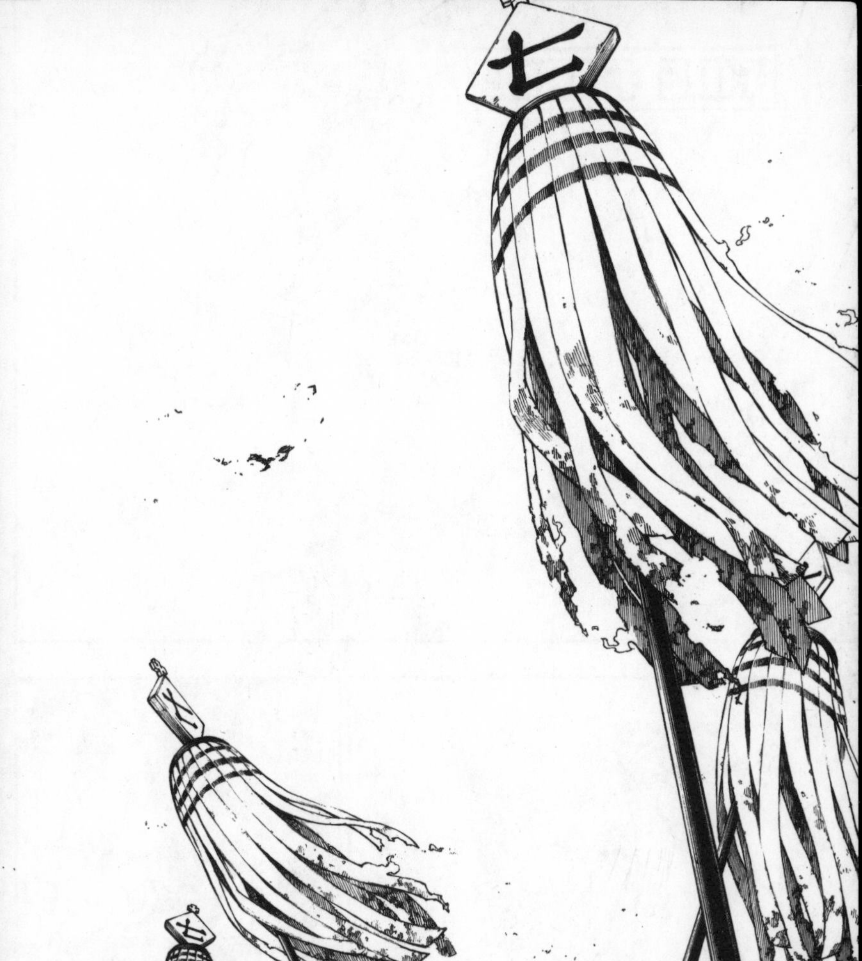
七

MOONLIGHT RESCUE

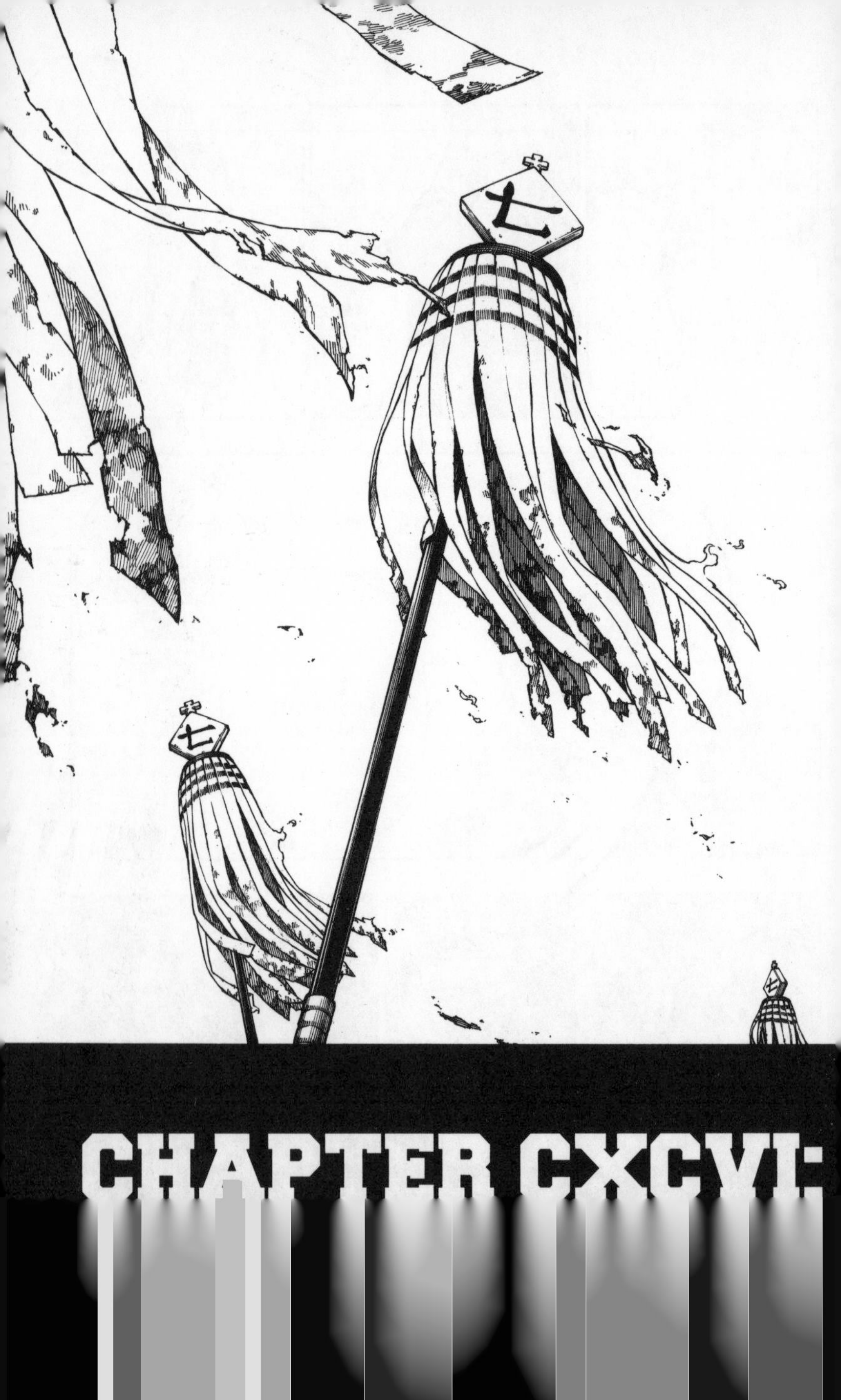
七
七

CHAPTER CXCVI:

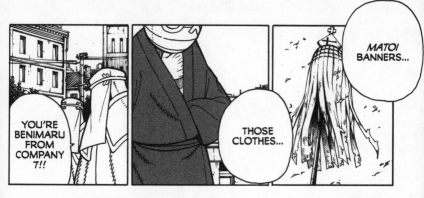

MATOI BANNERS...
THOSE CLOTHES...
YOU'RE BENIMARU FROM COMPANY 7!!
ONE MOMENT, SEE VOO PLAY.
I AM MOONLITE MASK.
MUCH AS ASAKUSA HATES THE EMPIRE, THERE'S NO POINT IN BECOMING THEIR ENEMY.
IS THAT WHY I HAVE TO WEAR THIS STUPID THING?
AND WEAR YOUR *HAPPI* COAT BACKWARDS. ...LISTEN, WAKA. YOU CAN THROW THEM OFF BY SAYING, "ONE MOMENT, SEE VOO PLAY."

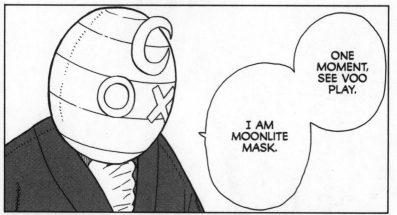

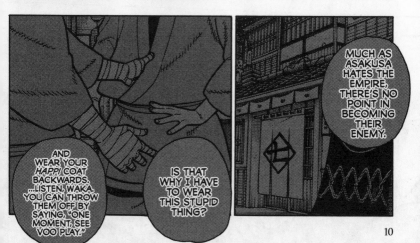

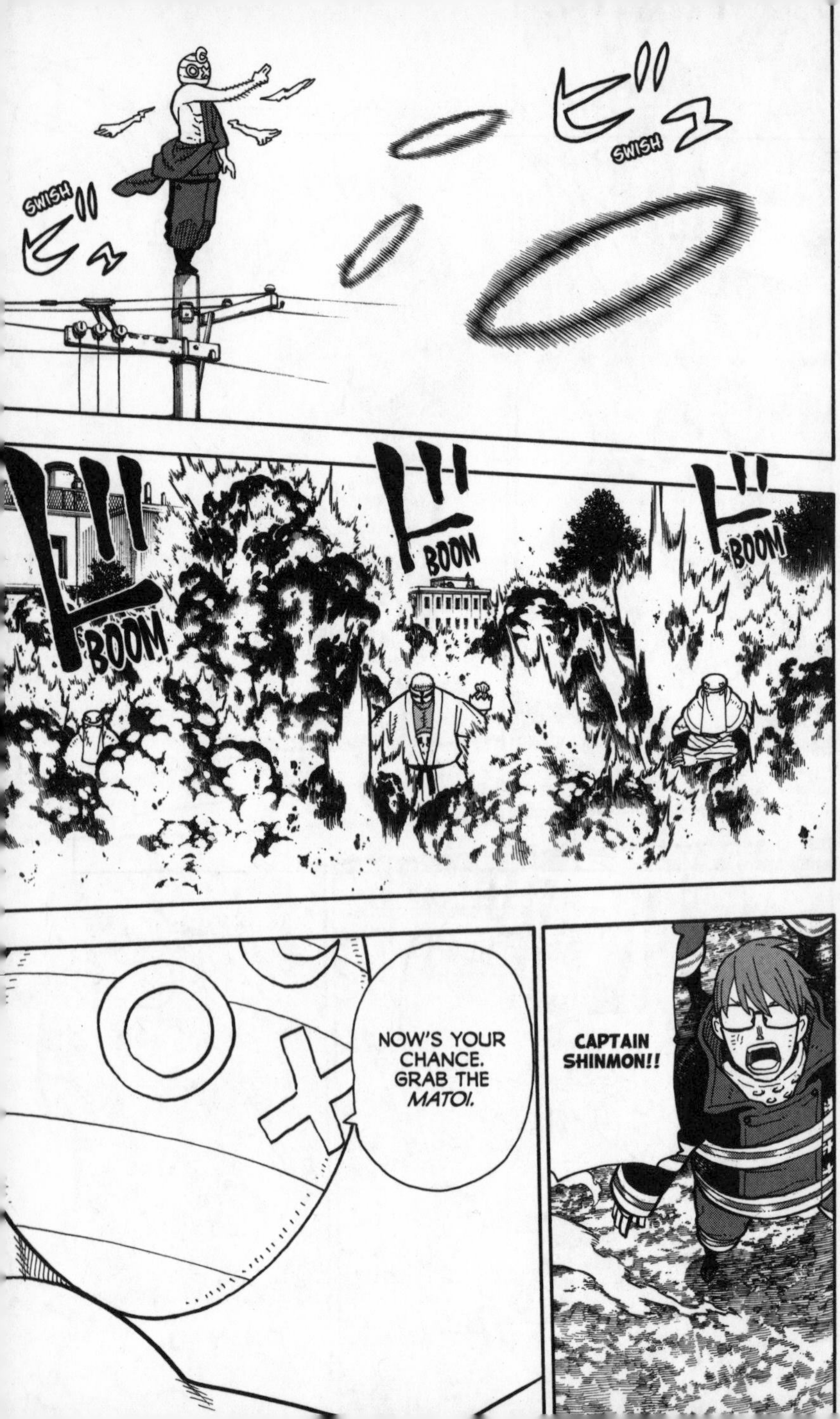
ビュ
SWISH
SWISH
ビュ
ド
BOOM
ド
BOOM
ド
BOOM
CAPTAIN SHINMON!!
NOW'S YOUR CHANCE. GRAB THE *MATOI.*

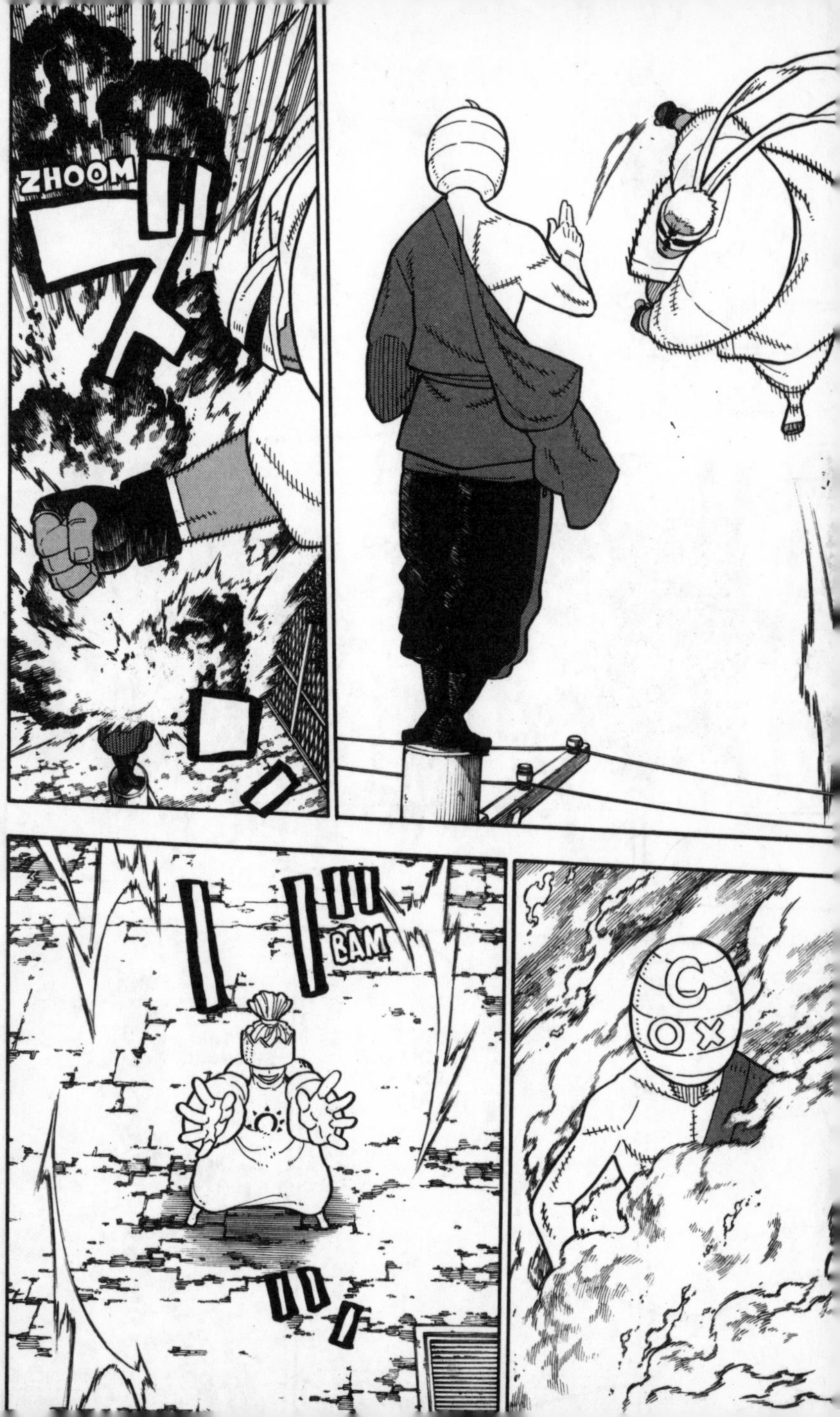
ZHOOM
C
O X
BAM

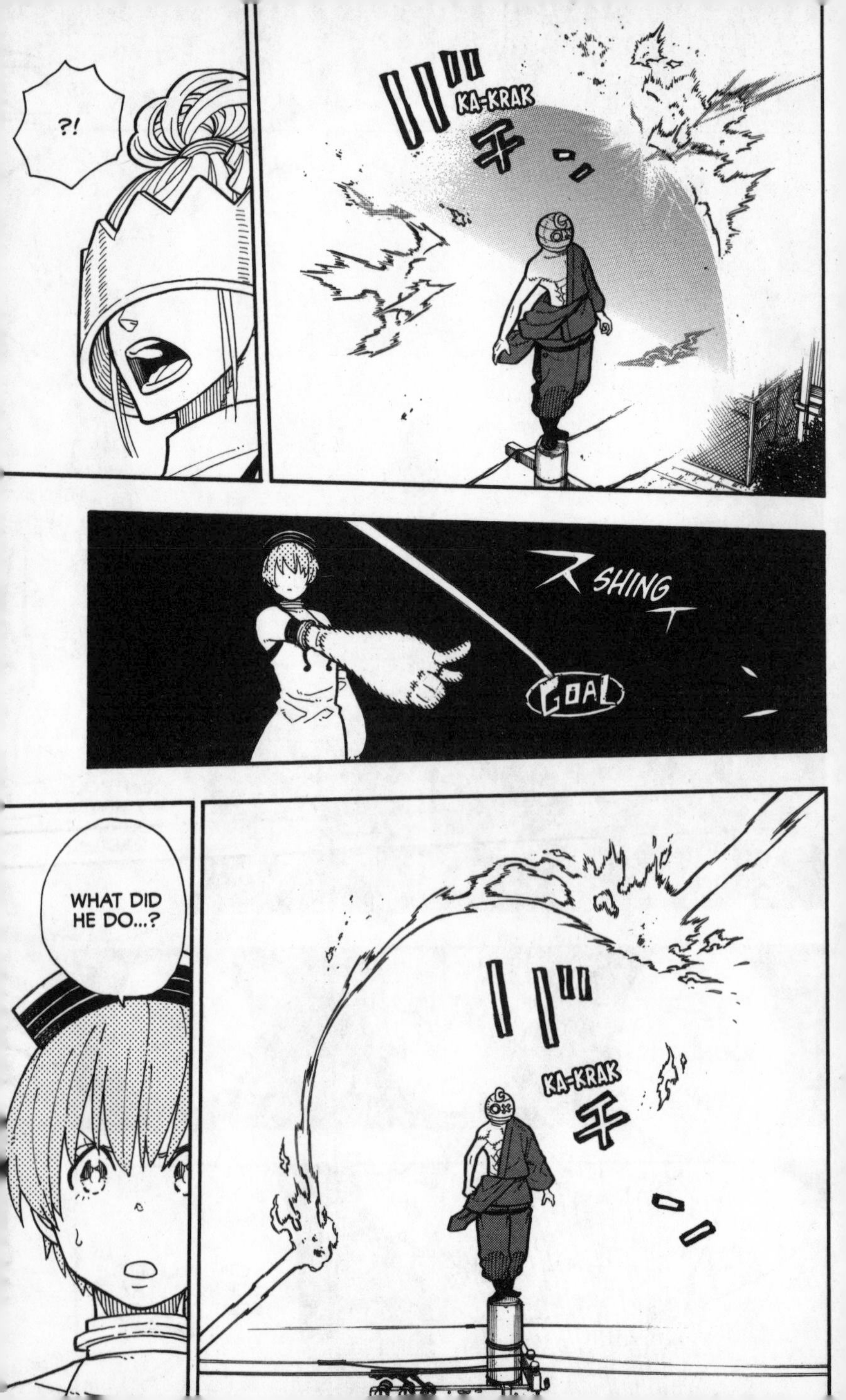
KA-KRAK
?!
SHING
GOAL
KA-KRAK
WHAT DID HE DO...?

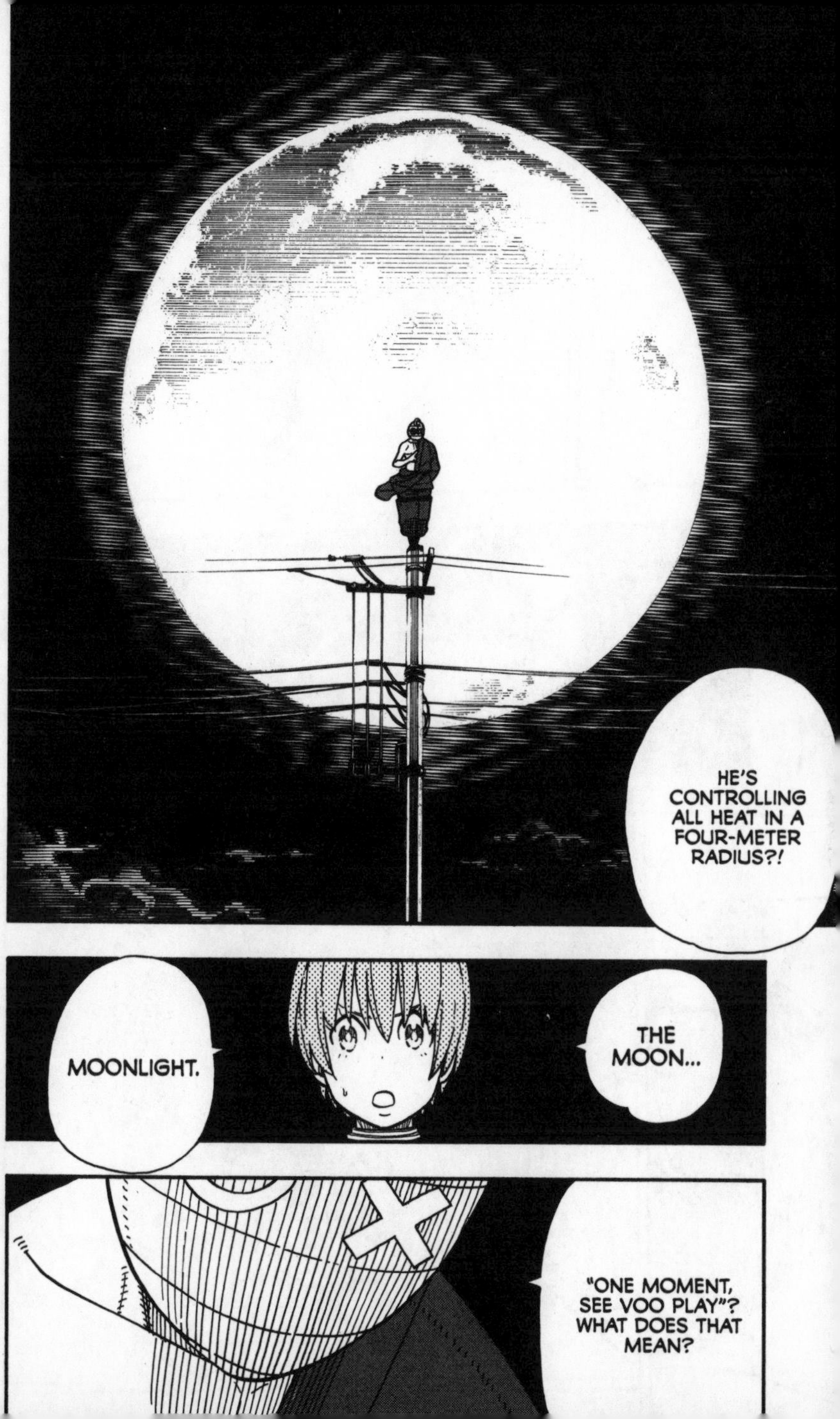
HE'S CONTROLLING ALL HEAT IN A FOUR-METER RADIUS?!
THE MOON...
MOONLIGHT.
"ONE MOMENT, SEE VOO PLAY"? WHAT DOES THAT MEAN?

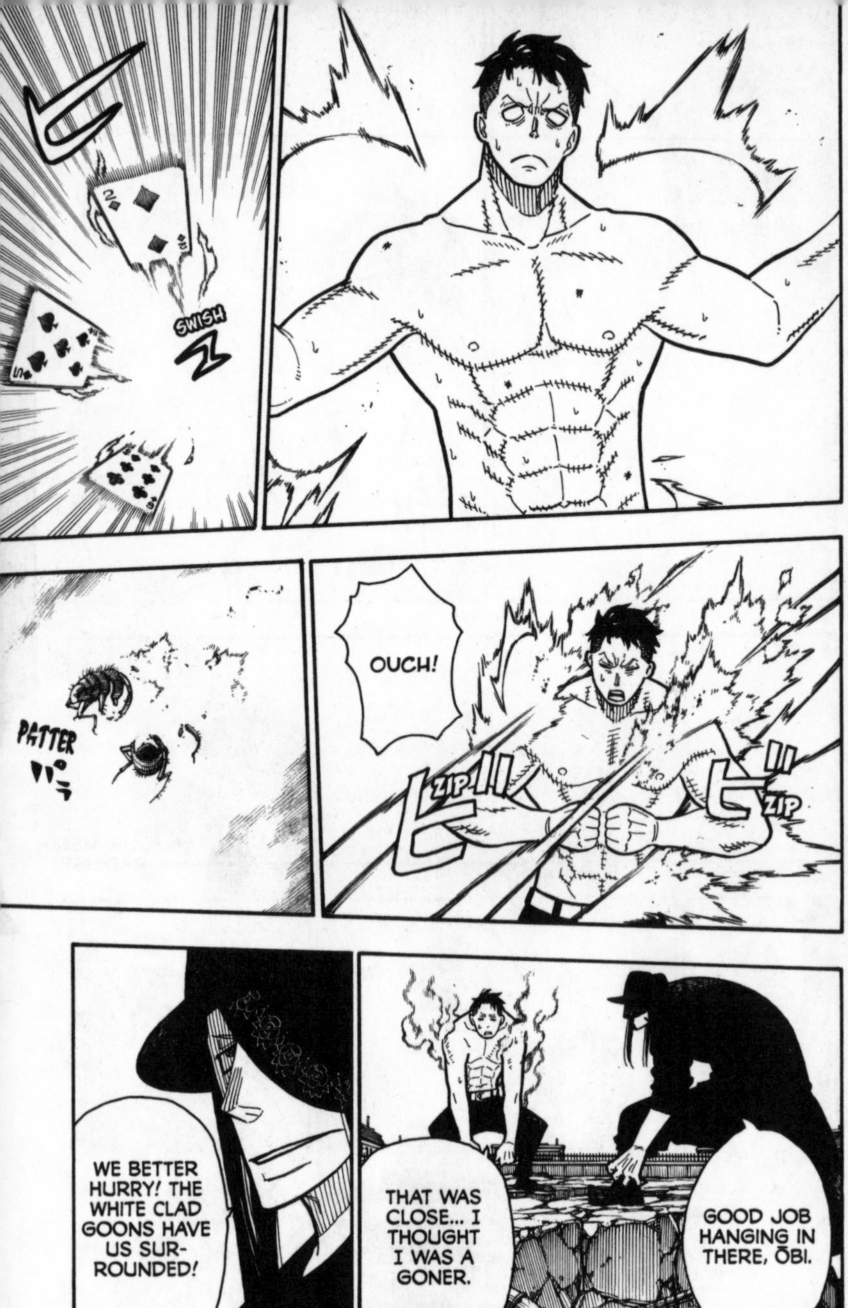
SWISH
OUCH!
ZIP
ZIP
PATTER
GOOD JOB HANGING IN THERE, ŌBI.
THAT WAS CLOSE... I THOUGHT I WAS A GONER.
WE BETTER HURRY! THE WHITE CLAD GOONS HAVE US SUR-ROUNDED!

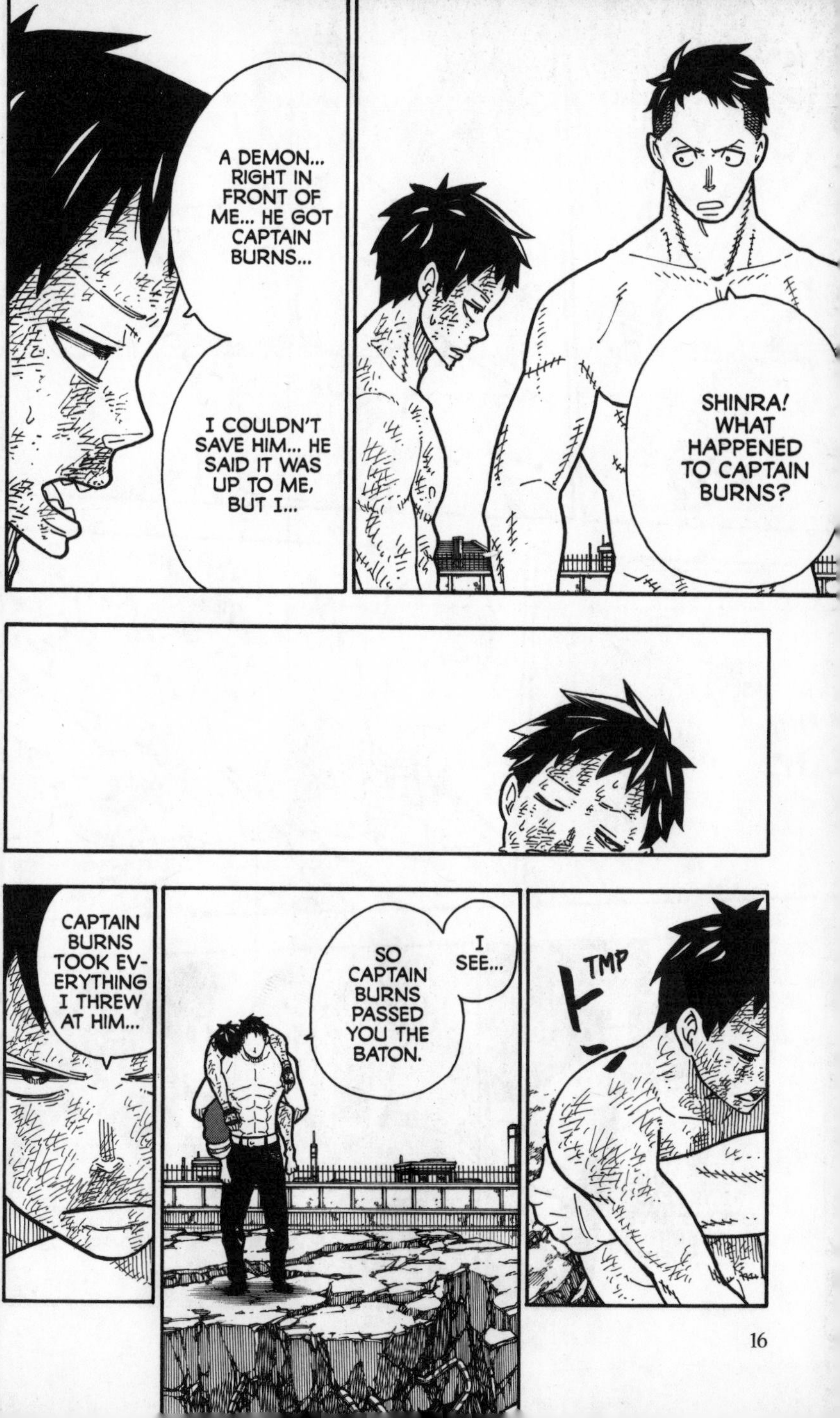
SHINRA! WHAT HAPPENED TO CAPTAIN BURNS?
A DEMON... RIGHT IN FRONT OF ME... HE GOT CAPTAIN BURNS...
I COULDN'T SAVE HIM... HE SAID IT WAS UP TO ME, BUT I...
TMP
I SEE...
SO CAPTAIN BURNS PASSED YOU THE BATON.
CAPTAIN BURNS TOOK EV-ERYTHING I THREW AT HIM...

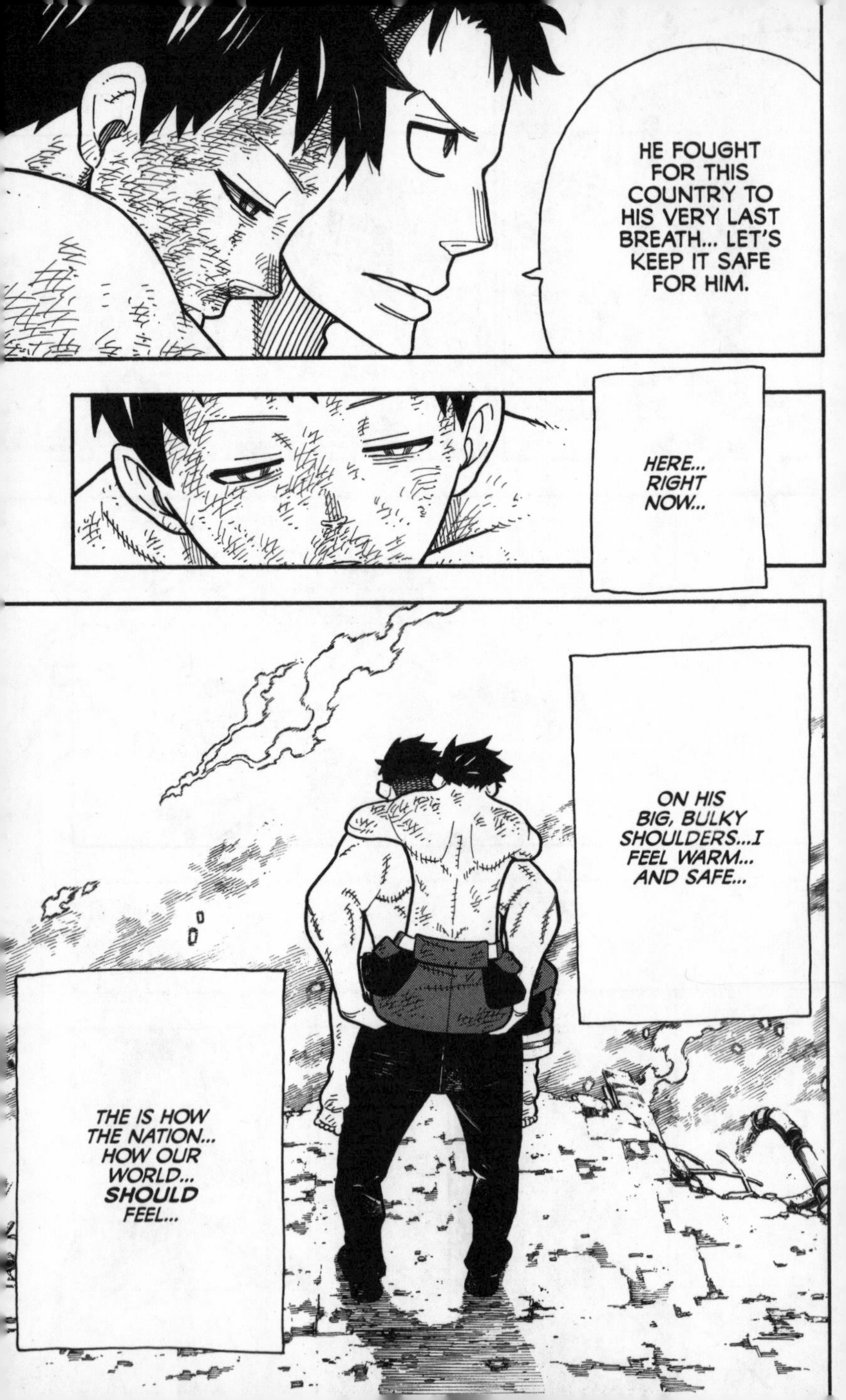
HE FOUGHT FOR THIS COUNTRY TO HIS VERY LAST BREATH... LET'S KEEP IT SAFE FOR HIM.
HERE... RIGHT NOW...
ON HIS BIG, BULKY SHOULDERS...I FEEL WARM... AND SAFE...
THE IS HOW THE NATION... HOW OUR WORLD... SHOULD FEEL...

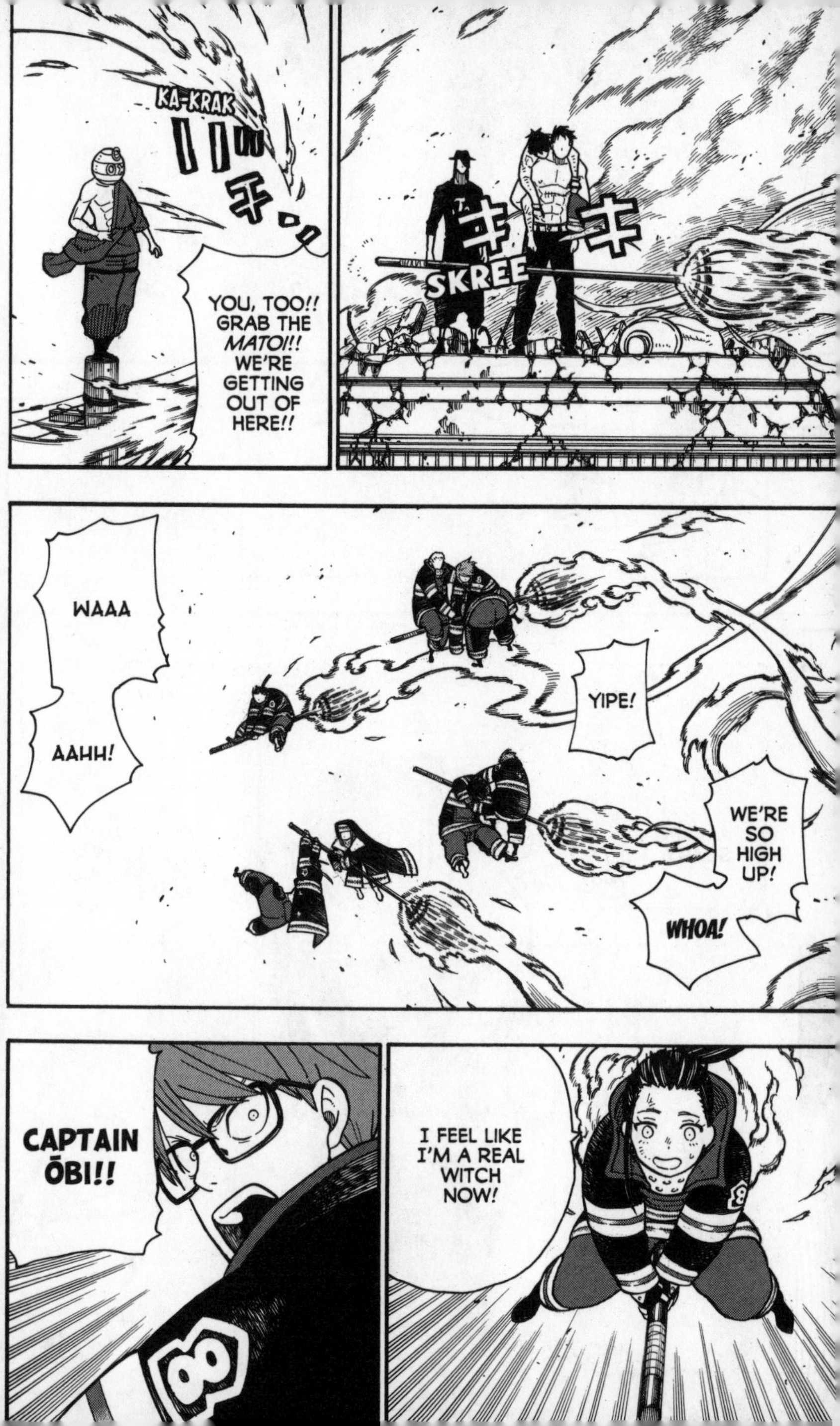
SKREE
KA-KRAK
YOU, TOO!! GRAB THE *MATOI*!! WE'RE GETTING OUT OF HERE!!
YIPE!
WE'RE SO HIGH UP!
WHOA!
WAAA
AAHH!
I FEEL LIKE I'M A REAL WITCH NOW!
CAPTAIN ŌBI!!

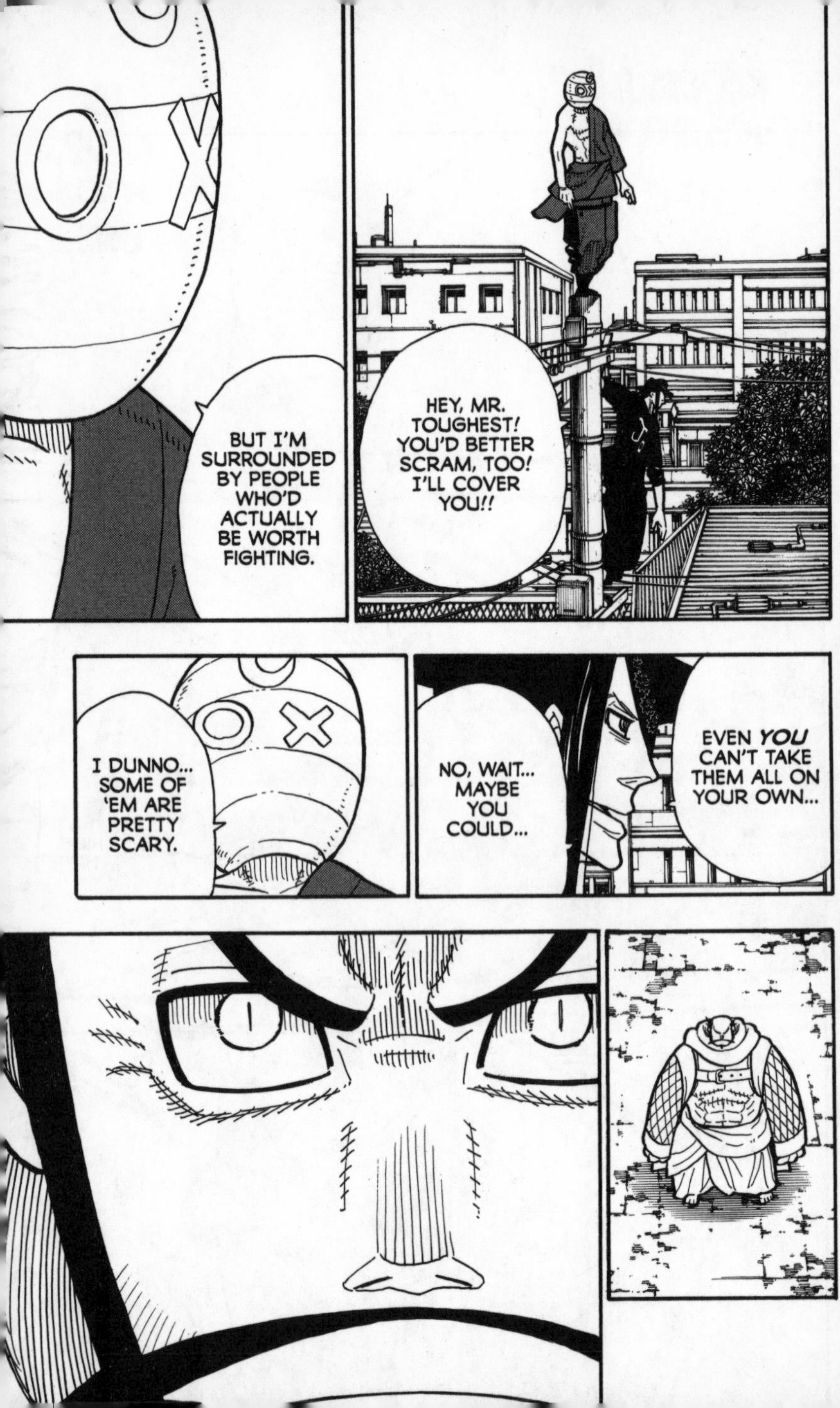
HEY, MR. TOUGHEST! YOU'D BETTER SCRAM, TOO! I'LL COVER YOU!!
BUT I'M SURROUNDED BY PEOPLE WHO'D ACTUALLY BE WORTH FIGHTING.
EVEN *YOU* CAN'T TAKE THEM ALL ON YOUR OWN...
NO, WAIT... MAYBE YOU COULD...
I DUNNO... SOME OF 'EM ARE PRETTY SCARY.

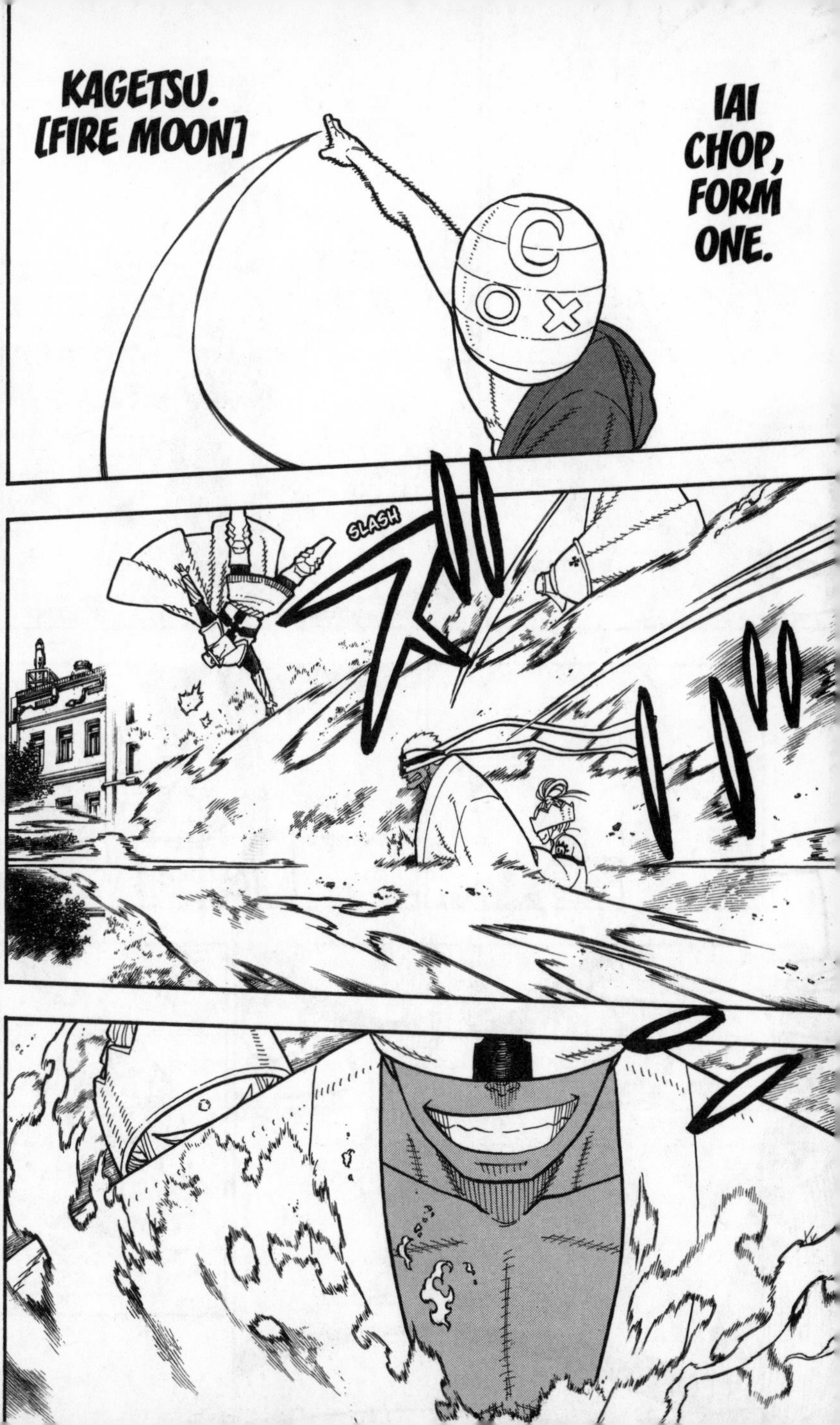
IAI CHOP, FORM ONE.
KAGETSU. [FIRE MOON]
SLASH

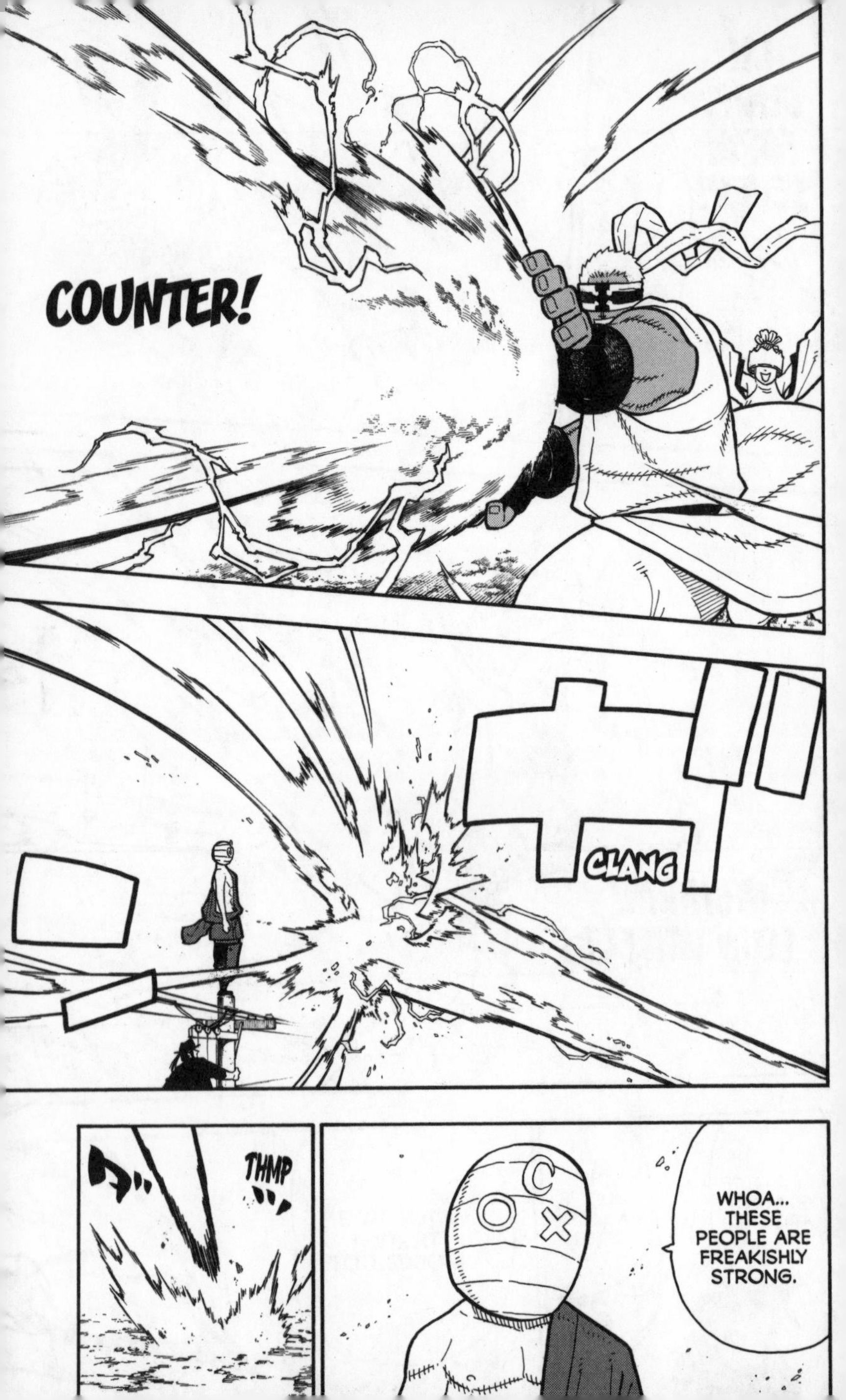COUNTER!
CLANG
WHOA... THESE PEOPLE ARE FREAKISHLY STRONG.
THMP

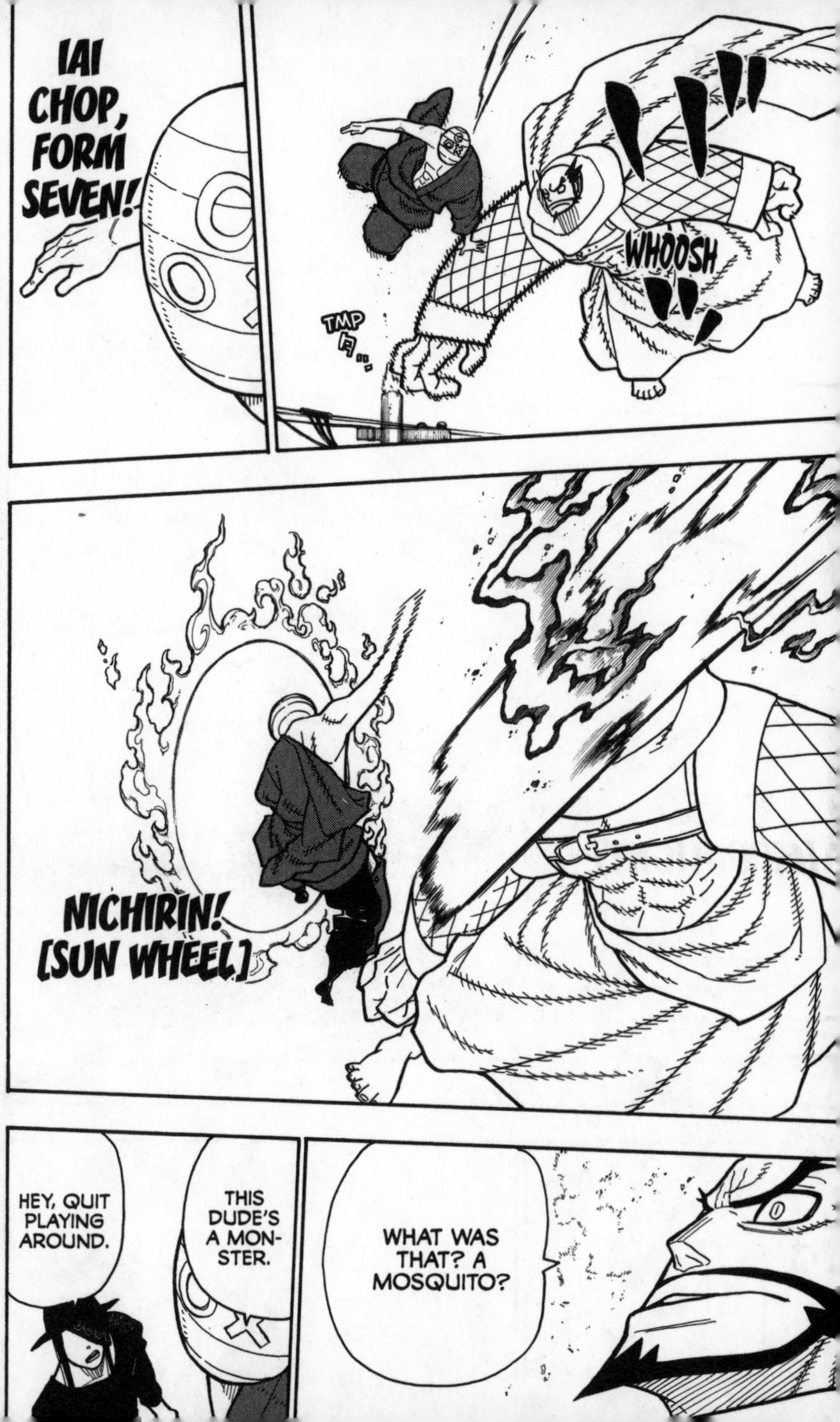
WHOOSH
TMP
IAI CHOP, FORM SEVEN!
NICHIRIN! [SUN WHEEL]
WHAT WAS THAT? A MOSQUITO?
THIS DUDE'S A MON-STER.
HEY, QUIT PLAYING AROUND.

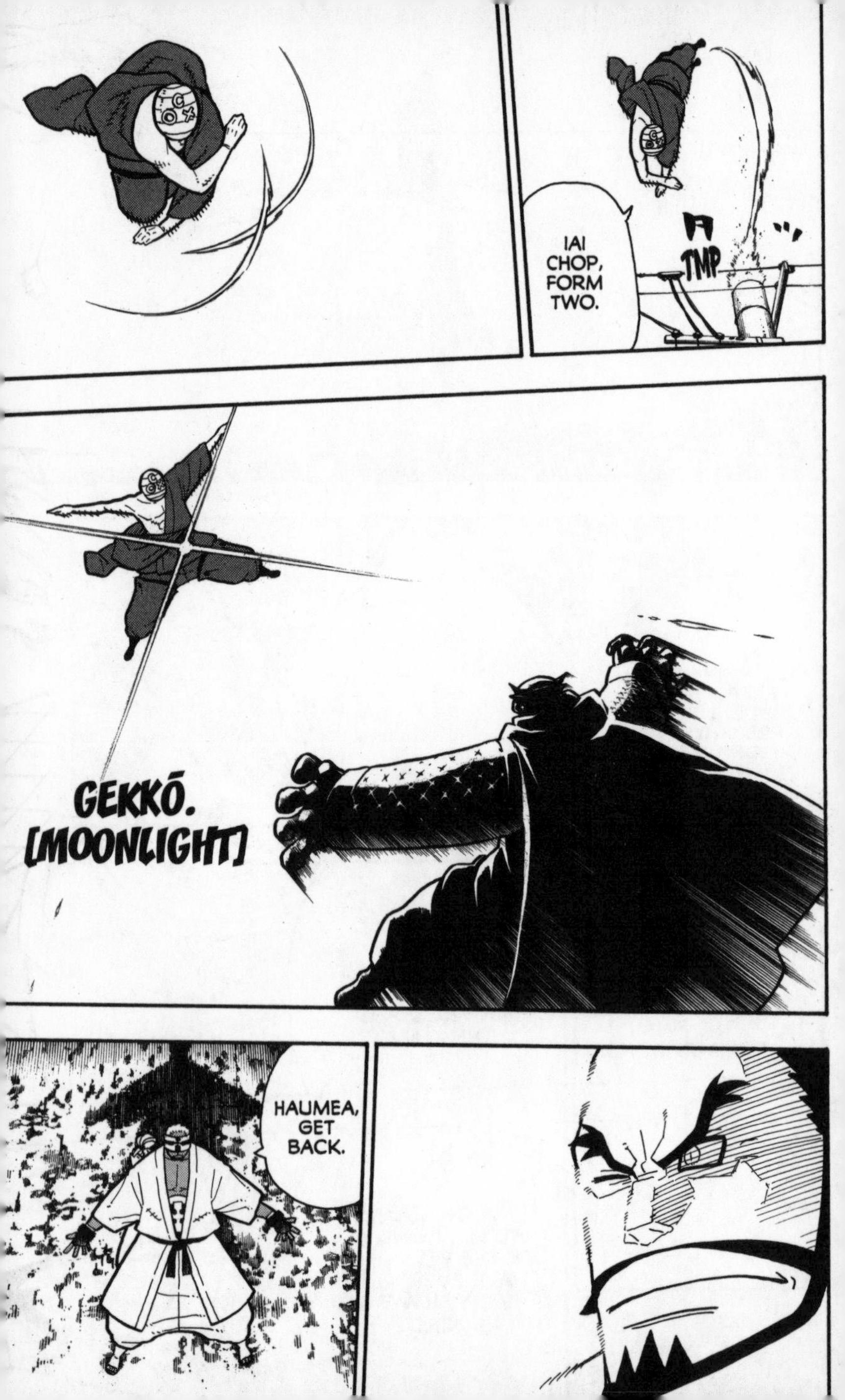
IAI CHOP, FORM TWO.
TMP
GEKKŌ. [MOONLIGHT]
HAUMEA, GET BACK.

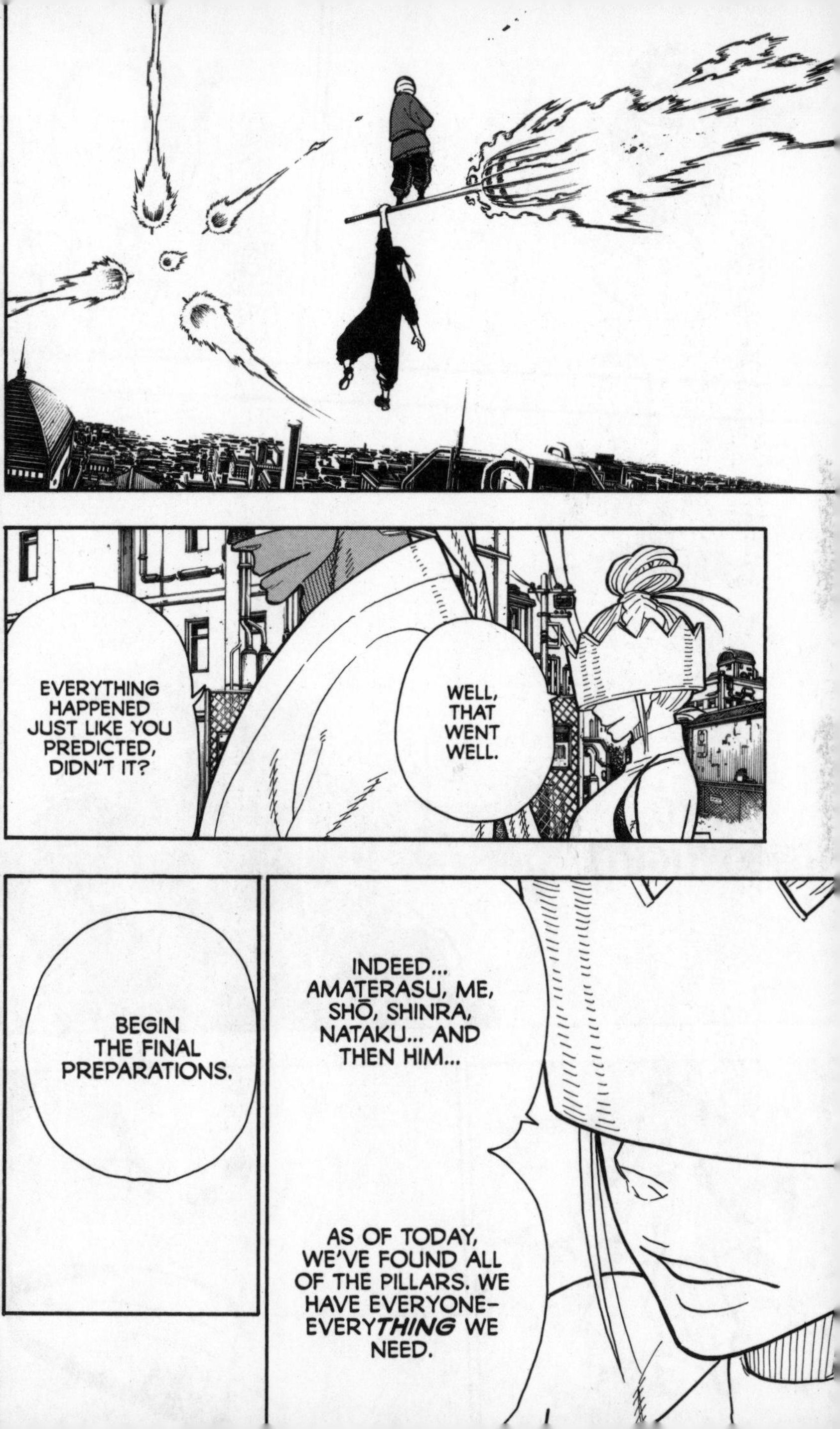
WELL, THAT WENT WELL.
EVERYTHING HAPPENED JUST LIKE YOU PREDICTED, DIDN'T IT?
INDEED... AMATERASU, ME, SHŌ, SHINRA, NATAKU... AND THEN HIM...
AS OF TODAY, WE'VE FOUND ALL OF THE PILLARS. WE HAVE EVERYONE– EVERYTHING WE NEED.
BEGIN THE FINAL PREPARATIONS.

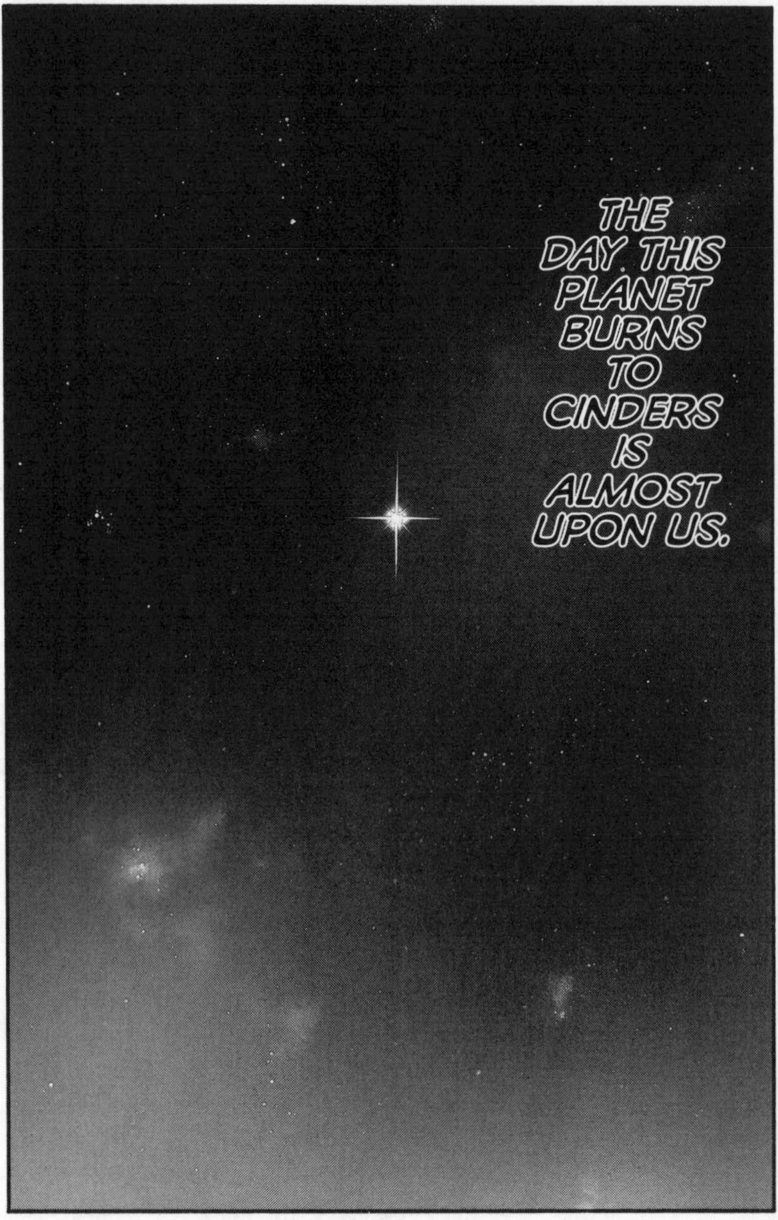
THE DAY THIS PLANET BURNS TO CINDERS IS ALMOST UPON US.

FIRE FORCE

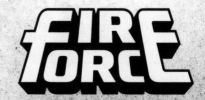

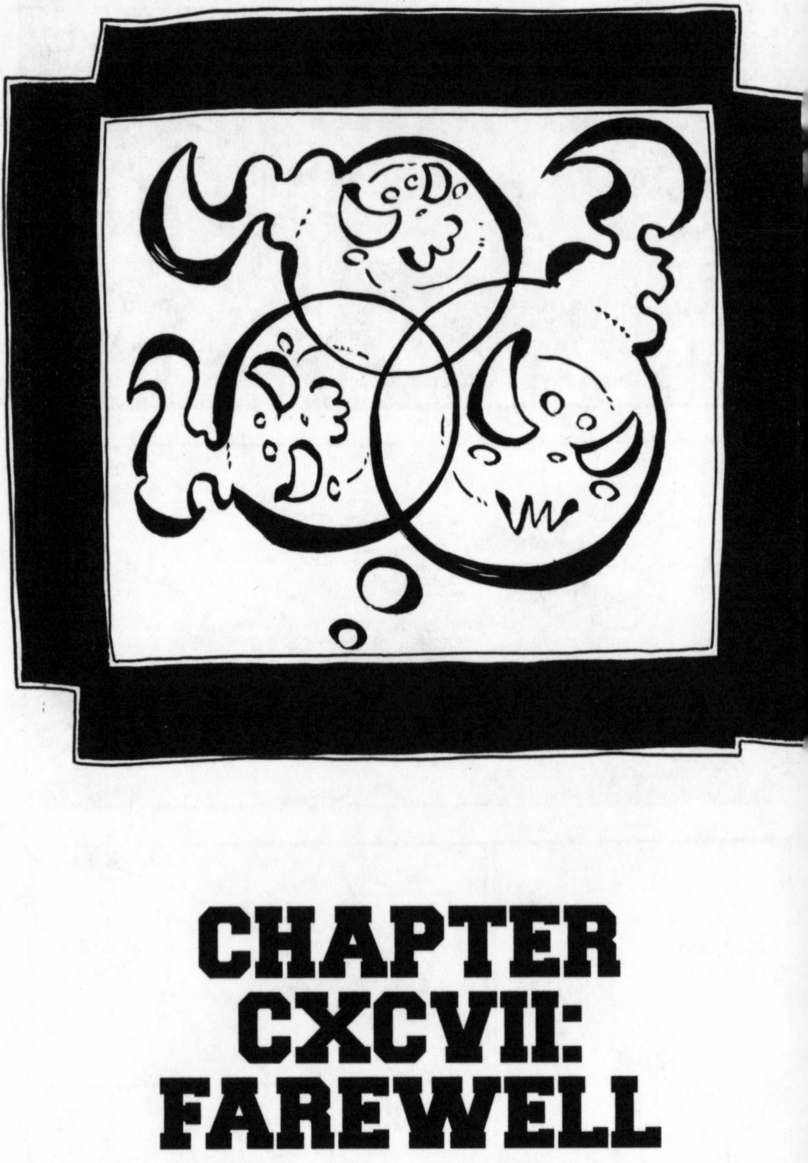

CHAPTER CXCVII: FAREWELL

Sign: Asakusa Handmade Udon Muranishi

Sign: Tsurukame Flagship Store

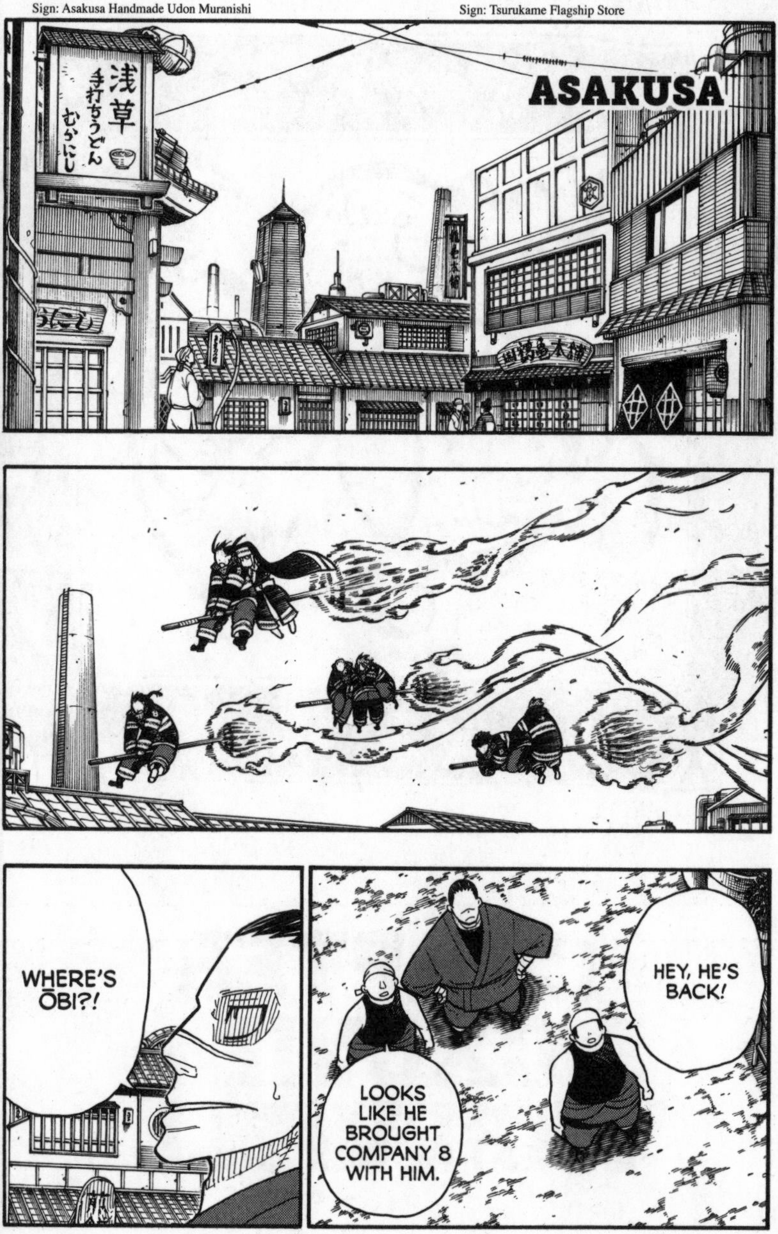
ASAKUSA
HEY, HE'S BACK!
LOOKS LIKE HE BROUGHT COMPANY 8 WITH HIM.
WHERE'S ŌBI?!

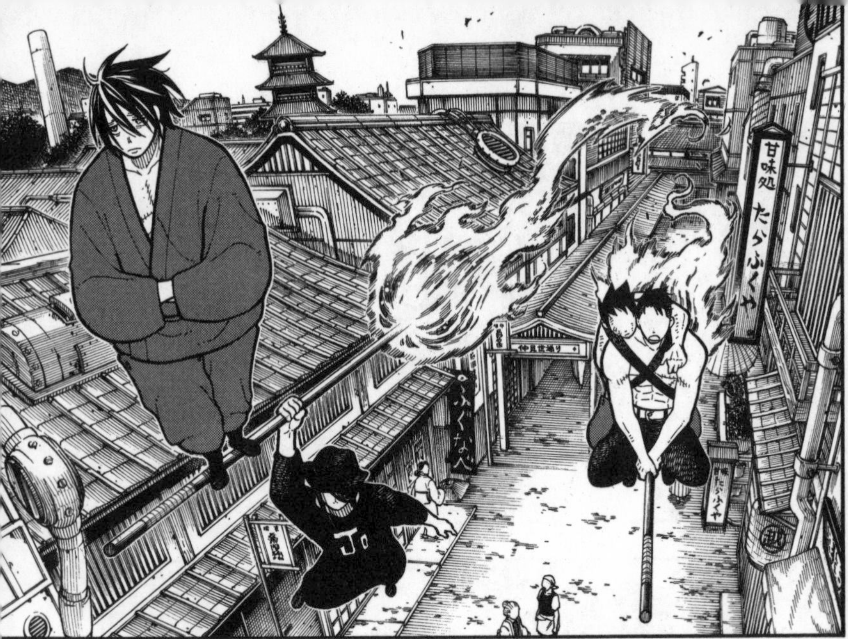
甘味処 たらふくや
仲見世通り
Sign: Blowfish Stew Sign: Nakamise Shopping Street Sign: Tarafukuya Sweets

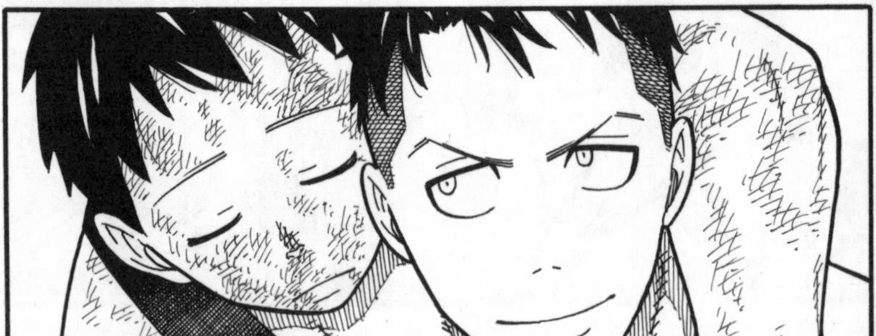

Sign: Asakusa Rusk

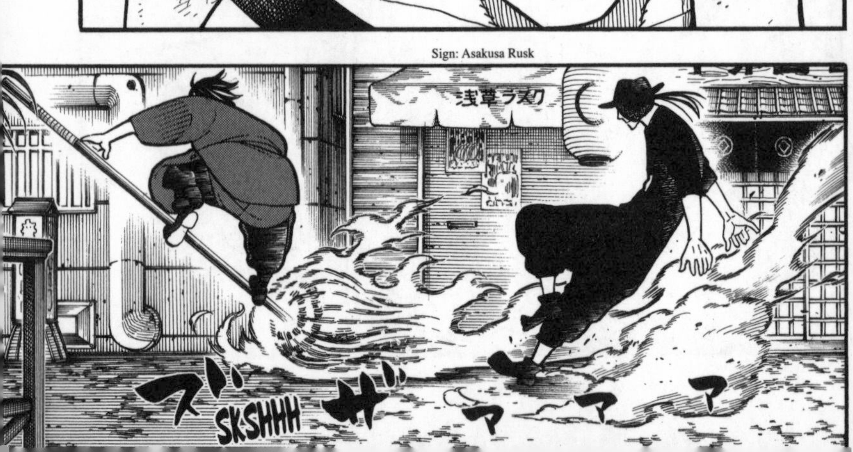
浅草ラスク
ズザァァァ
SKSHHH

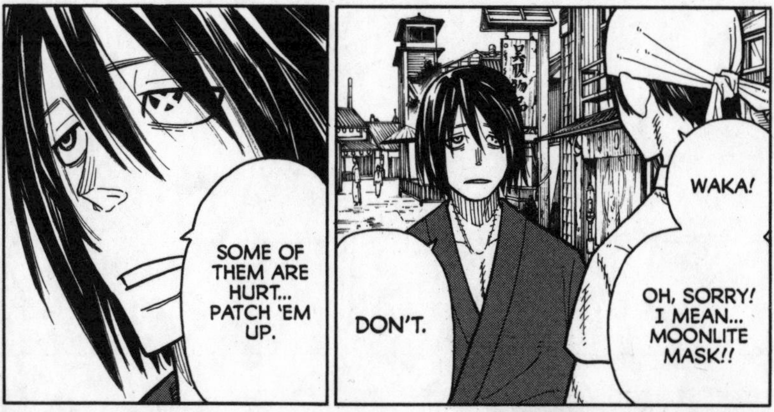
WAKA!
OH, SORRY! I MEAN... MOONLITE MASK!!
DON'T.
SOME OF THEM ARE HURT... PATCH 'EM UP.

Sign: Dry Goods

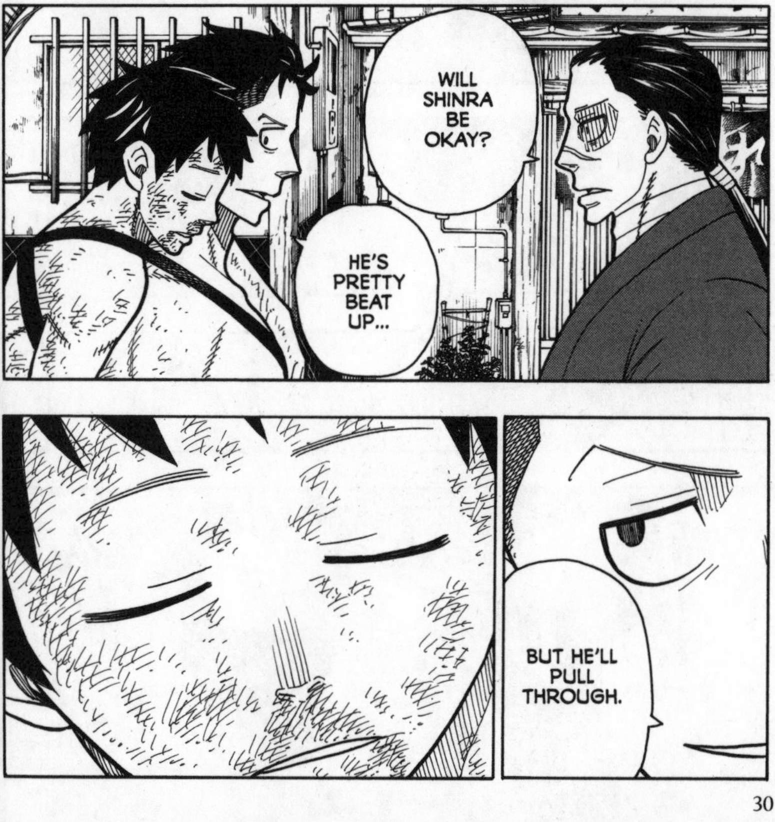
WILL SHINRA BE OKAY?
HE'S PRETTY BEAT UP...
BUT HE'LL PULL THROUGH.

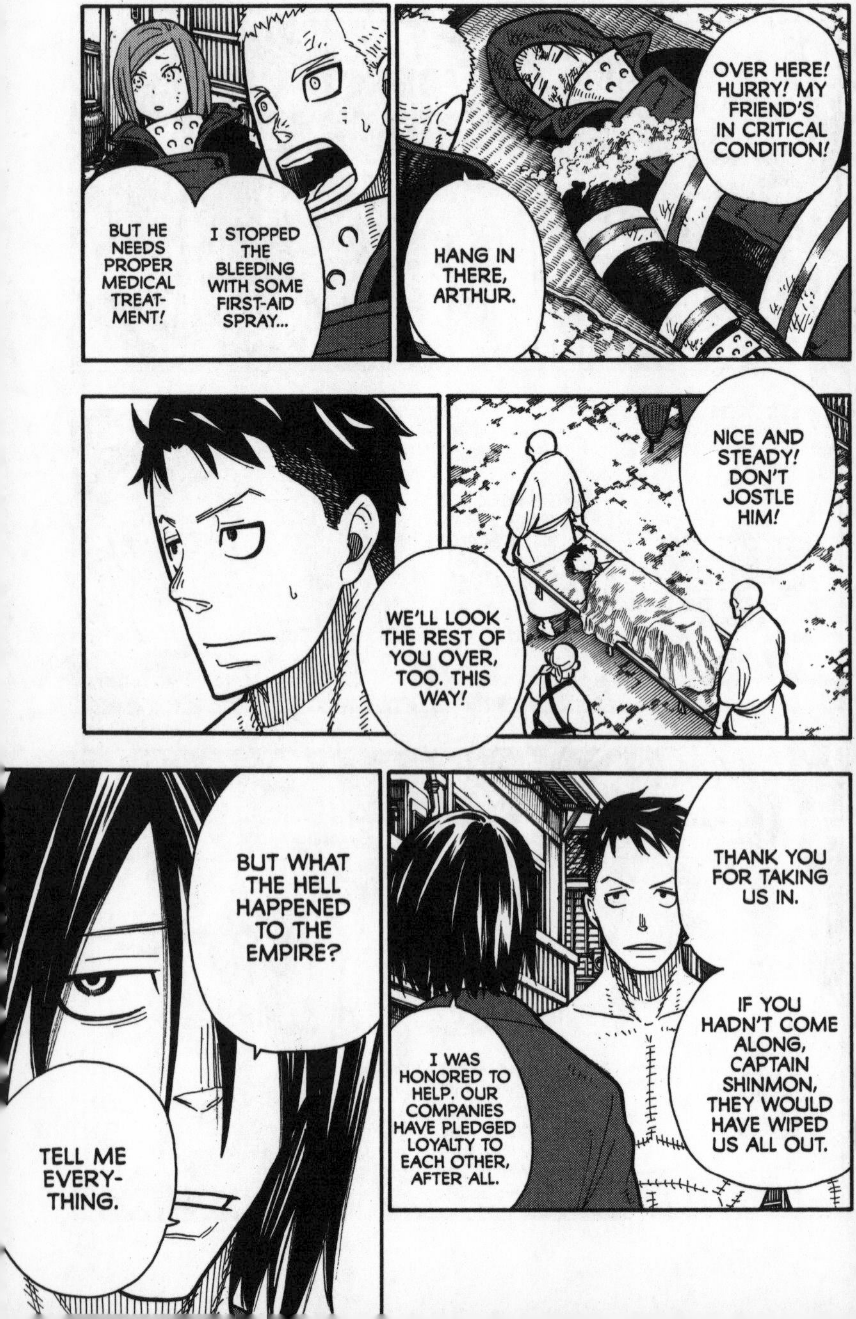

OVER HERE! HURRY! MY FRIEND'S IN CRITICAL CONDITION!
HANG IN THERE, ARTHUR.
I STOPPED THE BLEEDING WITH SOME FIRST-AID SPRAY...
BUT HE NEEDS PROPER MEDICAL TREATMENT!
NICE AND STEADY! DON'T JOSTLE HIM!
WE'LL LOOK THE REST OF YOU OVER, TOO. THIS WAY!
THANK YOU FOR TAKING US IN.
IF YOU HADN'T COME ALONG, CAPTAIN SHINMON, THEY WOULD HAVE WIPED US ALL OUT.
I WAS HONORED TO HELP. OUR COMPANIES HAVE PLEDGED LOYALTY TO EACH OTHER, AFTER ALL.
BUT WHAT THE HELL HAPPENED TO THE EMPIRE?
TELL ME EVERYTHING.

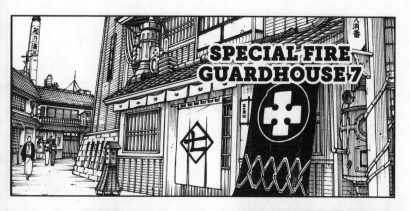

SPECIAL FIRE GUARDHOUSE 7
THE HOLY SOL TEMPLE HAS JOINED FORCES WITH THE EVANGELIST.
SO COMPANY 8 HAD NO CHOICE BUT TO SECEDE FROM THE EMPIRE.
YOUR HUNCH WAS RIGHT, WAKA.
DAMN... IF ONLY MY INSTINCTS WERE THIS GOOD WHEN I'M GAMBLING.
IS WHAT YOU JUST TOLD ME TRUE?

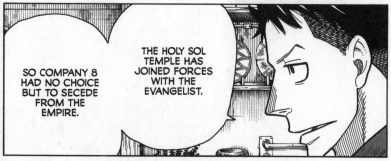

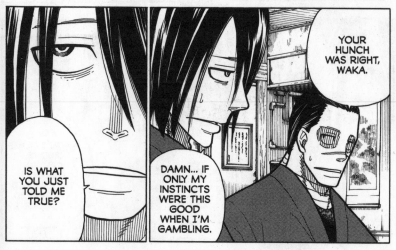

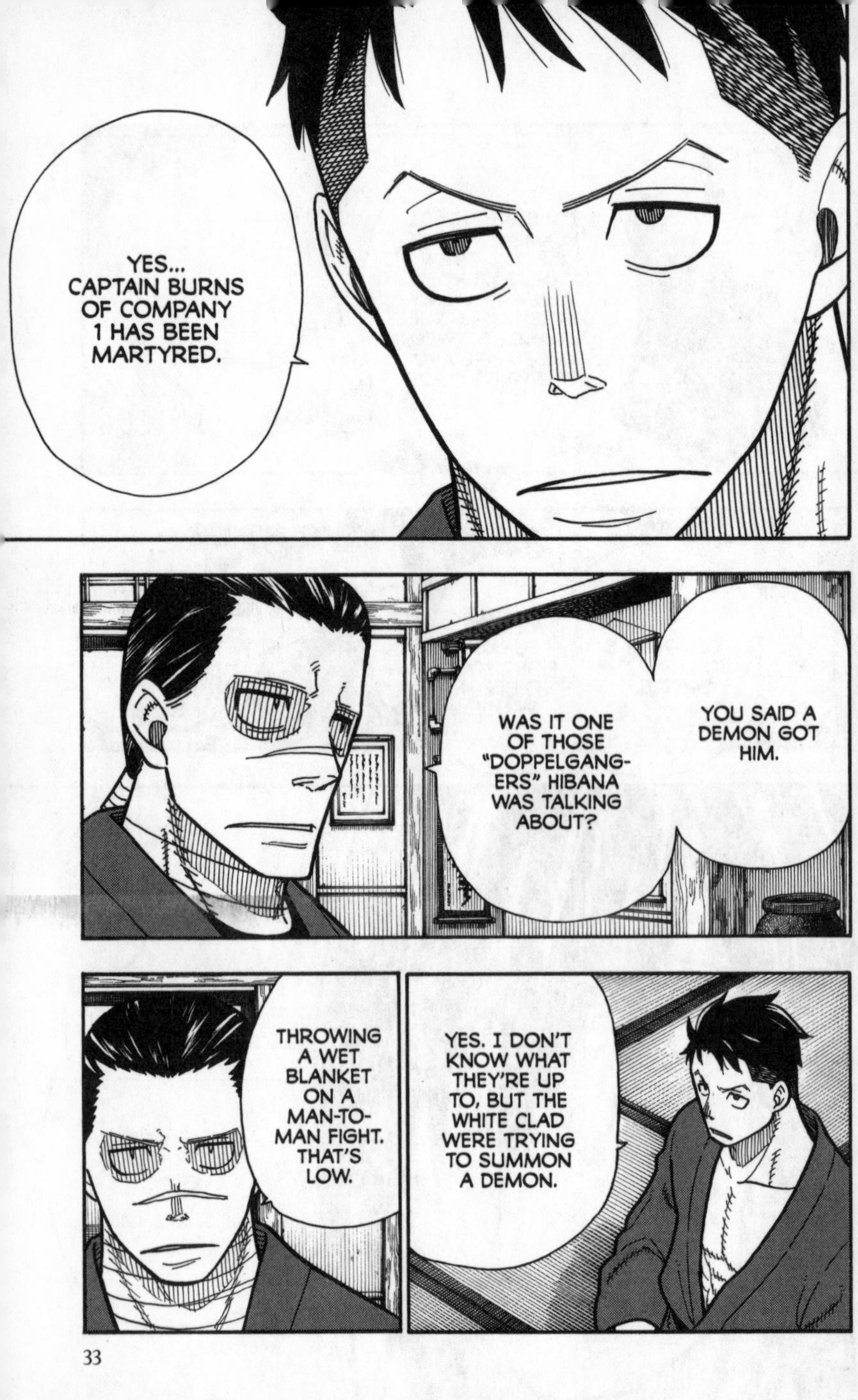
YES... CAPTAIN BURNS OF COMPANY 1 HAS BEEN MARTYRED.
YOU SAID A DEMON GOT HIM.
WAS IT ONE OF THOSE "DOPPELGANG-ERS" HIBANA WAS TALKING ABOUT?
YES. I DON'T KNOW WHAT THEY'RE UP TO, BUT THE WHITE CLAD WERE TRYING TO SUMMON A DEMON.
THROWING A WET BLANKET ON A MAN-TO-MAN FIGHT. THAT'S LOW.

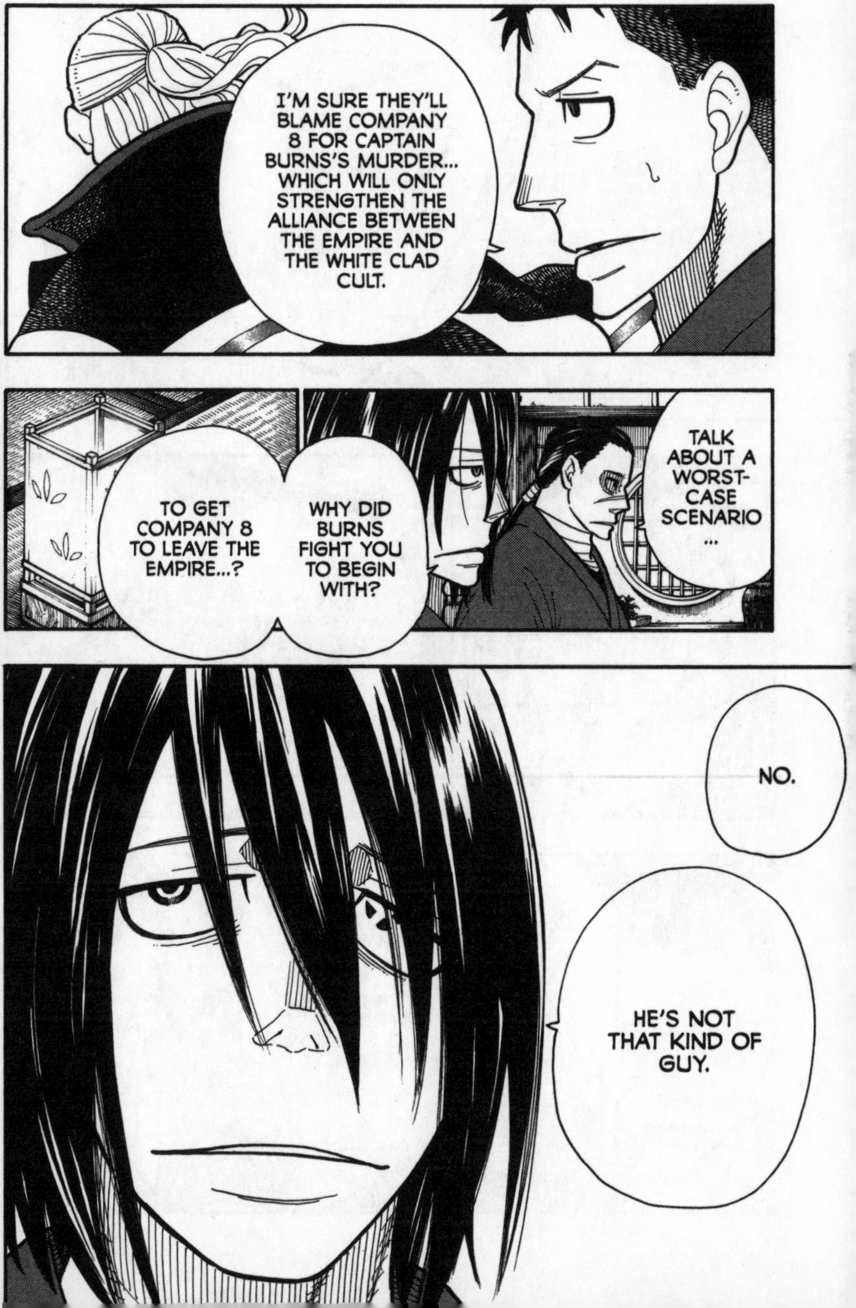
I'M SURE THEY'LL BLAME COMPANY 8 FOR CAPTAIN BURNS'S MURDER... WHICH WILL ONLY STRENGTHEN THE ALLIANCE BETWEEN THE EMPIRE AND THE WHITE CLAD CULT.
TALK ABOUT A WORST-CASE SCENARIO...
WHY DID BURNS FIGHT YOU TO BEGIN WITH?
TO GET COMPANY 8 TO LEAVE THE EMPIRE...?
NO.
HE'S NOT THAT KIND OF GUY.

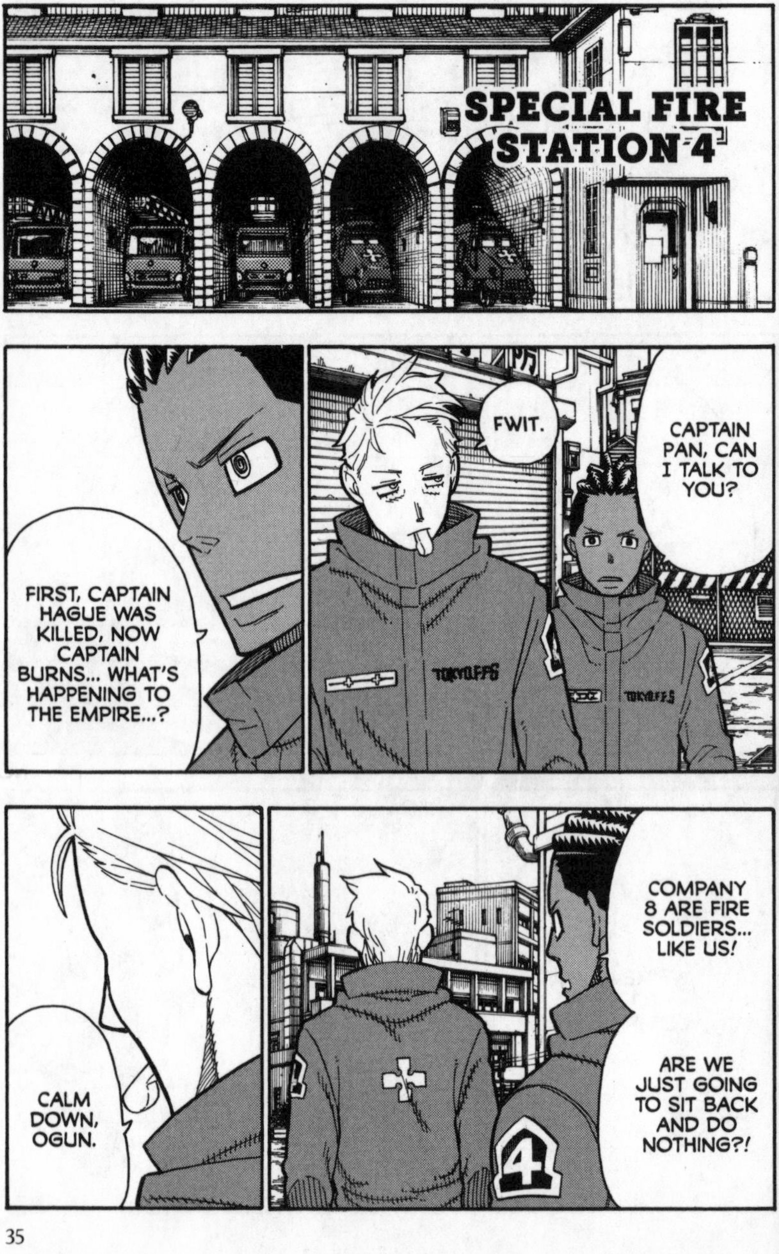
SPECIAL FIRE STATION 4
CAPTAIN PAN, CAN I TALK TO YOU?
FWIT.
FIRST, CAPTAIN HAGUE WAS KILLED, NOW CAPTAIN BURNS... WHAT'S HAPPENING TO THE EMPIRE...?
COMPANY 8 ARE FIRE SOLDIERS... LIKE US!
ARE WE JUST GOING TO SIT BACK AND DO NOTHING?!
CALM DOWN, OGUN.

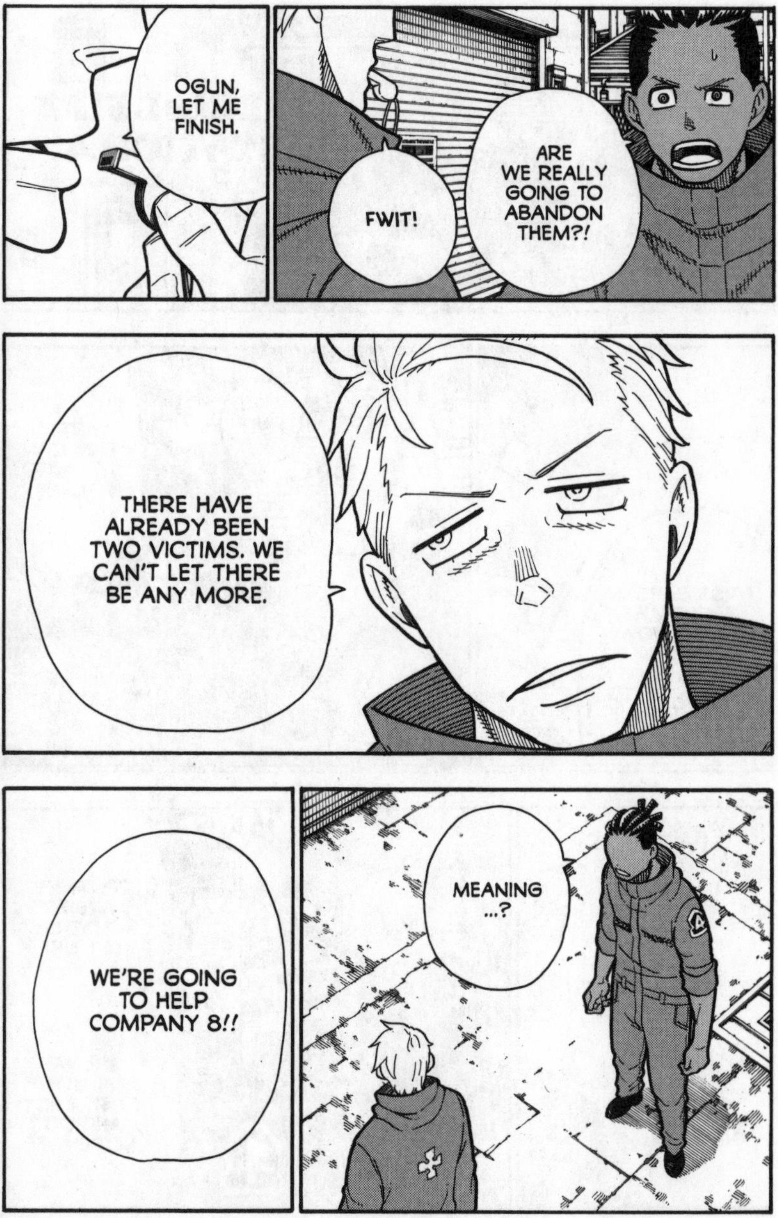
ARE WE REALLY GOING TO ABANDON THEM?!
FWIT!
OGUN, LET ME FINISH.
THERE HAVE ALREADY BEEN TWO VICTIMS. WE CAN'T LET THERE BE ANY MORE.
MEANING ...?
WE'RE GOING TO HELP COMPANY 8!!

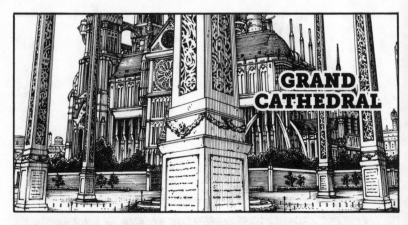

GRAND
CATHEDRAL

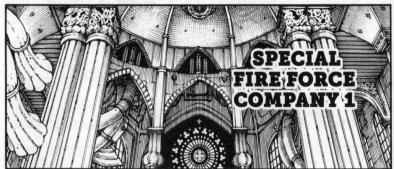

SPECIAL
FIRE FORCE
COMPANY 1

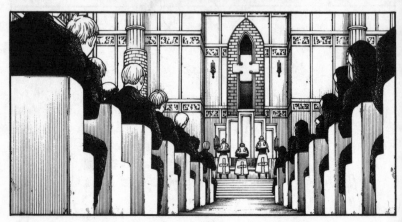

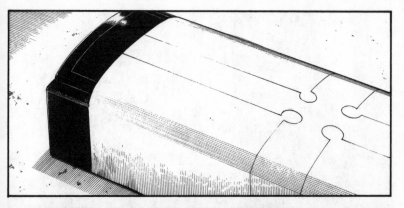

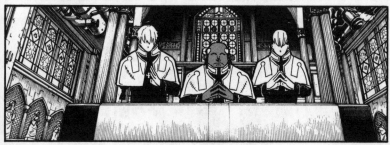

REST IN PEACE, BURNS.

...

WHY ARE WE PRAYING IN FRONT OF THIS COFFIN? THERE'S NOTHING IN IT...

LÁTOM.

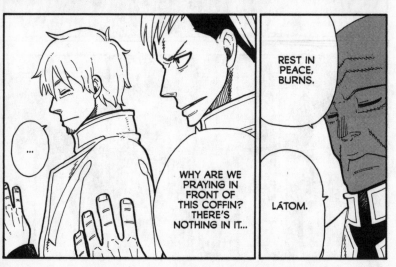

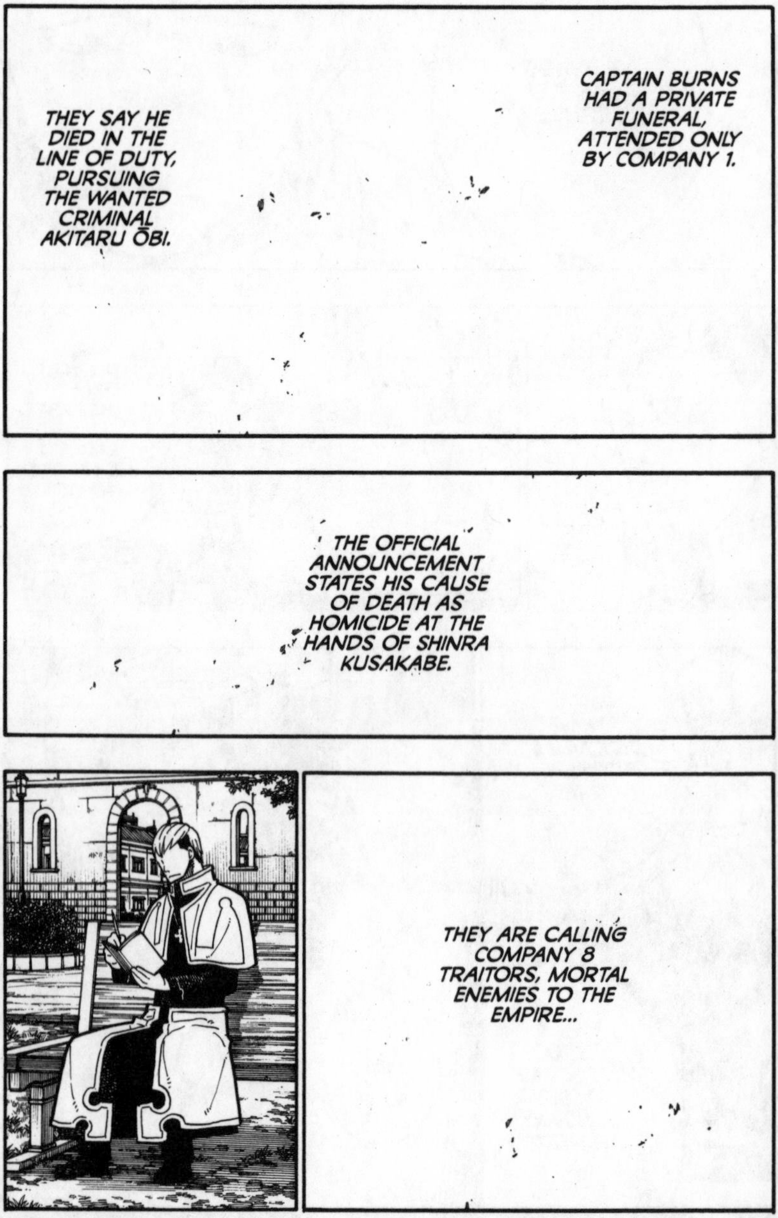
CAPTAIN BURNS HAD A PRIVATE FUNERAL, ATTENDED ONLY BY COMPANY 1.
THEY SAY HE DIED IN THE LINE OF DUTY, PURSUING THE WANTED CRIMINAL AKITARU ŌBI.
THE OFFICIAL ANNOUNCEMENT STATES HIS CAUSE OF DEATH AS HOMICIDE AT THE HANDS OF SHINRA KUSAKABE.
THEY ARE CALLING COMPANY 8 TRAITORS, MORTAL ENEMIES TO THE EMPIRE...

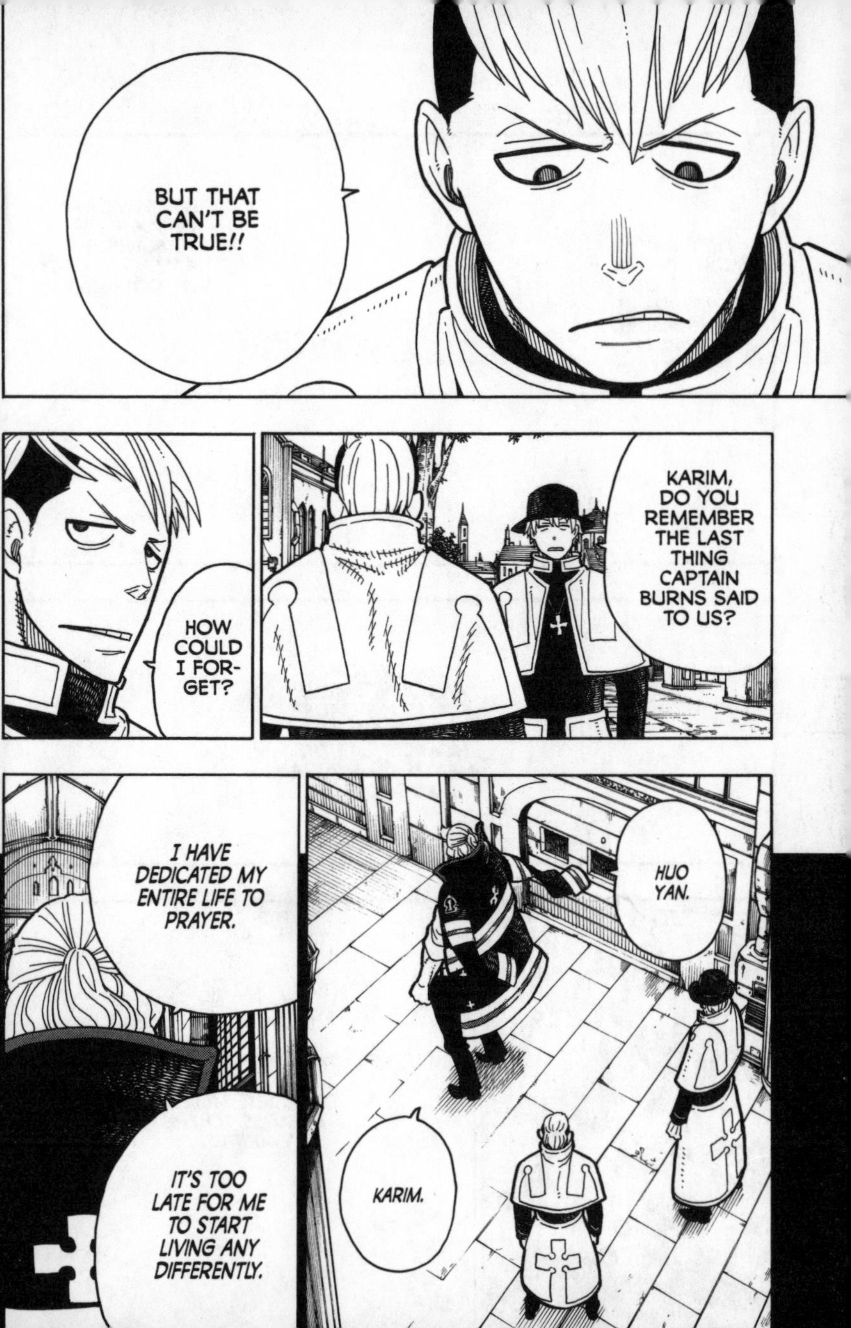
BUT THAT CAN'T BE TRUE!!
KARIM, DO YOU REMEMBER THE LAST THING CAPTAIN BURNS SAID TO US?
HOW COULD I FOR-GET?
HUO YAN.
KARIM.
I HAVE DEDICATED MY ENTIRE LIFE TO PRAYER.
IT'S TOO LATE FOR ME TO START LIVING ANY DIFFERENTLY.

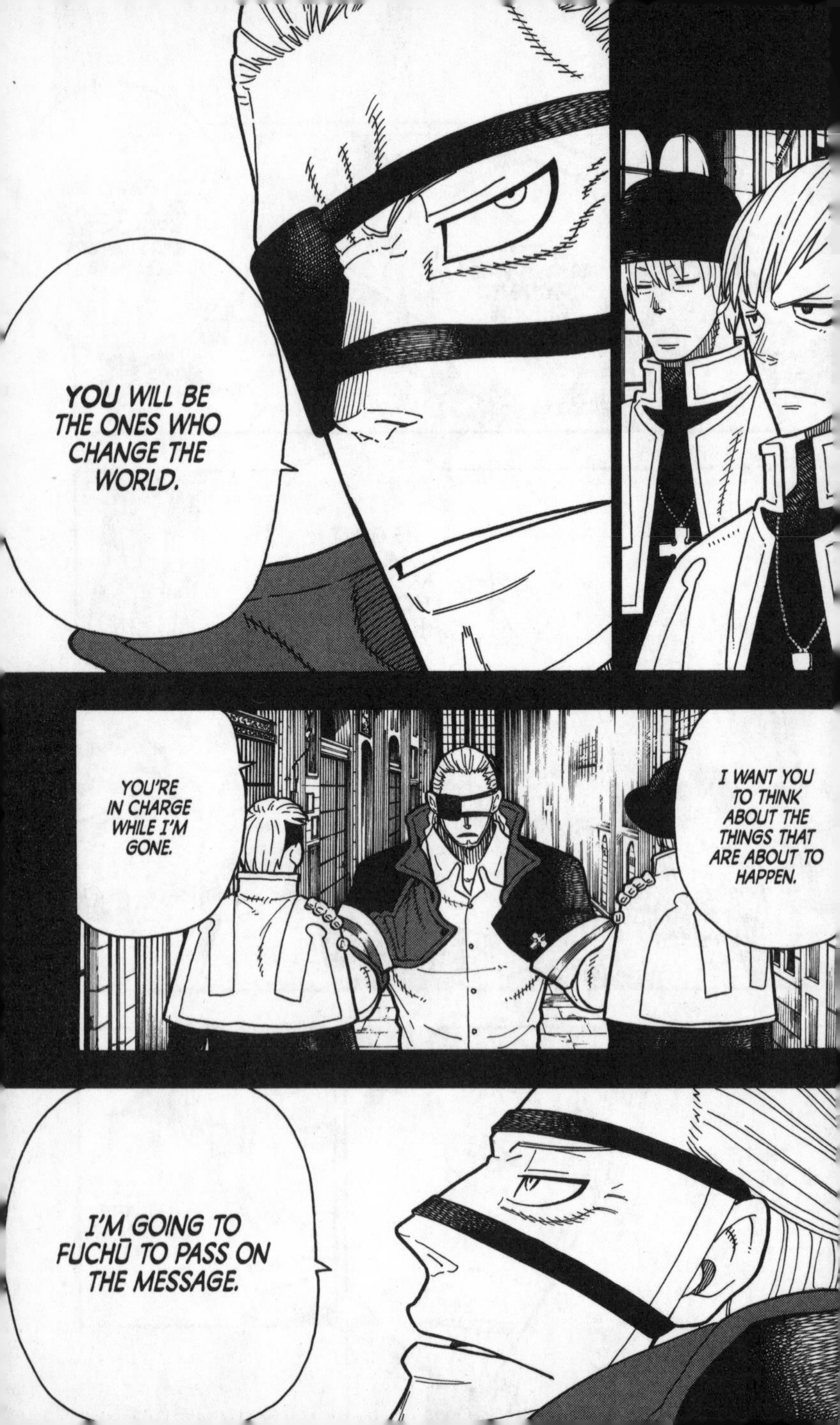
YOU WILL BE THE ONES WHO CHANGE THE WORLD.
I WANT YOU TO THINK ABOUT THE THINGS THAT ARE ABOUT TO HAPPEN.
YOU'RE IN CHARGE WHILE I'M GONE.
I'M GOING TO FUCHŪ TO PASS ON THE MESSAGE.

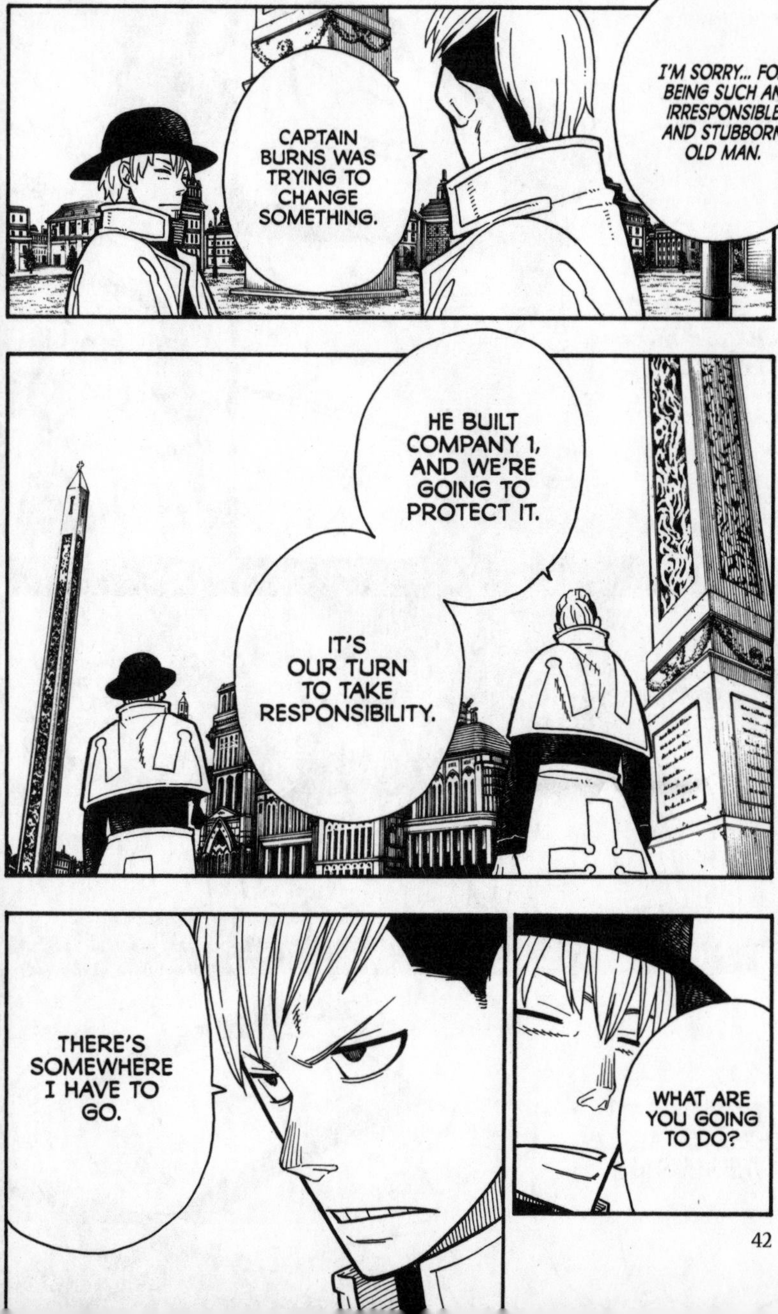
I'M SORRY... FOR BEING SUCH AN IRRESPONSIBLE AND STUBBORN OLD MAN.
CAPTAIN BURNS WAS TRYING TO CHANGE SOMETHING.
HE BUILT COMPANY 1, AND WE'RE GOING TO PROTECT IT.
IT'S OUR TURN TO TAKE RESPONSIBILITY.
WHAT ARE YOU GOING TO DO?
THERE'S SOMEWHERE I HAVE TO GO.

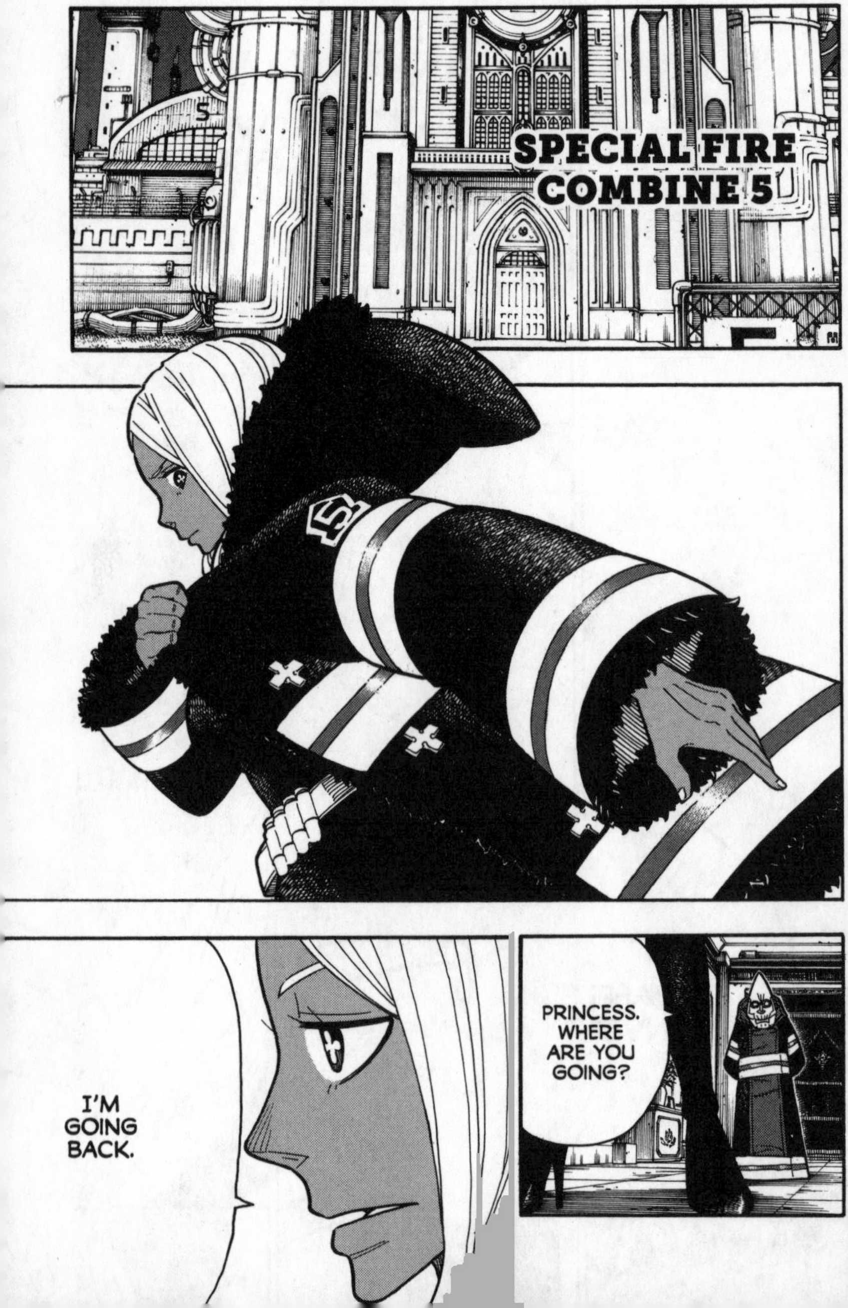
SPECIAL FIRE COMBINE 5
PRINCESS. WHERE ARE YOU GOING?
I'M GOING BACK.

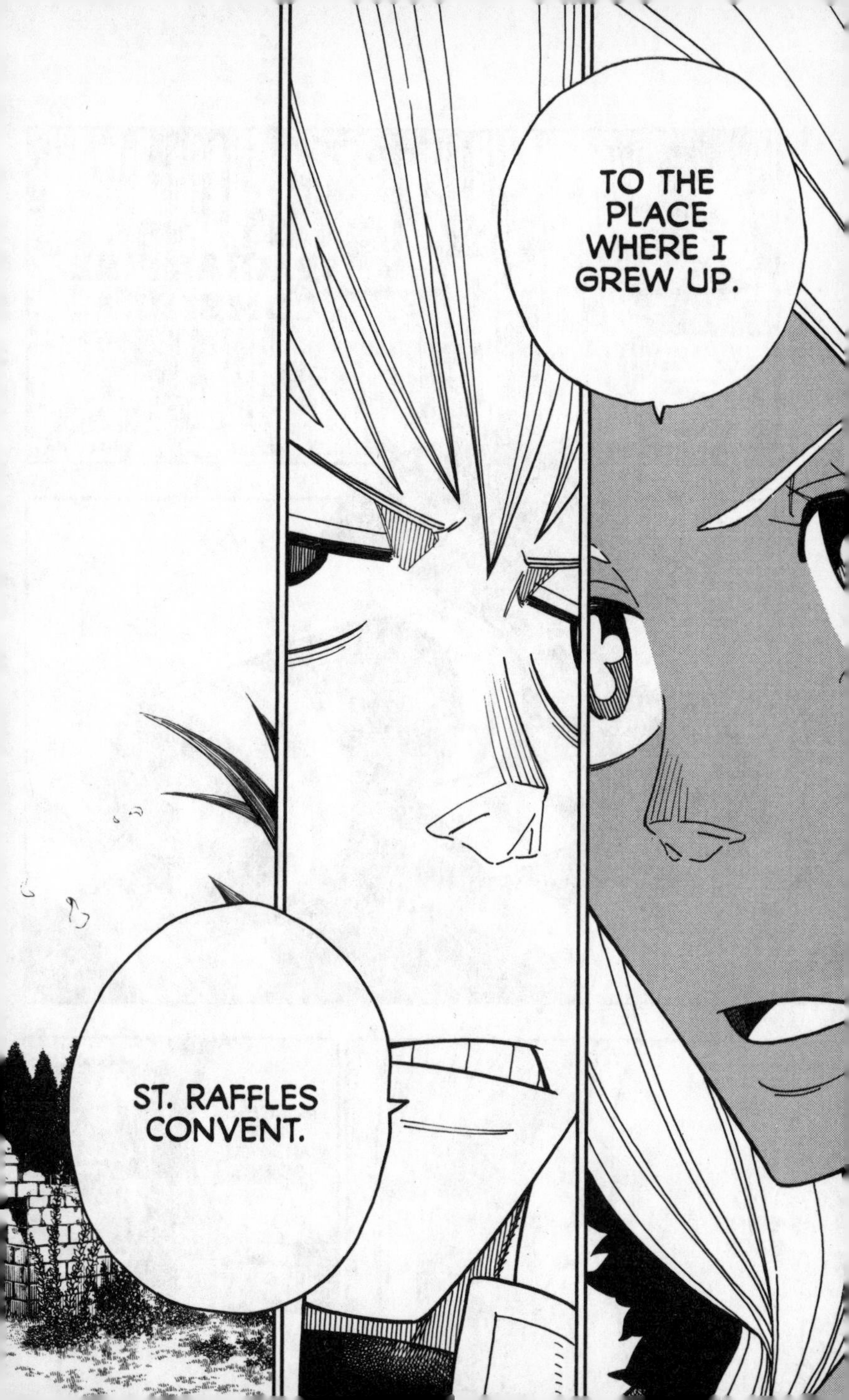
TO THE PLACE WHERE I GREW UP.
ST. RAFFLES CONVENT.

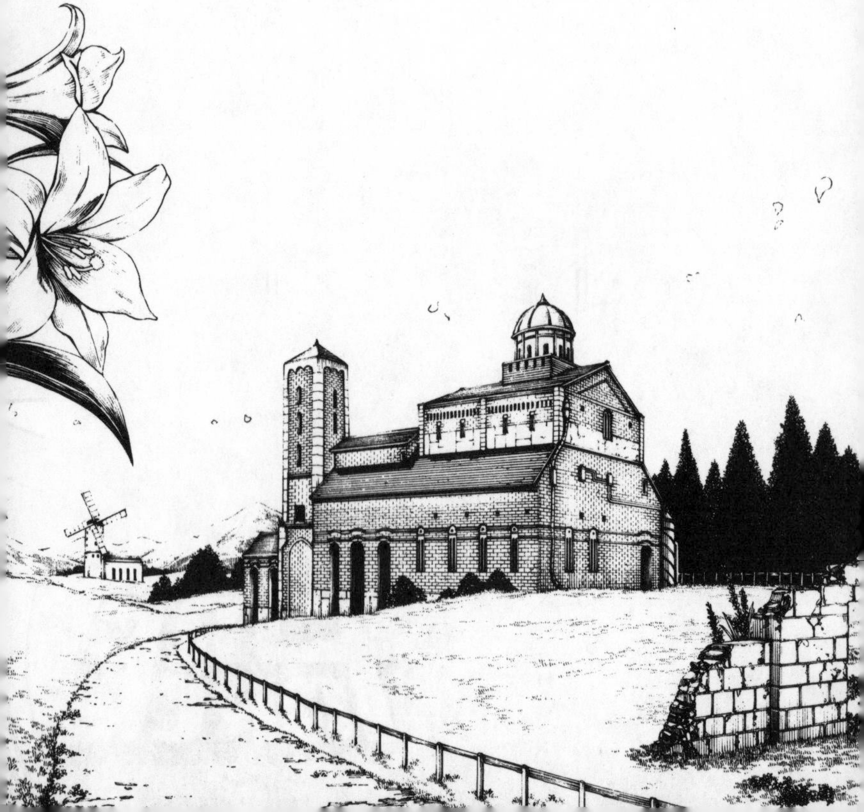

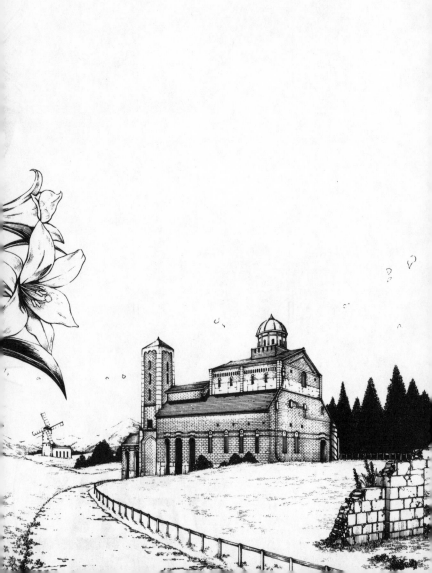

FIRE FORCE

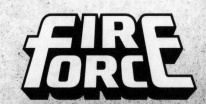

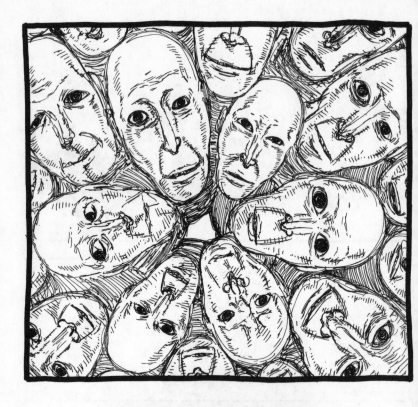

CHAPTER CXCVIII: FLOWER GARDEN MEMORIES

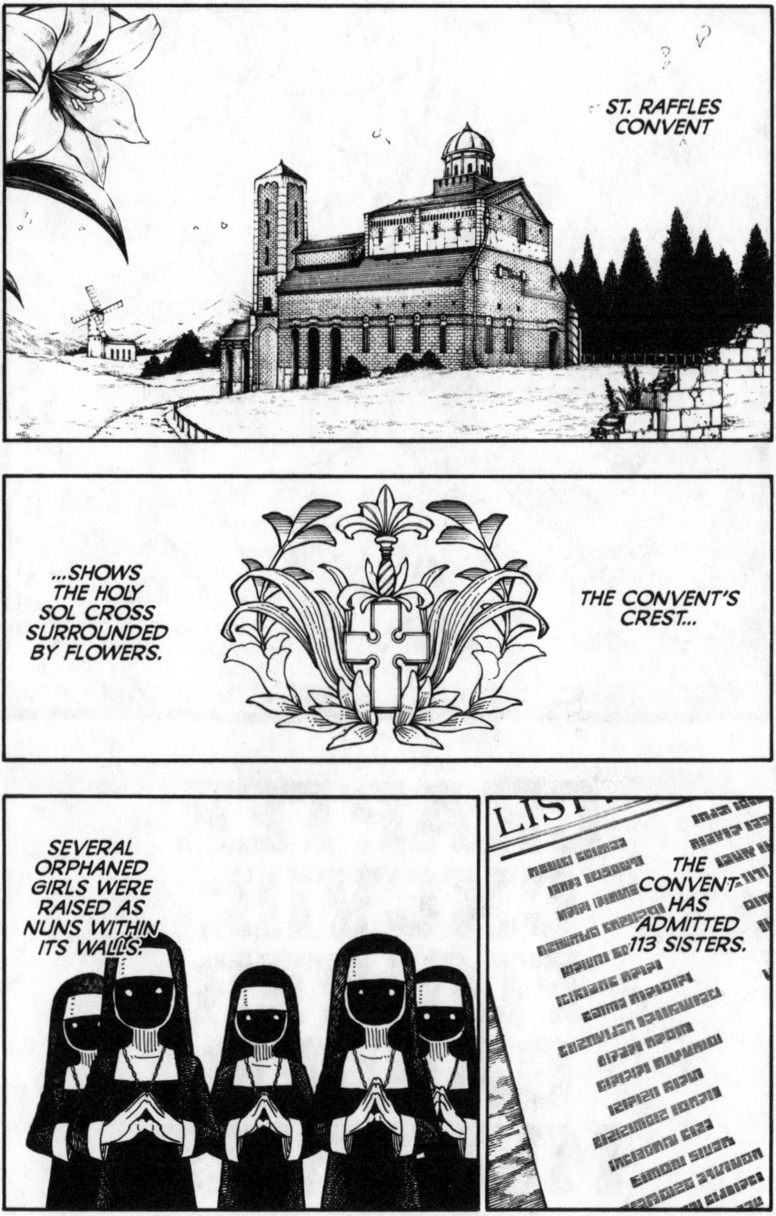
ST. RAFFLES CONVENT
THE CONVENT'S CREST...
...SHOWS THE HOLY SOL CROSS SURROUNDED BY FLOWERS.
LIST
THE CONVENT HAS ADMITTED 113 SISTERS.
SEVERAL ORPHANED GIRLS WERE RAISED AS NUNS WITHIN ITS WALLS.

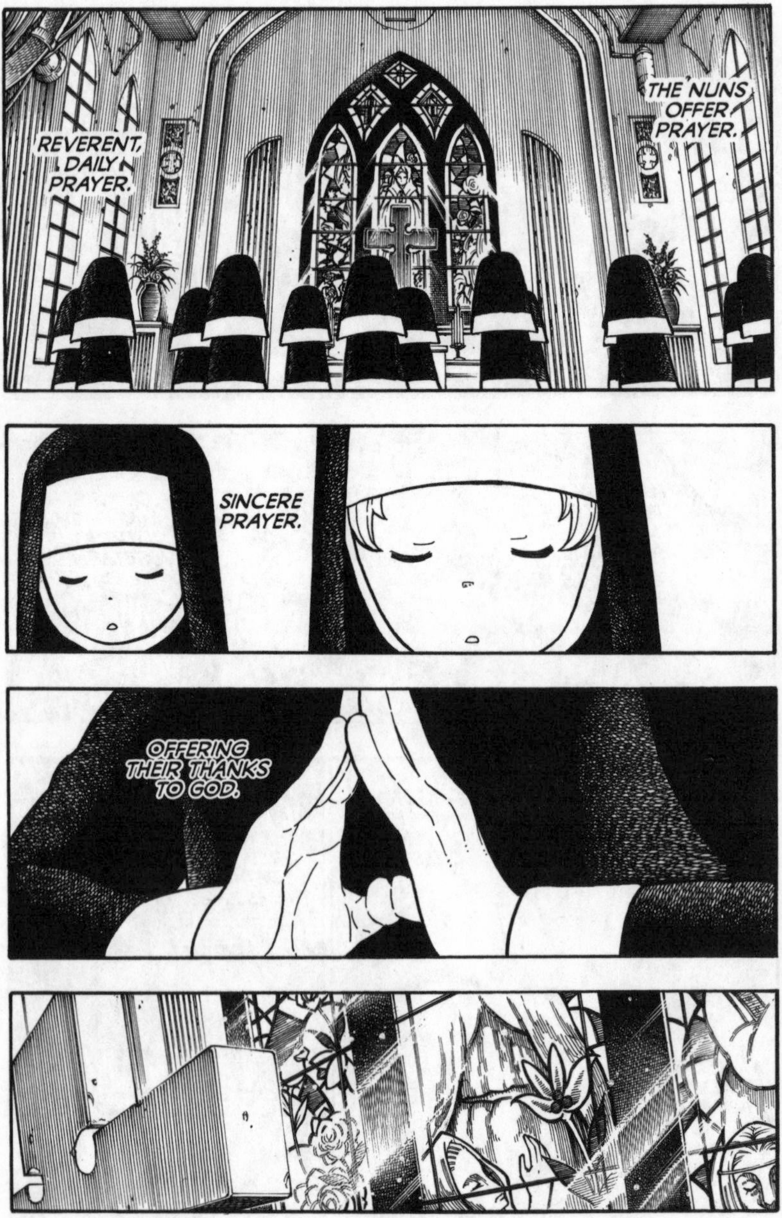
THE NUNS OFFER PRAYER.
REVERENT, DAILY PRAYER.
SINCERE PRAYER.
OFFERING THEIR THANKS TO GOD.

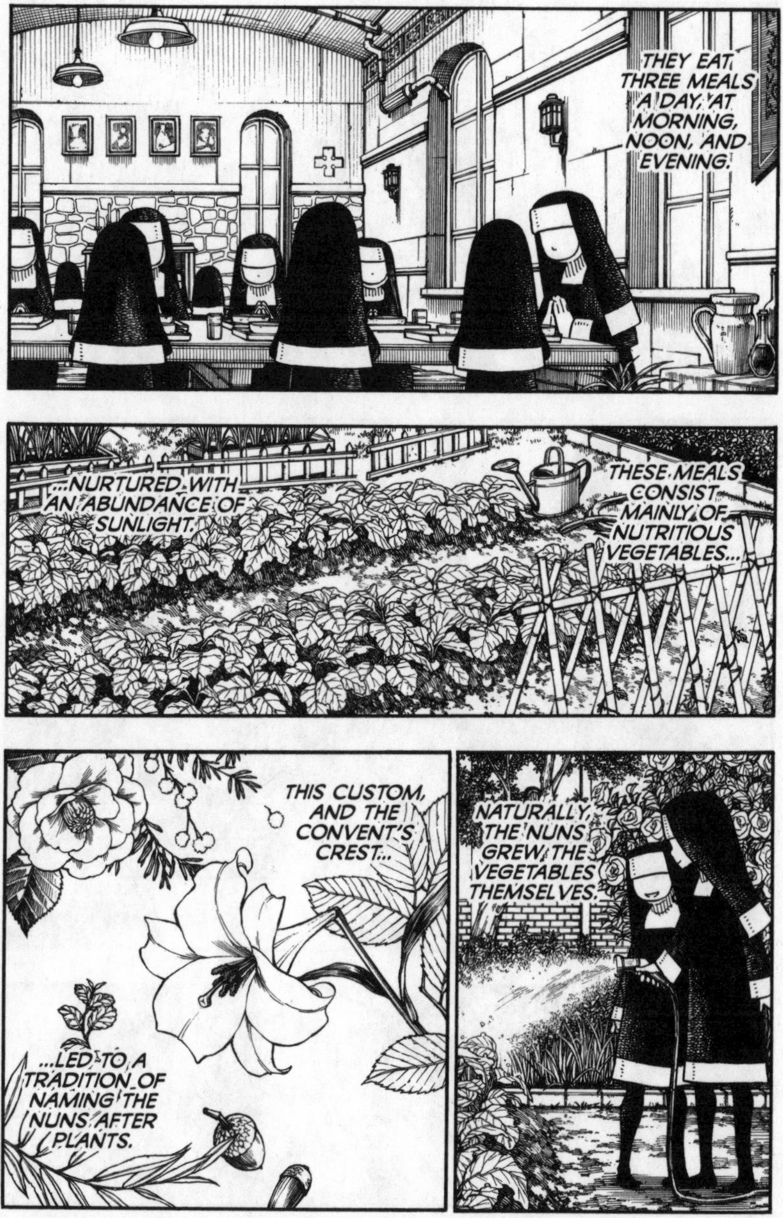
THEY EAT THREE MEALS A DAY, AT MORNING, NOON, AND EVENING.
THESE MEALS CONSIST MAINLY OF NUTRITIOUS VEGETABLES...
...NURTURED WITH AN ABUNDANCE OF SUNLIGHT.
NATURALLY, THE NUNS GREW THE VEGETABLES THEMSELVES.
THIS CUSTOM, AND THE CONVENT'S CREST...
...LED TO A TRADITION OF NAMING THE NUNS AFTER PLANTS.

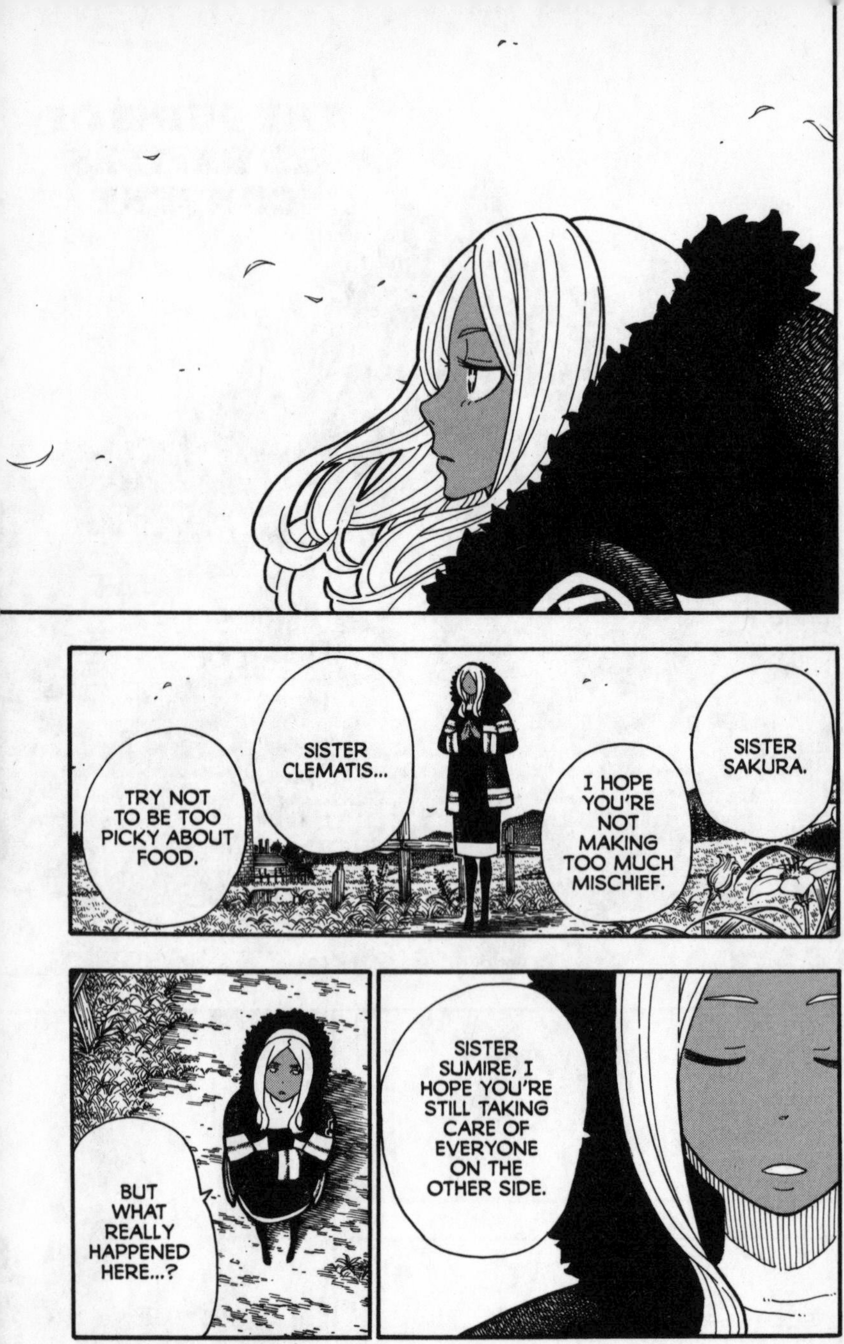
SISTER SAKURA.
I HOPE YOU'RE NOT MAKING TOO MUCH MISCHIEF.
SISTER CLEMATIS...
TRY NOT TO BE TOO PICKY ABOUT FOOD.
SISTER SUMIRE, I HOPE YOU'RE STILL TAKING CARE OF EVERYONE ON THE OTHER SIDE.
BUT WHAT REALLY HAPPENED HERE...?

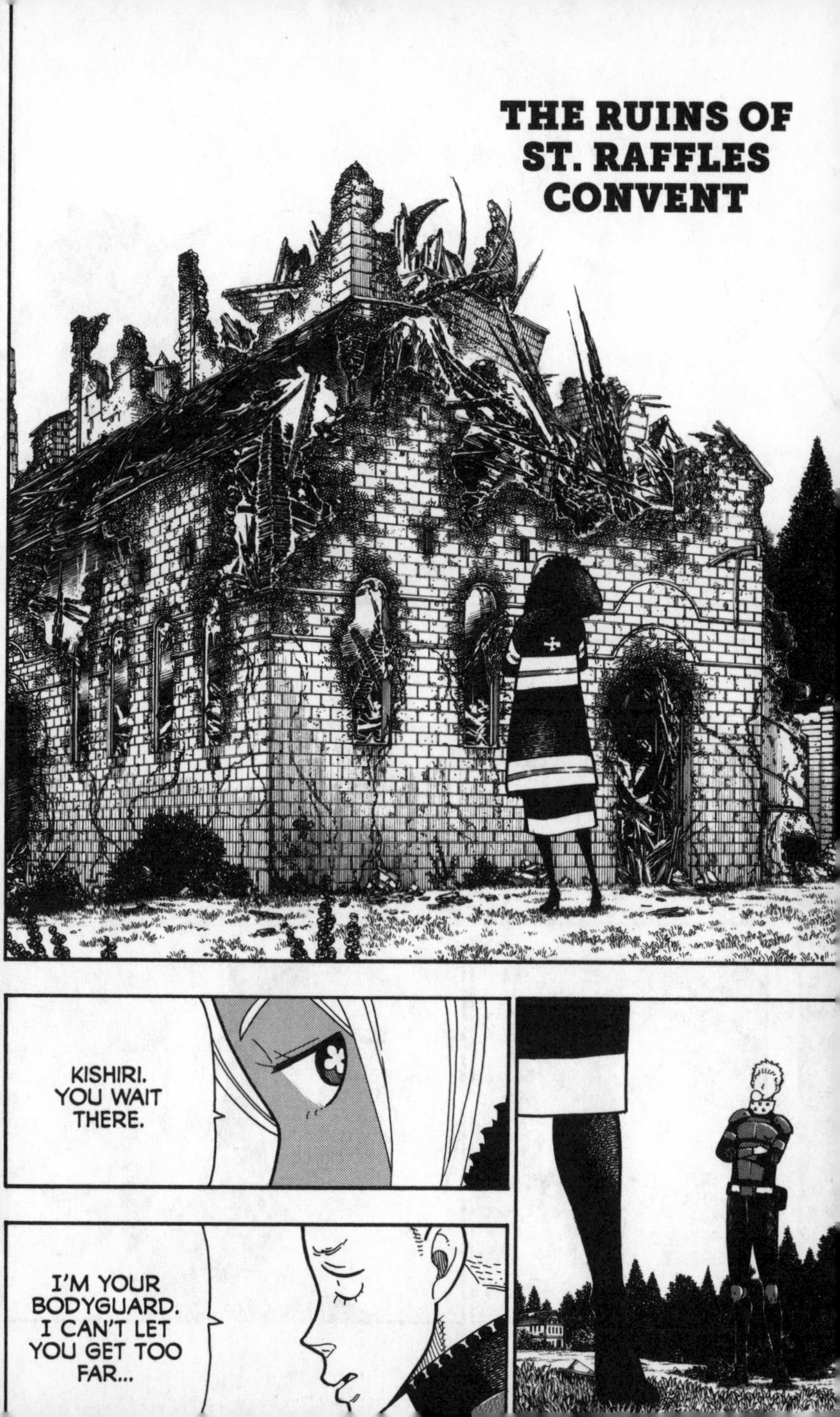
THE RUINS OF ST. RAFFLES CONVENT
KISHIRI. YOU WAIT THERE.
I'M YOUR BODYGUARD. I CAN'T LET YOU GET TOO FAR...

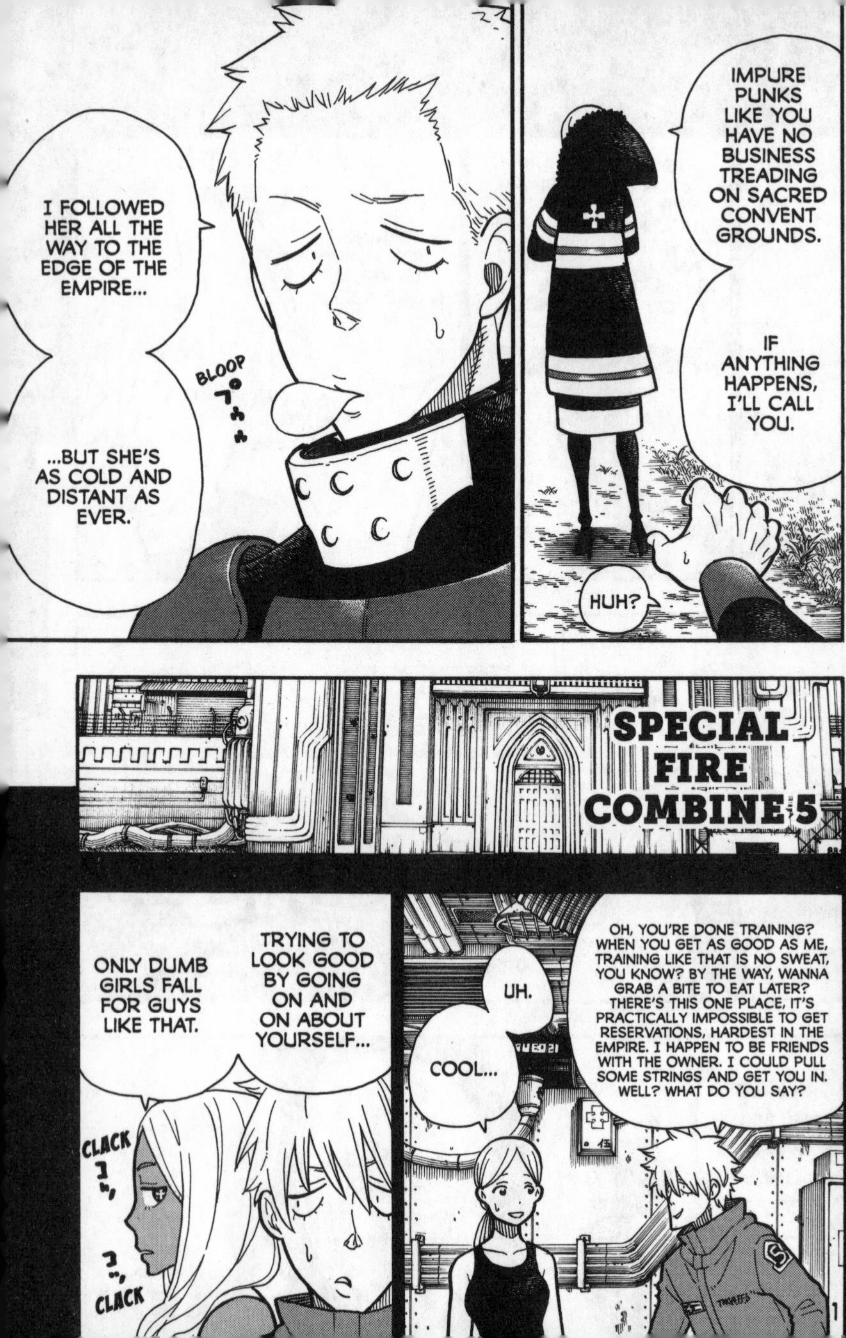
IMPURE PUNKS LIKE YOU HAVE NO BUSINESS TREADING ON SACRED CONVENT GROUNDS.
IF ANYTHING HAPPENS, I'LL CALL YOU.
HUH?
I FOLLOWED HER ALL THE WAY TO THE EDGE OF THE EMPIRE...
...BUT SHE'S AS COLD AND DISTANT AS EVER.
BLOOP
SPECIAL FIRE COMBINE 5
OH, YOU'RE DONE TRAINING? WHEN YOU GET AS GOOD AS ME, TRAINING LIKE THAT IS NO SWEAT, YOU KNOW? BY THE WAY, WANNA GRAB A BITE TO EAT LATER? THERE'S THIS ONE PLACE, IT'S PRACTICALLY IMPOSSIBLE TO GET RESERVATIONS, HARDEST IN THE EMPIRE. I HAPPEN TO BE FRIENDS WITH THE OWNER. I COULD PULL SOME STRINGS AND GET YOU IN. WELL? WHAT DO YOU SAY?
UH.
COOL...
TRYING TO LOOK GOOD BY GOING ON AND ON ABOUT YOURSELF...
ONLY DUMB GIRLS FALL FOR GUYS LIKE THAT.
CLACK
CLACK

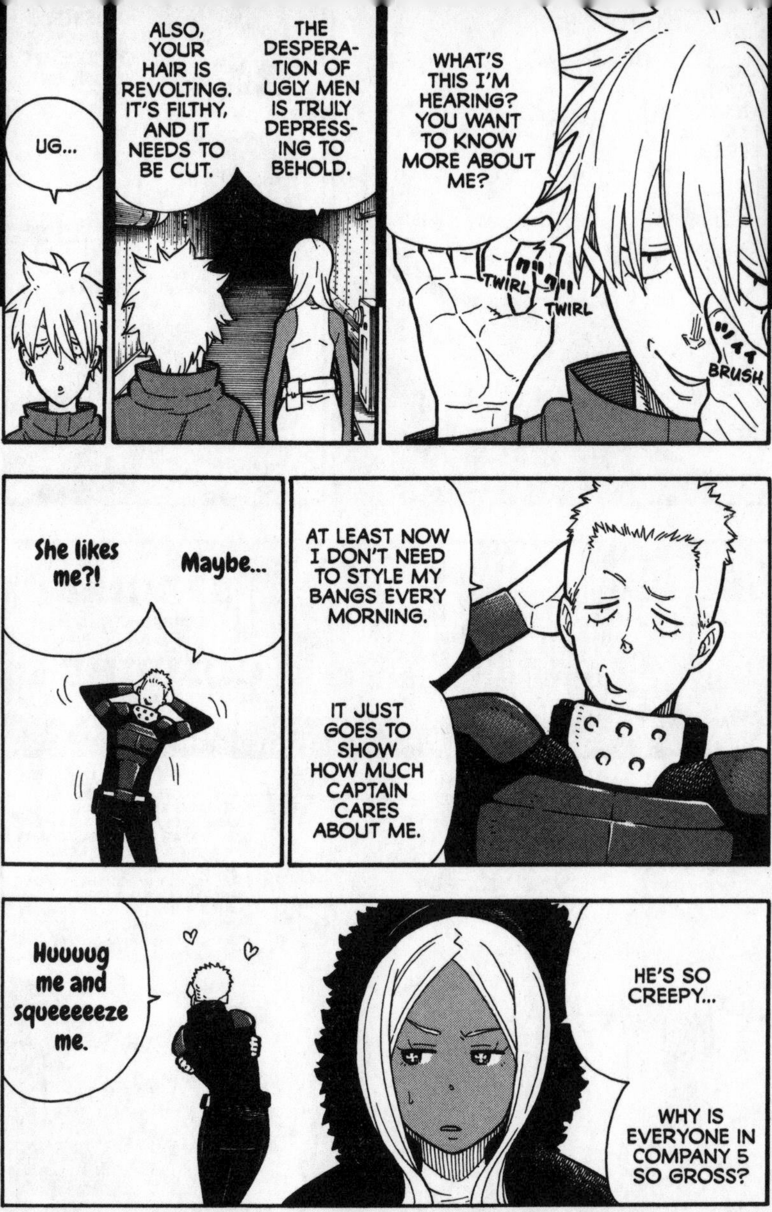
WHAT'S THIS I'M HEARING? YOU WANT TO KNOW MORE ABOUT ME?
TWIRL
TWIRL
BRUSH
THE DESPERATION OF UGLY MEN IS TRULY DEPRESSING TO BEHOLD.
ALSO, YOUR HAIR IS REVOLTING. IT'S FILTHY, AND IT NEEDS TO BE CUT.
UG...
AT LEAST NOW I DON'T NEED TO STYLE MY BANGS EVERY MORNING.
IT JUST GOES TO SHOW HOW MUCH CAPTAIN CARES ABOUT ME.
Maybe...
She likes me?!
HE'S SO CREEPY...
WHY IS EVERYONE IN COMPANY 5 SO GROSS?
Huuuug me and squeeeeeze me.

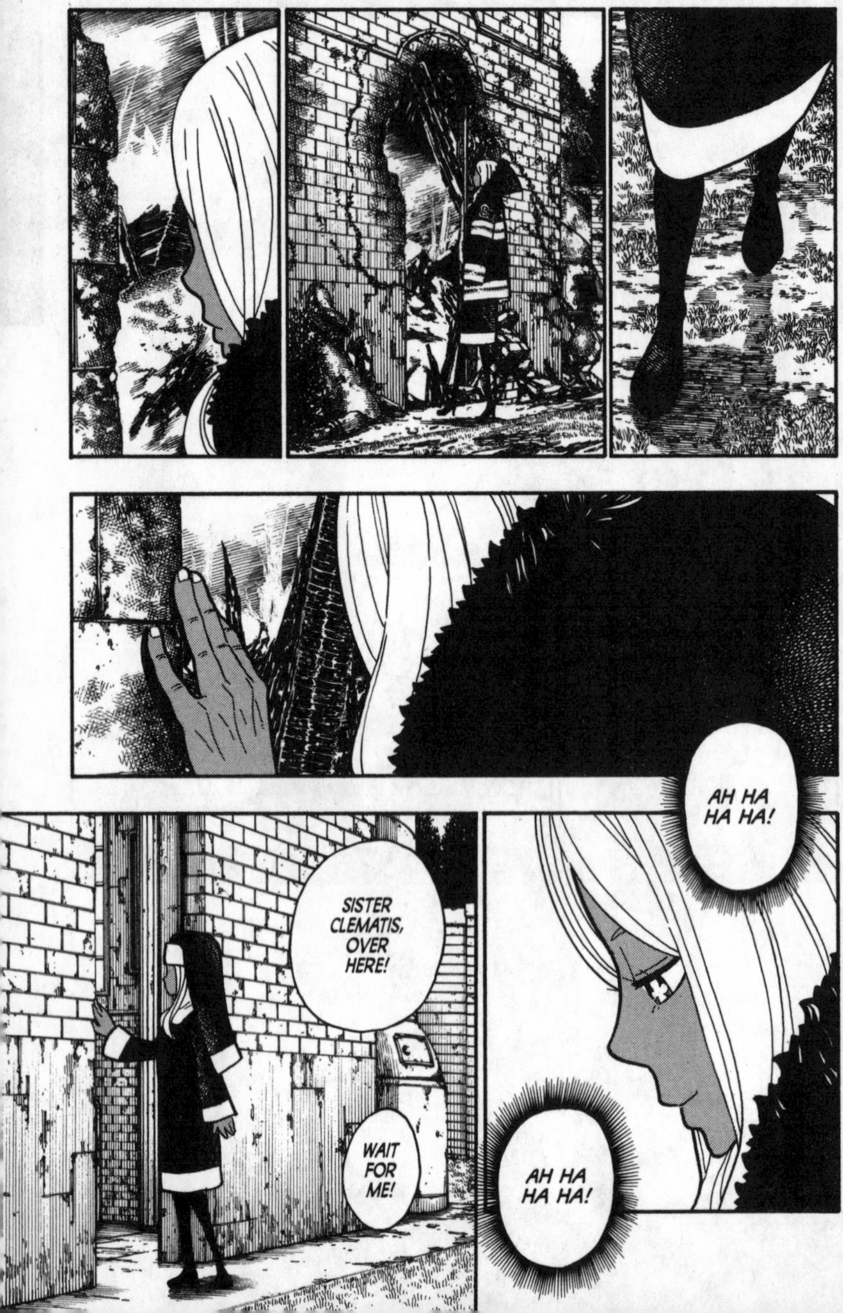
AH HA HA HA!
AH HA HA HA!
SISTER CLEMATIS, OVER HERE!
WAIT FOR ME!

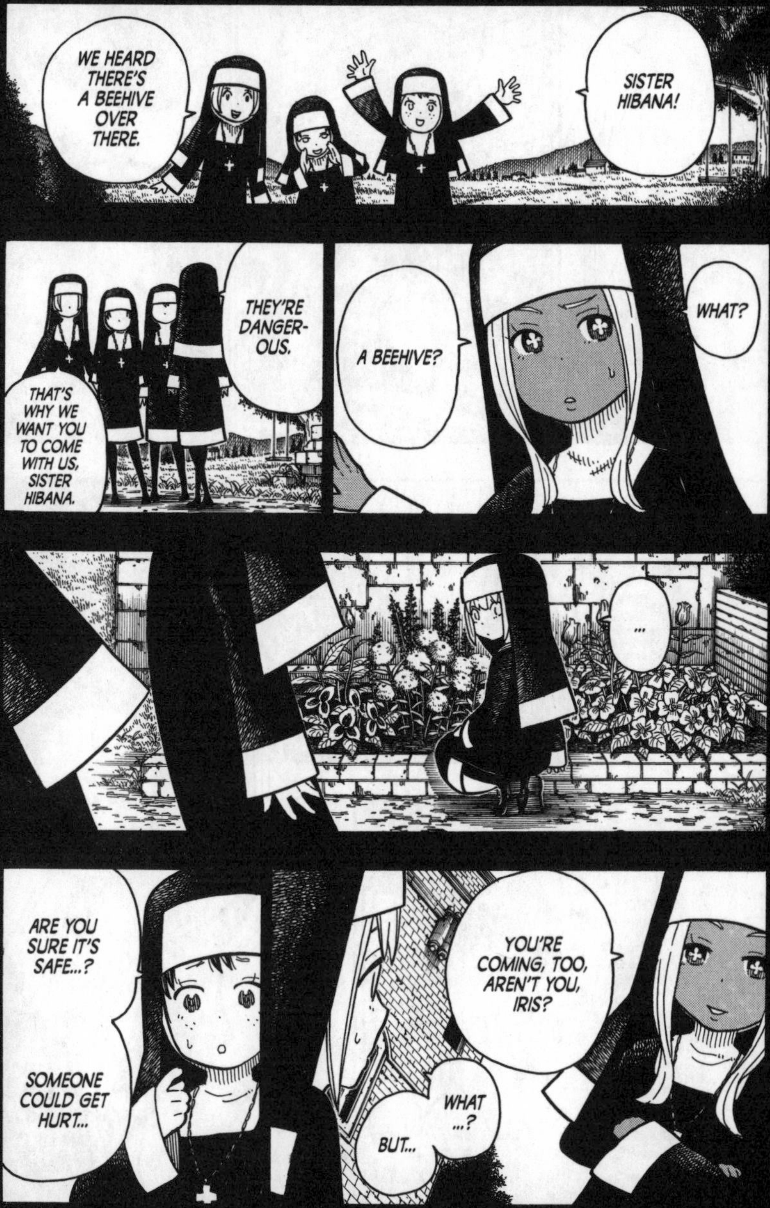
SISTER HIBANA!
WE HEARD THERE'S A BEEHIVE OVER THERE.
WHAT?
A BEEHIVE?
THEY'RE DANGER-OUS.
THAT'S WHY WE WANT YOU TO COME WITH US, SISTER HIBANA.
...
YOU'RE COMING, TOO, AREN'T YOU, IRIS?
WHAT ...?
BUT...
ARE YOU SURE IT'S SAFE...?
SOMEONE COULD GET HURT...

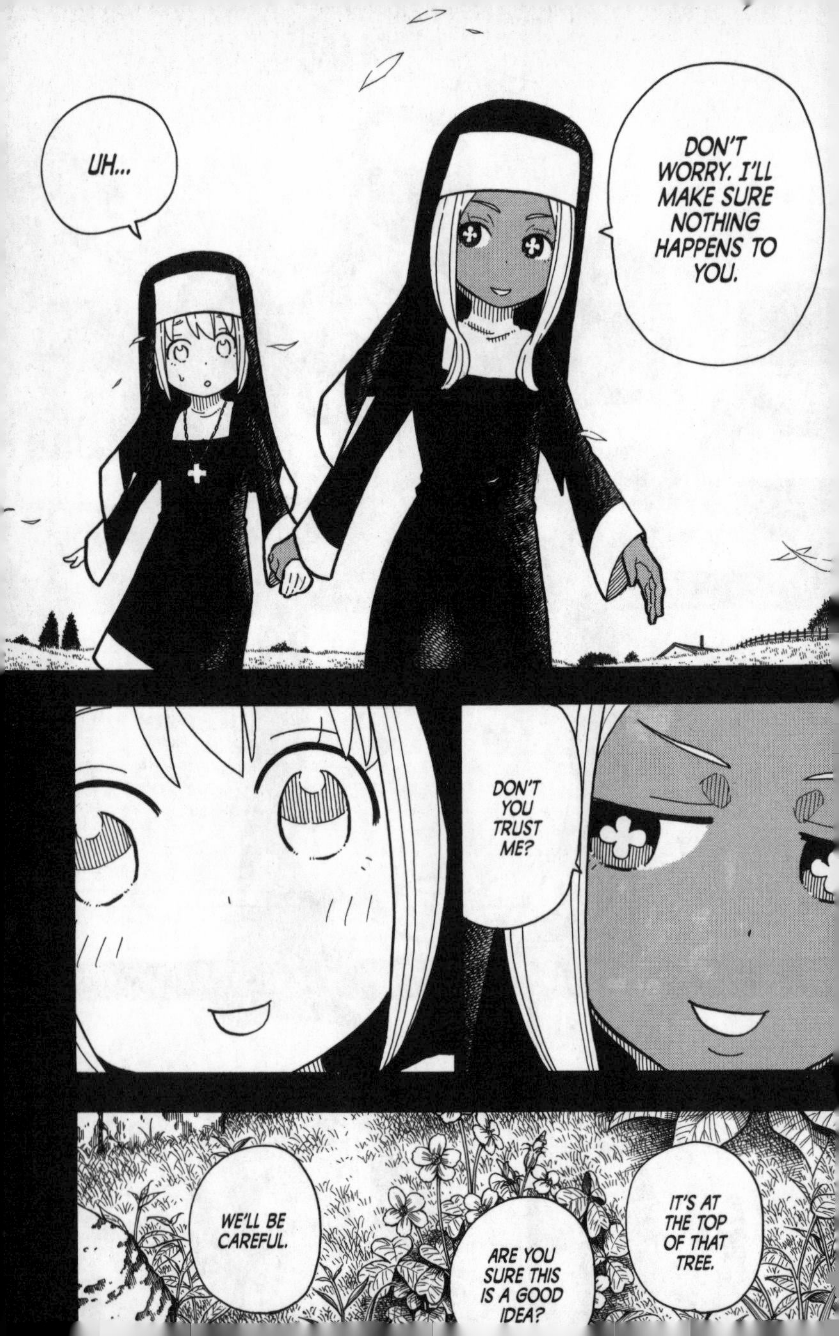
DON'T WORRY. I'LL MAKE SURE NOTHING HAPPENS TO YOU.
UH...
DON'T YOU TRUST ME?
IT'S AT THE TOP OF THAT TREE.
ARE YOU SURE THIS IS A GOOD IDEA?
WE'LL BE CAREFUL.

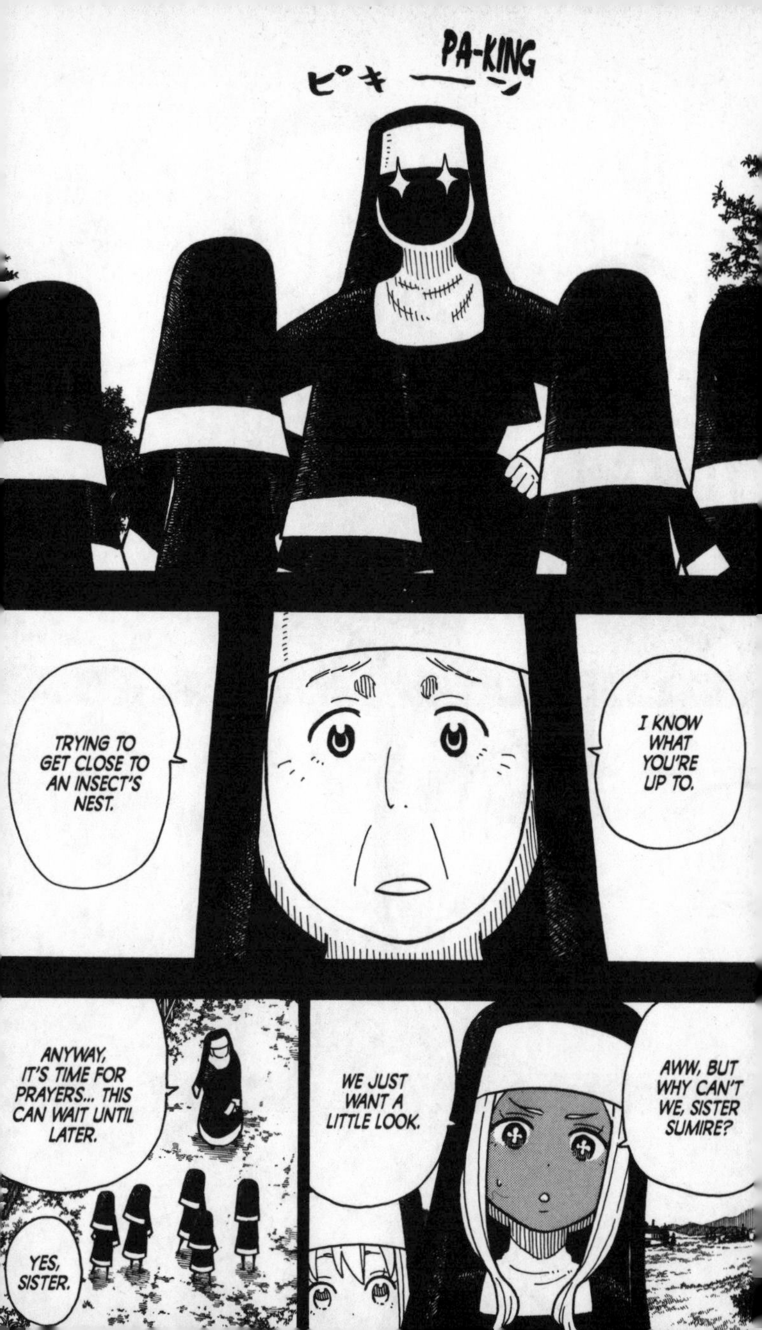
ピキーン
PA-KING
I KNOW WHAT YOU'RE UP TO.
TRYING TO GET CLOSE TO AN INSECT'S NEST.
AWW, BUT WHY CAN'T WE, SISTER SUMIRE?
WE JUST WANT A LITTLE LOOK.
ANYWAY, IT'S TIME FOR PRAYERS... THIS CAN WAIT UNTIL LATER.
YES, SISTER.

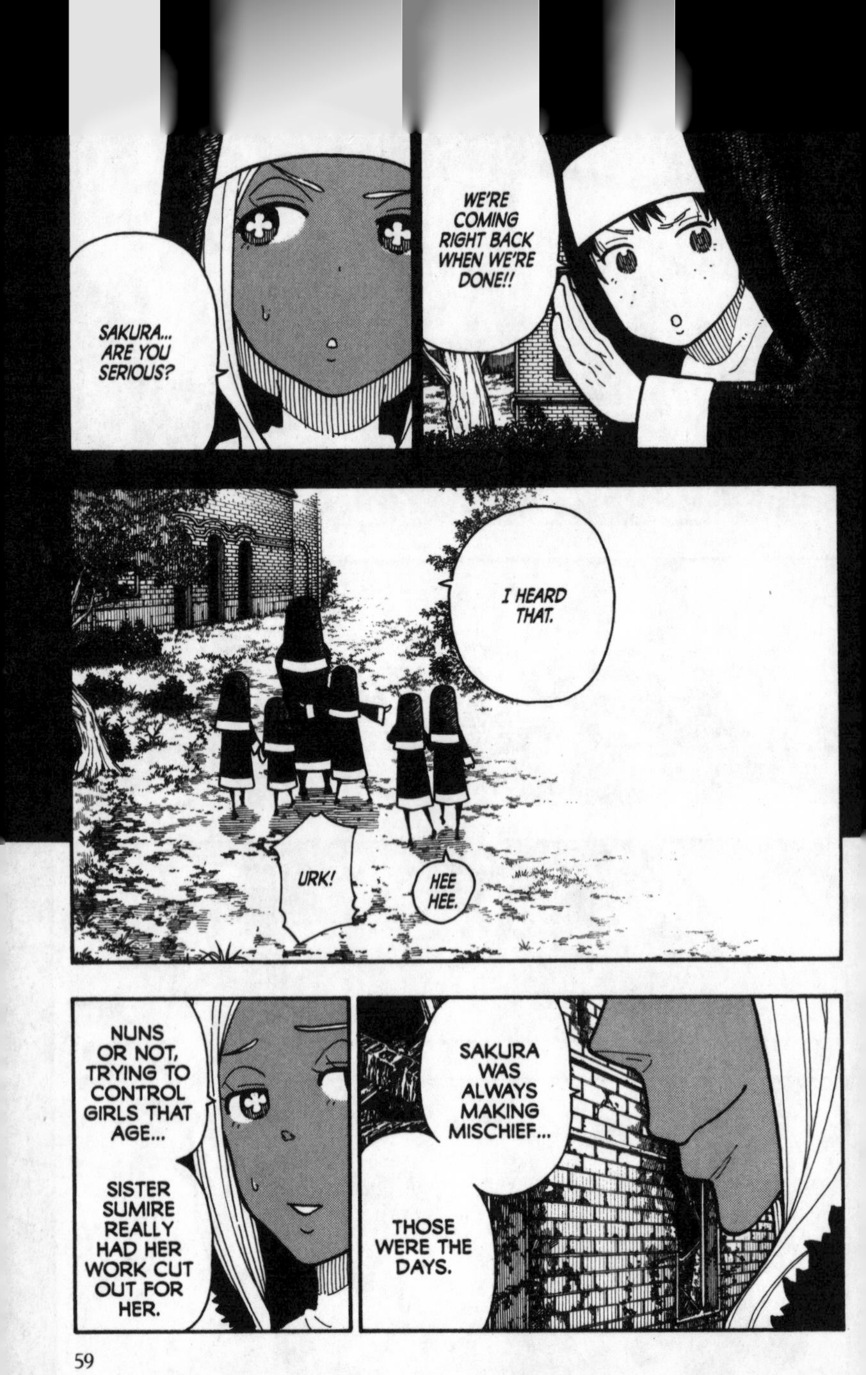
WE'RE COMING RIGHT BACK WHEN WE'RE DONE!!
SAKURA... ARE YOU SERIOUS?
I HEARD THAT.
HEE HEE.
URK!
SAKURA WAS ALWAYS MAKING MISCHIEF...
THOSE WERE THE DAYS.
NUNS OR NOT, TRYING TO CONTROL GIRLS THAT AGE...
SISTER SUMIRE REALLY HAD HER WORK CUT OUT FOR HER.

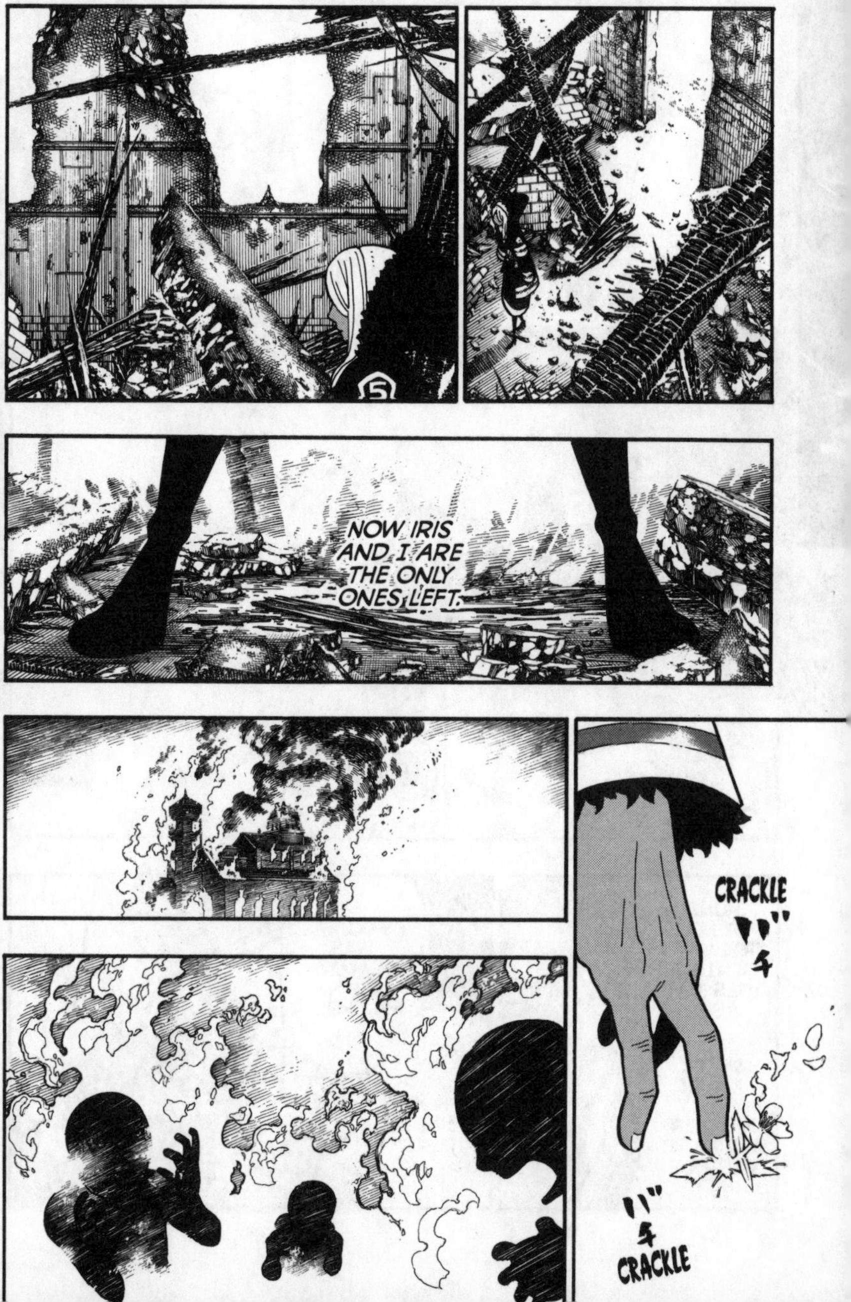
NOW IRIS AND I ARE THE ONLY ONES LEFT.
CRACKLE
バチ
バチ
CRACKLE

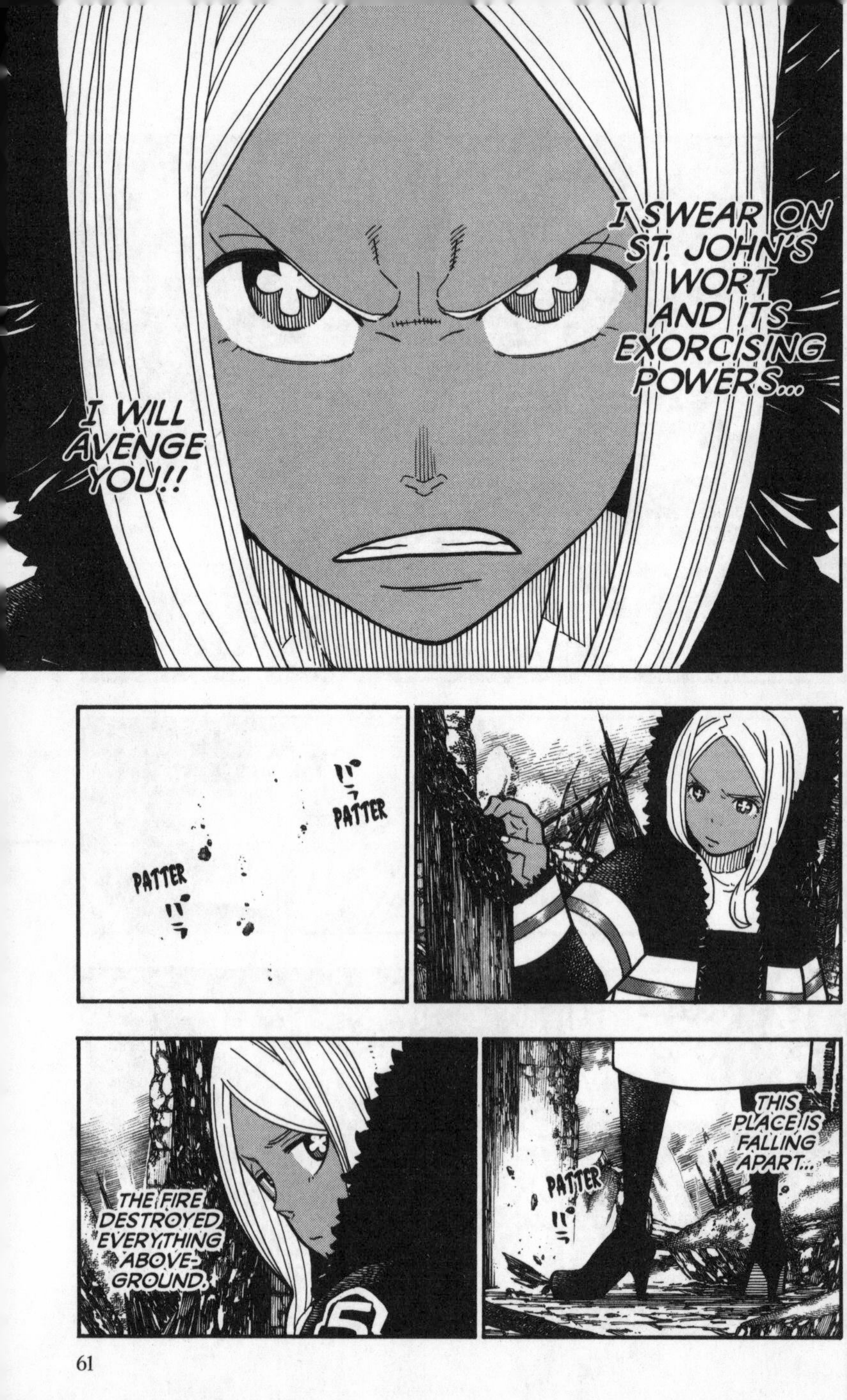
I SWEAR ON ST. JOHN'S WORT AND ITS EXORCISING POWERS...
I WILL AVENGE YOU!!
PATTER
PATTER
THIS PLACE IS FALLING APART...
PATTER
THE FIRE DESTROYED EVERYTHING ABOVE-GROUND.

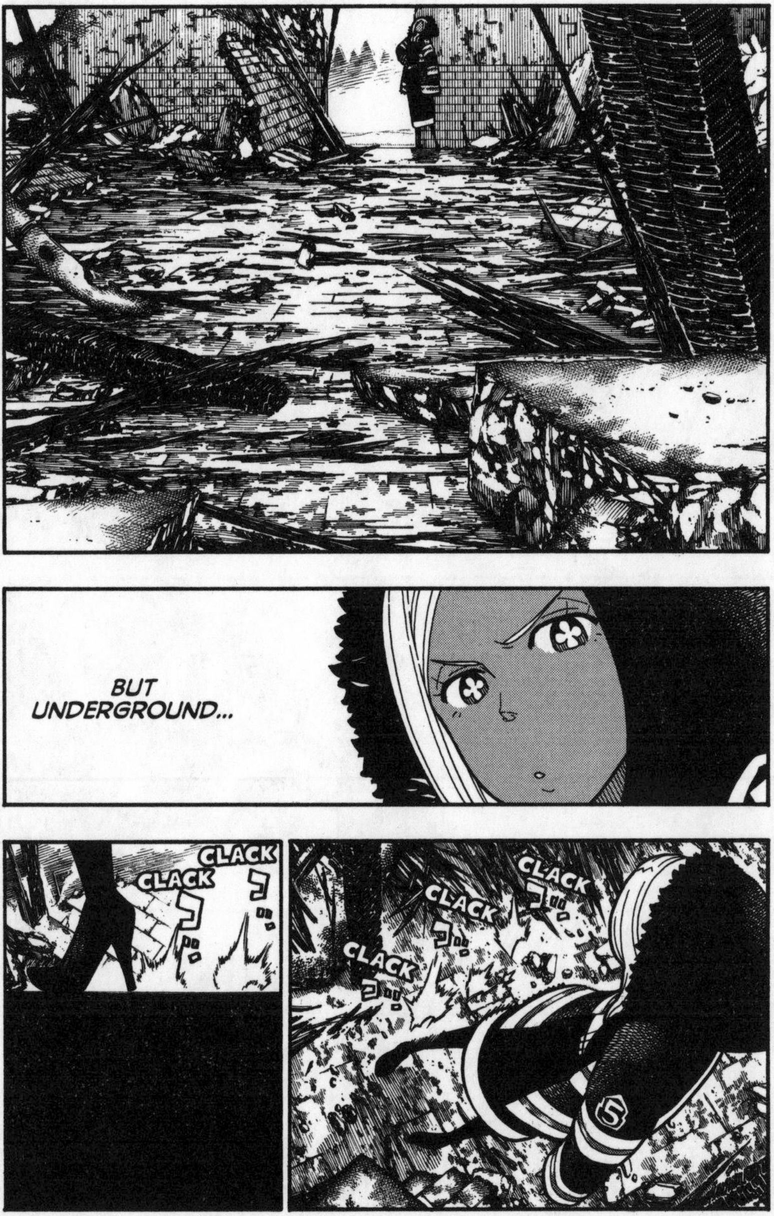
BUT UNDERGROUND...
CLACK
CLACK
CLACK
CLACK
CLACK

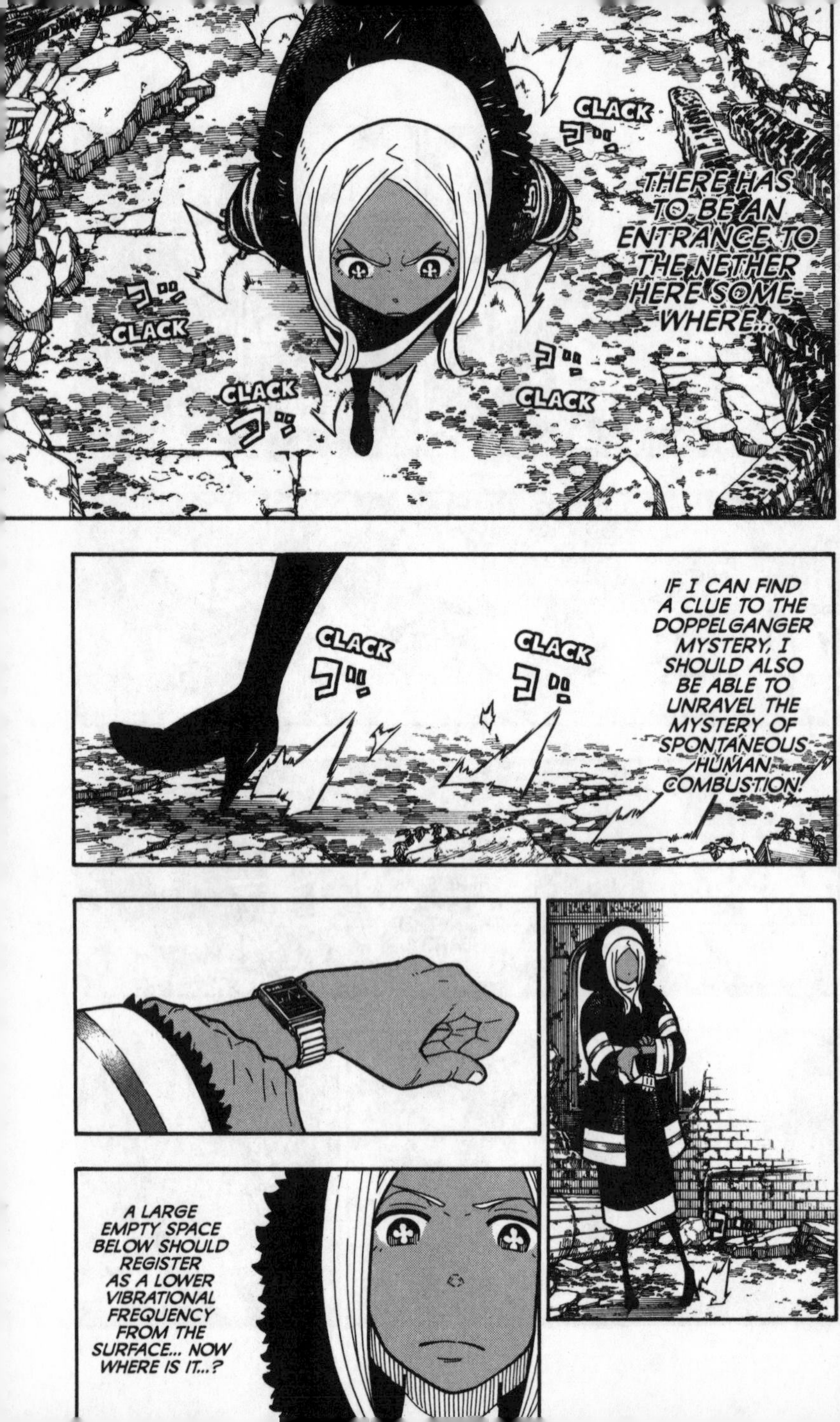
CLACK
THERE HAS TO BE AN ENTRANCE TO THE NETHER HERE SOME-WHERE...
CLACK
CLACK
CLACK
IF I CAN FIND A CLUE TO THE DOPPELGANGER MYSTERY, I SHOULD ALSO BE ABLE TO UNRAVEL THE MYSTERY OF SPONTANEOUS HUMAN COMBUSTION!
CLACK
CLACK
A LARGE EMPTY SPACE BELOW SHOULD REGISTER AS A LOWER VIBRATIONAL FREQUENCY FROM THE SURFACE... NOW WHERE IS IT...?

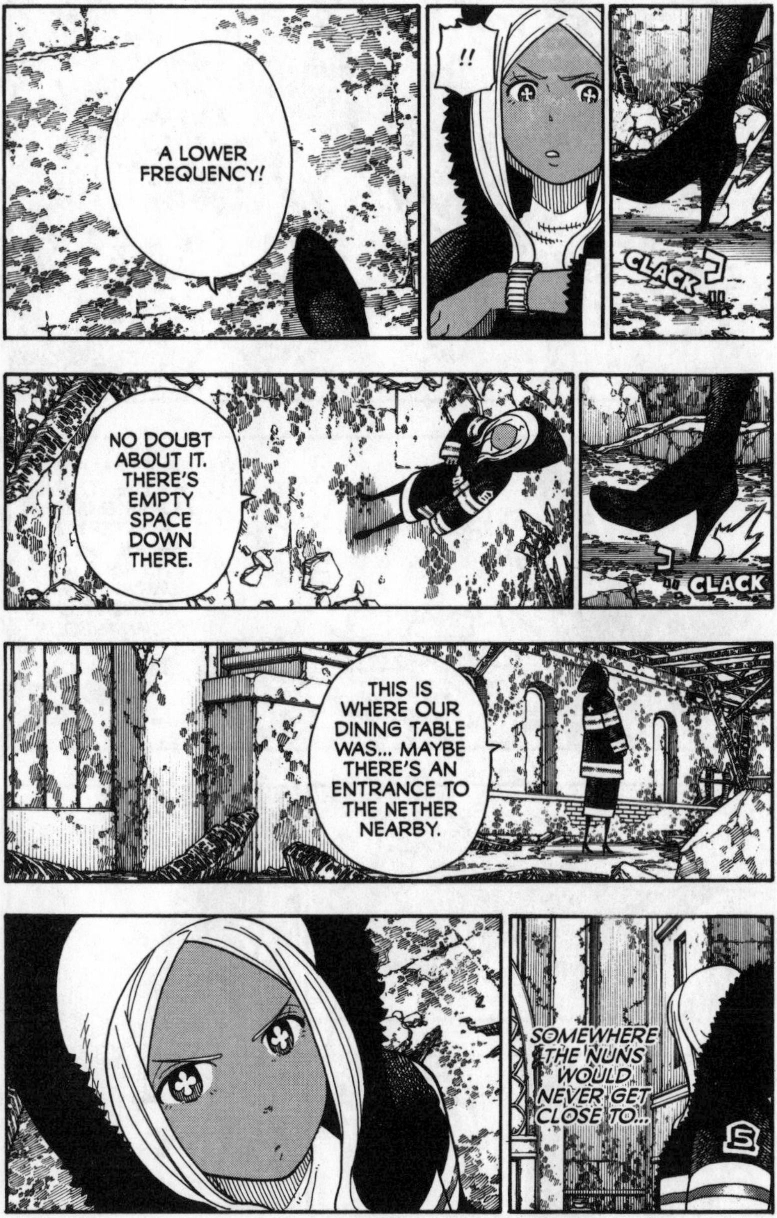
CLACK
!!
A LOWER FREQUENCY!
CLACK
NO DOUBT ABOUT IT. THERE'S EMPTY SPACE DOWN THERE.
THIS IS WHERE OUR DINING TABLE WAS... MAYBE THERE'S AN ENTRANCE TO THE NETHER NEARBY.
SOMEWHERE THE NUNS WOULD NEVER GET CLOSE TO...

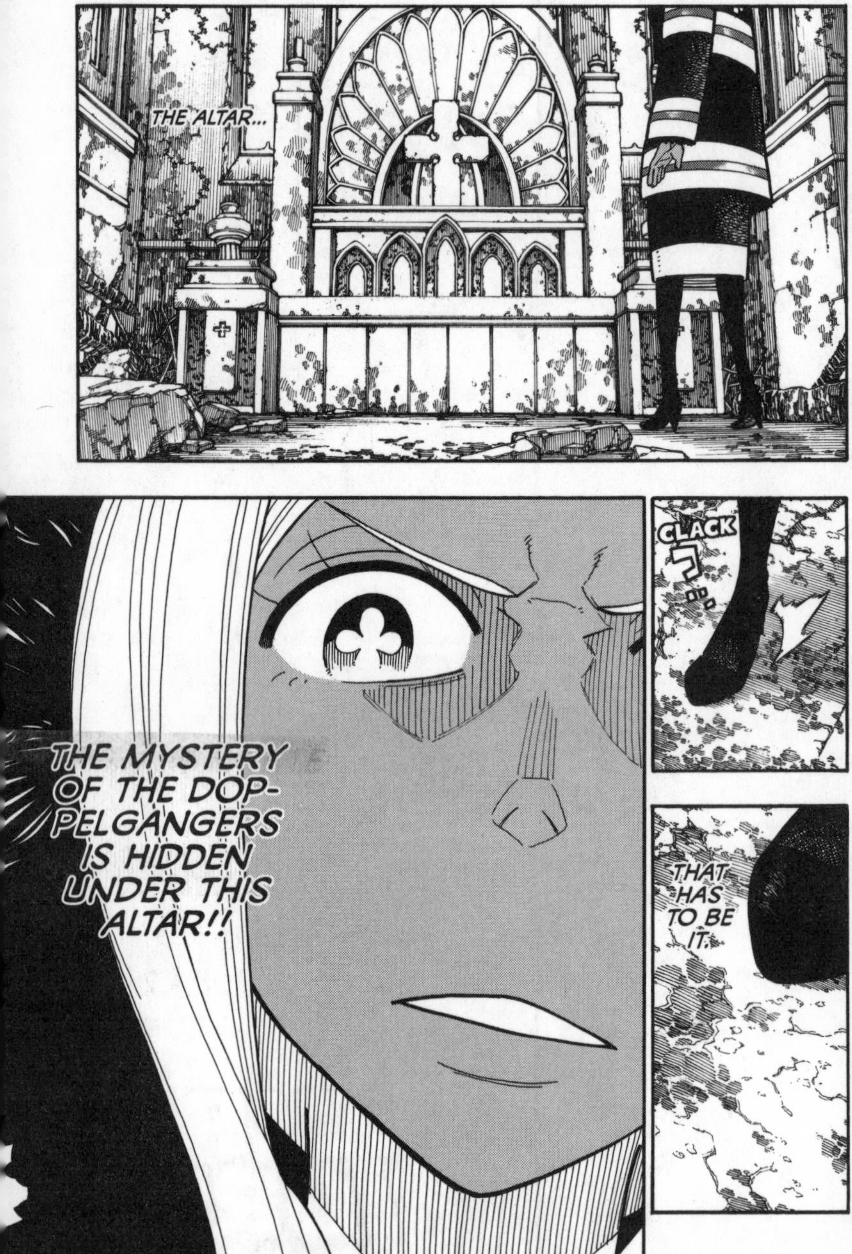
THE ALTAR...
CLACK
THAT HAS TO BE IT.
THE MYSTERY OF THE DOP-PELGANGERS IS HIDDEN UNDER THIS ALTAR!!

FIRE FORCE

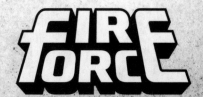

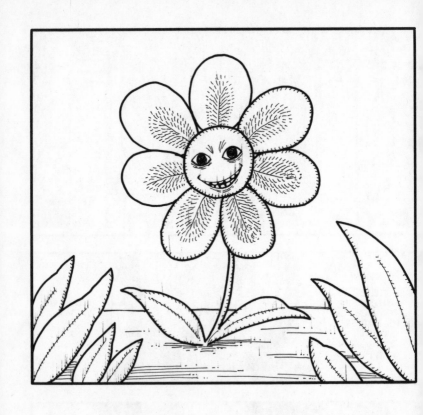

CHAPTER CXCIX: SLUMBERING TRUTH

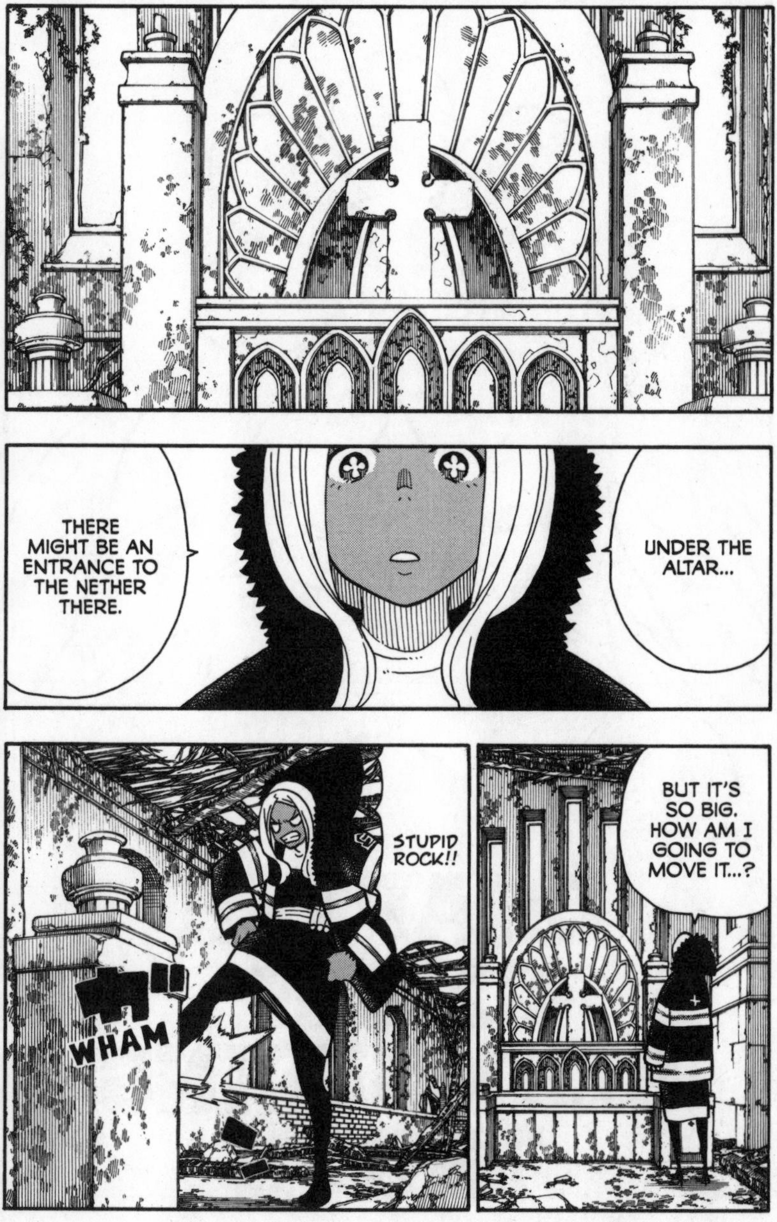
UNDER THE ALTAR...
THERE MIGHT BE AN ENTRANCE TO THE NETHER THERE.
BUT IT'S SO BIG. HOW AM I GOING TO MOVE IT...?
STUPID ROCK!!
WHAM

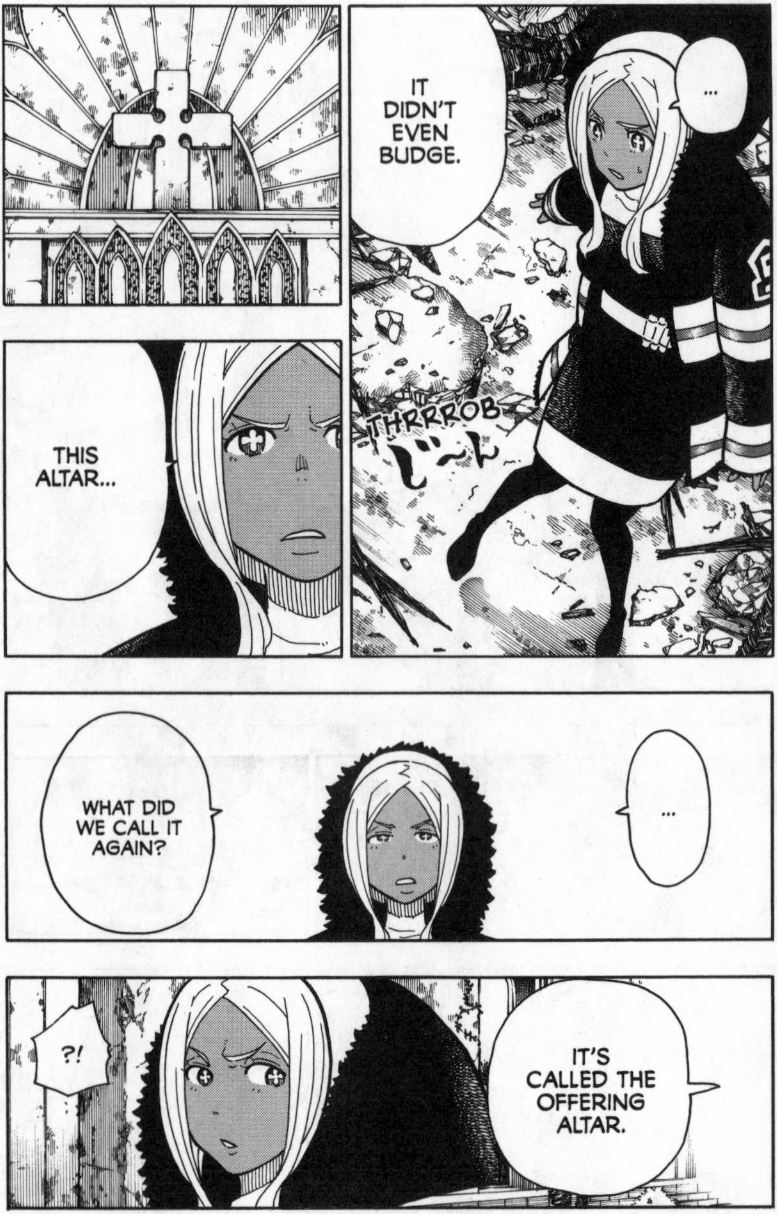
...
IT DIDN'T EVEN BUDGE.
THRRROB
じ~ん
THIS ALTAR...
...
WHAT DID WE CALL IT AGAIN?
IT'S CALLED THE OFFERING ALTAR.
?!

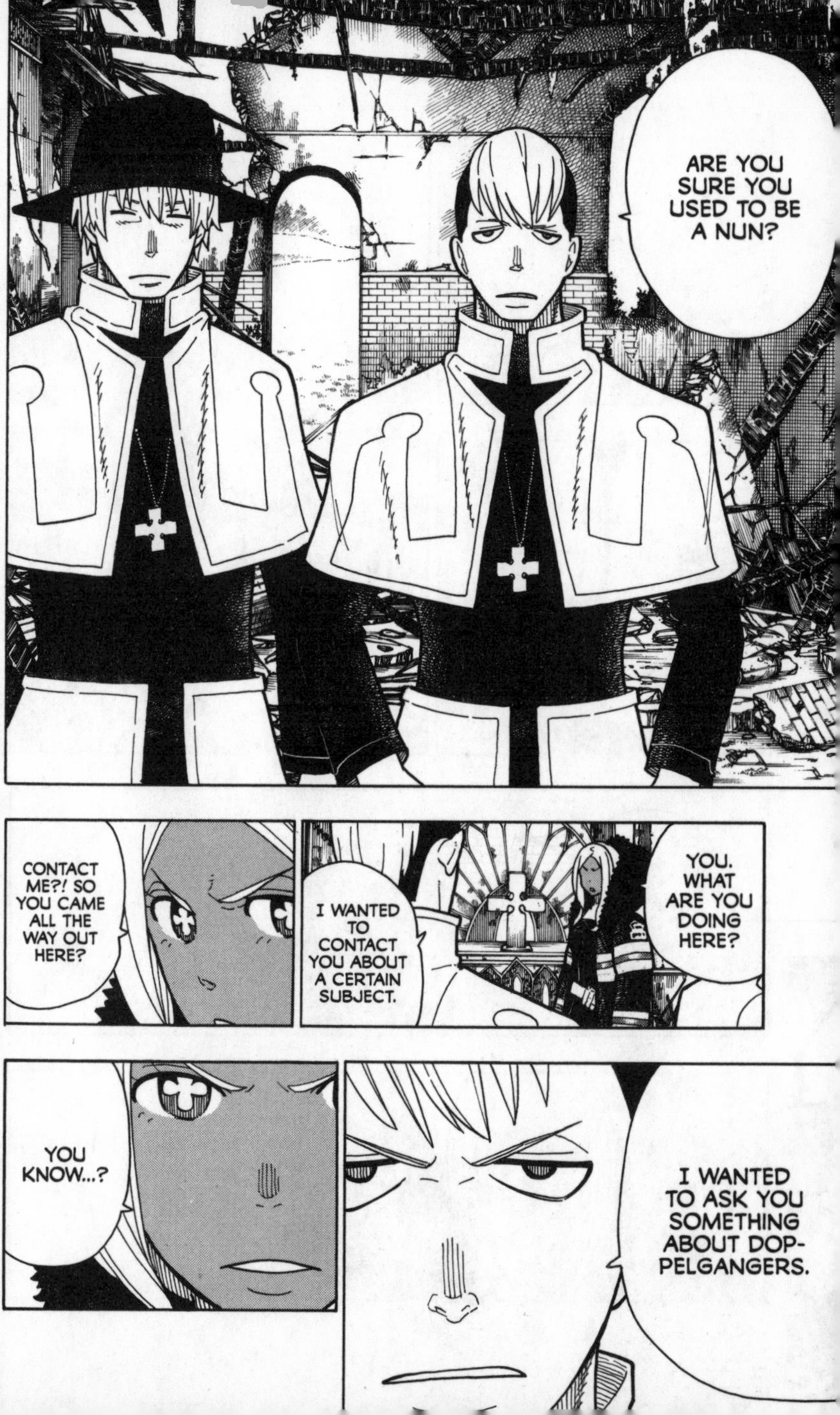
ARE YOU SURE YOU USED TO BE A NUN?
YOU. WHAT ARE YOU DOING HERE?
I WANTED TO CONTACT YOU ABOUT A CERTAIN SUBJECT.
CONTACT ME?! SO YOU CAME ALL THE WAY OUT HERE?
I WANTED TO ASK YOU SOMETHING ABOUT DOP-PELGANGERS.
YOU KNOW...?

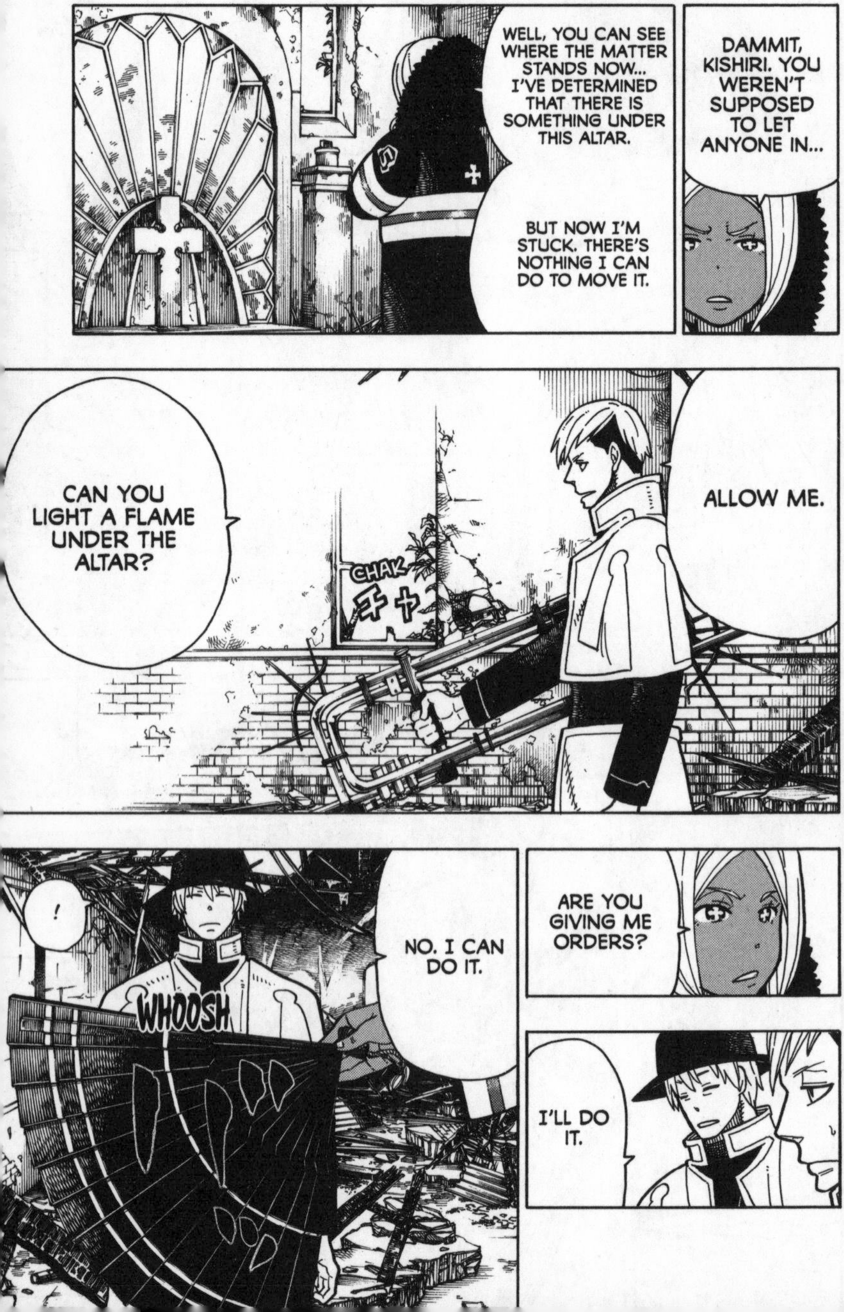
DAMMIT, KISHIRI. YOU WEREN'T SUPPOSED TO LET ANYONE IN...
WELL, YOU CAN SEE WHERE THE MATTER STANDS NOW... I'VE DETERMINED THAT THERE IS SOMETHING UNDER THIS ALTAR.
BUT NOW I'M STUCK. THERE'S NOTHING I CAN DO TO MOVE IT.
ALLOW ME.
CHAK
チャ
CAN YOU LIGHT A FLAME UNDER THE ALTAR?
ARE YOU GIVING ME ORDERS?
I'LL DO IT.
NO. I CAN DO IT.
!
WHOOSH

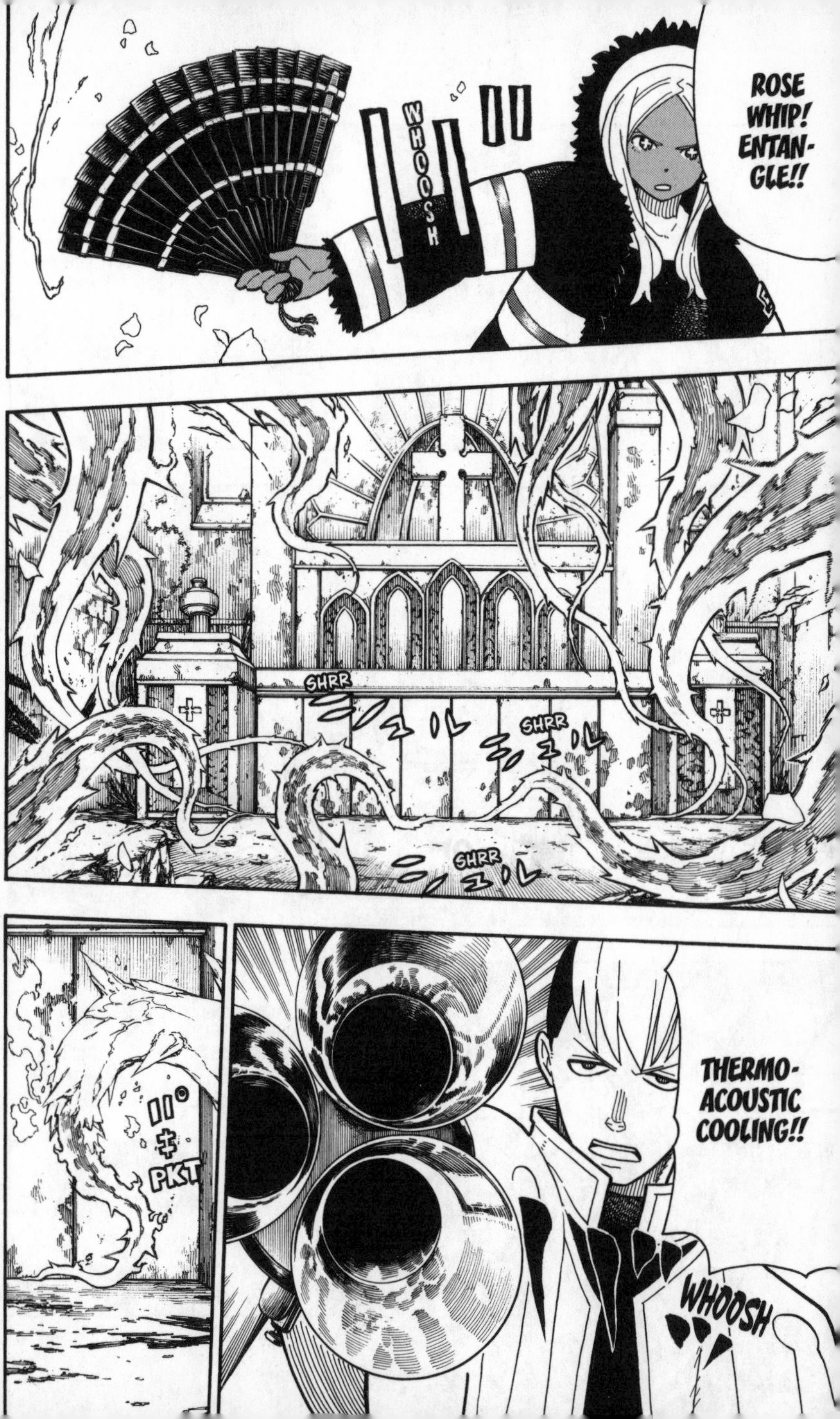
ROSE WHIP! ENTAN-GLE!!
WHOOSH
SHRR
SHRR
SHRR
THERMO-ACOUSTIC COOLING!!
WHOOSH
PKT

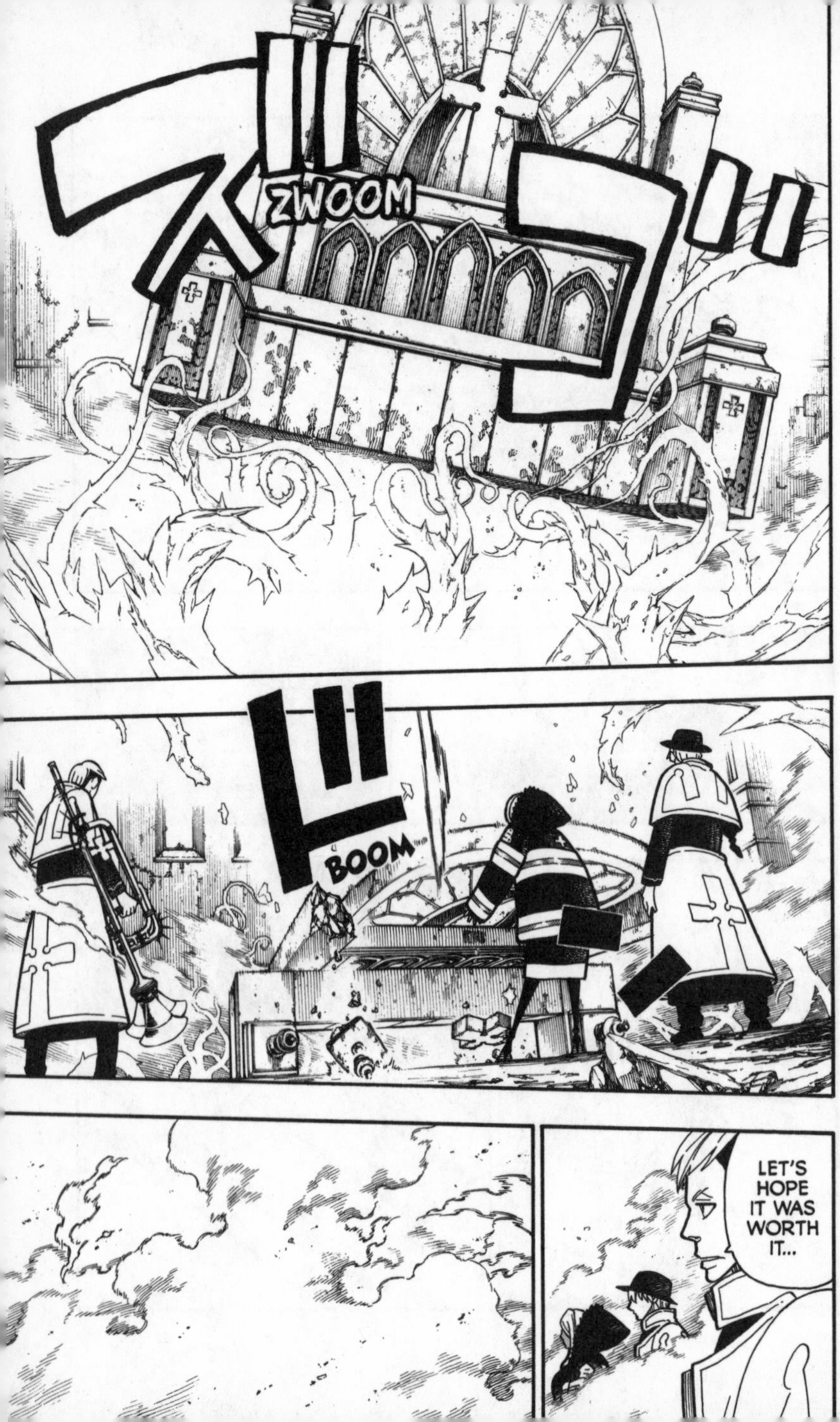
ZWOOM
BOOM
LET'S HOPE IT WAS WORTH IT...

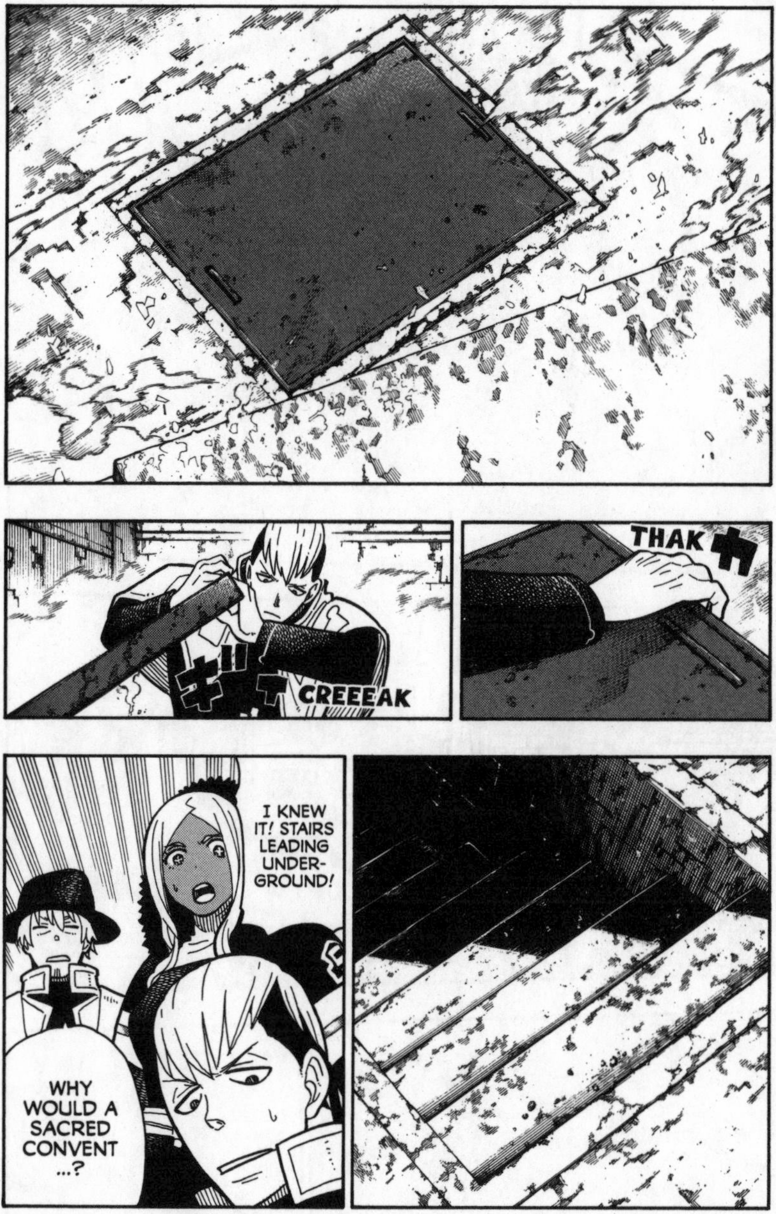
THAK
CREEEAK
I KNEW IT! STAIRS LEADING UNDER-GROUND!
WHY WOULD A SACRED CONVENT ...?

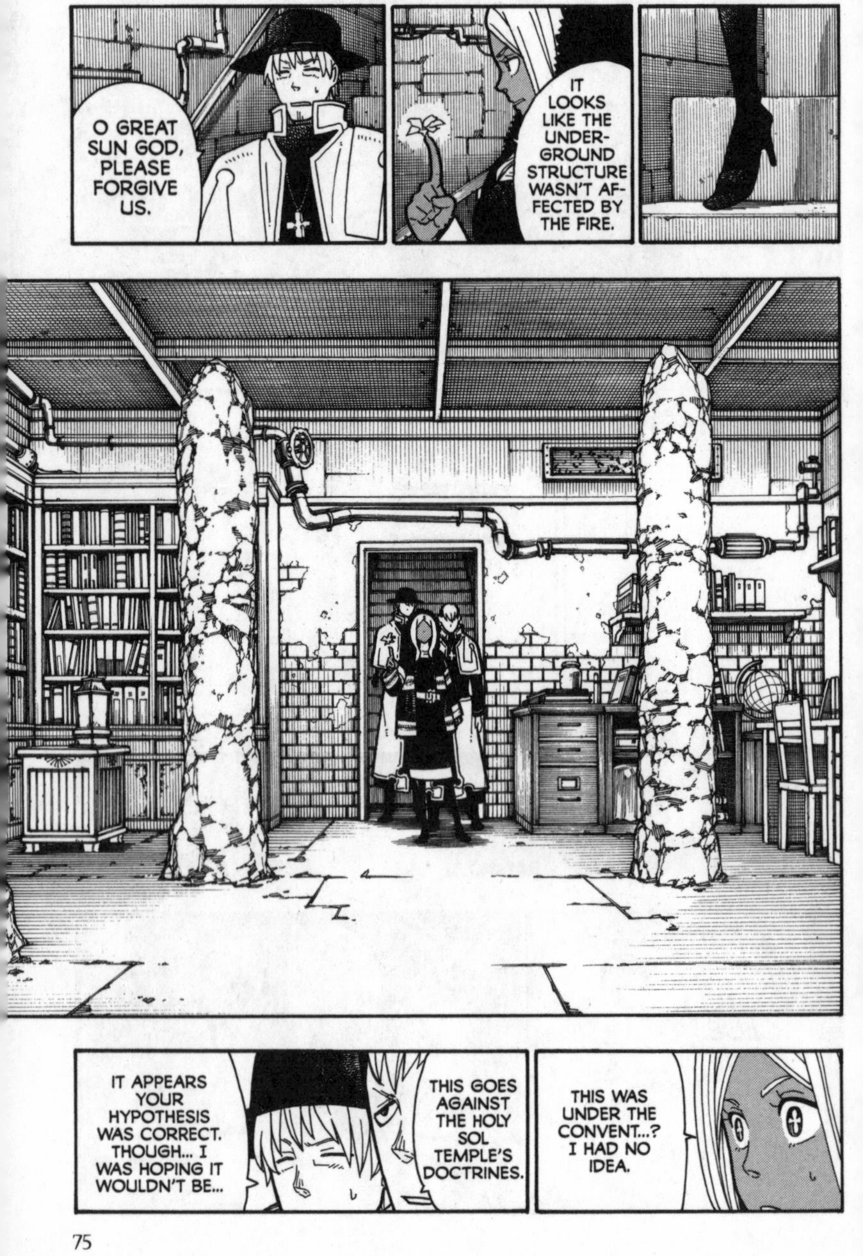
IT LOOKS LIKE THE UNDER-GROUND STRUCTURE WASN'T AF-FECTED BY THE FIRE.
O GREAT SUN GOD, PLEASE FORGIVE US.
THIS WAS UNDER THE CONVENT...? I HAD NO IDEA.
THIS GOES AGAINST THE HOLY SOL TEMPLE'S DOCTRINES.
IT APPEARS YOUR HYPOTHESIS WAS CORRECT. THOUGH... I WAS HOPING IT WOULDN'T BE...

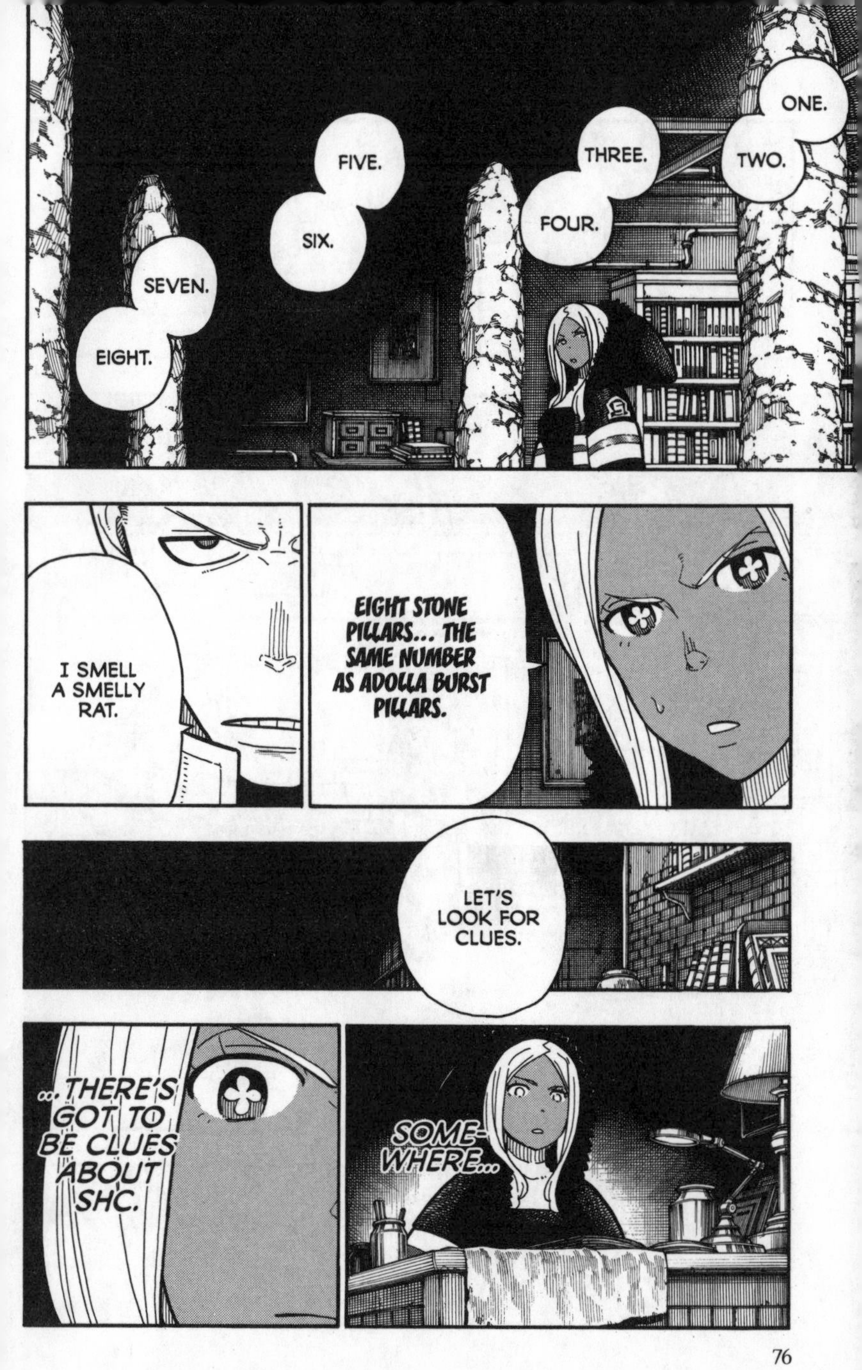
ONE.
TWO.
THREE.
FOUR.
FIVE.
SIX.
SEVEN.
EIGHT.
EIGHT STONE PILLARS... THE SAME NUMBER AS ADOLLA BURST PILLARS.
I SMELL A SMELLY RAT.
LET'S LOOK FOR CLUES.
SOME-WHERE...
...THERE'S GOT TO BE CLUES ABOUT SHC.

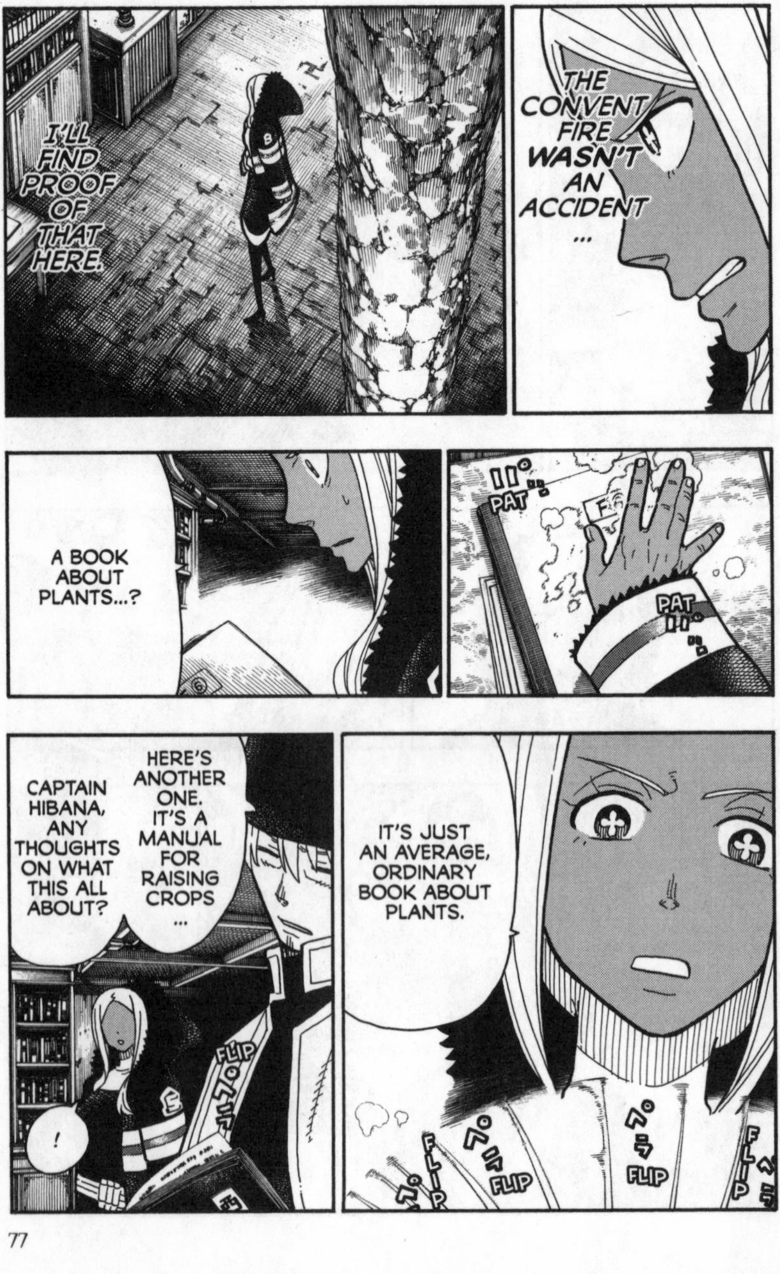
THE CONVENT FIRE WASN'T AN ACCIDENT ...
I'LL FIND PROOF OF THAT HERE.
PAT
PAT
A BOOK ABOUT PLANTS...?
IT'S JUST AN AVERAGE, ORDINARY BOOK ABOUT PLANTS.
FLIP
FLIP
FLIP
FLIP
HERE'S ANOTHER ONE. IT'S A MANUAL FOR RAISING CROPS ...
CAPTAIN HIBANA, ANY THOUGHTS ON WHAT THIS ALL ABOUT?
FLIP
!

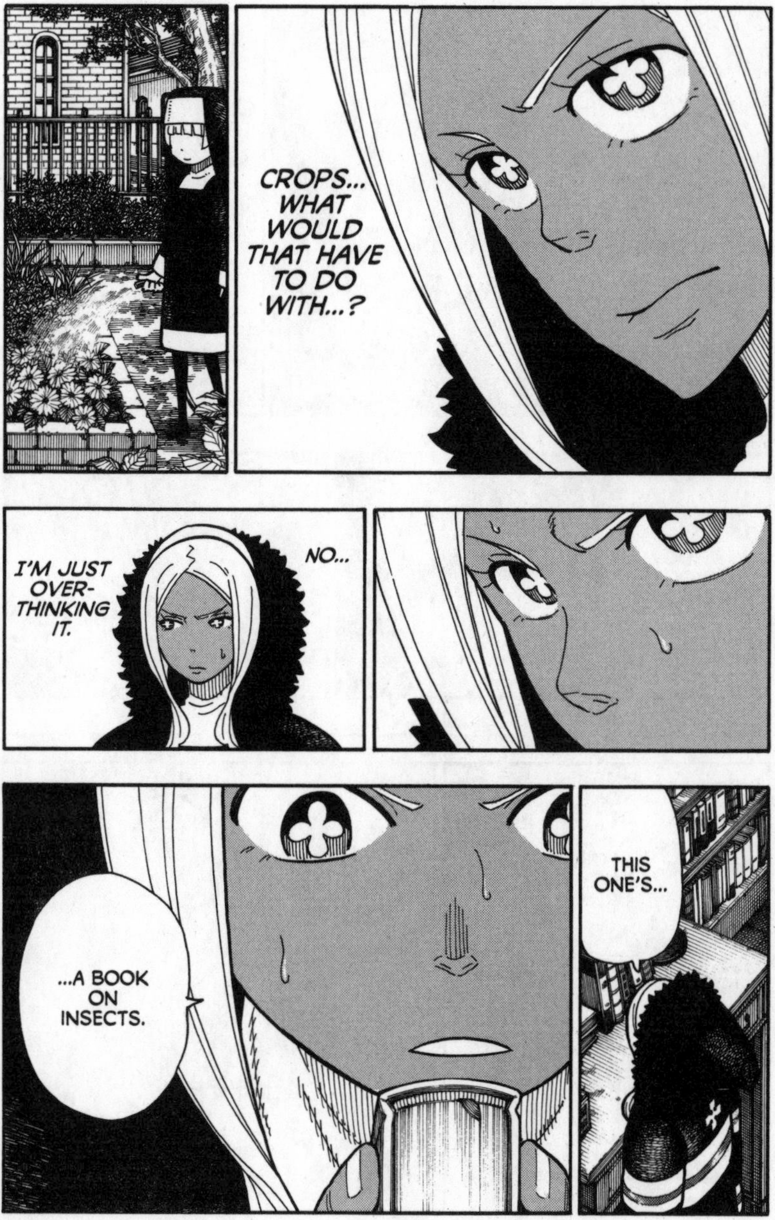
CROPS... WHAT WOULD THAT HAVE TO DO WITH...?
NO...
I'M JUST OVER-THINKING IT.
THIS ONE'S...
...A BOOK ON INSECTS.

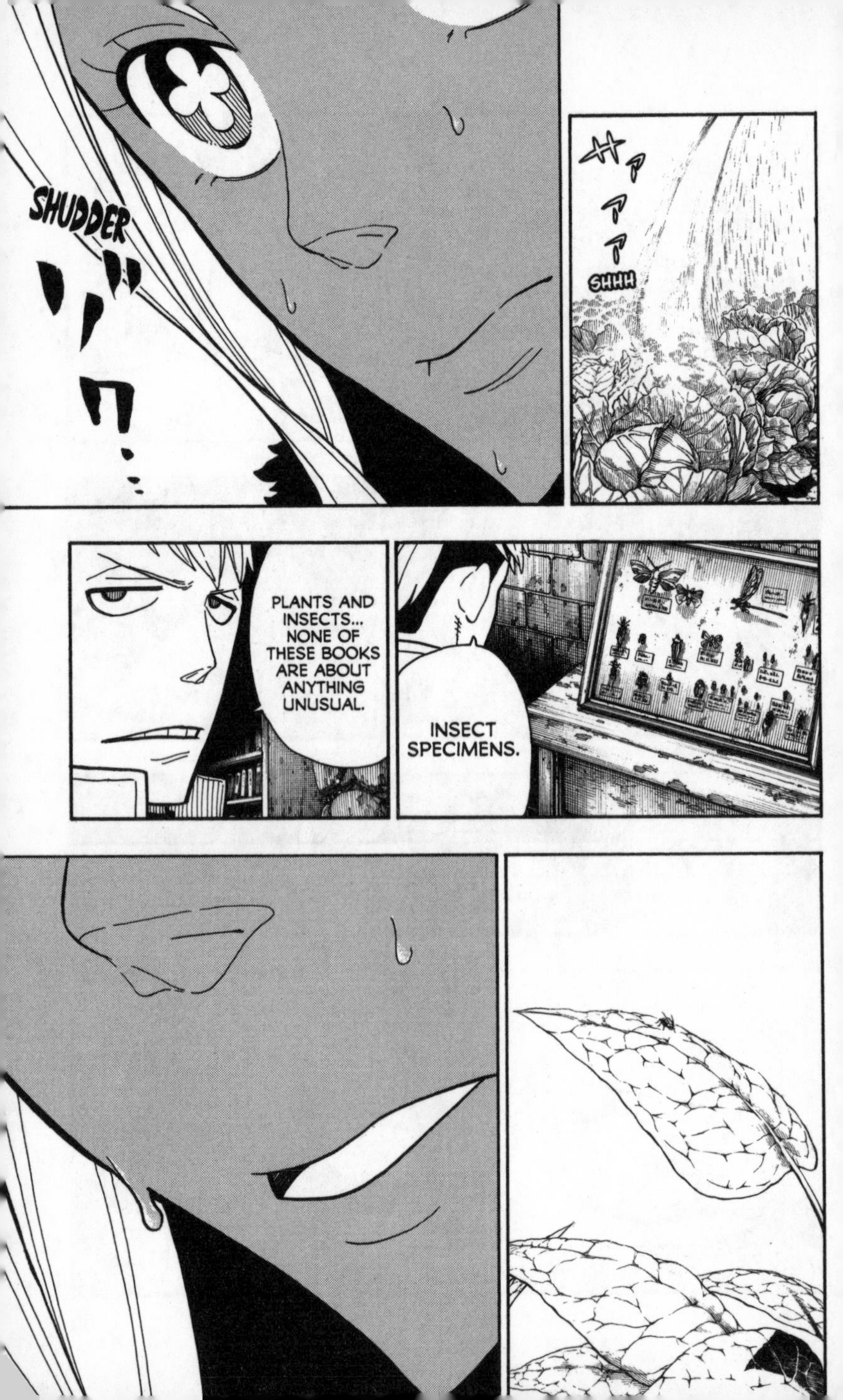
SHHH
SHUDDER
INSECT SPECIMENS.
PLANTS AND INSECTS... NONE OF THESE BOOKS ARE ABOUT ANYTHING UNUSUAL.

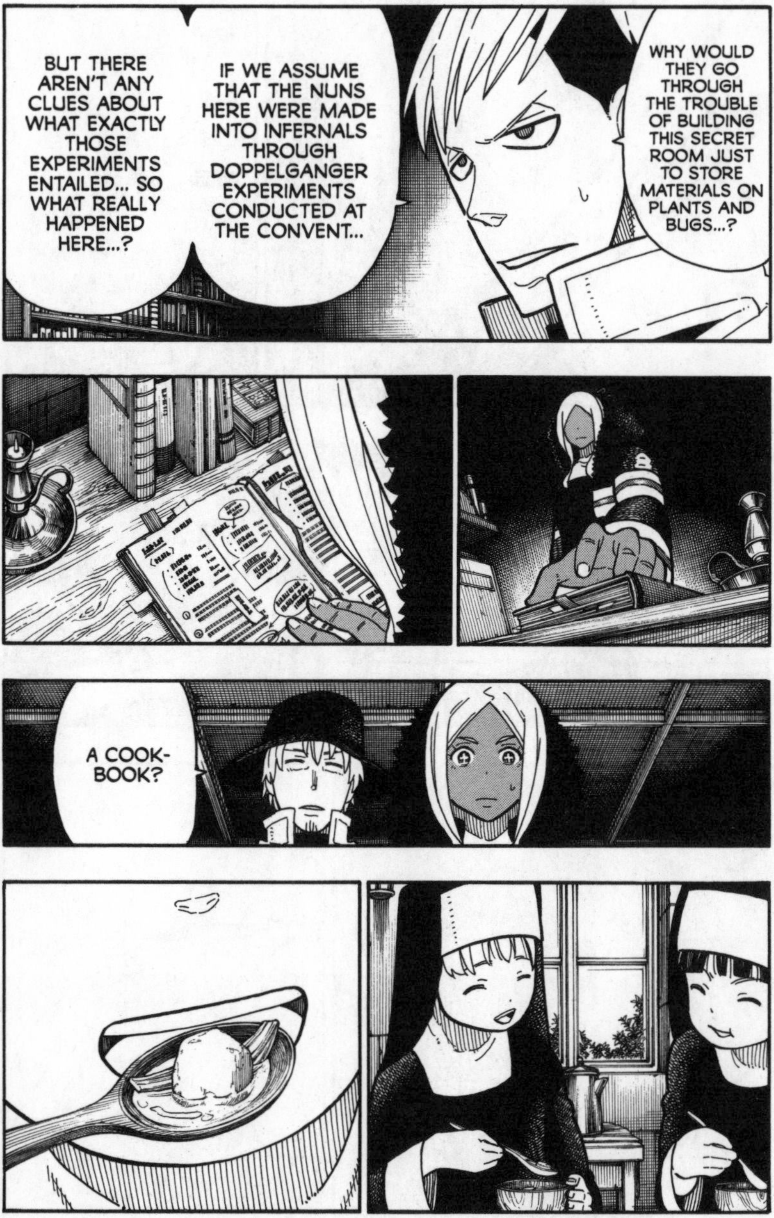
WHY WOULD THEY GO THROUGH THE TROUBLE OF BUILDING THIS SECRET ROOM JUST TO STORE MATERIALS ON PLANTS AND BUGS...?
IF WE ASSUME THAT THE NUNS HERE WERE MADE INTO INFERNALS THROUGH DOPPELGANGER EXPERIMENTS CONDUCTED AT THE CONVENT...
BUT THERE AREN'T ANY CLUES ABOUT WHAT EXACTLY THOSE EXPERIMENTS ENTAILED... SO WHAT REALLY HAPPENED HERE...?
A COOK-BOOK?

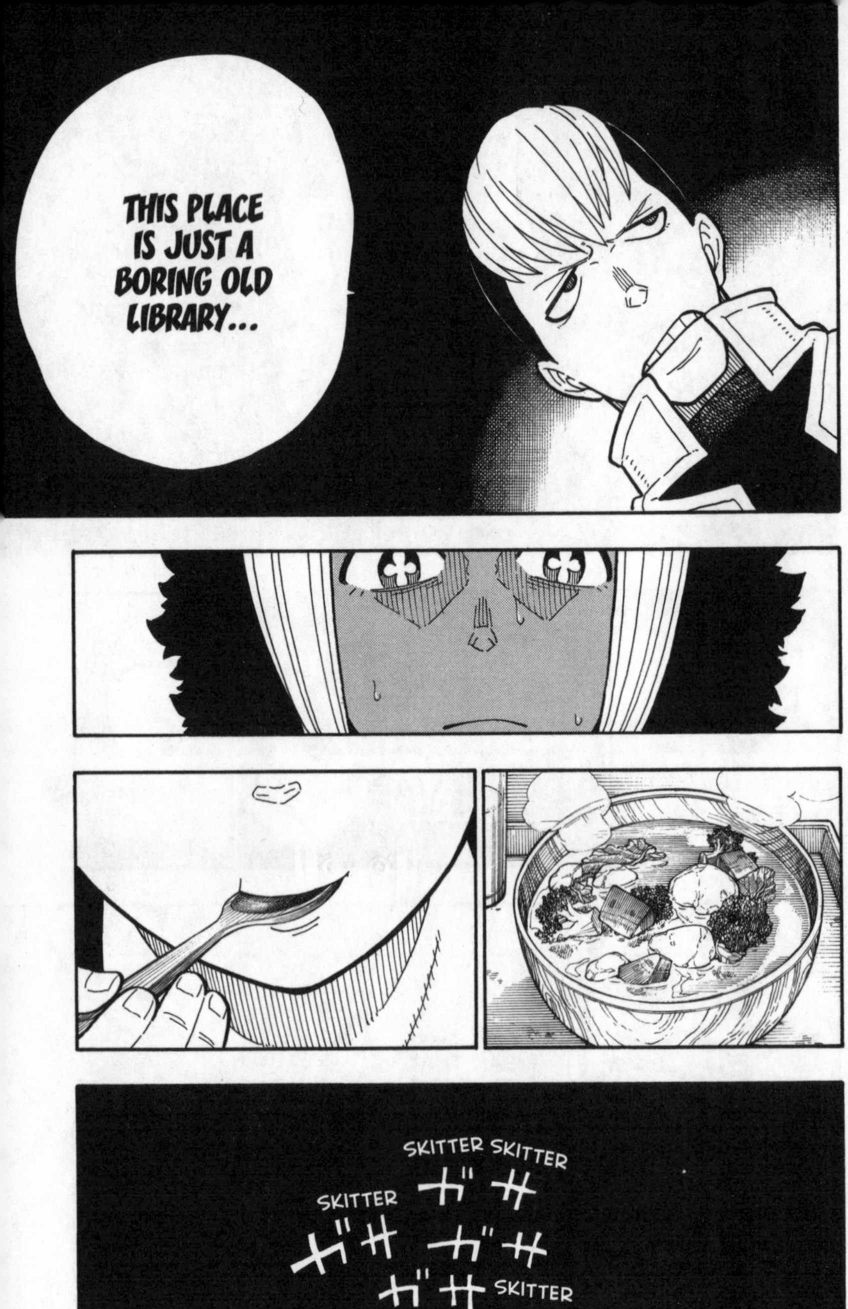
THIS PLACE IS JUST A BORING OLD LIBRARY...
SKITTER SKITTER
ガサ
SKITTER
ガサ ガサ
ガサ
SKITTER

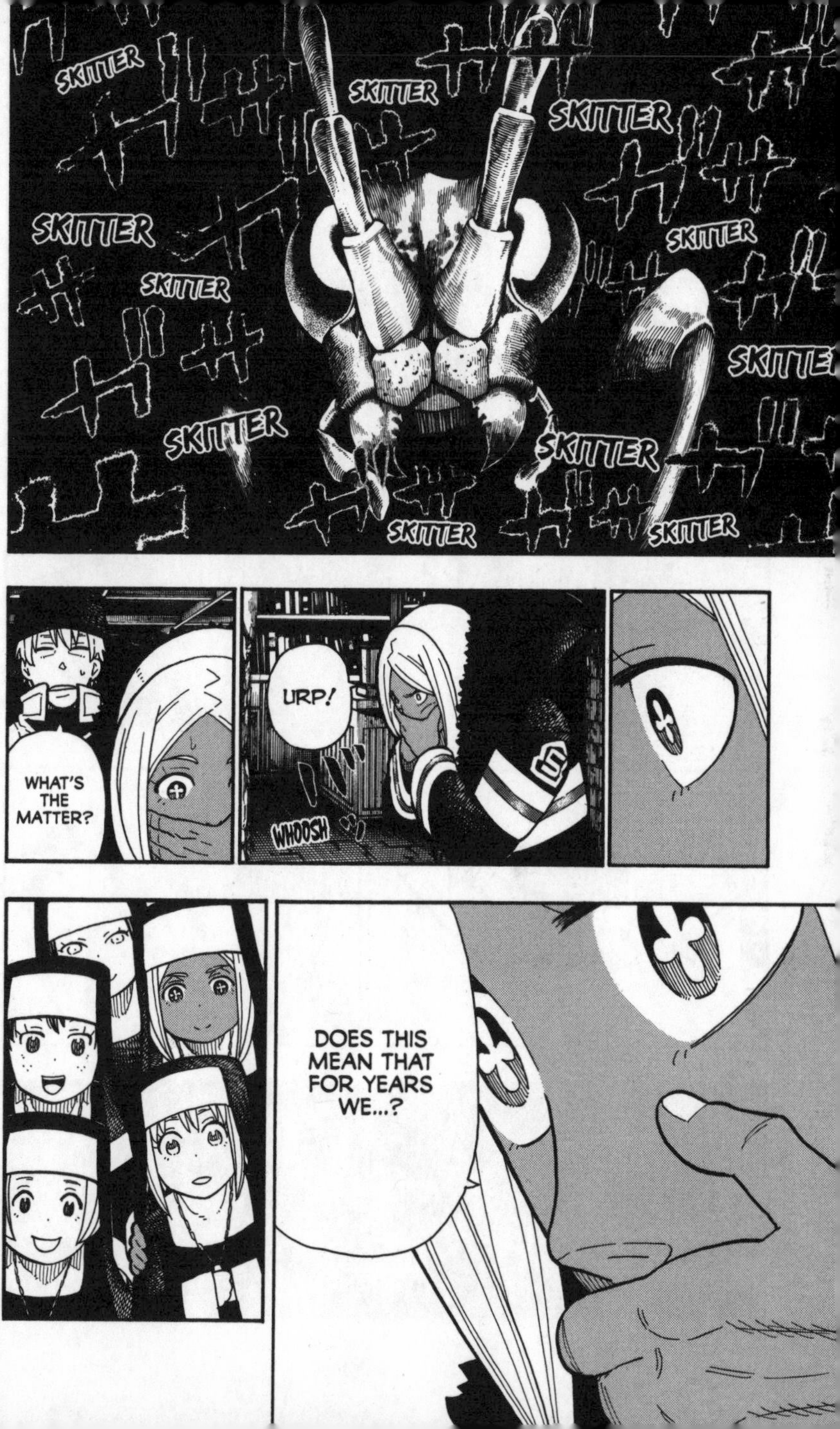
SKITTER
SKITTER
SKITTER
SKITTER
SKITTE
SKITTER
SKITTER
SKITTER
SKITTER
SKITTER
SKITTER
URP!
WHOOSH
WHAT'S THE MATTER?
DOES THIS MEAN THAT FOR YEARS WE...?

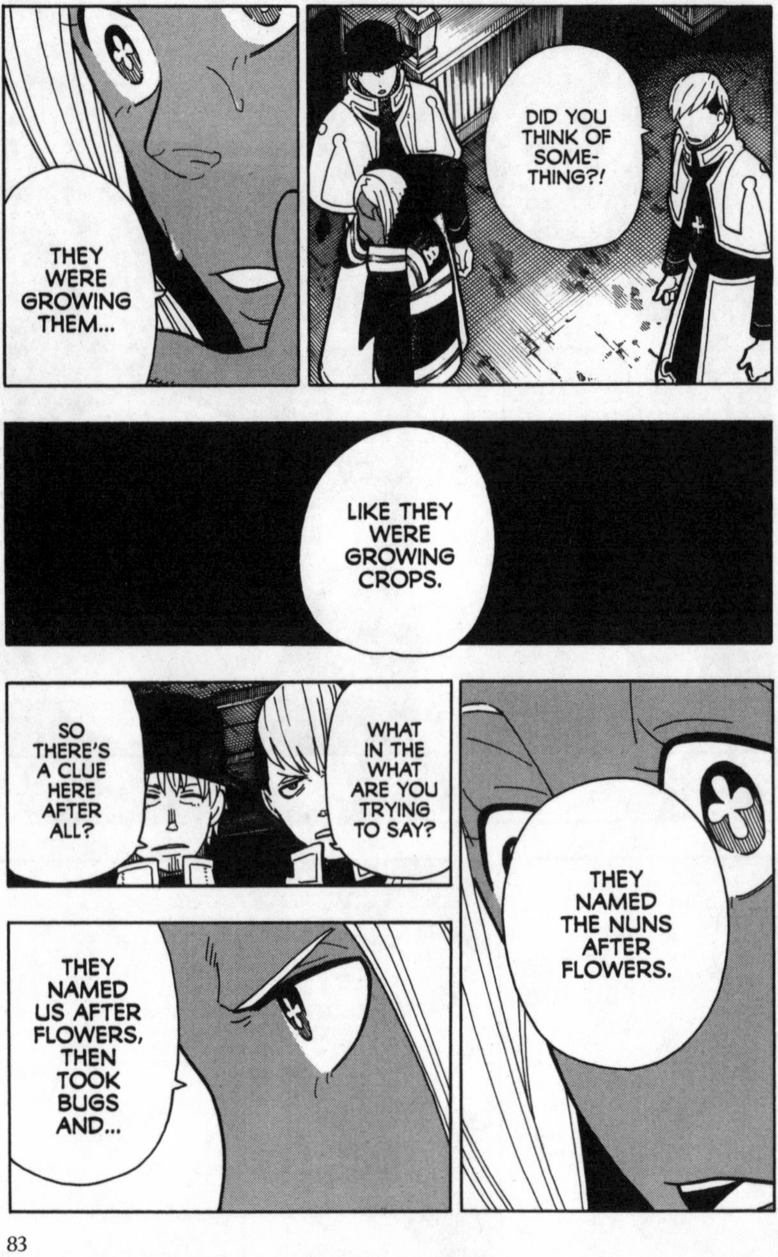
DID YOU THINK OF SOME-THING?!
THEY WERE GROWING THEM...
LIKE THEY WERE GROWING CROPS.
THEY NAMED THE NUNS AFTER FLOWERS.
WHAT IN THE WHAT ARE YOU TRYING TO SAY?
SO THERE'S A CLUE HERE AFTER ALL?
THEY NAMED US AFTER FLOWERS, THEN TOOK BUGS AND...

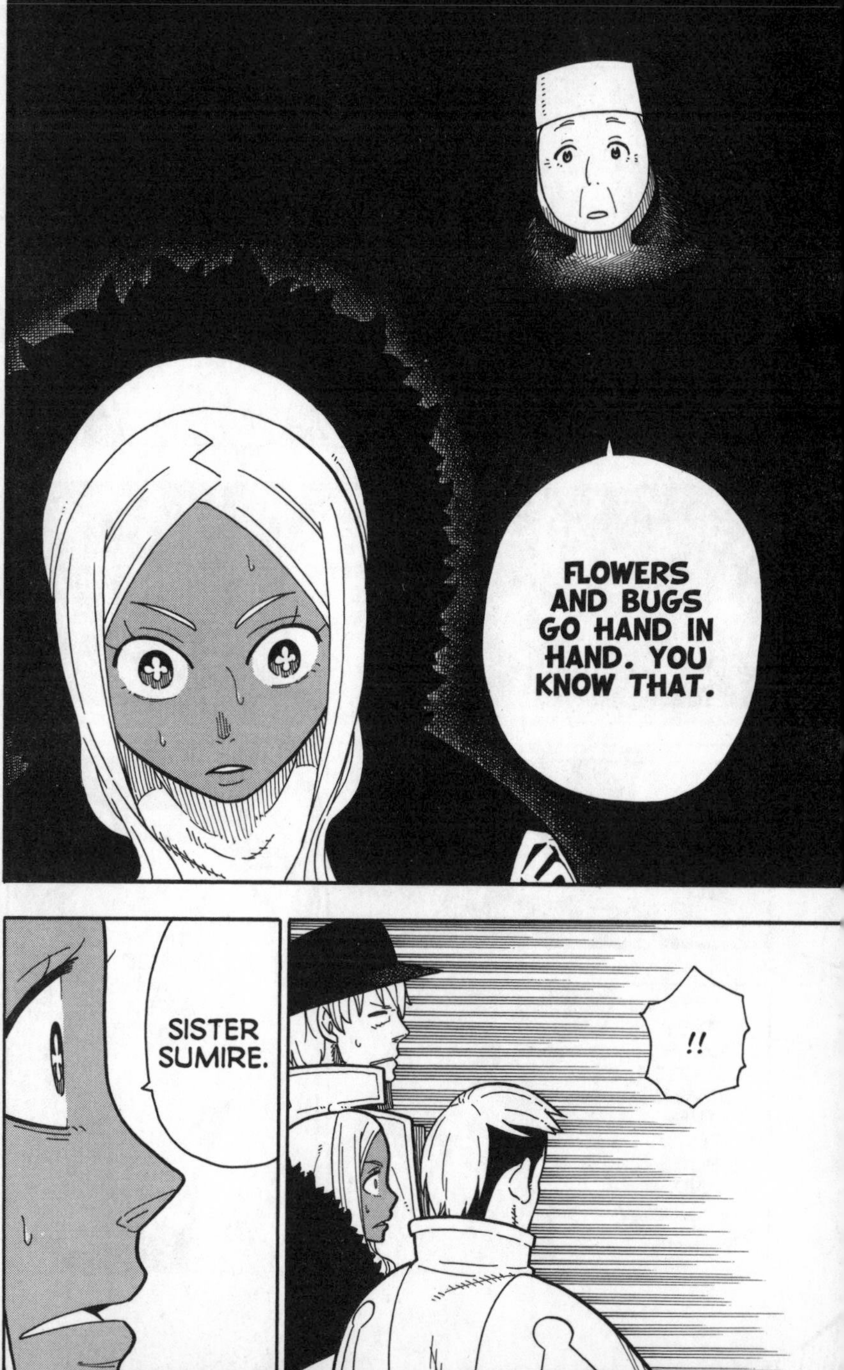
FLOWERS AND BUGS GO HAND IN HAND. YOU KNOW THAT.
!!
SISTER SUMIRE.

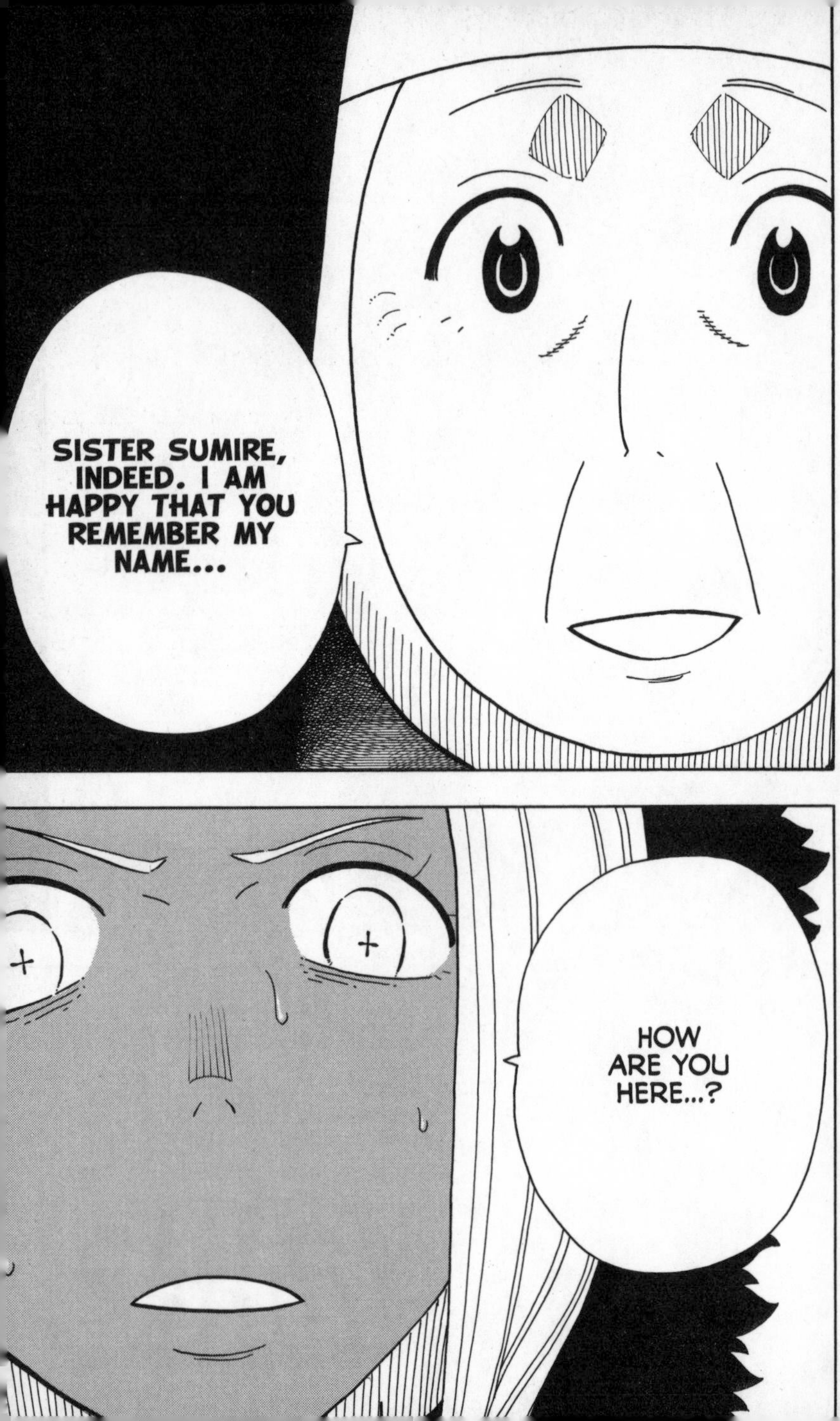
SISTER SUMIRE, INDEED. I AM HAPPY THAT YOU REMEMBER MY NAME...
HOW ARE YOU HERE...?

FIRE FORCE

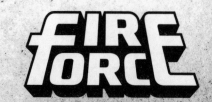

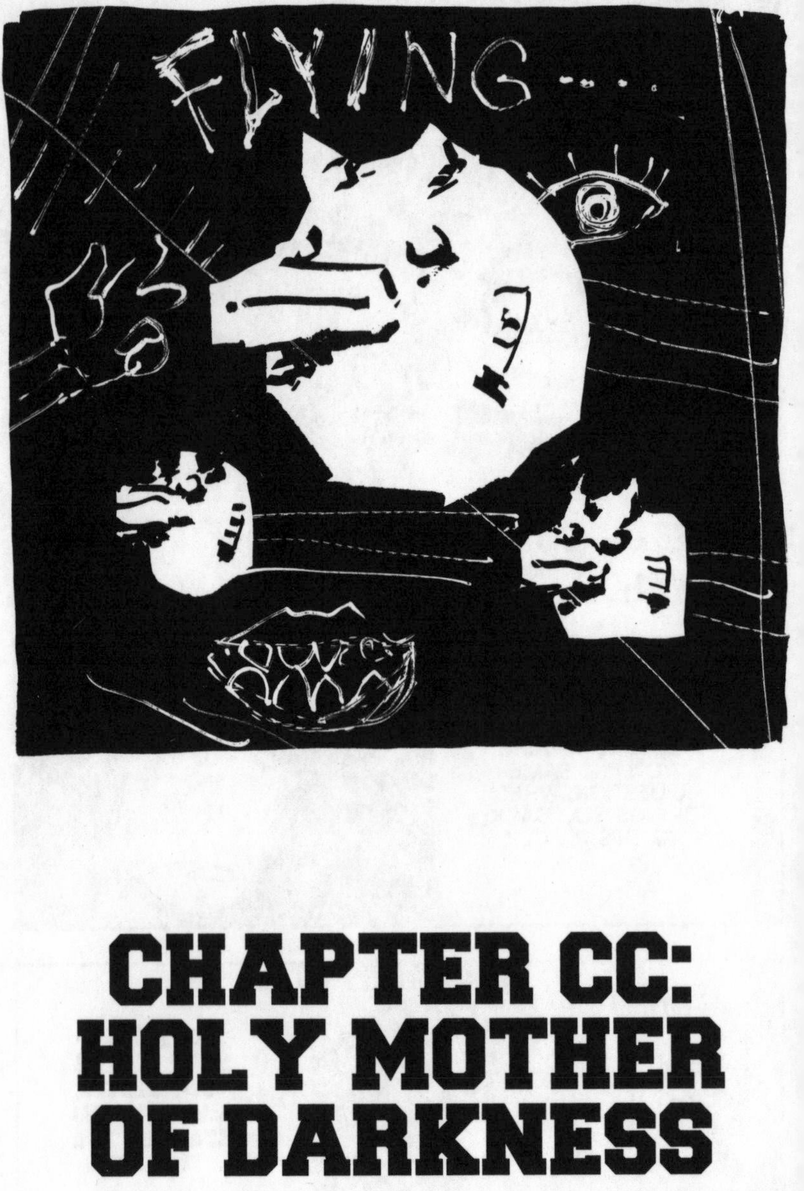
FLYING...

CHAPTER CC: HOLY MOTHER OF DARKNESS

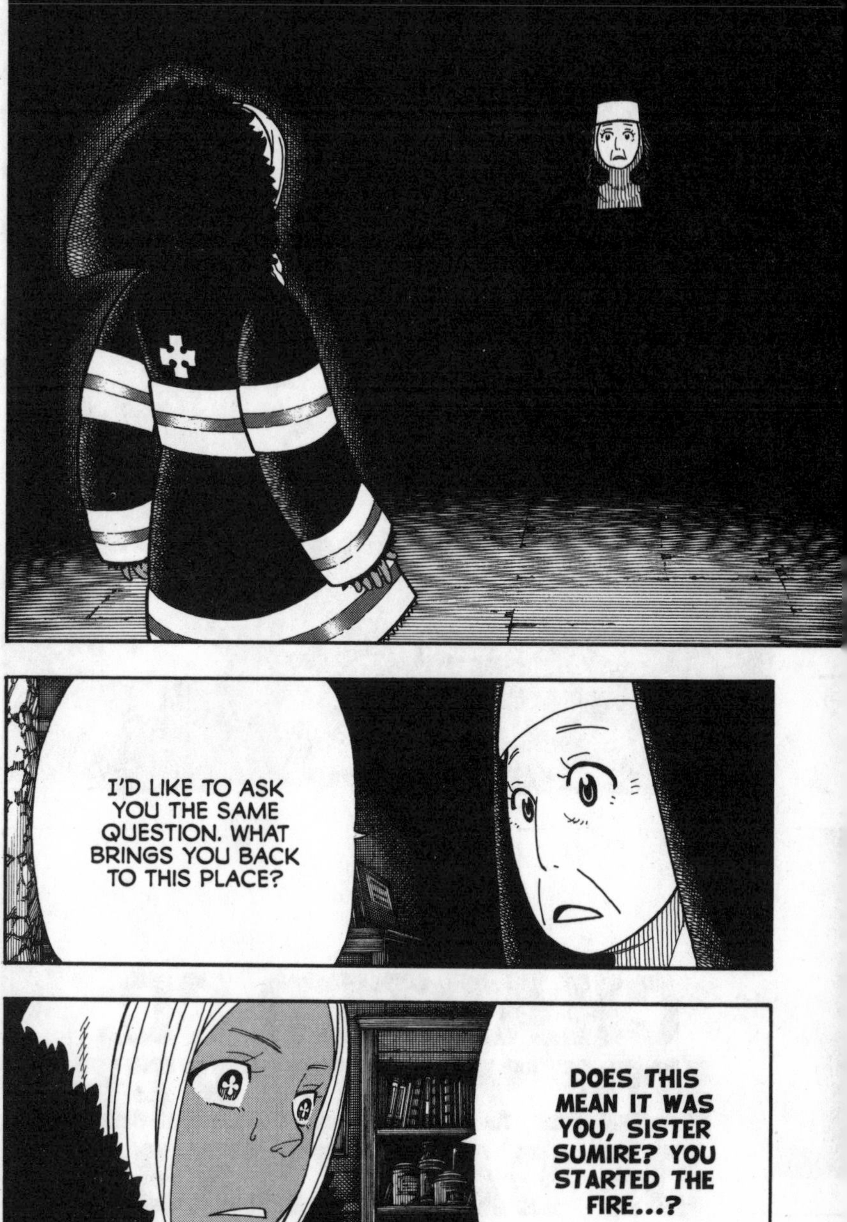
I'D LIKE TO ASK YOU THE SAME QUESTION. WHAT BRINGS YOU BACK TO THIS PLACE?
DOES THIS MEAN IT WAS YOU, SISTER SUMIRE? YOU STARTED THE FIRE...?

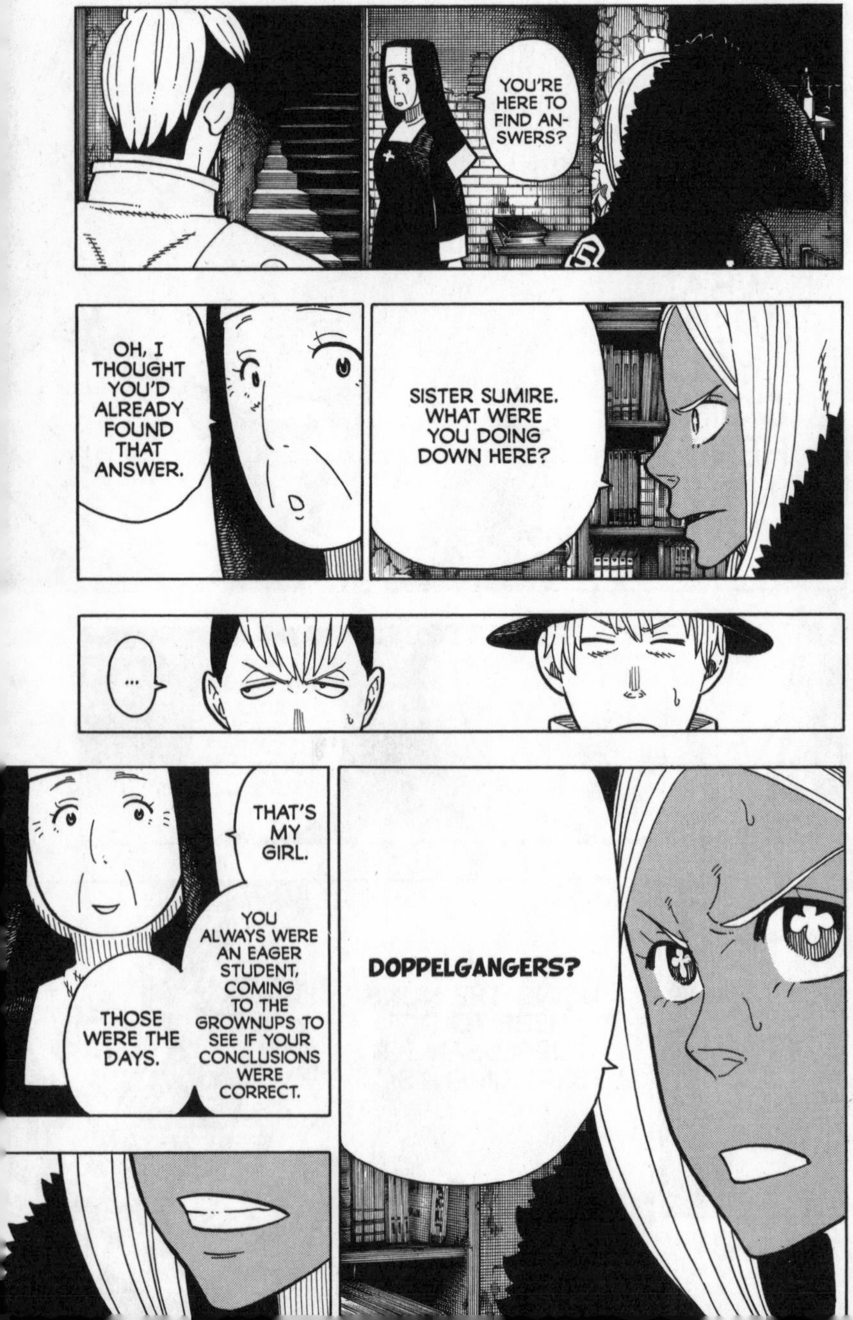
YOU'RE HERE TO FIND AN-SWERS?
SISTER SUMIRE. WHAT WERE YOU DOING DOWN HERE?
OH, I THOUGHT YOU'D ALREADY FOUND THAT ANSWER.
...
DOPPELGANGERS?
THAT'S MY GIRL.
YOU ALWAYS WERE AN EAGER STUDENT, COMING TO THE GROWNUPS TO SEE IF YOUR CONCLUSIONS WERE CORRECT.
THOSE WERE THE DAYS.

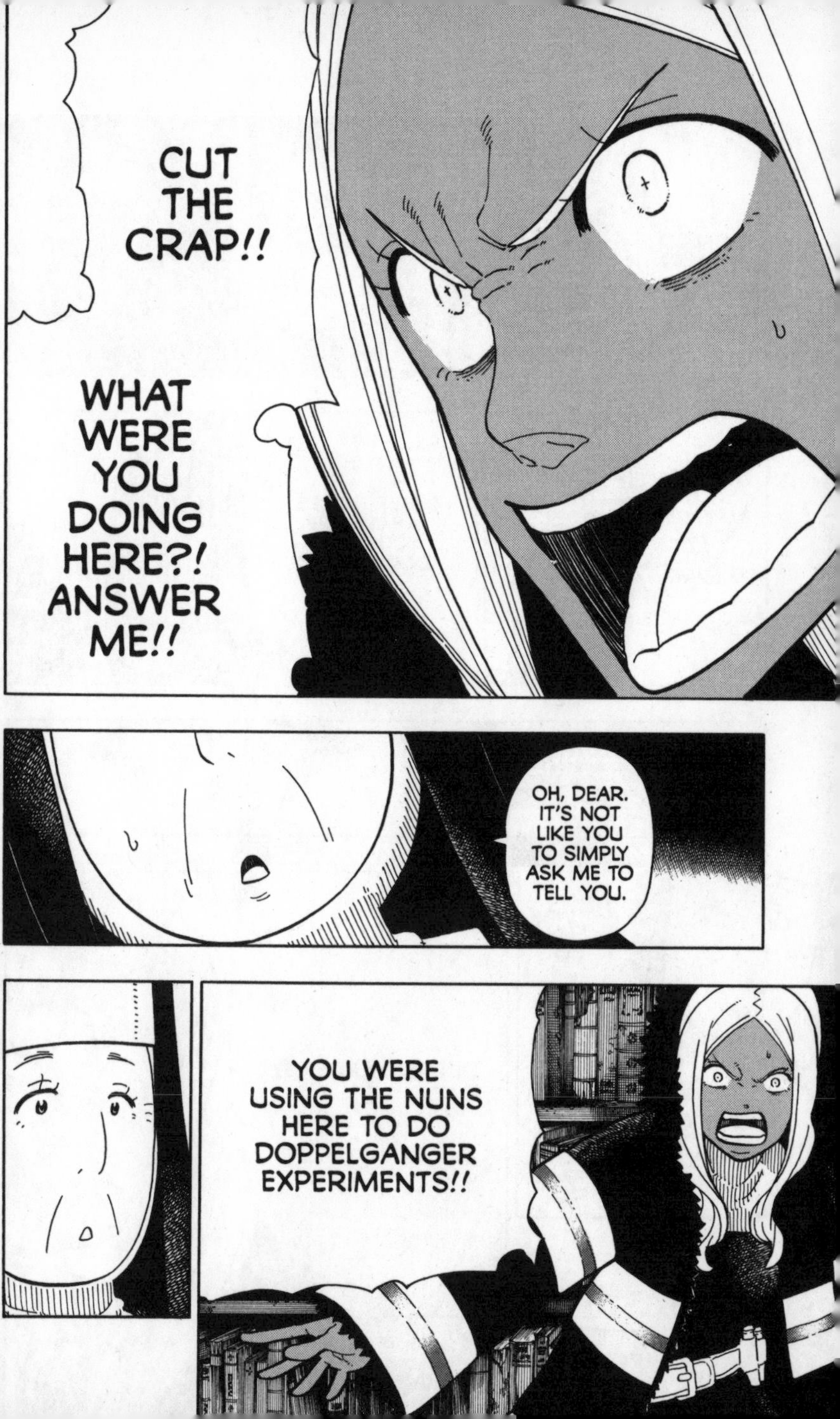
CUT THE CRAP!!
WHAT WERE YOU DOING HERE?! ANSWER ME!!
OH, DEAR. IT'S NOT LIKE YOU TO SIMPLY ASK ME TO TELL YOU.
YOU WERE USING THE NUNS HERE TO DO DOPPELGANGER EXPERIMENTS!!

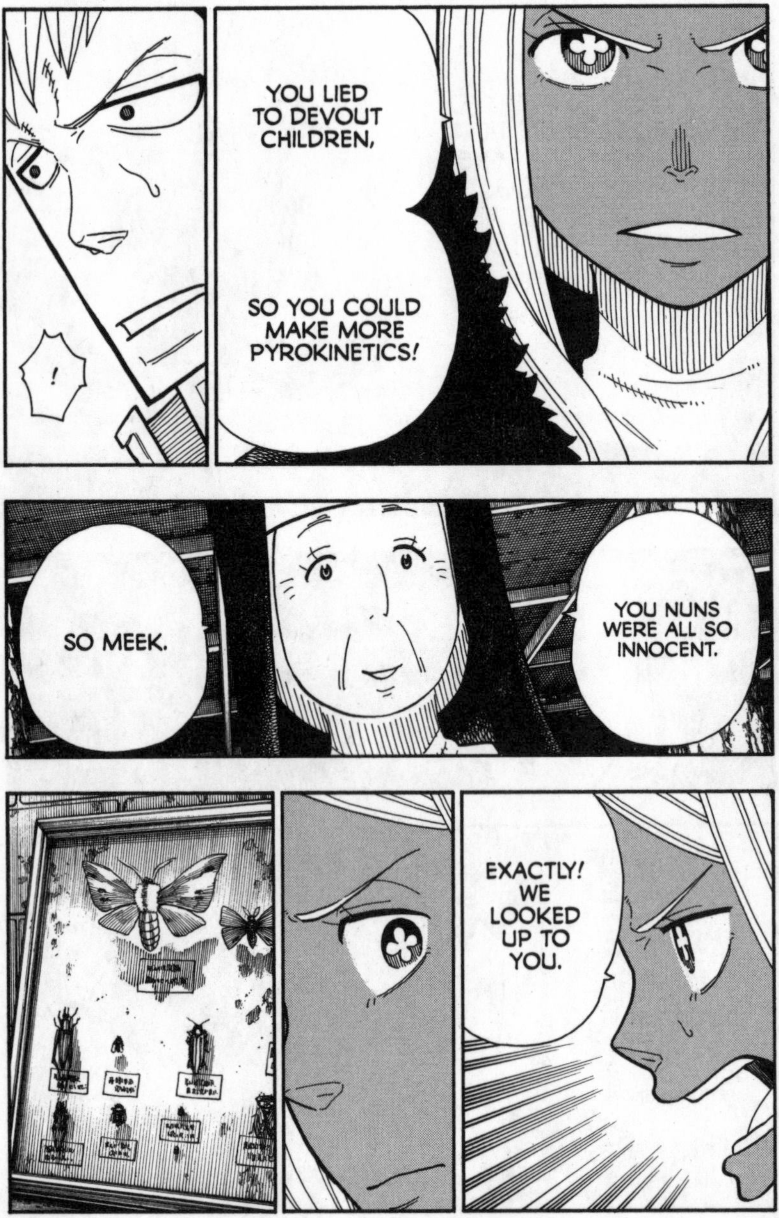
YOU LIED TO DEVOUT CHILDREN,
SO YOU COULD MAKE MORE PYROKINETICS!
!
YOU NUNS WERE ALL SO INNOCENT.
SO MEEK.
EXACTLY! WE LOOKED UP TO YOU.

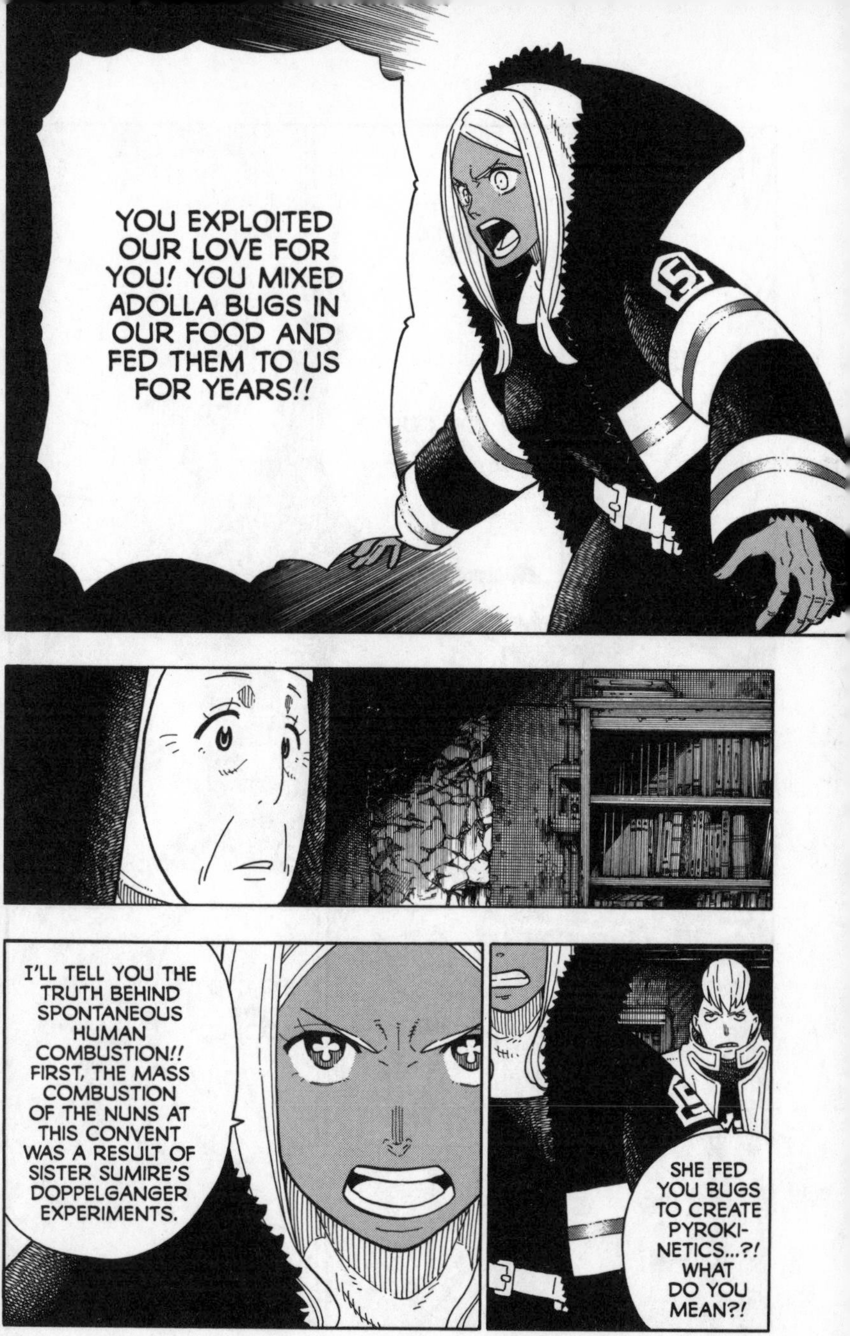
YOU EXPLOITED OUR LOVE FOR YOU! YOU MIXED ADOLLA BUGS IN OUR FOOD AND FED THEM TO US FOR YEARS!!
SHE FED YOU BUGS TO CREATE PYROKI-NETICS...?! WHAT DO YOU MEAN?!
I'LL TELL YOU THE TRUTH BEHIND SPONTANEOUS HUMAN COMBUSTION!! FIRST, THE MASS COMBUSTION OF THE NUNS AT THIS CONVENT WAS A RESULT OF SISTER SUMIRE'S DOPPELGANGER EXPERIMENTS.

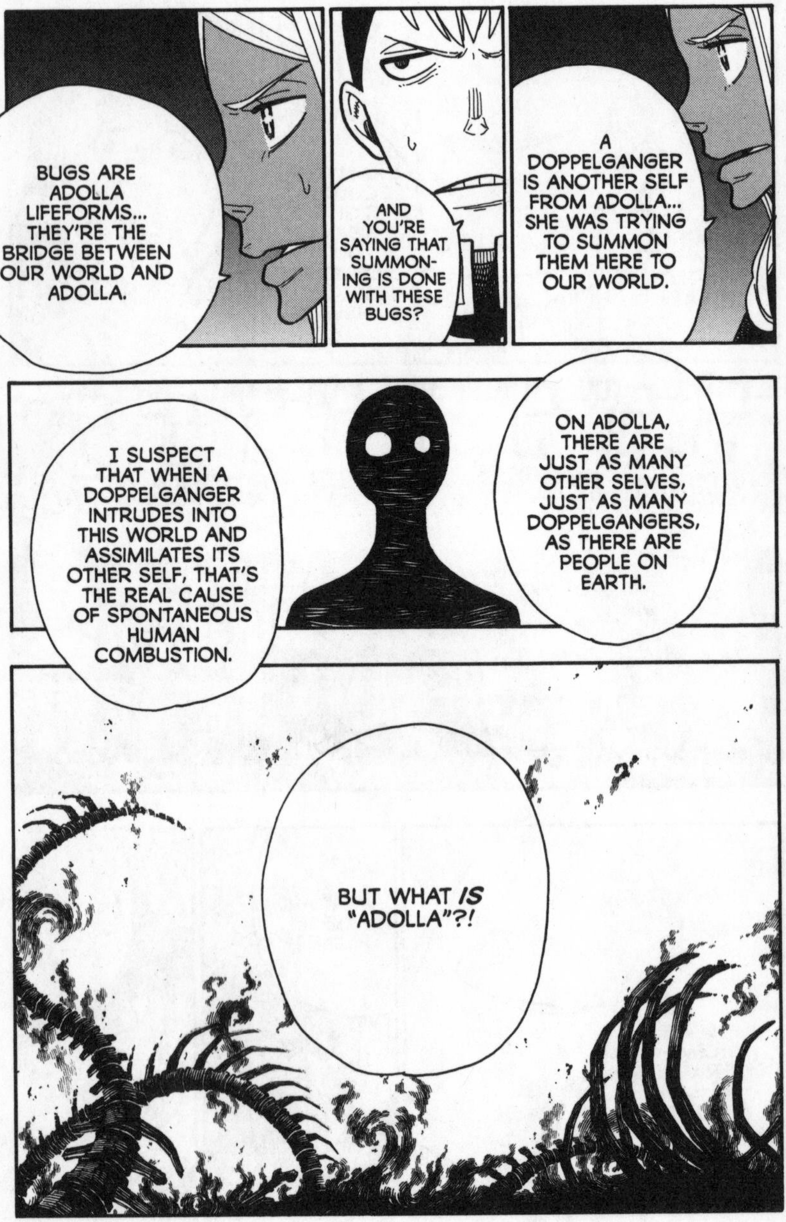
A DOPPELGANGER IS ANOTHER SELF FROM ADOLLA... SHE WAS TRYING TO SUMMON THEM HERE TO OUR WORLD.
AND YOU'RE SAYING THAT SUMMONING IS DONE WITH THESE BUGS?
BUGS ARE ADOLLA LIFEFORMS... THEY'RE THE BRIDGE BETWEEN OUR WORLD AND ADOLLA.
ON ADOLLA, THERE ARE JUST AS MANY OTHER SELVES, JUST AS MANY DOPPELGANGERS, AS THERE ARE PEOPLE ON EARTH.
I SUSPECT THAT WHEN A DOPPELGANGER INTRUDES INTO THIS WORLD AND ASSIMILATES ITS OTHER SELF, THAT'S THE REAL CAUSE OF SPONTANEOUS HUMAN COMBUSTION.
BUT WHAT *IS* "ADOLLA"?!

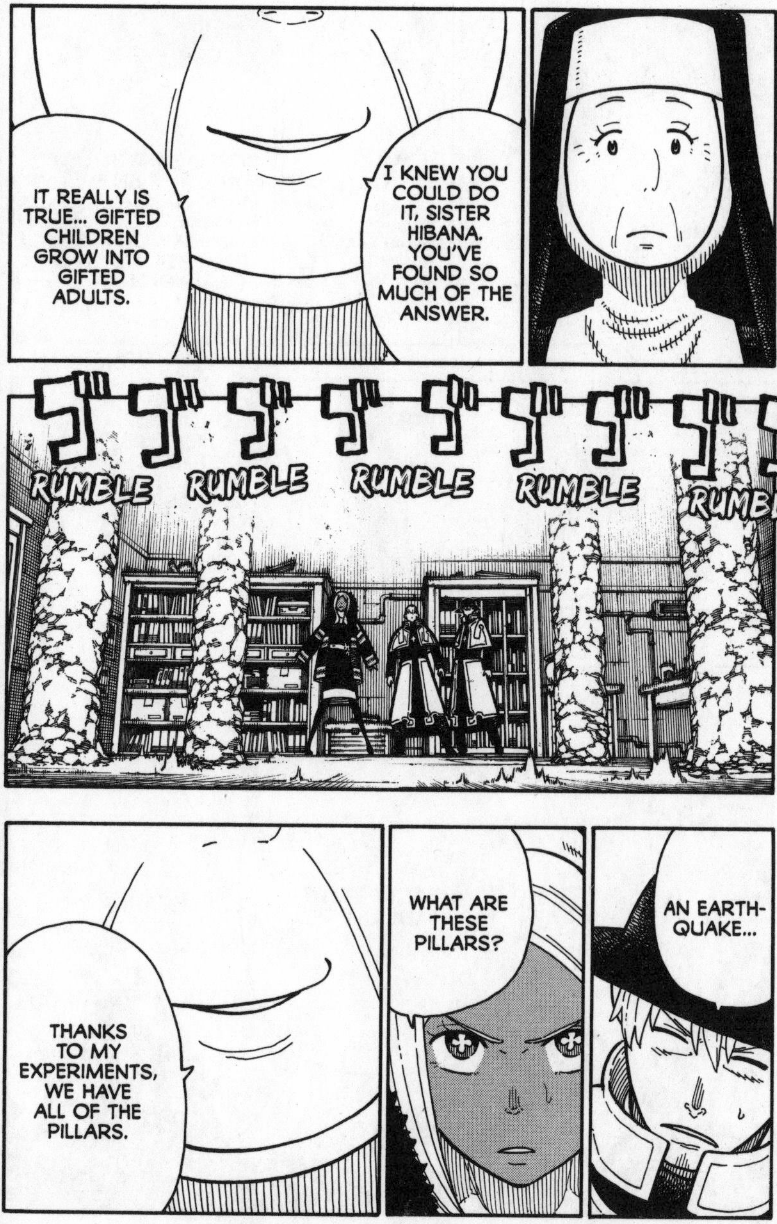
I KNEW YOU COULD DO IT, SISTER HIBANA. YOU'VE FOUND SO MUCH OF THE ANSWER.
IT REALLY IS TRUE... GIFTED CHILDREN GROW INTO GIFTED ADULTS.
ゴゴゴゴゴゴゴゴゴ
RUMBLE RUMBLE RUMBLE RUMBLE RUMBLE
AN EARTH-QUAKE...
WHAT ARE THESE PILLARS?
THANKS TO MY EXPERIMENTS, WE HAVE ALL OF THE PILLARS.

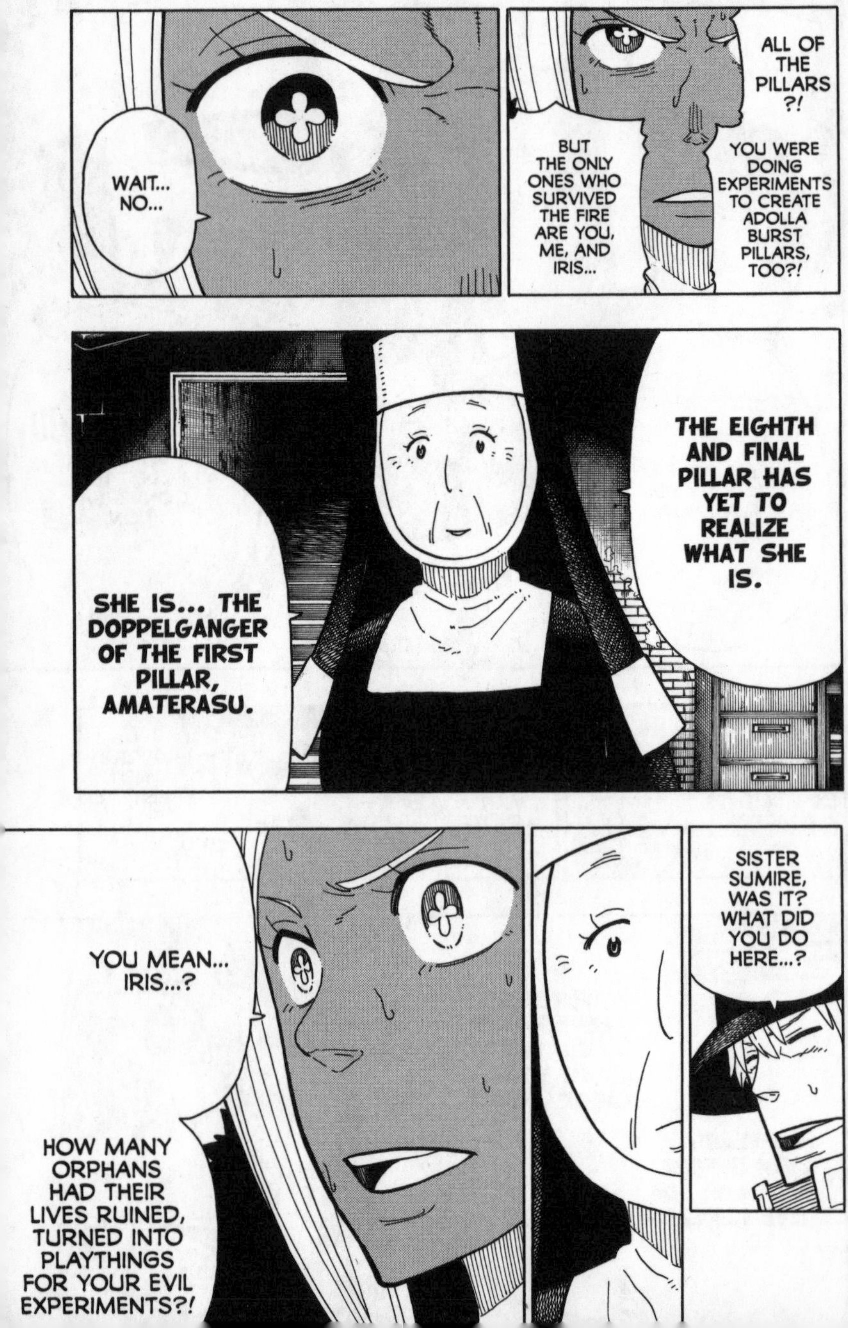
ALL OF THE PILLARS?!
YOU WERE DOING EXPERIMENTS TO CREATE ADOLLA BURST PILLARS, TOO?!
BUT THE ONLY ONES WHO SURVIVED THE FIRE ARE YOU, ME, AND IRIS...
WAIT... NO...
THE EIGHTH AND FINAL PILLAR HAS YET TO REALIZE WHAT SHE IS.
SHE IS... THE DOPPELGANGER OF THE FIRST PILLAR, AMATERASU.
SISTER SUMIRE, WAS IT? WHAT DID YOU DO HERE...?
YOU MEAN... IRIS...?
HOW MANY ORPHANS HAD THEIR LIVES RUINED, TURNED INTO PLAYTHINGS FOR YOUR EVIL EXPERIMENTS?!

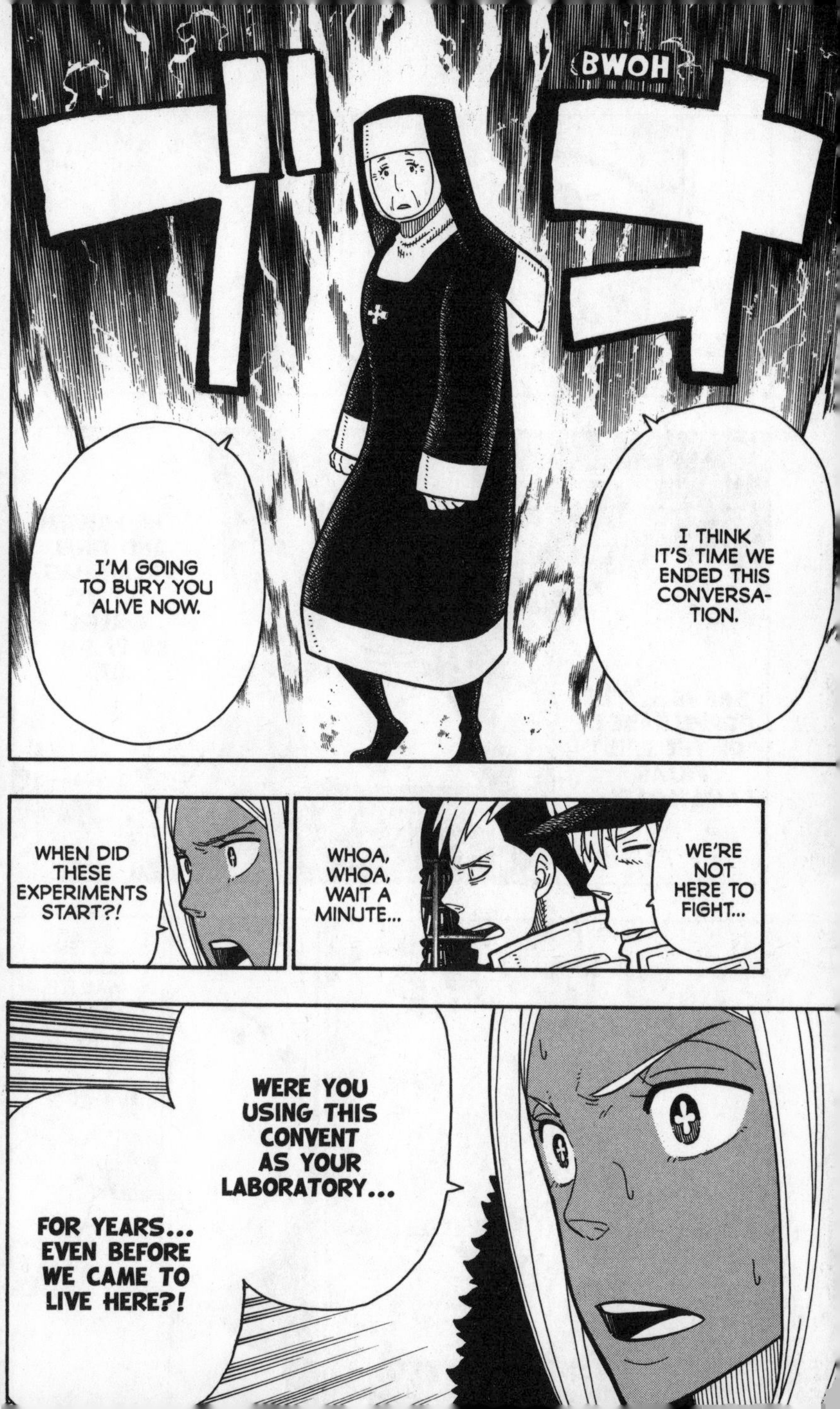
BWOH
ブオ
I THINK IT'S TIME WE ENDED THIS CONVERSA-TION.
I'M GOING TO BURY YOU ALIVE NOW.
WE'RE NOT HERE TO FIGHT...
WHOA, WHOA, WAIT A MINUTE...
WHEN DID THESE EXPERIMENTS START?!
WERE YOU USING THIS CONVENT AS YOUR LABORATORY...
FOR YEARS... EVEN BEFORE WE CAME TO LIVE HERE?!

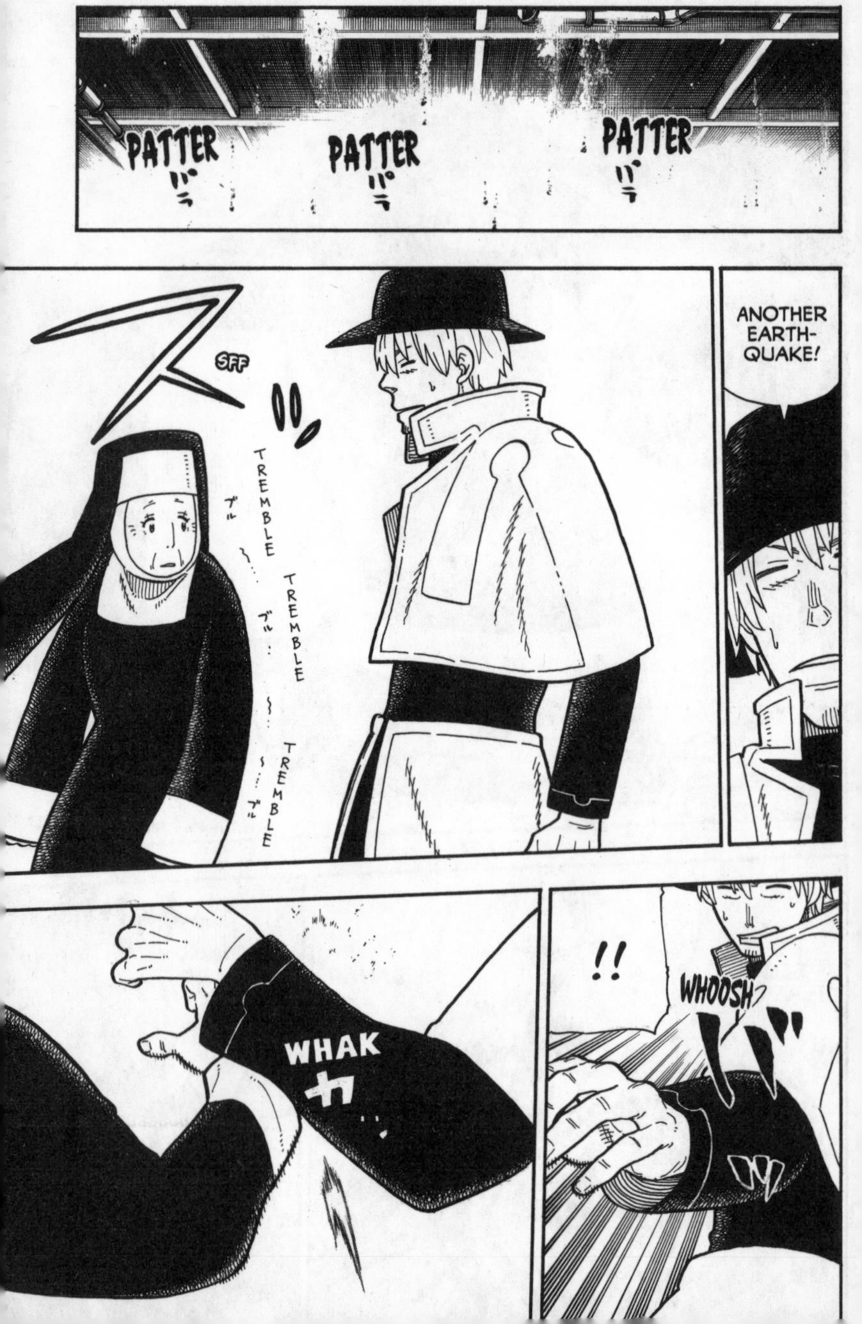
PATTER
PATTER
PATTER
ANOTHER EARTH-QUAKE!
SFF
TREMBLE
TREMBLE
TREMBLE
!!
WHOOSH
WHAK

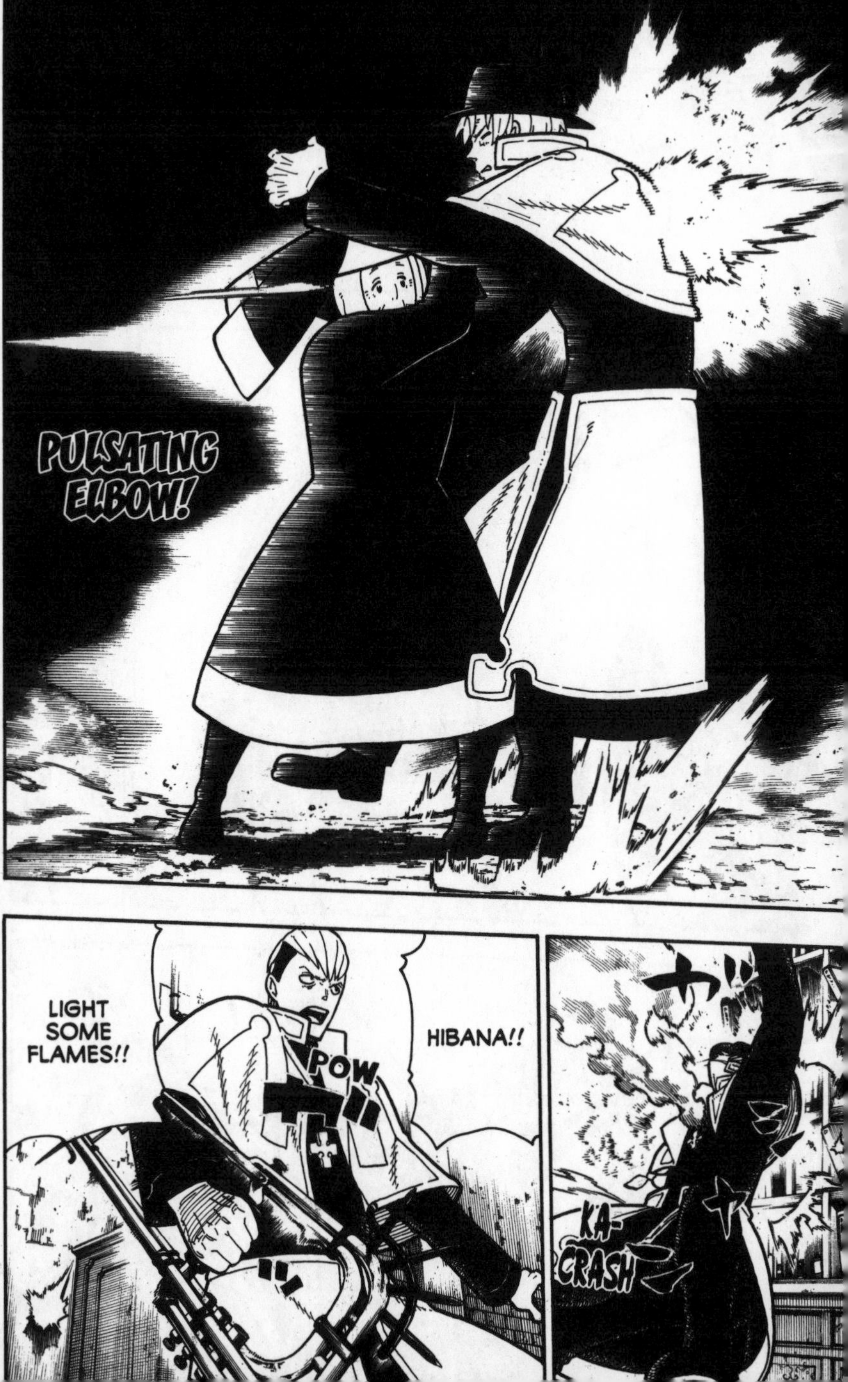
PULSATING ELBOW!
KA-CRASH
HIBANA!!
LIGHT SOME FLAMES!!
POW
!!

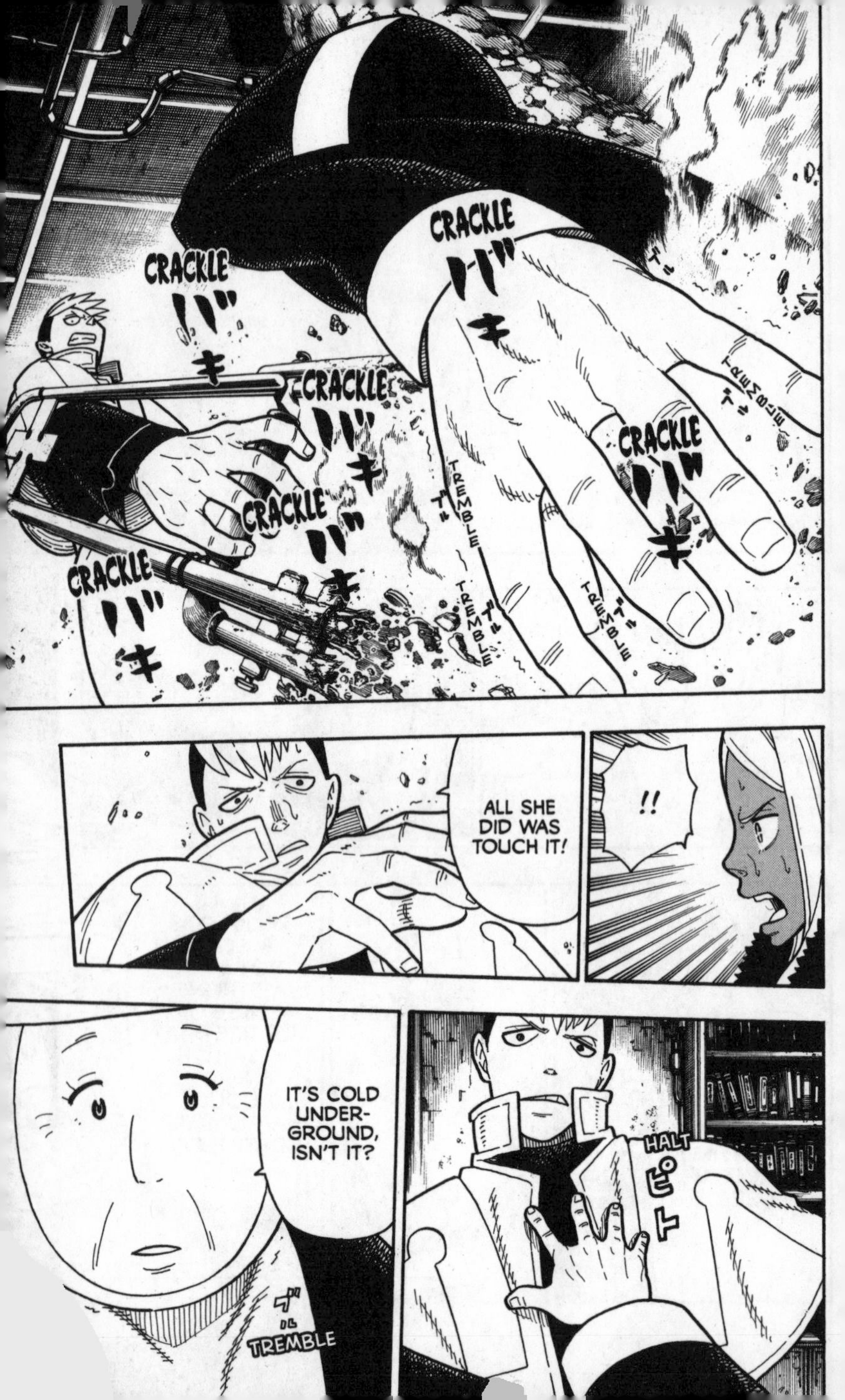
CRACKLE
TREMBLE
CRACKLE
CRACKLE
CRACKLE
TREMBLE
TREMBLE
TREMBLE
CRACKLE
CRACKLE
!!
ALL SHE DID WAS TOUCH IT!
HALT
IT'S COLD UNDERGROUND, ISN'T IT?
TREMBLE

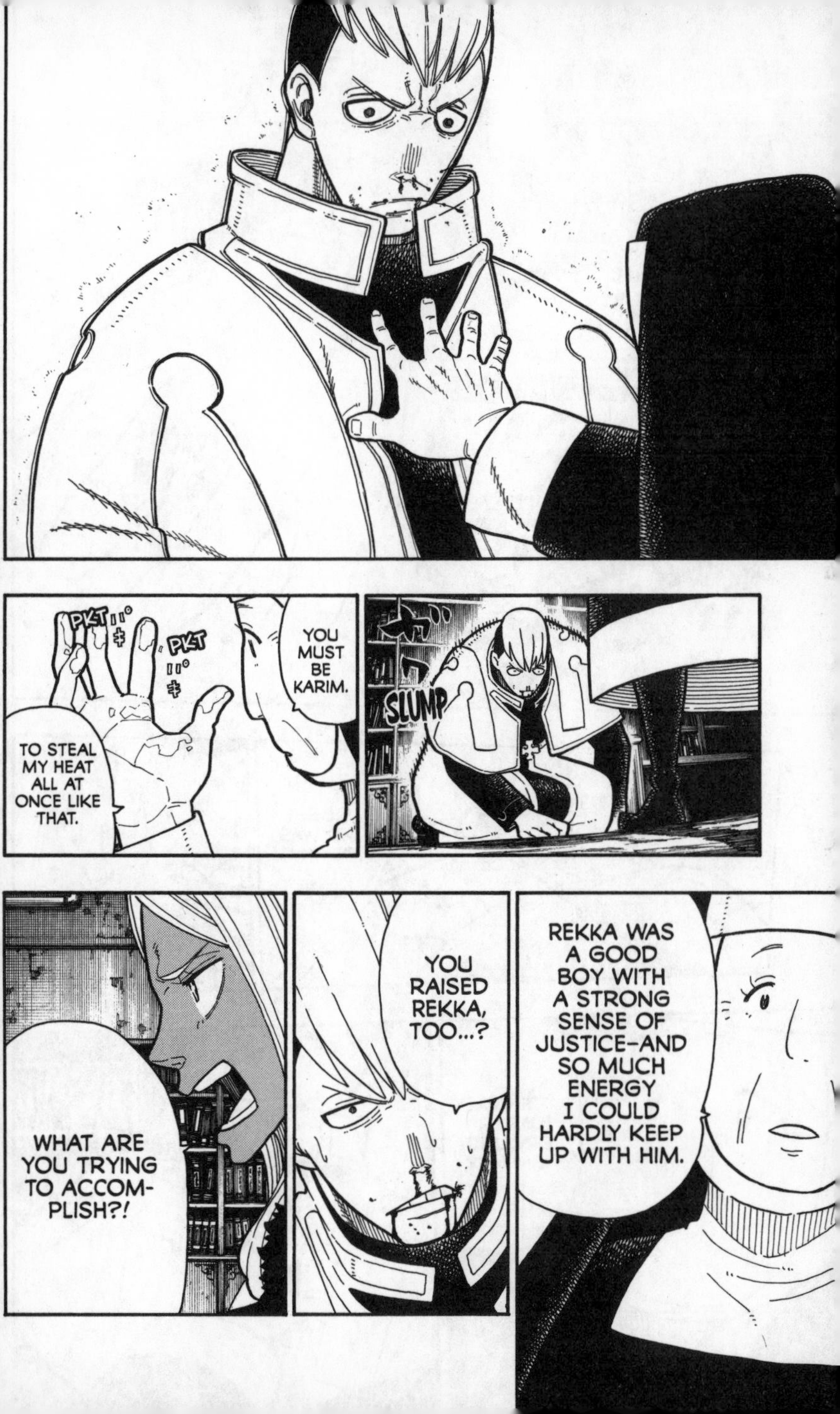
SLUMP
YOU MUST BE KARIM.
PKT
PKT
TO STEAL MY HEAT ALL AT ONCE LIKE THAT.
REKKA WAS A GOOD BOY WITH A STRONG SENSE OF JUSTICE–AND SO MUCH ENERGY I COULD HARDLY KEEP UP WITH HIM.
YOU RAISED REKKA, TOO...?
WHAT ARE YOU TRYING TO ACCOMPLISH?!

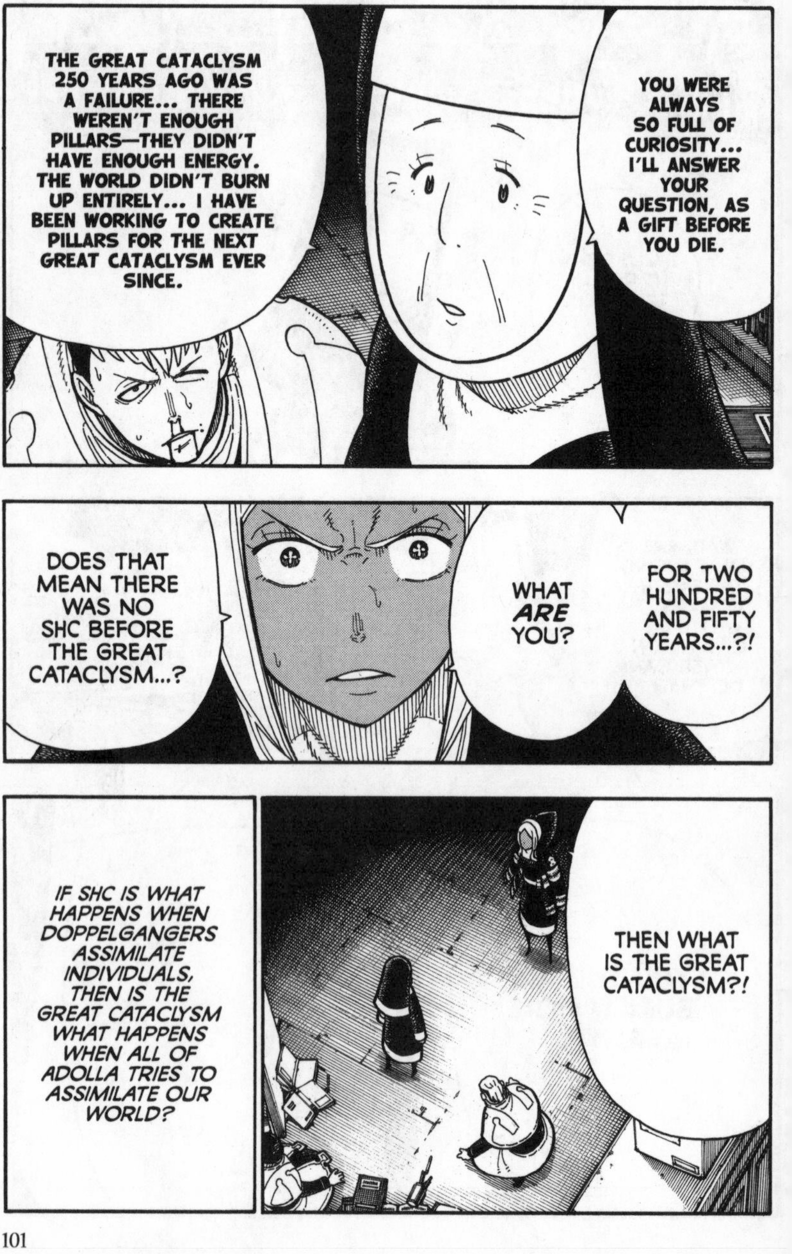
YOU WERE ALWAYS SO FULL OF CURIOSITY... I'LL ANSWER YOUR QUESTION, AS A GIFT BEFORE YOU DIE.
THE GREAT CATACLYSM 250 YEARS AGO WAS A FAILURE... THERE WEREN'T ENOUGH PILLARS—THEY DIDN'T HAVE ENOUGH ENERGY. THE WORLD DIDN'T BURN UP ENTIRELY... I HAVE BEEN WORKING TO CREATE PILLARS FOR THE NEXT GREAT CATACLYSM EVER SINCE.
FOR TWO HUNDRED AND FIFTY YEARS...?!
WHAT *ARE* YOU?
DOES THAT MEAN THERE WAS NO SHC BEFORE THE GREAT CATACLYSM...?
THEN WHAT IS THE GREAT CATACLYSM?!
IF SHC IS WHAT HAPPENS WHEN DOPPELGANGERS ASSIMILATE INDIVIDUALS, THEN IS THE GREAT CATACLYSM WHAT HAPPENS WHEN ALL OF ADOLLA TRIES TO ASSIMILATE OUR WORLD?

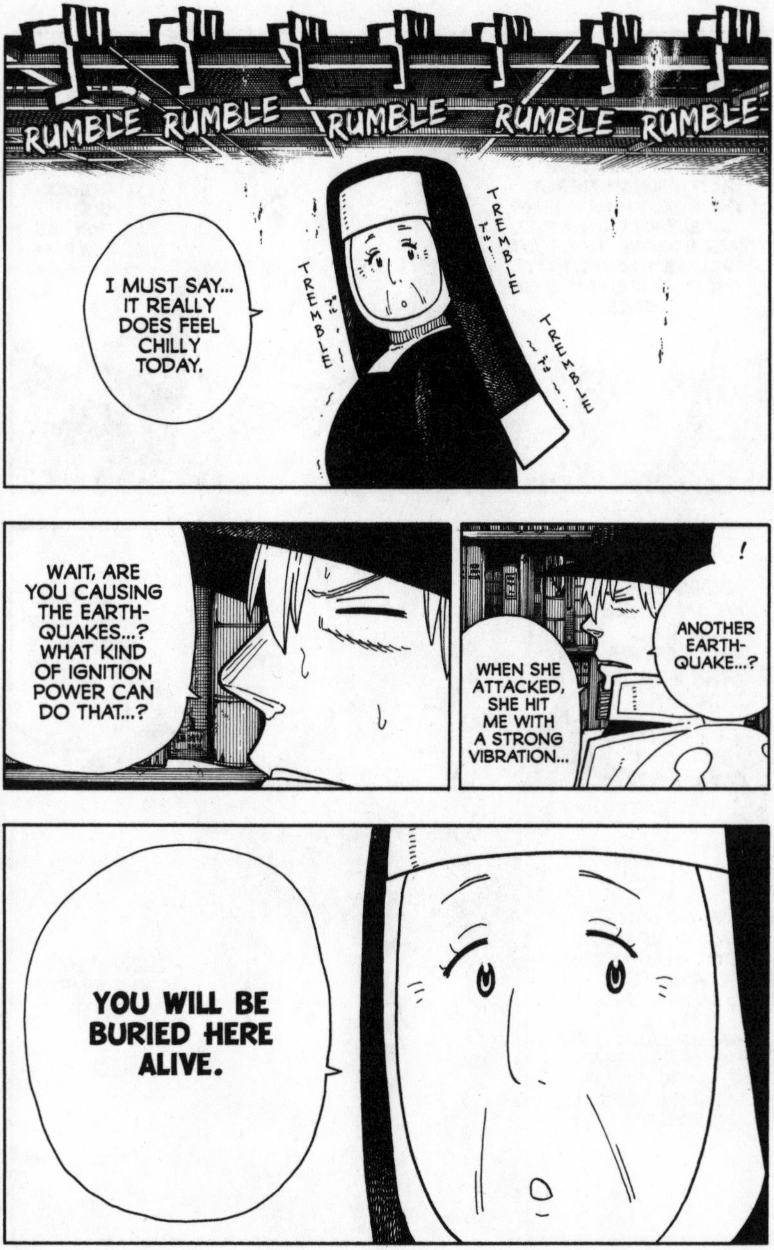
RUMBLE RUMBLE RUMBLE RUMBLE RUMBLE
TREMBLE
TREMBLE
TREMBLE
I MUST SAY... IT REALLY DOES FEEL CHILLY TODAY.
!
ANOTHER EARTHQUAKE...?
WHEN SHE ATTACKED, SHE HIT ME WITH A STRONG VIBRATION...
WAIT, ARE YOU CAUSING THE EARTHQUAKES...? WHAT KIND OF IGNITION POWER CAN DO THAT...?
YOU WILL BE BURIED HERE ALIVE.

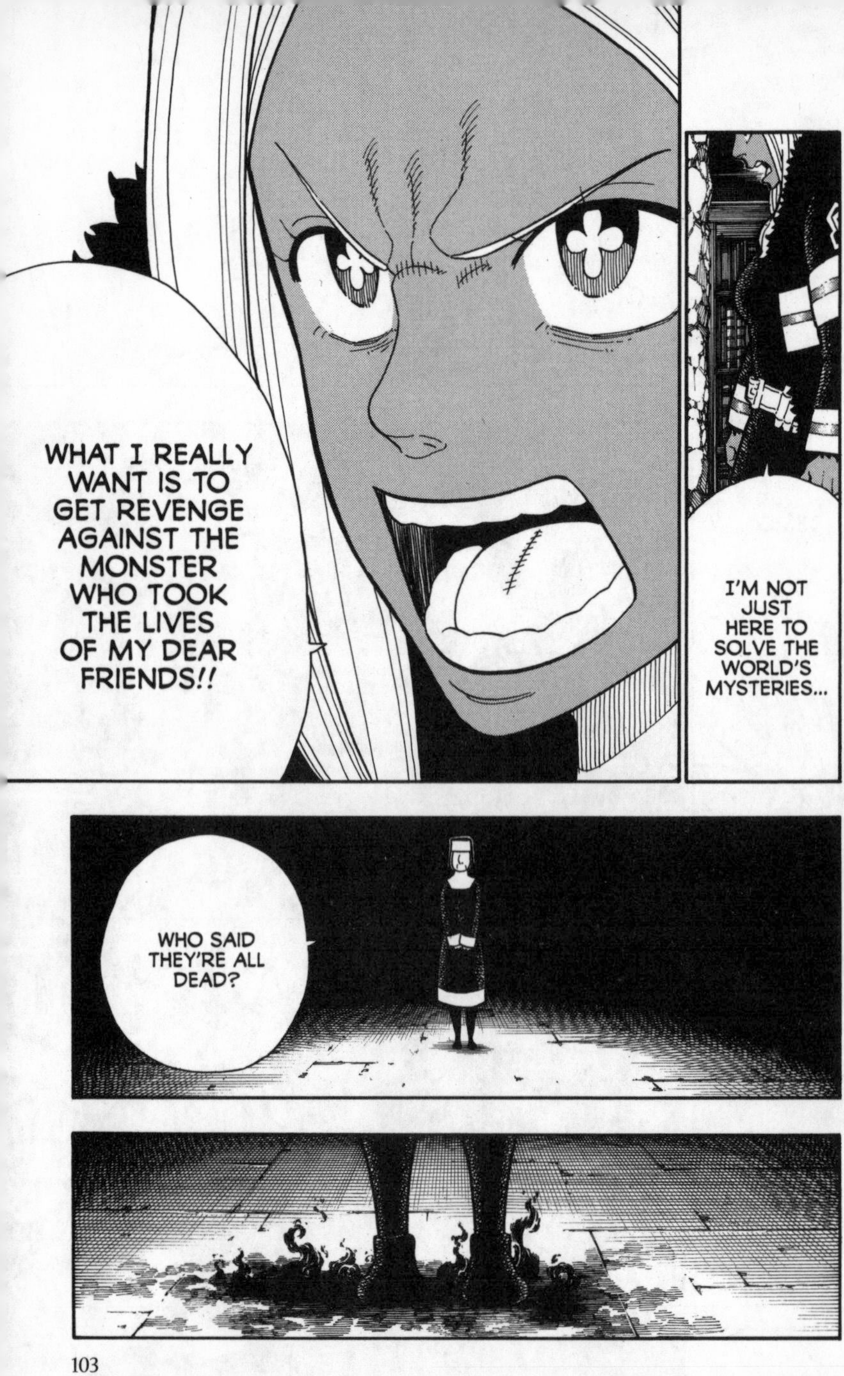
I'M NOT JUST HERE TO SOLVE THE WORLD'S MYSTERIES...
WHAT I REALLY WANT IS TO GET REVENGE AGAINST THE MONSTER WHO TOOK THE LIVES OF MY DEAR FRIENDS!!
WHO SAID THEY'RE ALL DEAD?

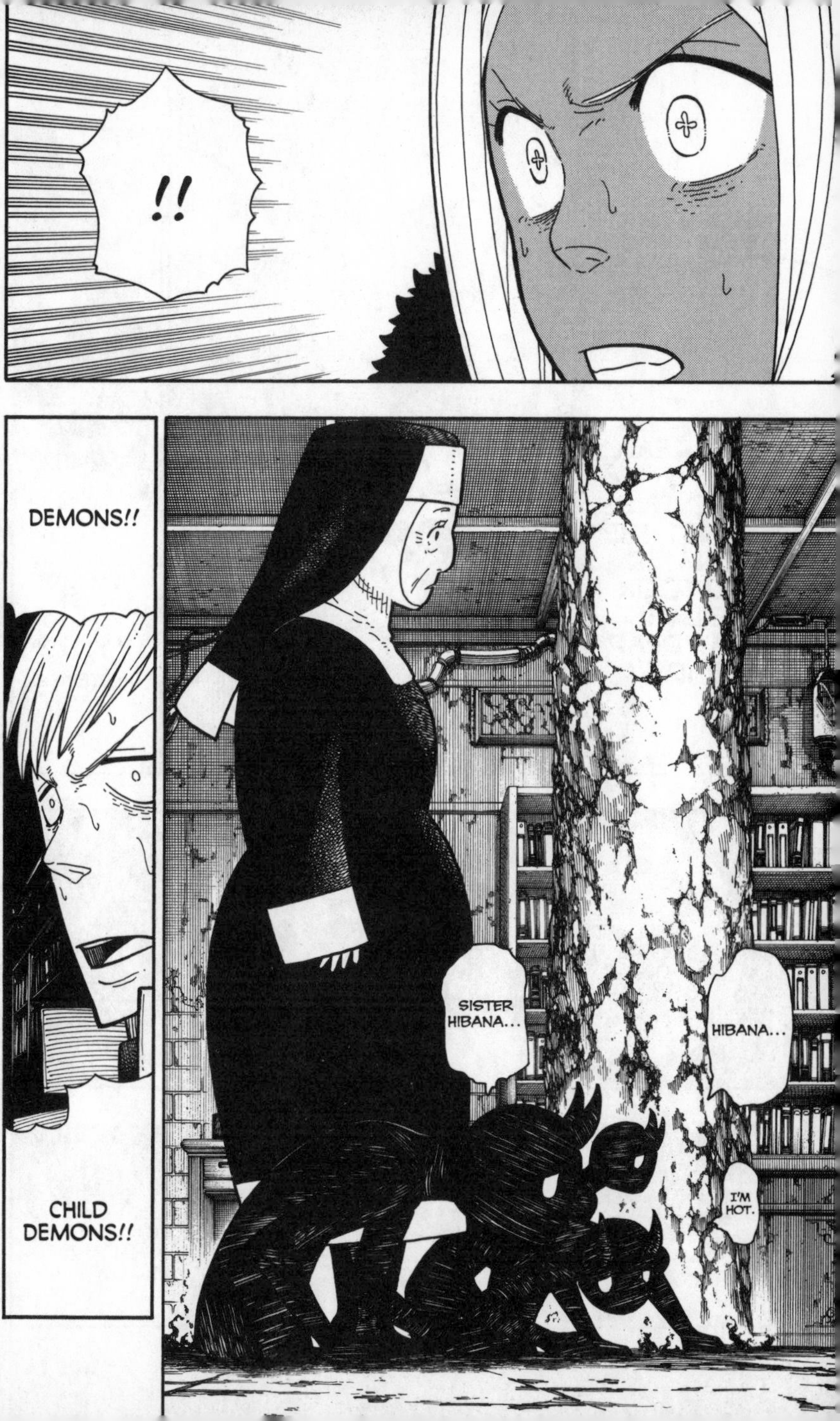
!!
HIBANA...
SISTER HIBANA...
I'M HOT.
DEMONS!!
CHILD DEMONS!!

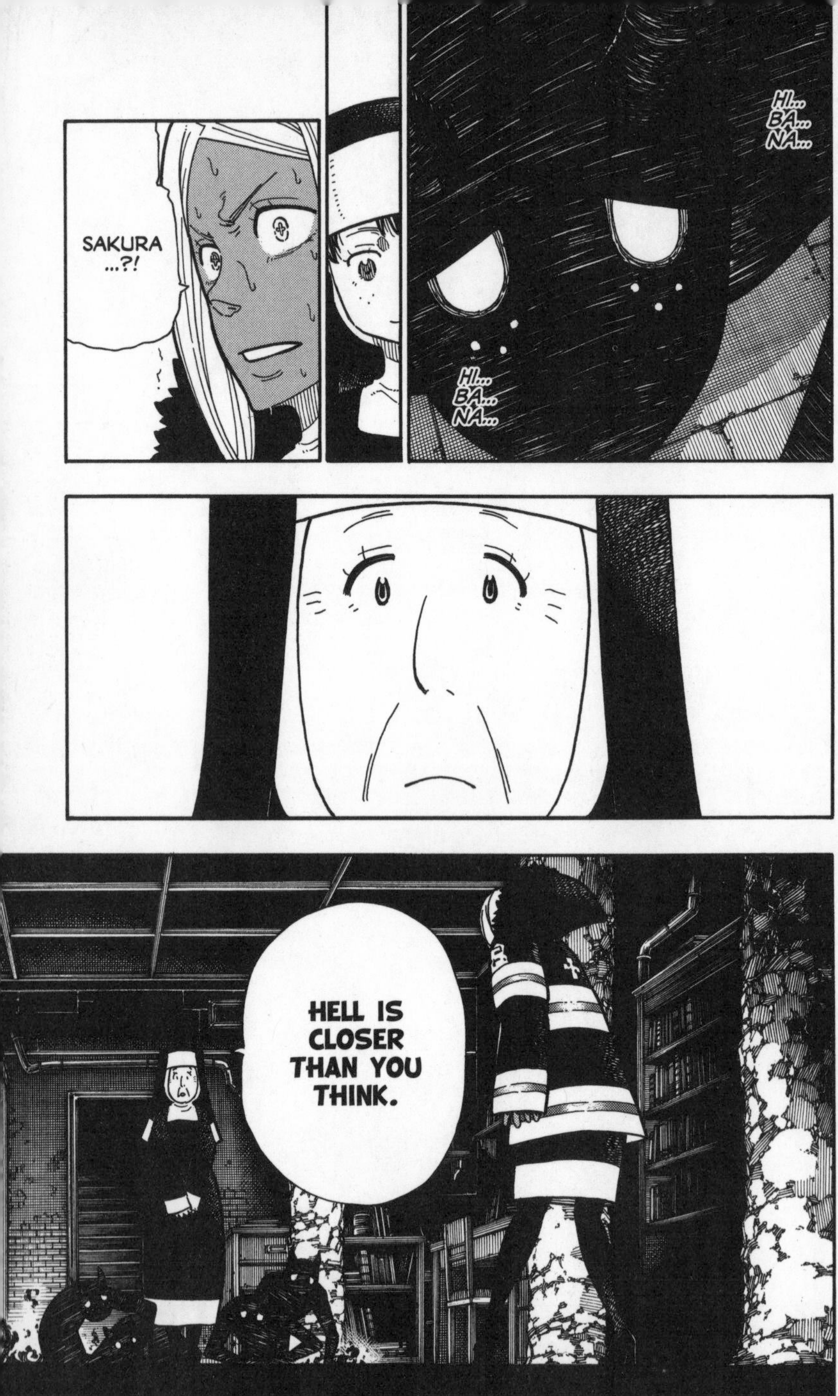
HI... BA... NA...
HI... BA... NA...
SAKURA ...?!
HELL IS CLOSER THAN YOU THINK.

FIRE FORCE

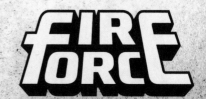

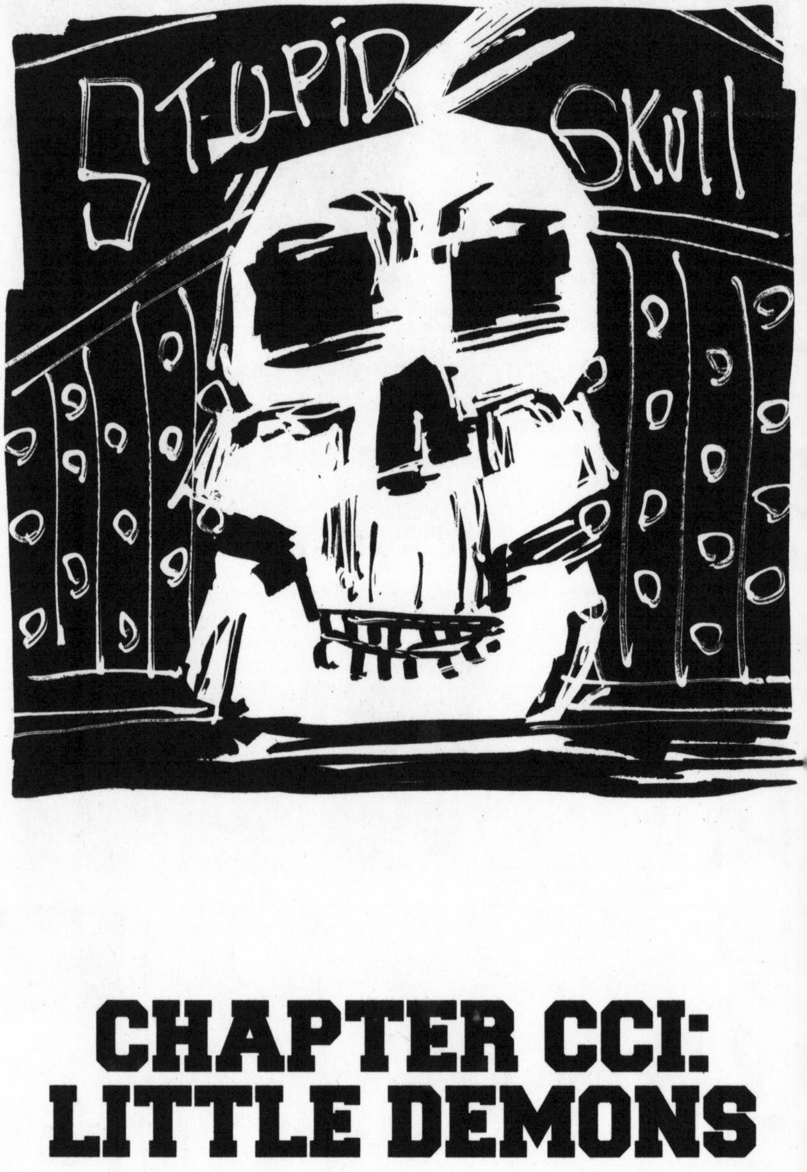
STUPID SKULL

CHAPTER CCI: LITTLE DEMONS

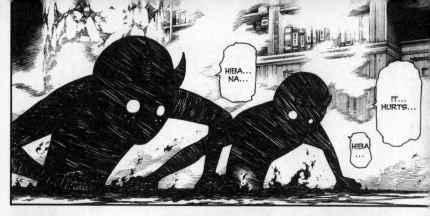

HIBA... NA...

IT... HURTS...

HIBA...

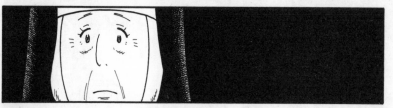

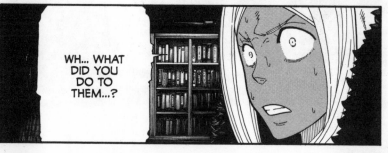

WH... WHAT DID YOU DO TO THEM...?

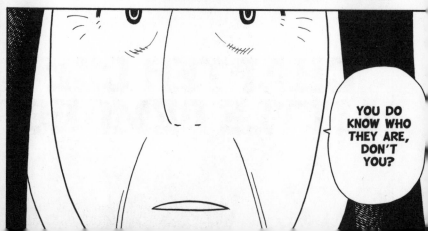

YOU DO KNOW WHO THEY ARE, DON'T YOU?

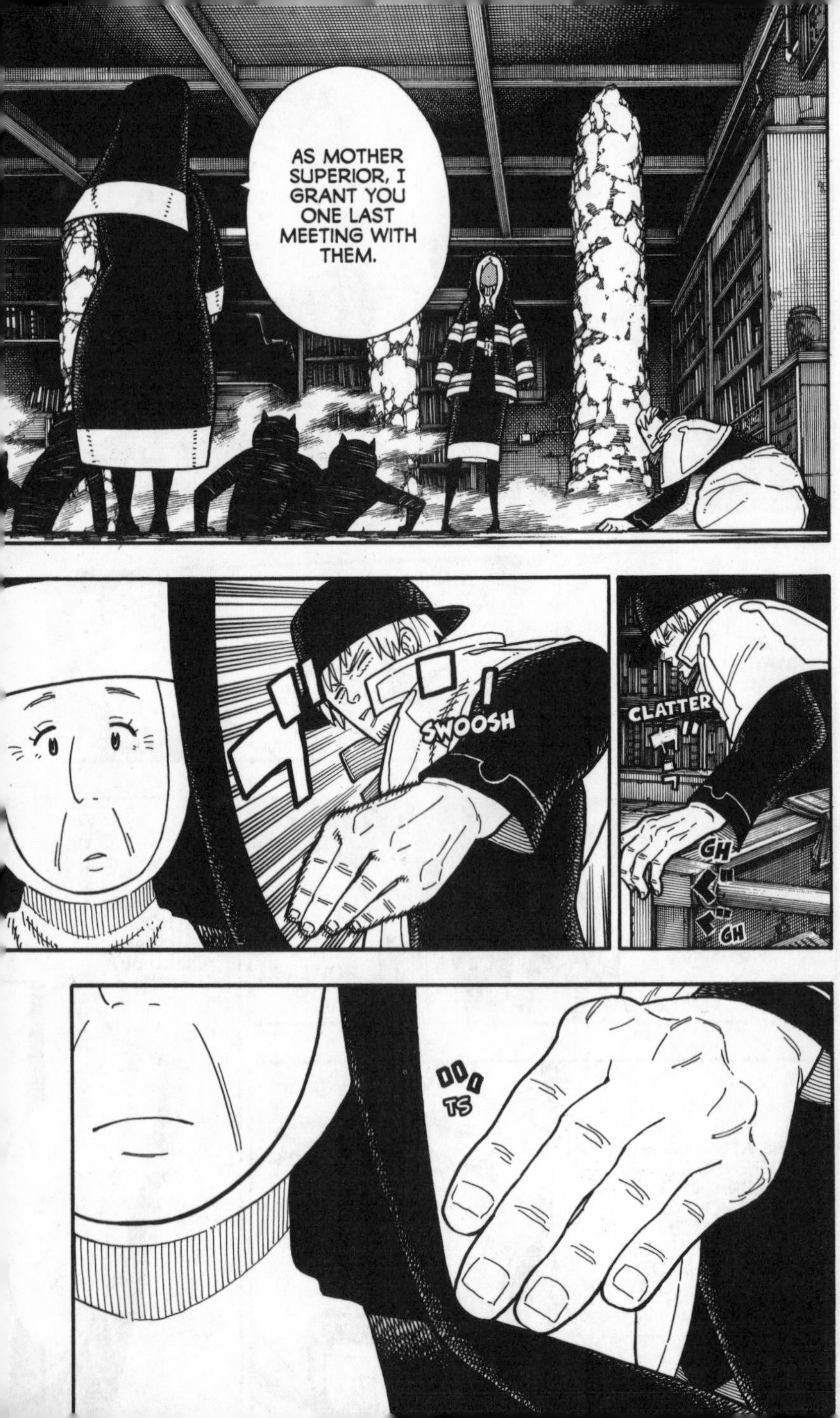
AS MOTHER SUPERIOR, I GRANT YOU ONE LAST MEETING WITH THEM.
CLATTER
GH
GH
SWOOSH
TS

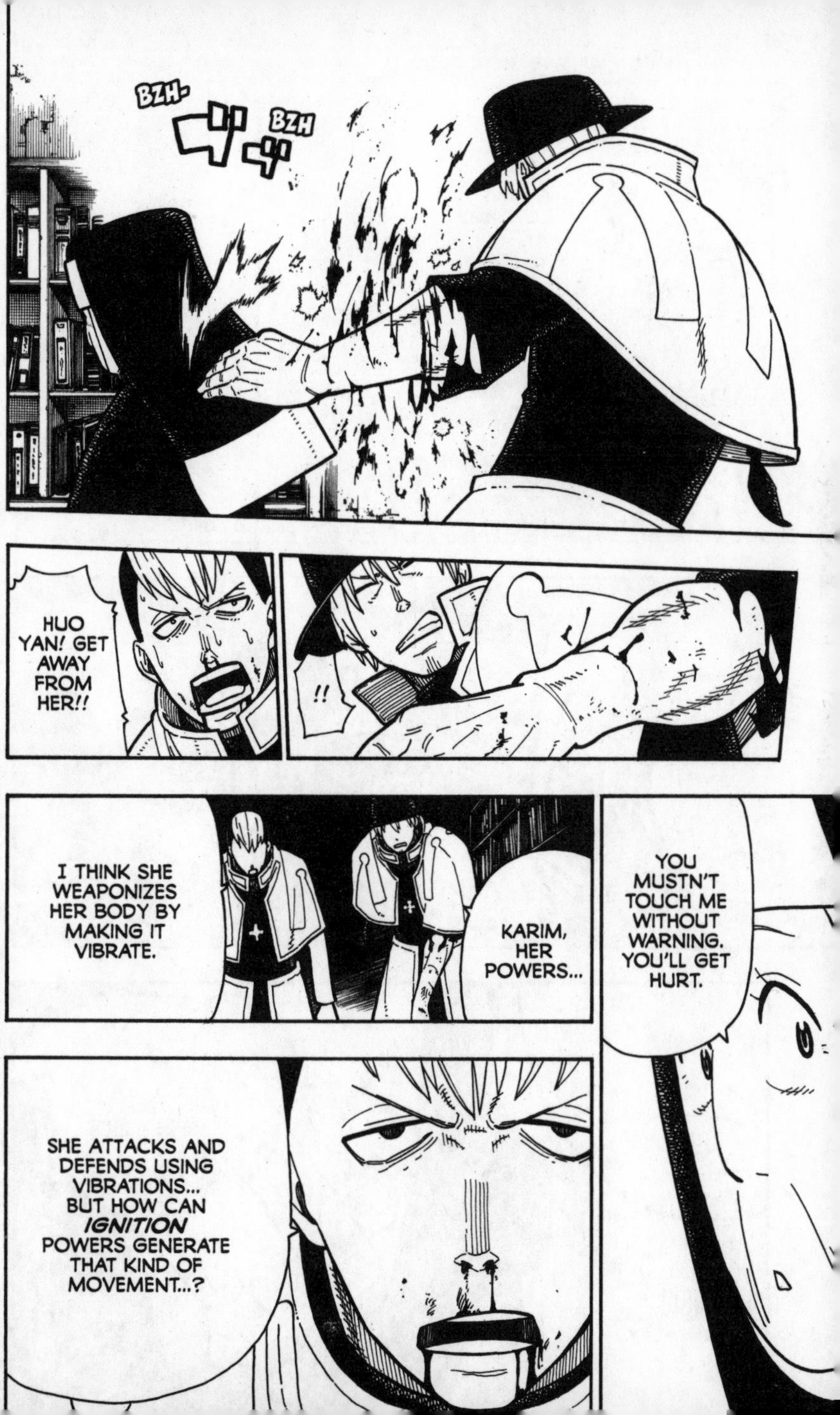
BZH-
BZH
!!
HUO YAN! GET AWAY FROM HER!!
YOU MUSTN'T TOUCH ME WITHOUT WARNING. YOU'LL GET HURT.
KARIM, HER POWERS...
I THINK SHE WEAPONIZES HER BODY BY MAKING IT VIBRATE.
SHE ATTACKS AND DEFENDS USING VIBRATIONS... BUT HOW CAN *IGNITION* POWERS GENERATE THAT KIND OF MOVEMENT...?

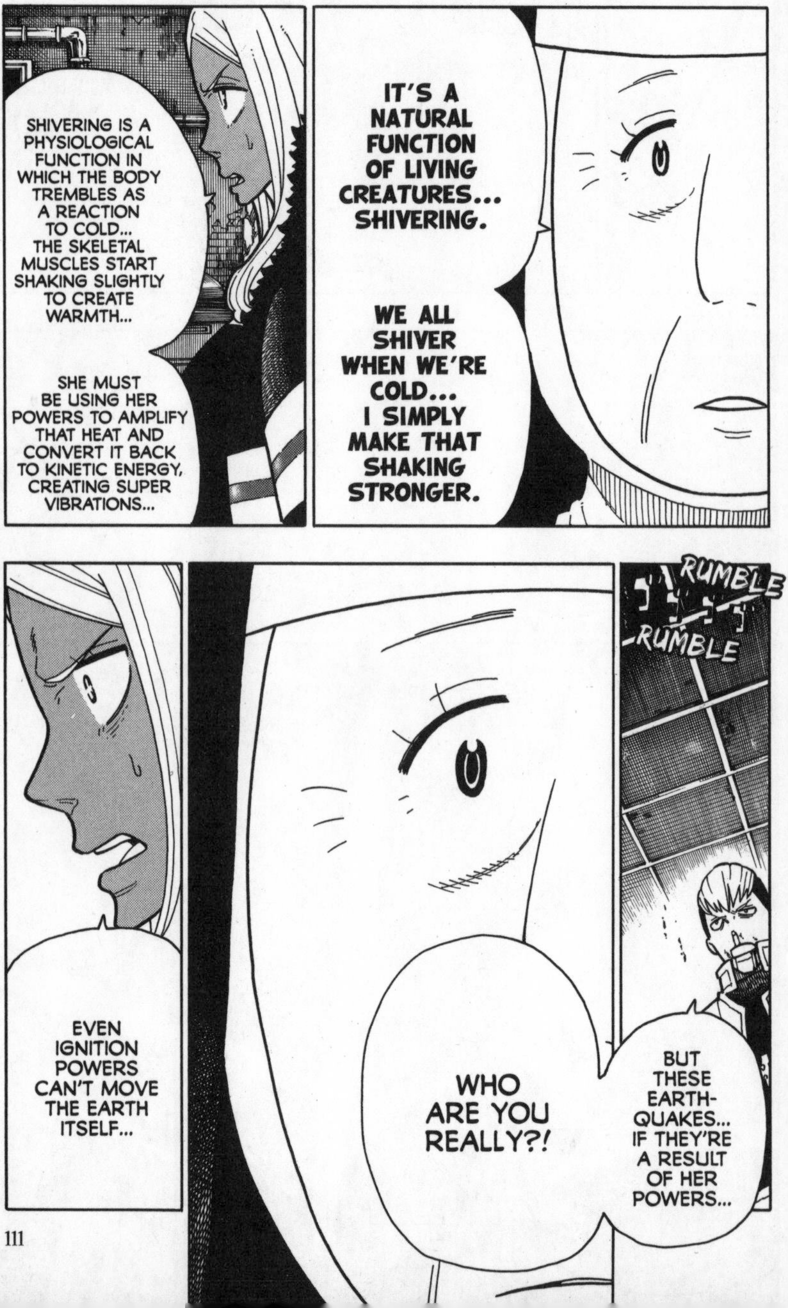
IT'S A NATURAL FUNCTION OF LIVING CREATURES... SHIVERING.
WE ALL SHIVER WHEN WE'RE COLD... I SIMPLY MAKE THAT SHAKING STRONGER.
SHIVERING IS A PHYSIOLOGICAL FUNCTION IN WHICH THE BODY TREMBLES AS A REACTION TO COLD... THE SKELETAL MUSCLES START SHAKING SLIGHTLY TO CREATE WARMTH...
SHE MUST BE USING HER POWERS TO AMPLIFY THAT HEAT AND CONVERT IT BACK TO KINETIC ENERGY, CREATING SUPER VIBRATIONS...
RUMBLE
RUMBLE
BUT THESE EARTH-QUAKES... IF THEY'RE A RESULT OF HER POWERS...
WHO ARE YOU REALLY?!
EVEN IGNITION POWERS CAN'T MOVE THE EARTH ITSELF...

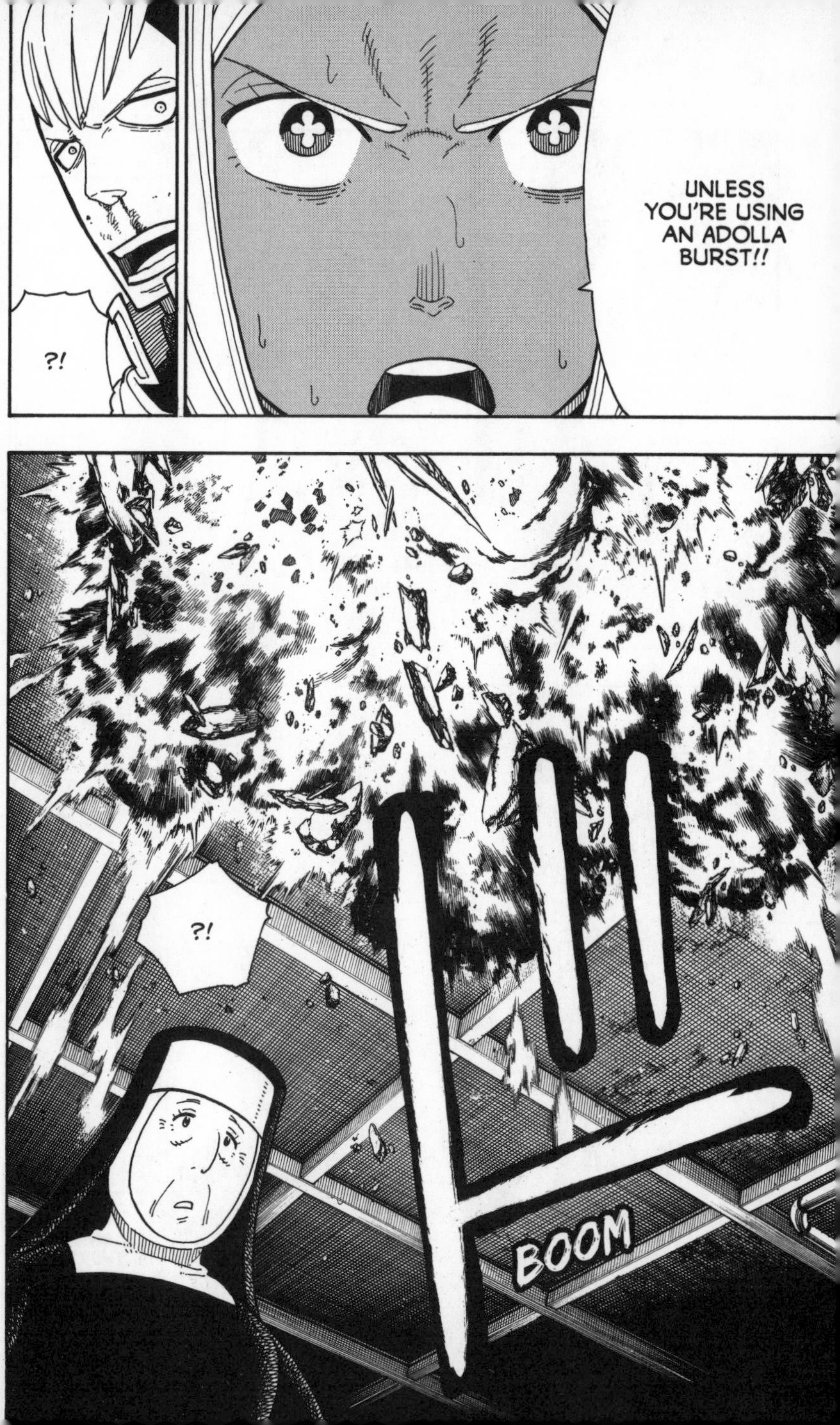
UNLESS YOU'RE USING AN ADOLLA BURST!!
?!
?!
BOOM

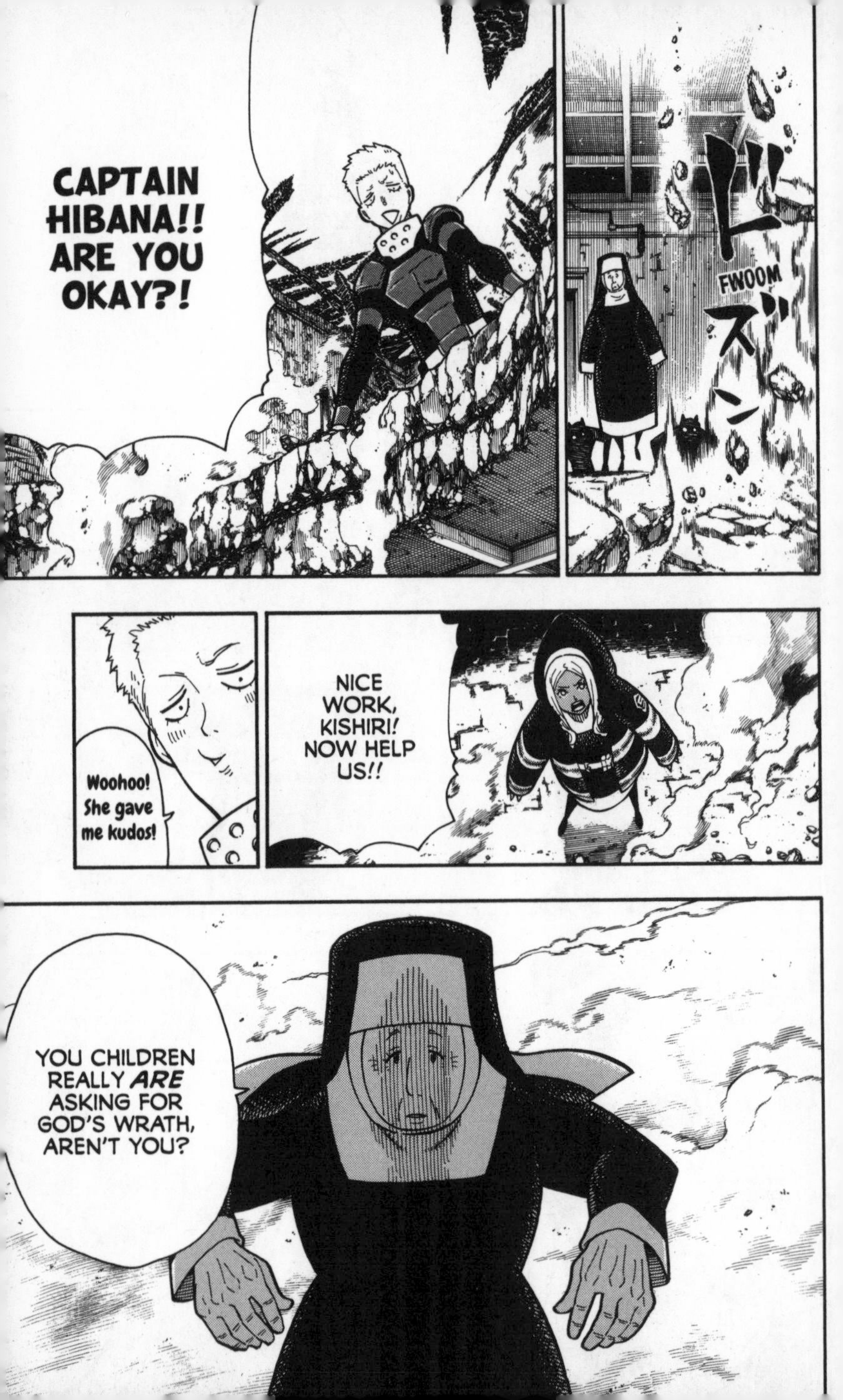
ドズン
FWOOM
CAPTAIN HIBANA!! ARE YOU OKAY?!
NICE WORK, KISHIRI! NOW HELP US!!
Woohoo! She gave me kudos!
YOU CHILDREN REALLY *ARE* ASKING FOR GOD'S WRATH, AREN'T YOU?

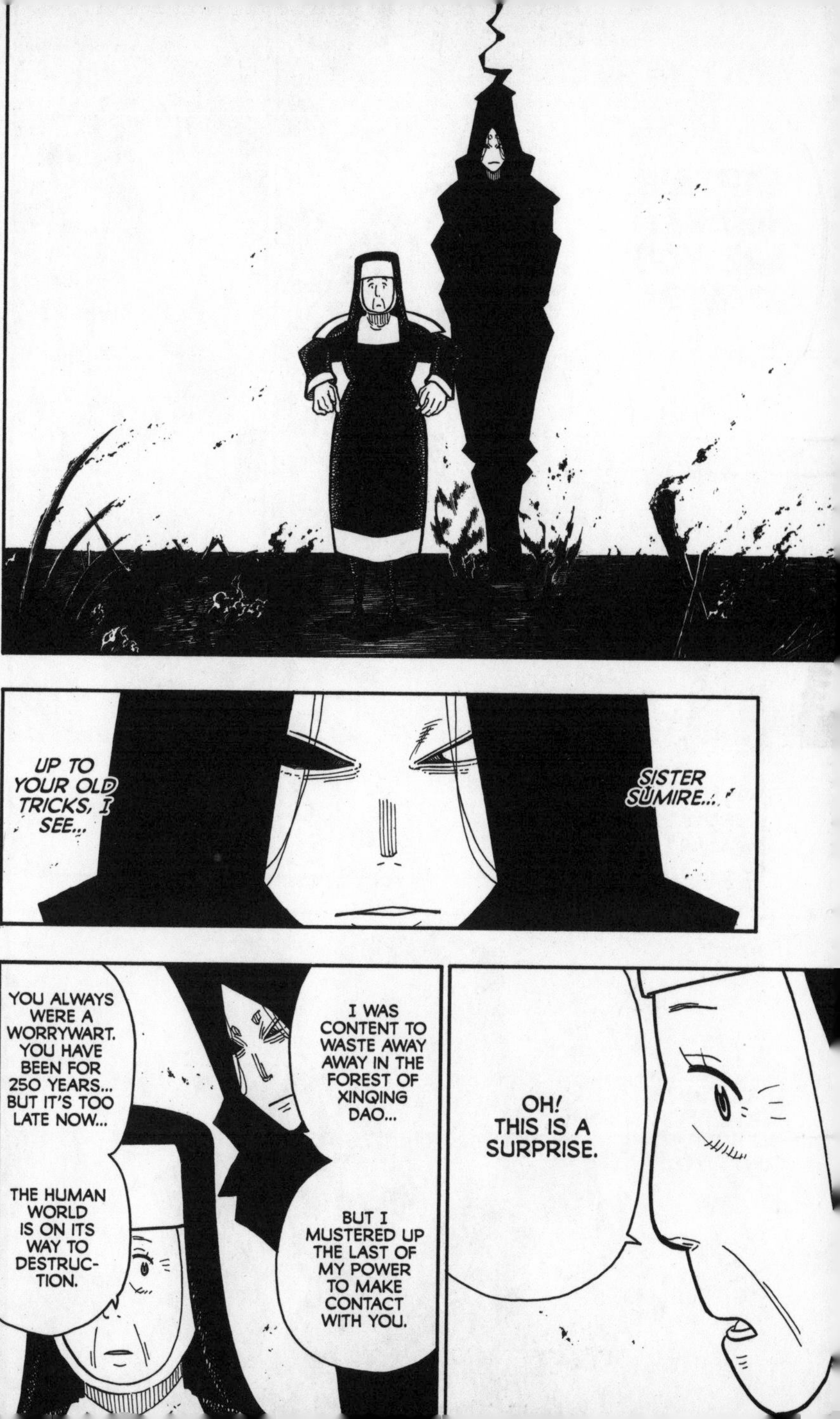
SISTER SUMIRE...
UP TO YOUR OLD TRICKS, I SEE...
OH! THIS IS A SURPRISE.
I WAS CONTENT TO WASTE AWAY AWAY IN THE FOREST OF XINQING DAO...
BUT I MUSTERED UP THE LAST OF MY POWER TO MAKE CONTACT WITH YOU.
YOU ALWAYS WERE A WORRYWART. YOU HAVE BEEN FOR 250 YEARS... BUT IT'S TOO LATE NOW...
THE HUMAN WORLD IS ON ITS WAY TO DESTRUC-TION.

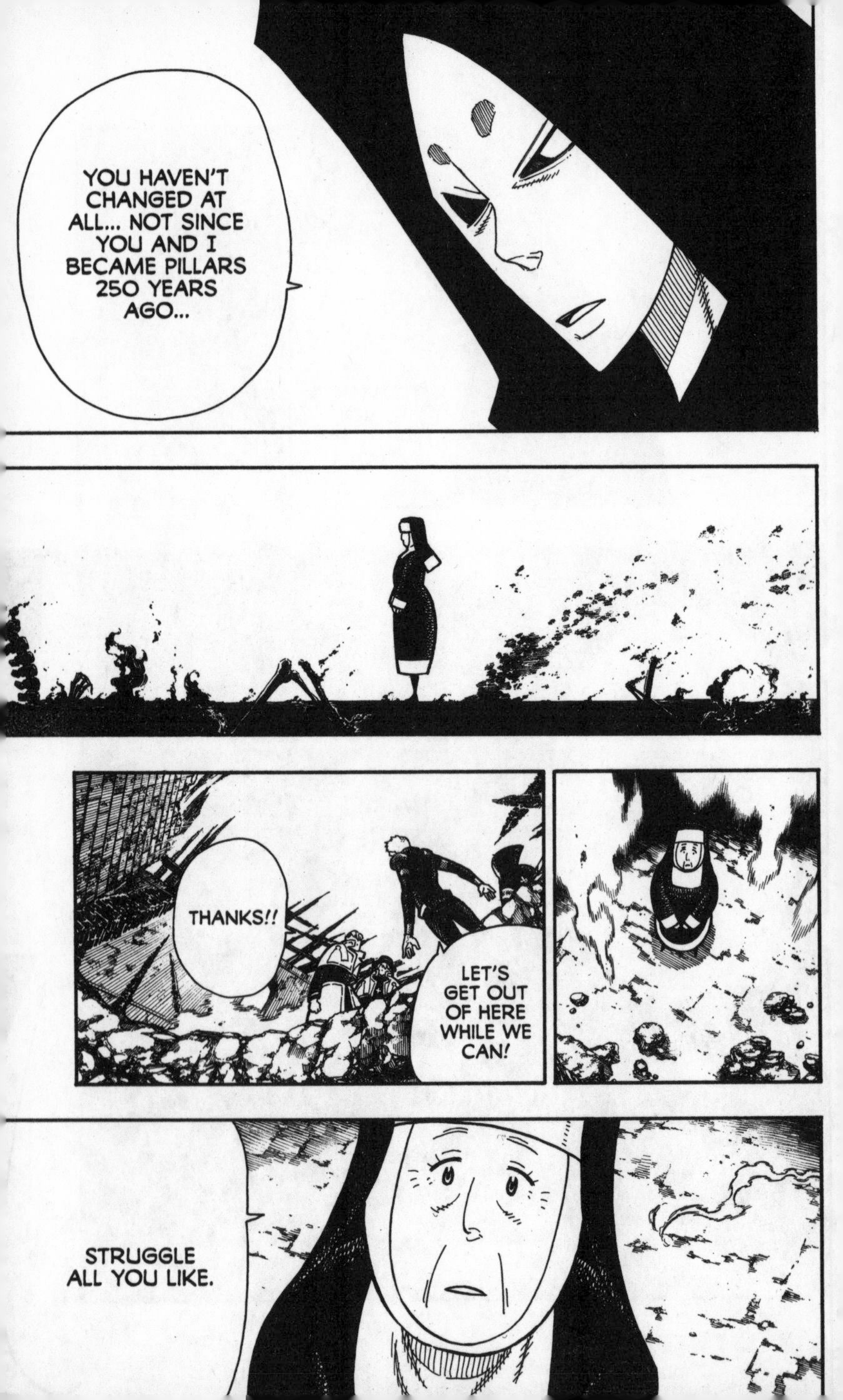
YOU HAVEN'T CHANGED AT ALL... NOT SINCE YOU AND I BECAME PILLARS 250 YEARS AGO...
THANKS!!
LET'S GET OUT OF HERE WHILE WE CAN!
STRUGGLE ALL YOU LIKE.

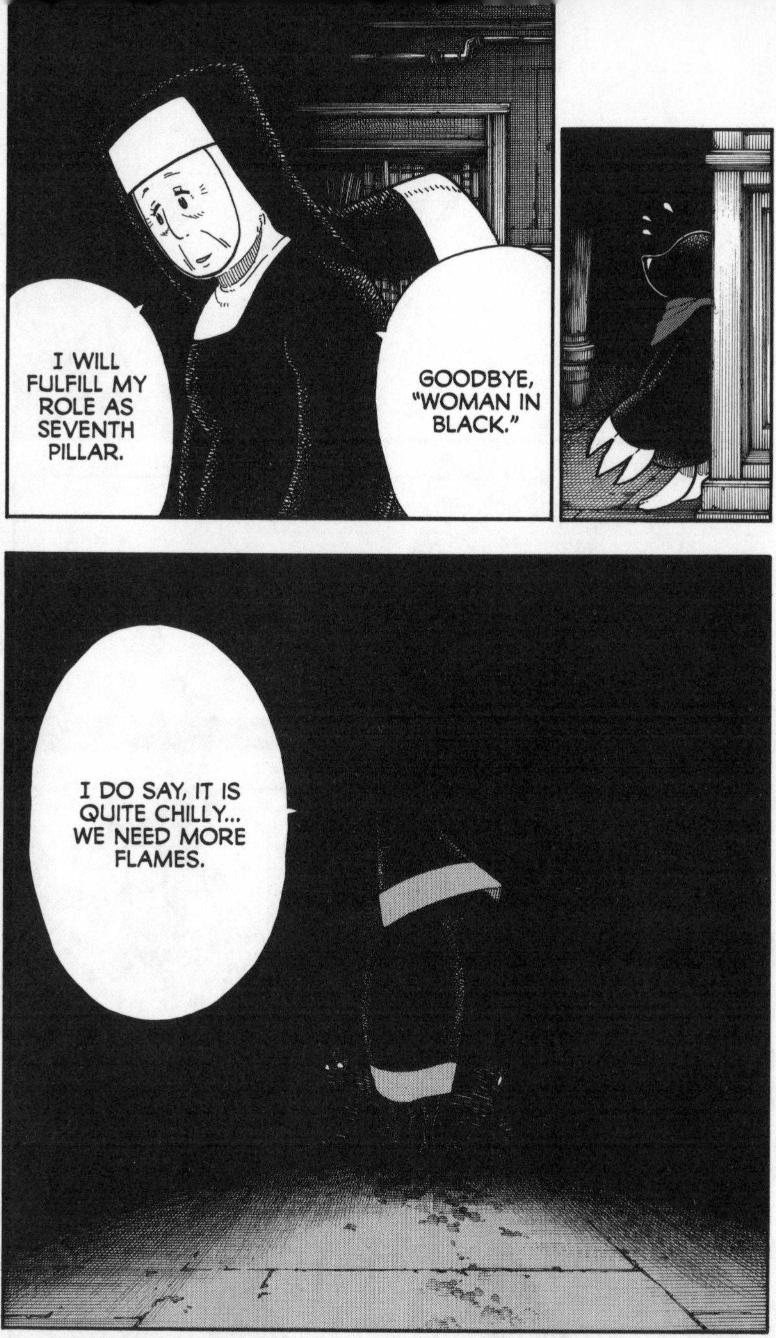
GOODBYE, "WOMAN IN BLACK."
I WILL FULFILL MY ROLE AS SEVENTH PILLAR.
I DO SAY, IT IS QUITE CHILLY... WE NEED MORE FLAMES.

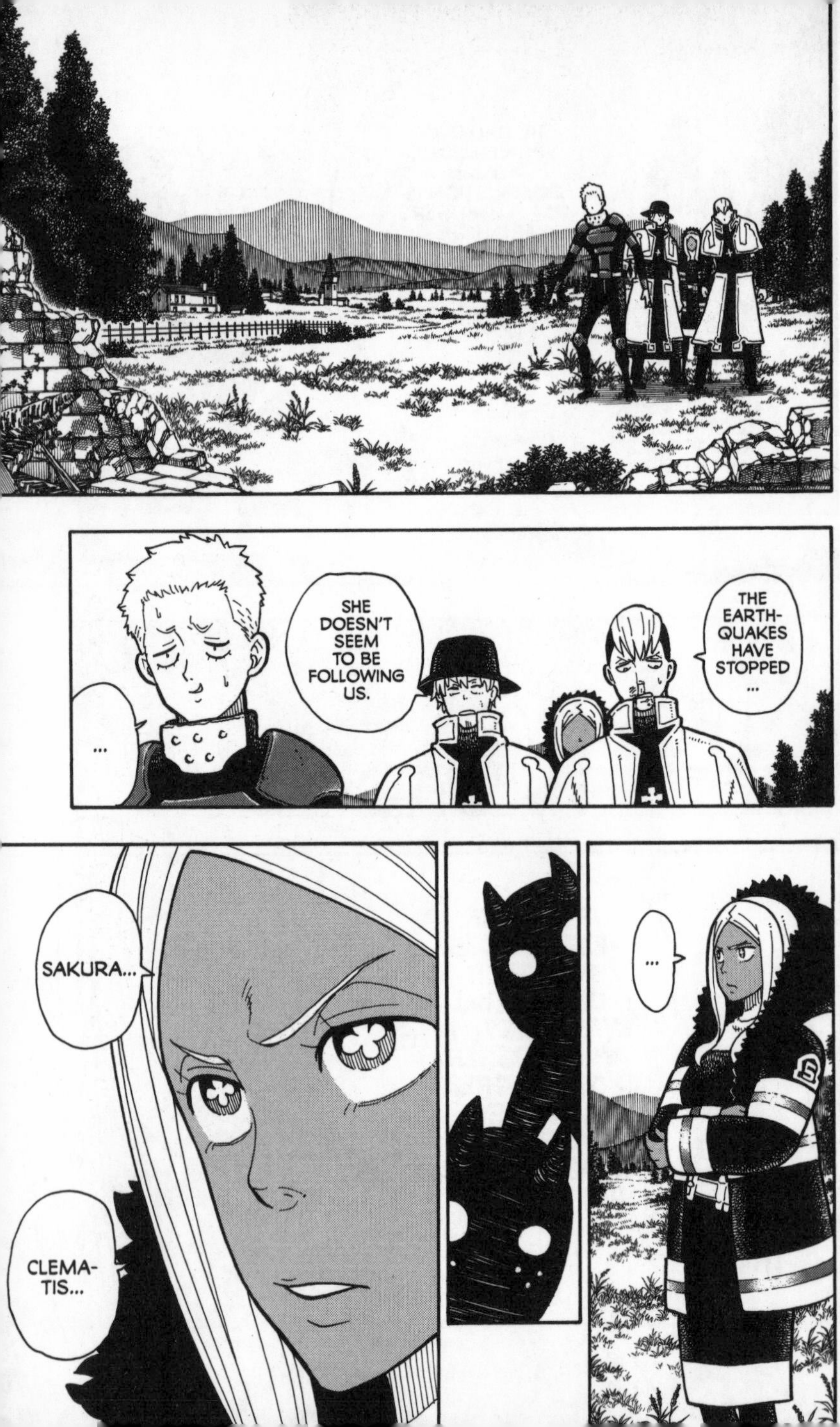

THE EARTH-QUAKES HAVE STOPPED ...
SHE DOESN'T SEEM TO BE FOLLOWING US.
...
...
SAKURA...
CLEMA-TIS...

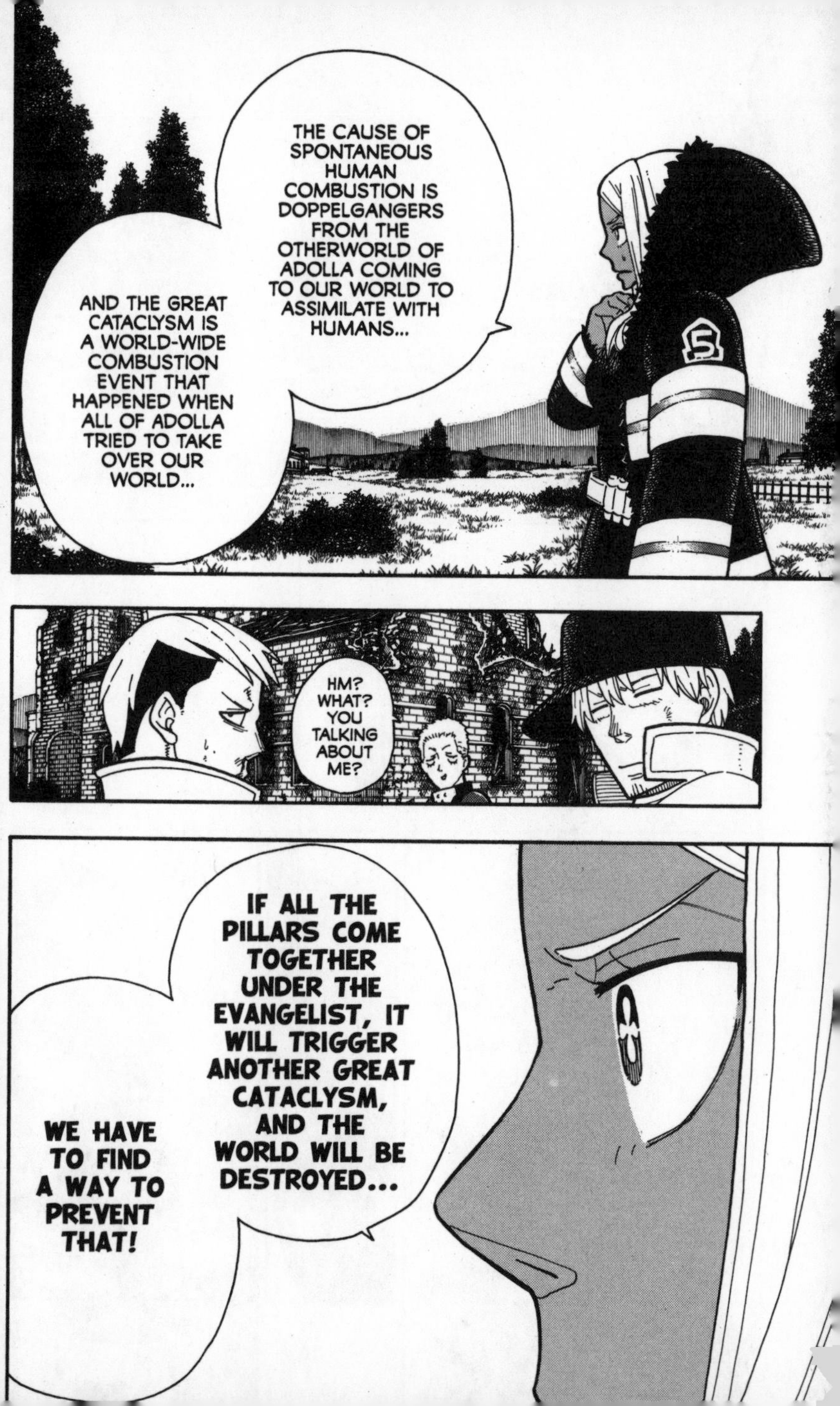
THE CAUSE OF SPONTANEOUS HUMAN COMBUSTION IS DOPPELGANGERS FROM THE OTHERWORLD OF ADOLLA COMING TO OUR WORLD TO ASSIMILATE WITH HUMANS...
AND THE GREAT CATACLYSM IS A WORLD-WIDE COMBUSTION EVENT THAT HAPPENED WHEN ALL OF ADOLLA TRIED TO TAKE OVER OUR WORLD...
HM? WHAT? YOU TALKING ABOUT ME?
IF ALL THE PILLARS COME TOGETHER UNDER THE EVANGELIST, IT WILL TRIGGER ANOTHER GREAT CATACLYSM, AND THE WORLD WILL BE DESTROYED...
WE HAVE TO FIND A WAY TO PREVENT THAT!

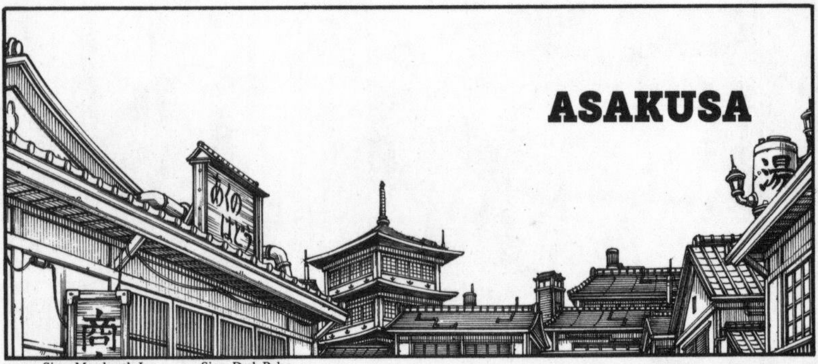
ASAKUSA

Sign: Merchant's Inn Sign: Dark Pulse Label: Bath

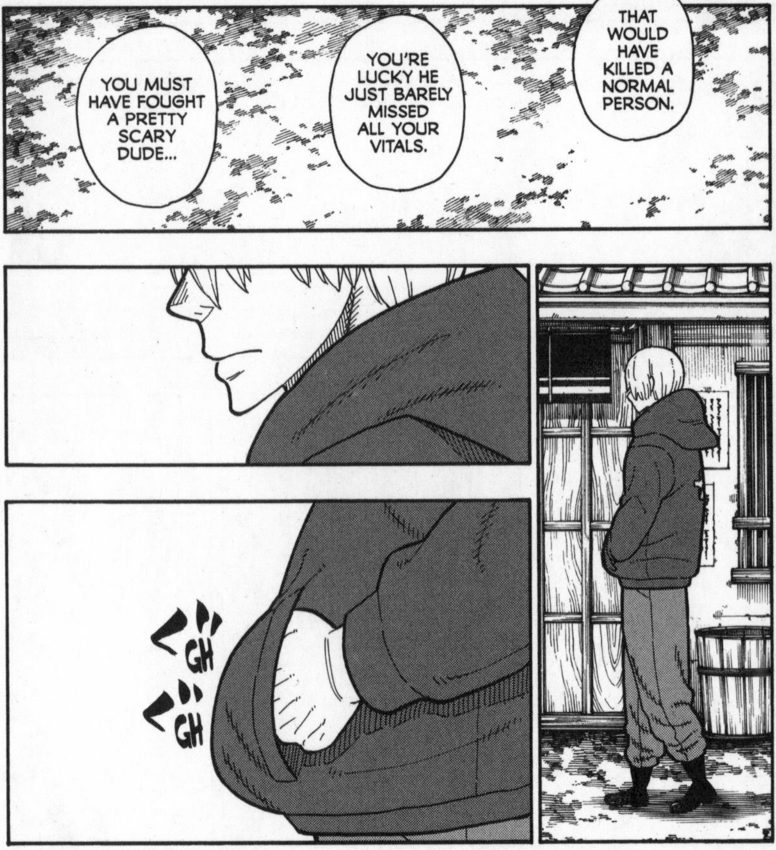
THAT WOULD HAVE KILLED A NORMAL PERSON.
YOU'RE LUCKY HE JUST BARELY MISSED ALL YOUR VITALS.
YOU MUST HAVE FOUGHT A PRETTY SCARY DUDE...
GH
GH

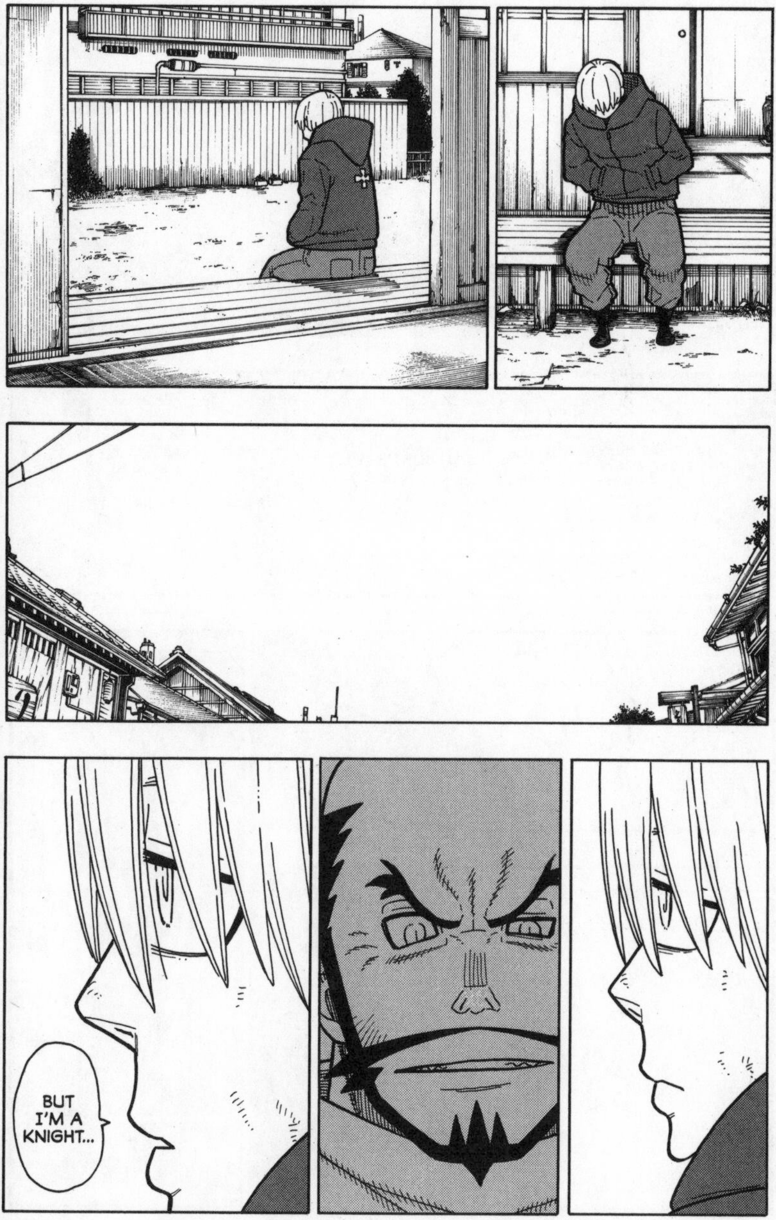
BUT I'M A KNIGHT...

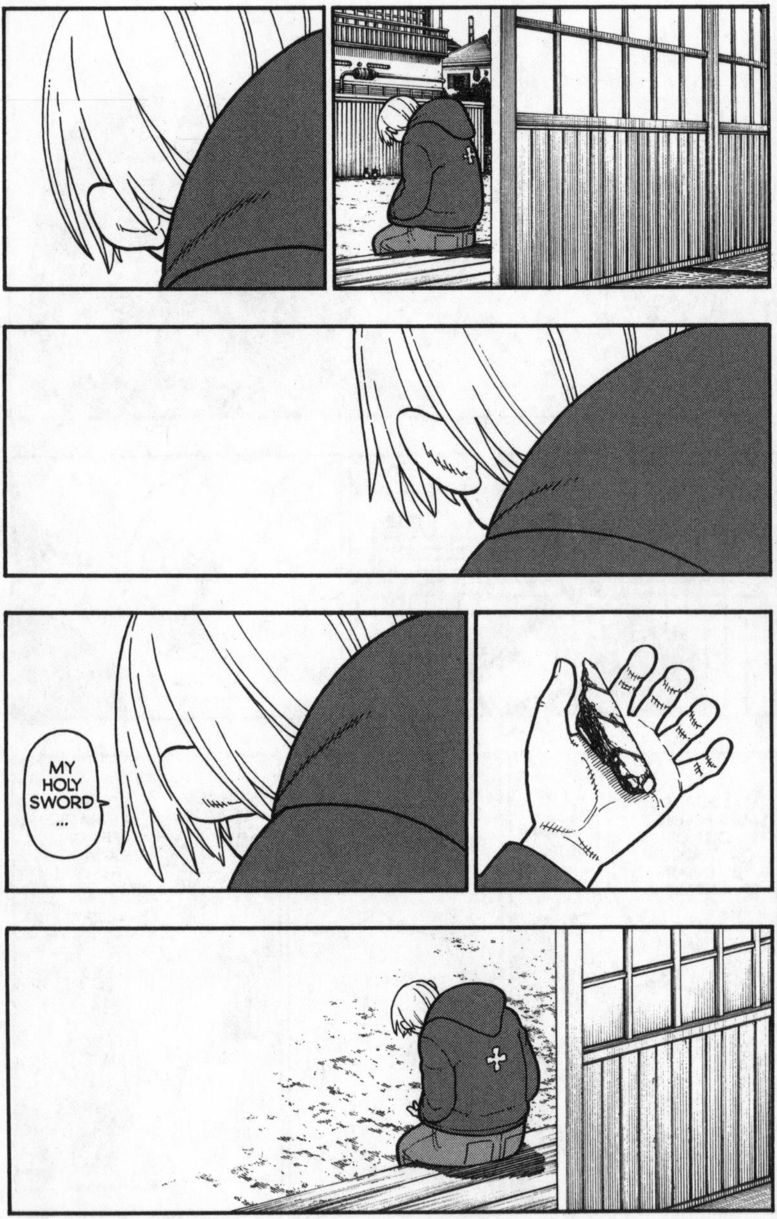
MY HOLY SWORD ...

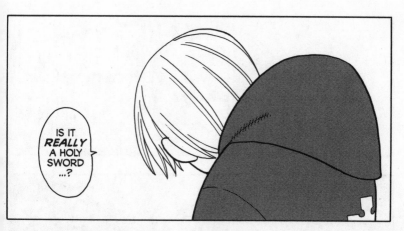

IS IT *REALLY* A HOLY SWORD ...?
...
SO THIS IS WHAT'S LEFT OF EXCALIBUR?
HIGH TEMPERATURE CARBON... THE STUFF THEY SELL AT HARDWARE STORES.
IT'S ORICHALCUM.
ORICHALCUM?
THE FANTASY METAL?
IT'S *LEGENDARY* METAL...
MY EXCALIBUR WAS FORGED OUT OF ORICHALCUM BY DWARF BLACKSMITHS.

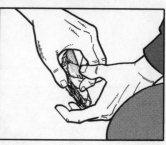

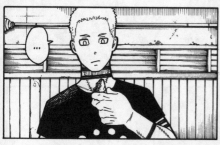

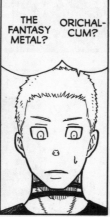

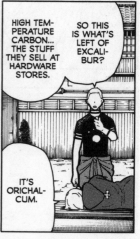

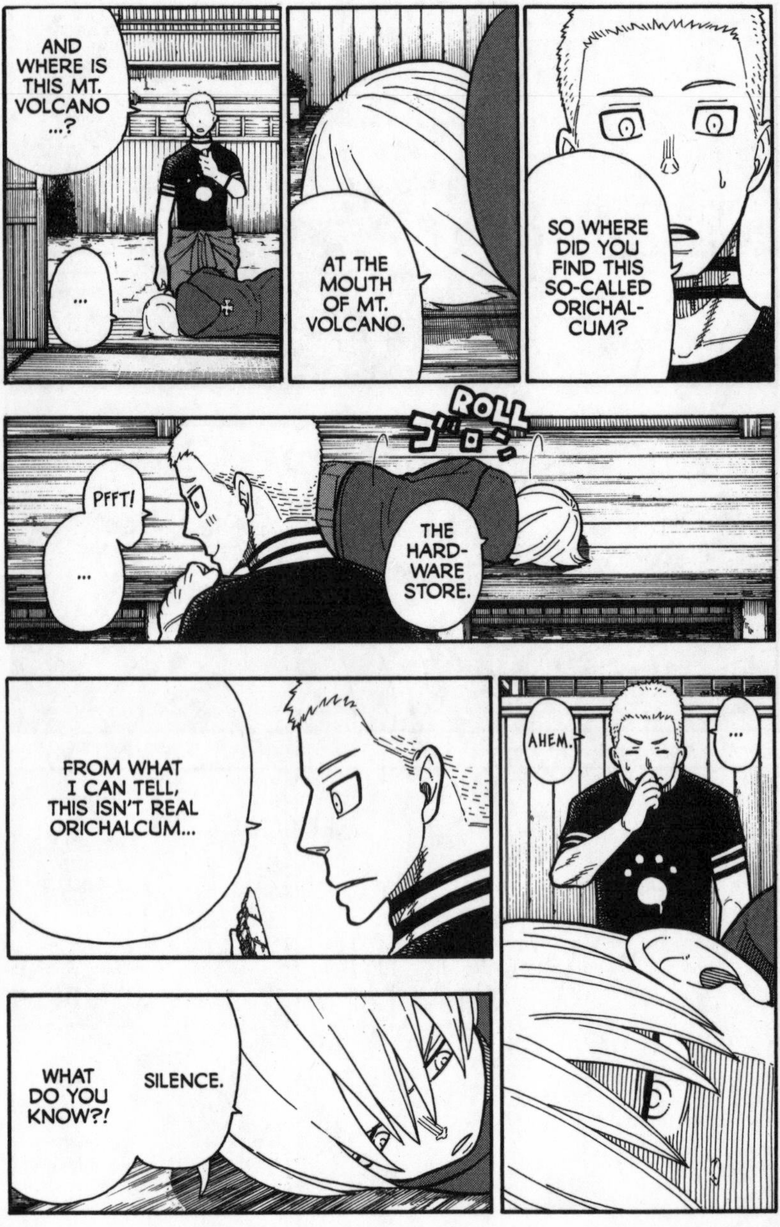
SO WHERE DID YOU FIND THIS SO-CALLED ORICHAL-CUM?
AT THE MOUTH OF MT. VOLCANO.
AND WHERE IS THIS MT. VOLCANO ...?
...
ROLL
THE HARD-WARE STORE.
PFFT!
...
...
AHEM.
FROM WHAT I CAN TELL, THIS ISN'T REAL ORICHALCUM...
SILENCE.
WHAT DO YOU KNOW?!

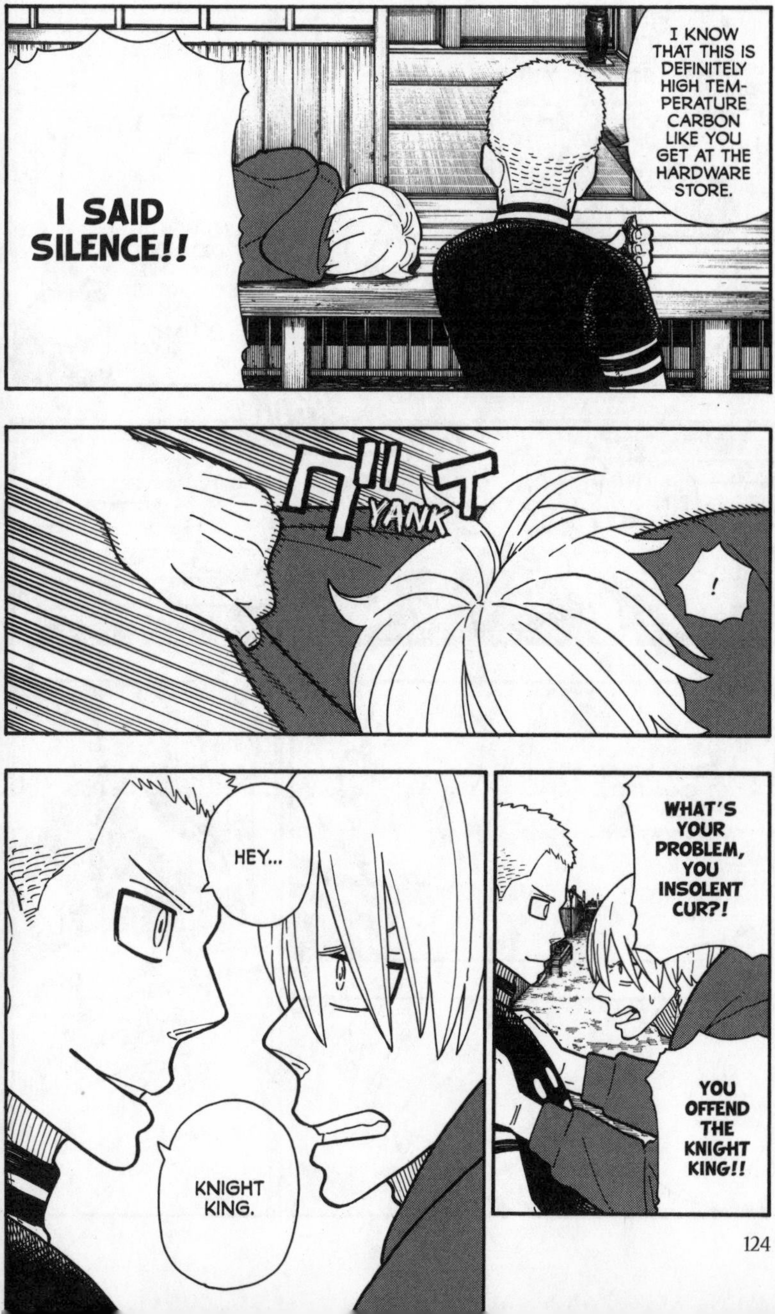
I KNOW THAT THIS IS DEFINITELY HIGH TEMPERATURE CARBON LIKE YOU GET AT THE HARDWARE STORE.
I SAID SILENCE!!
YANK
!
WHAT'S YOUR PROBLEM, YOU INSOLENT CUR?!
YOU OFFEND THE KNIGHT KING!!
HEY...
KNIGHT KING.

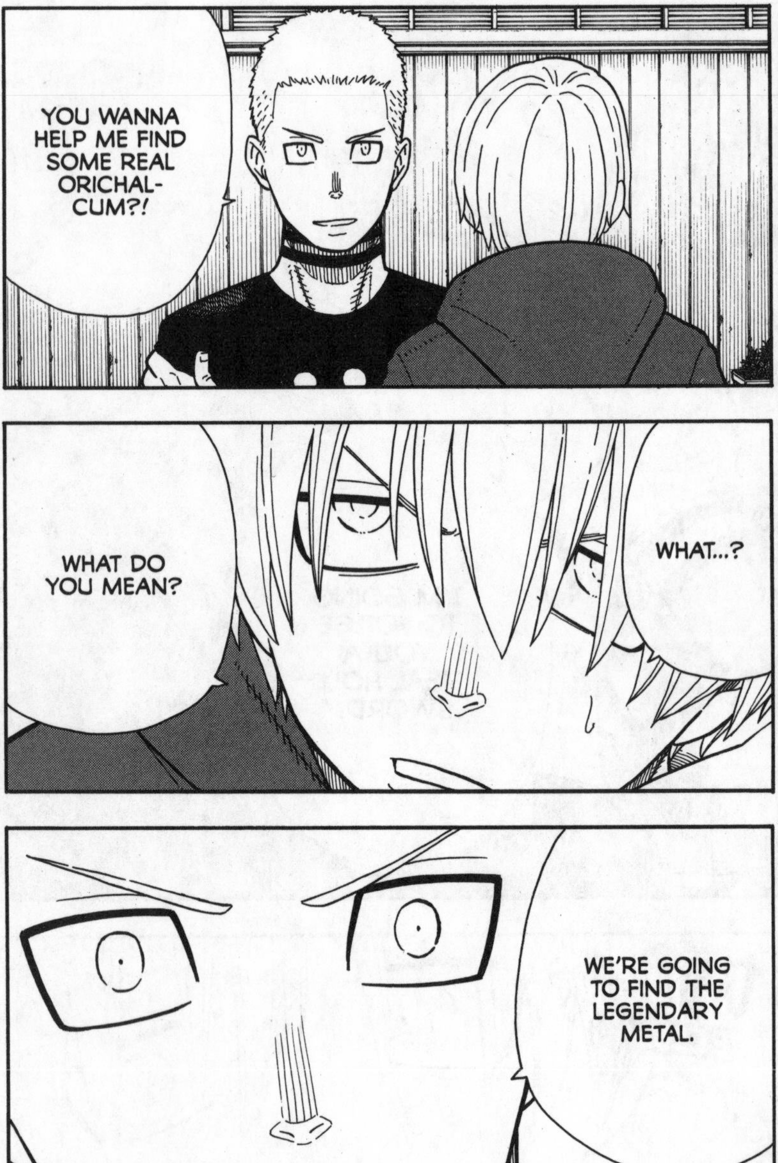
YOU WANNA HELP ME FIND SOME REAL ORICHAL-CUM?!
WHAT...?
WHAT DO YOU MEAN?
WE'RE GOING TO FIND THE LEGENDARY METAL.

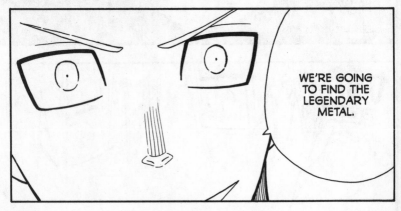

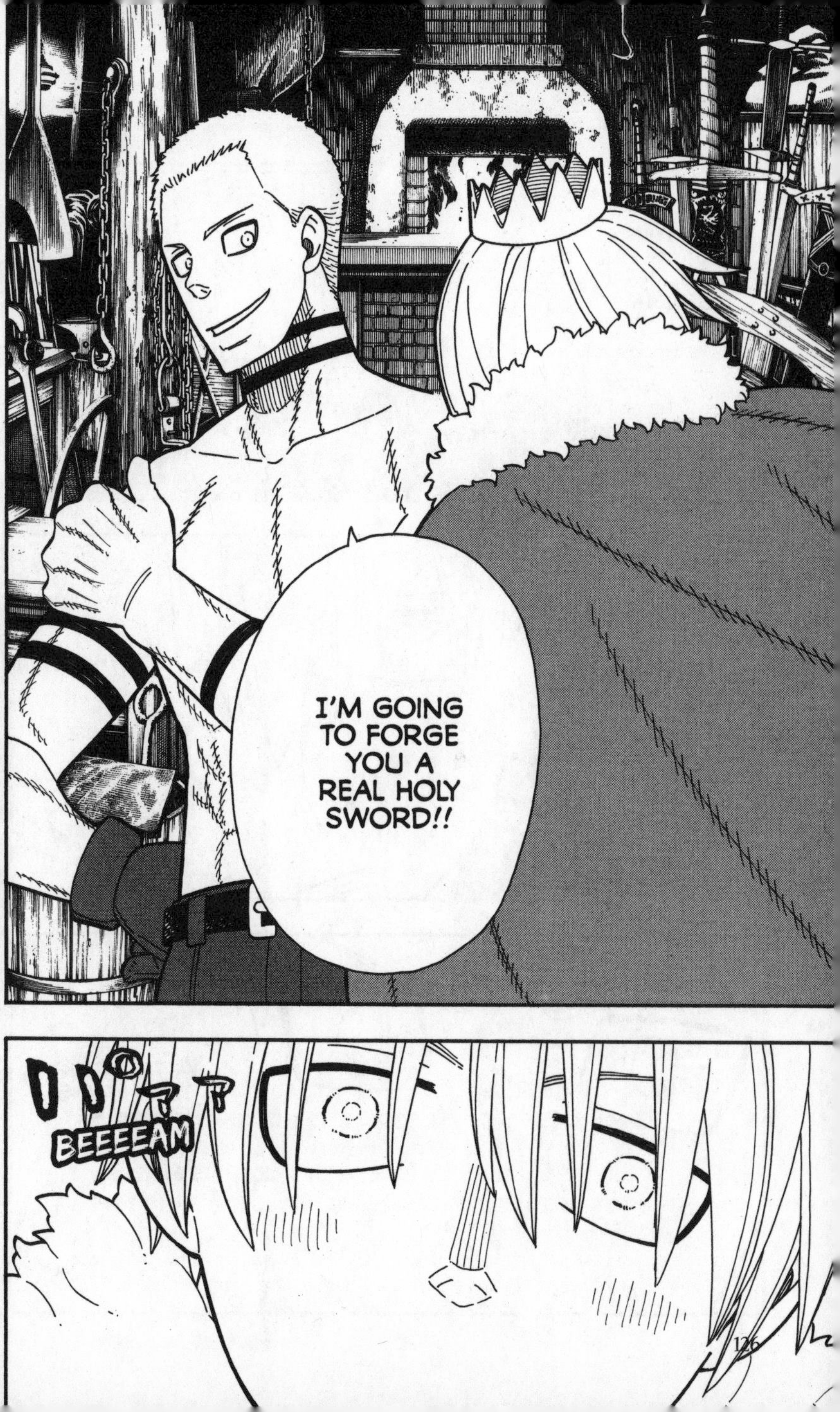
I'M GOING TO FORGE YOU A REAL HOLY SWORD!!
BEEEEEAM

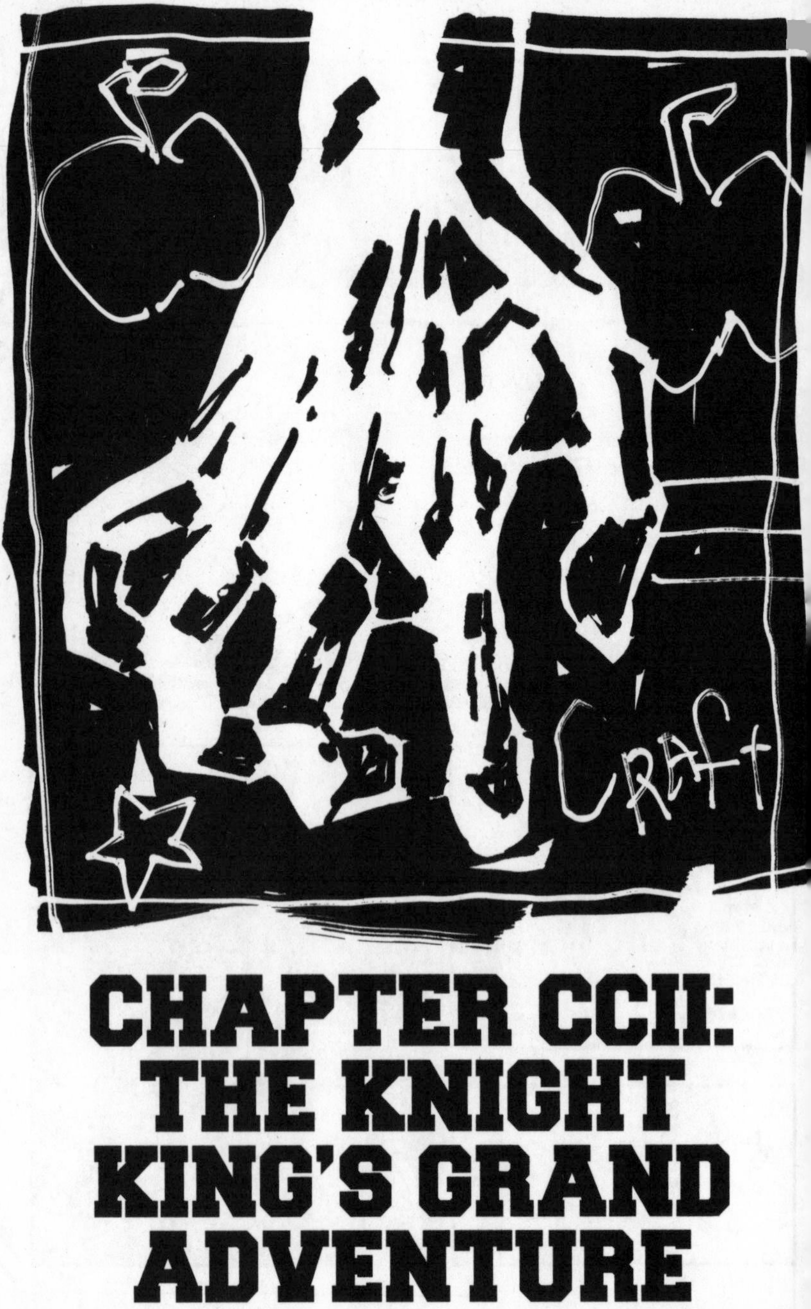
CRAFT

CHAPTER CCII: THE KNIGHT KING'S GRAND ADVENTURE

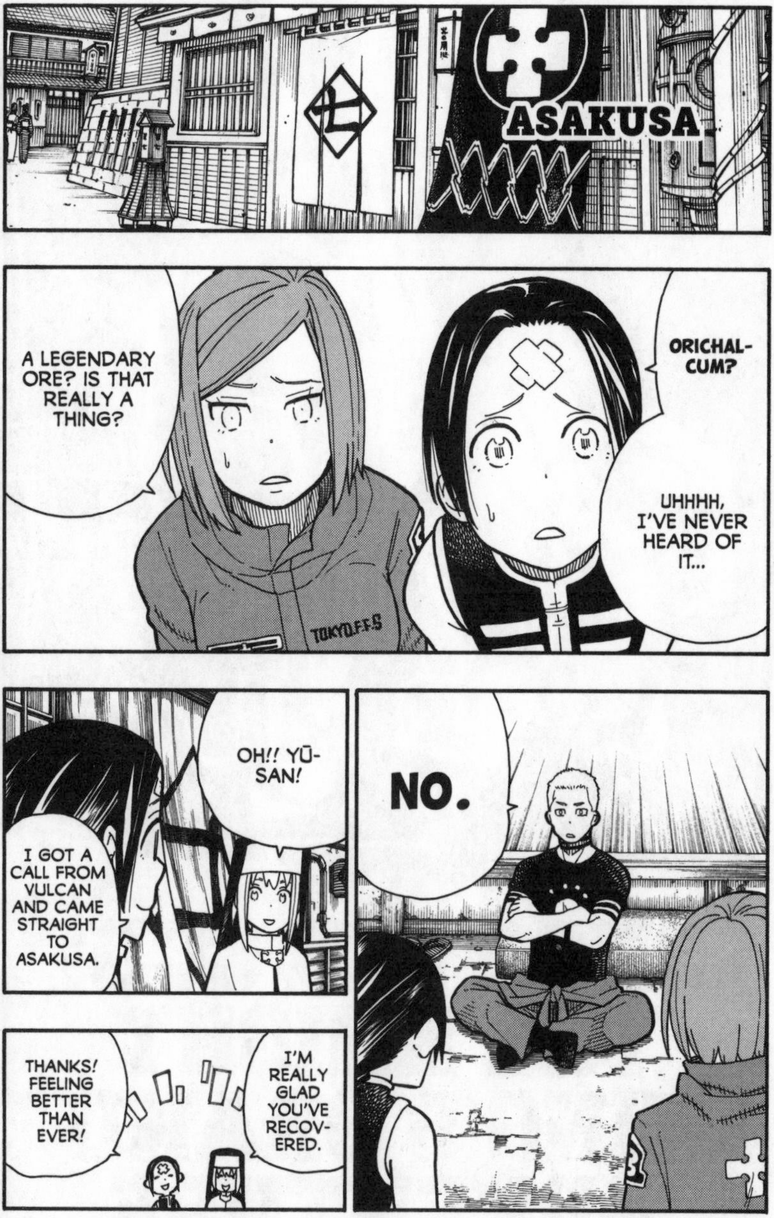
ASAKUSA
ORICHAL-CUM?
UHHHH, I'VE NEVER HEARD OF IT...
A LEGENDARY ORE? IS THAT REALLY A THING?
NO.
OH!! YŪ-SAN!
I GOT A CALL FROM VULCAN AND CAME STRAIGHT TO ASAKUSA.
I'M REALLY GLAD YOU'VE RECOV-ERED.
THANKS! FEELING BETTER THAN EVER!

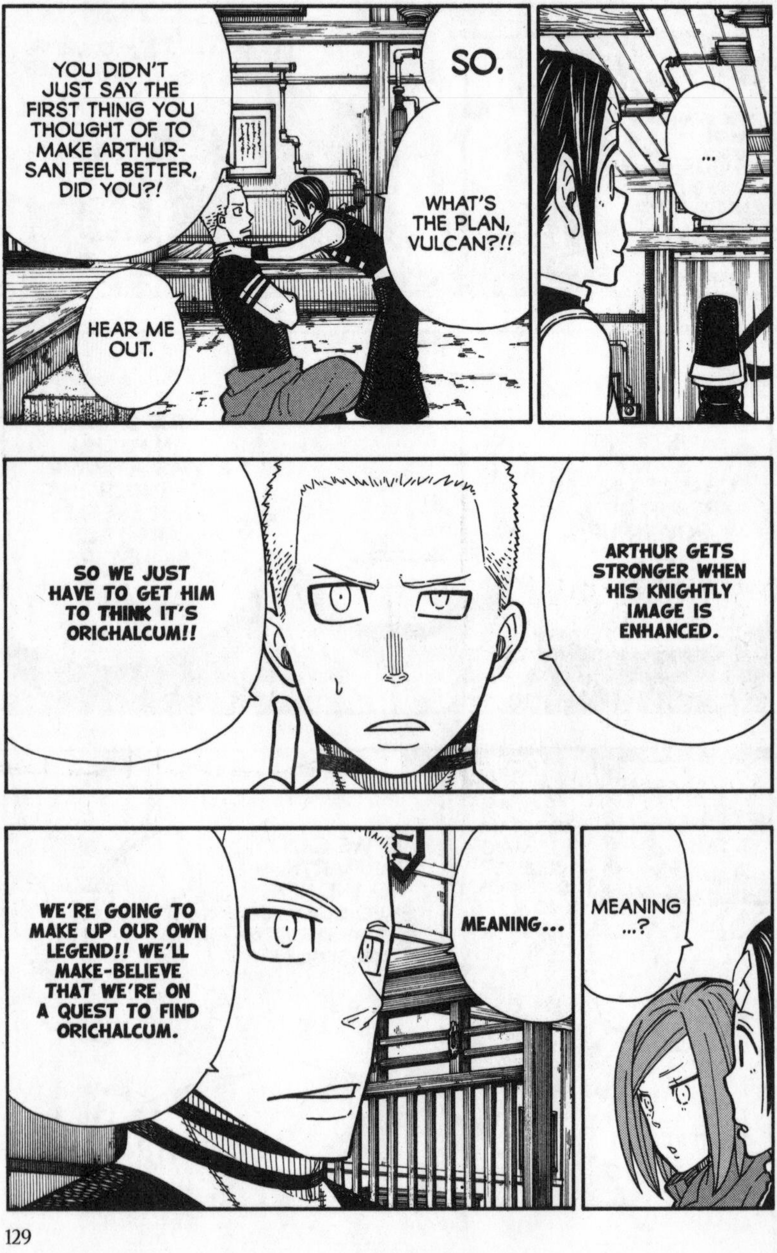
...
SO.
WHAT'S THE PLAN, VULCAN?!!
YOU DIDN'T JUST SAY THE FIRST THING YOU THOUGHT OF TO MAKE ARTHUR-SAN FEEL BETTER, DID YOU?!
HEAR ME OUT.
ARTHUR GETS STRONGER WHEN HIS KNIGHTLY IMAGE IS ENHANCED.
SO WE JUST HAVE TO GET HIM TO THINK IT'S ORICHALCUM!!
MEANING ...?
MEANING...
WE'RE GOING TO MAKE UP OUR OWN LEGEND!! WE'LL MAKE-BELIEVE THAT WE'RE ON A QUEST TO FIND ORICHALCUM.

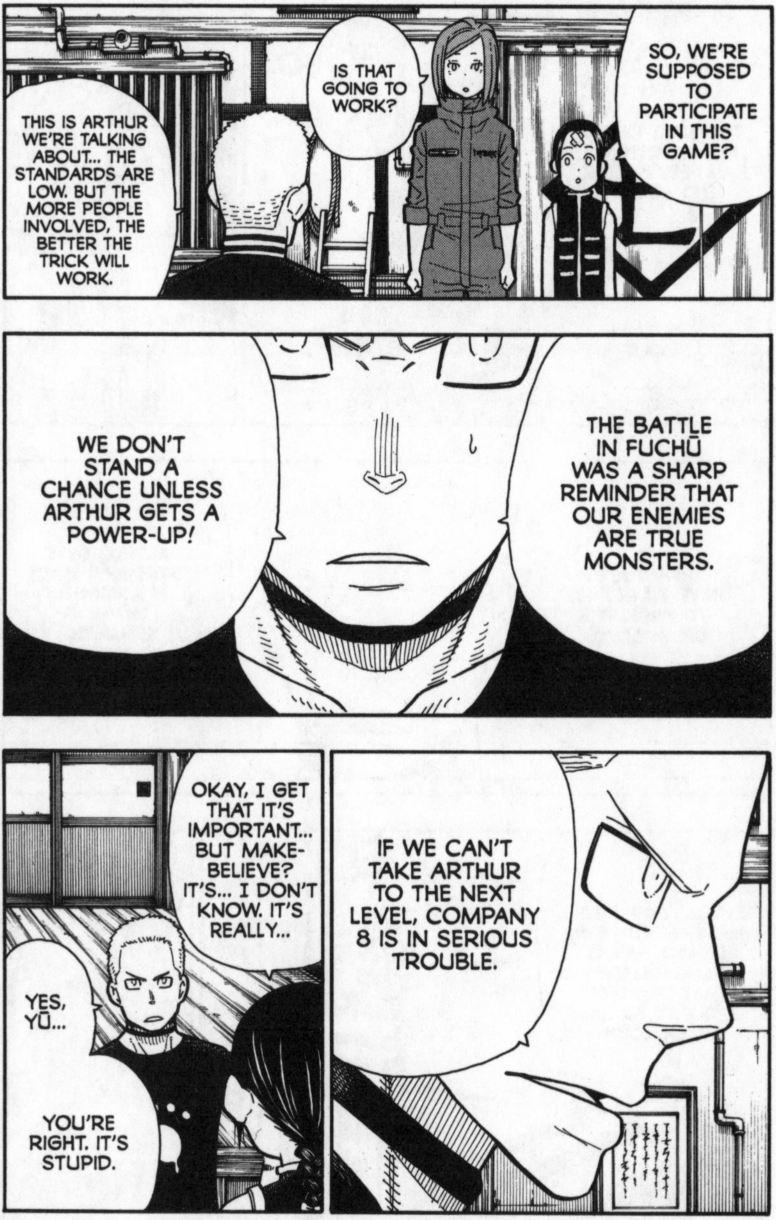
SO, WE'RE SUPPOSED TO PARTICIPATE IN THIS GAME?
IS THAT GOING TO WORK?
THIS IS ARTHUR WE'RE TALKING ABOUT... THE STANDARDS ARE LOW. BUT THE MORE PEOPLE INVOLVED, THE BETTER THE TRICK WILL WORK.
THE BATTLE IN FUCHŪ WAS A SHARP REMINDER THAT OUR ENEMIES ARE TRUE MONSTERS.
WE DON'T STAND A CHANCE UNLESS ARTHUR GETS A POWER-UP!
IF WE CAN'T TAKE ARTHUR TO THE NEXT LEVEL, COMPANY 8 IS IN SERIOUS TROUBLE.
OKAY, I GET THAT IT'S IMPORTANT... BUT MAKE-BELIEVE? IT'S... I DON'T KNOW. IT'S REALLY...
YES, YŪ...
YOU'RE RIGHT. IT'S STUPID.

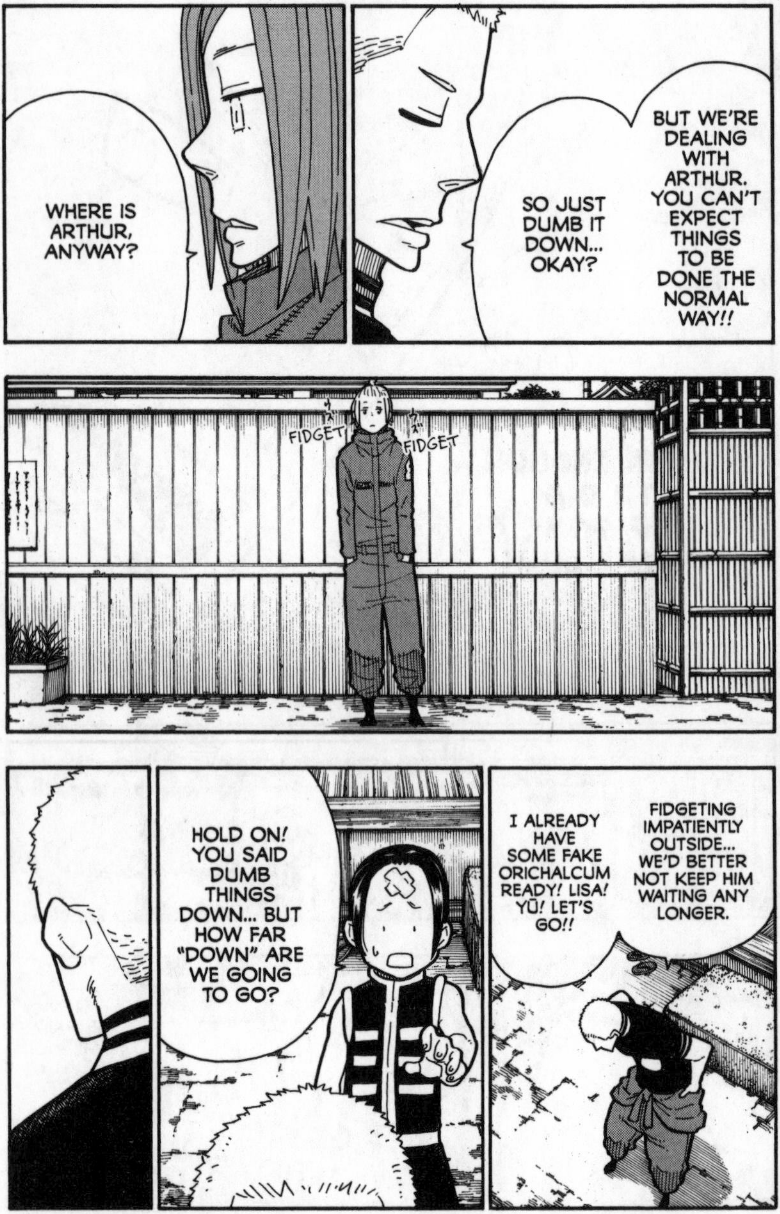
BUT WE'RE DEALING WITH ARTHUR. YOU CAN'T EXPECT THINGS TO BE DONE THE NORMAL WAY!!
SO JUST DUMB IT DOWN... OKAY?
WHERE IS ARTHUR, ANYWAY?
FIDGET
FIDGET
FIDGETING IMPATIENTLY OUTSIDE... WE'D BETTER NOT KEEP HIM WAITING ANY LONGER.
I ALREADY HAVE SOME FAKE ORICHALCUM READY! LISA! YŪ! LET'S GO!!
HOLD ON! YOU SAID DUMB THINGS DOWN... BUT HOW FAR "DOWN" ARE WE GOING TO GO?

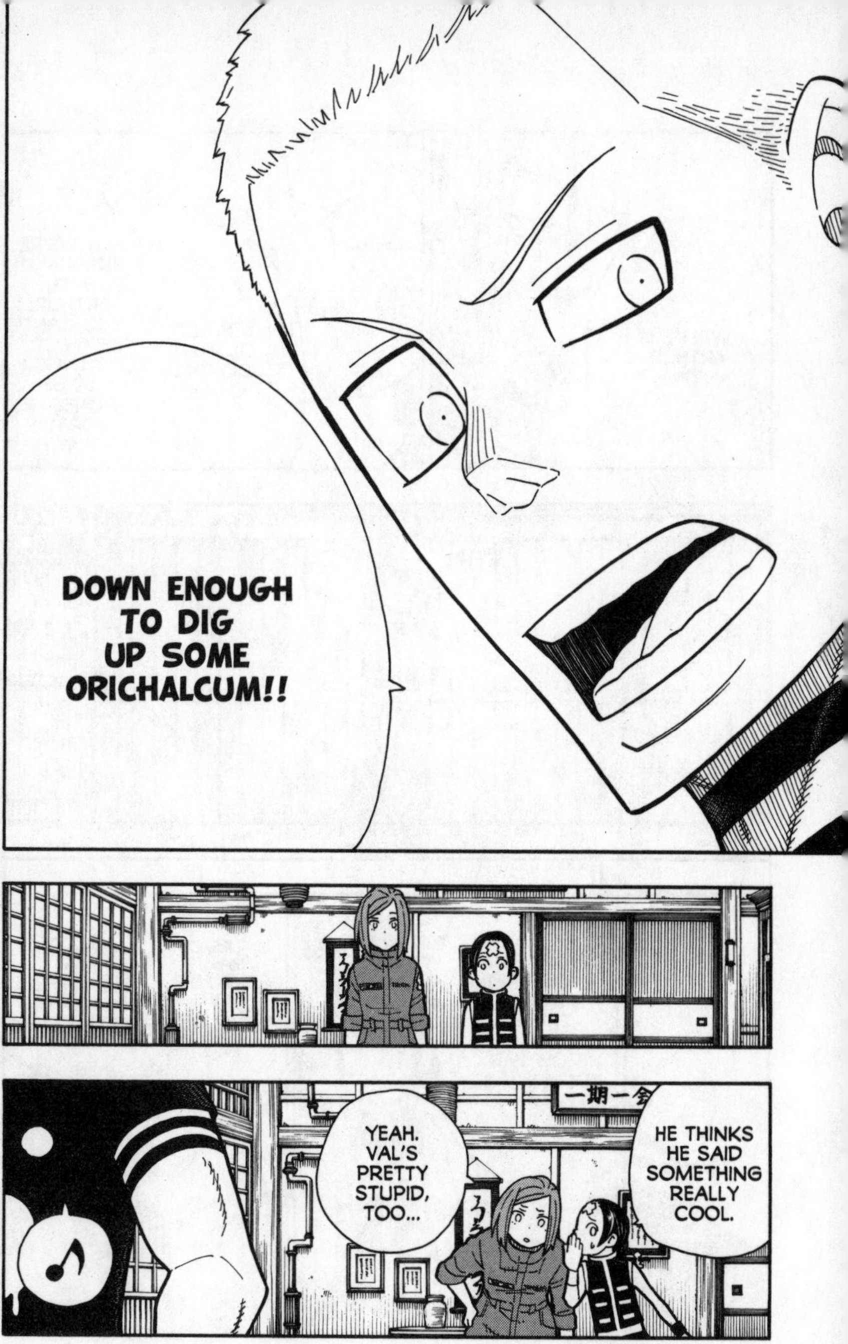
DOWN ENOUGH TO DIG UP SOME ORICHALCUM!!
HE THINKS HE SAID SOMETHING REALLY COOL.
YEAH. VAL'S PRETTY STUPID, TOO...

Sign: Once in a Lifetime

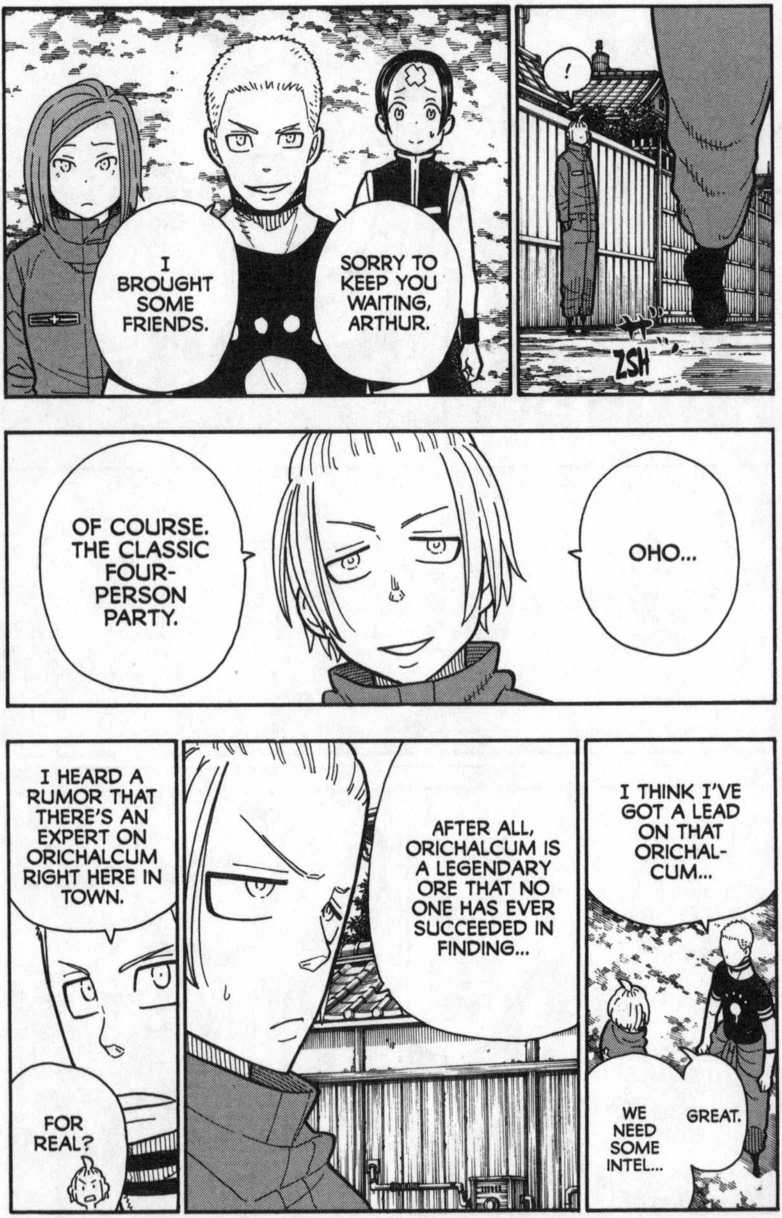
!
ZSH
SORRY TO KEEP YOU WAITING, ARTHUR.
I BROUGHT SOME FRIENDS.
OHO...
OF COURSE. THE CLASSIC FOUR-PERSON PARTY.
I THINK I'VE GOT A LEAD ON THAT ORICHALCUM...
GREAT.
WE NEED SOME INTEL...
AFTER ALL, ORICHALCUM IS A LEGENDARY ORE THAT NO ONE HAS EVER SUCCEEDED IN FINDING...
I HEARD A RUMOR THAT THERE'S AN EXPERT ON ORICHALCUM RIGHT HERE IN TOWN.
FOR REAL?

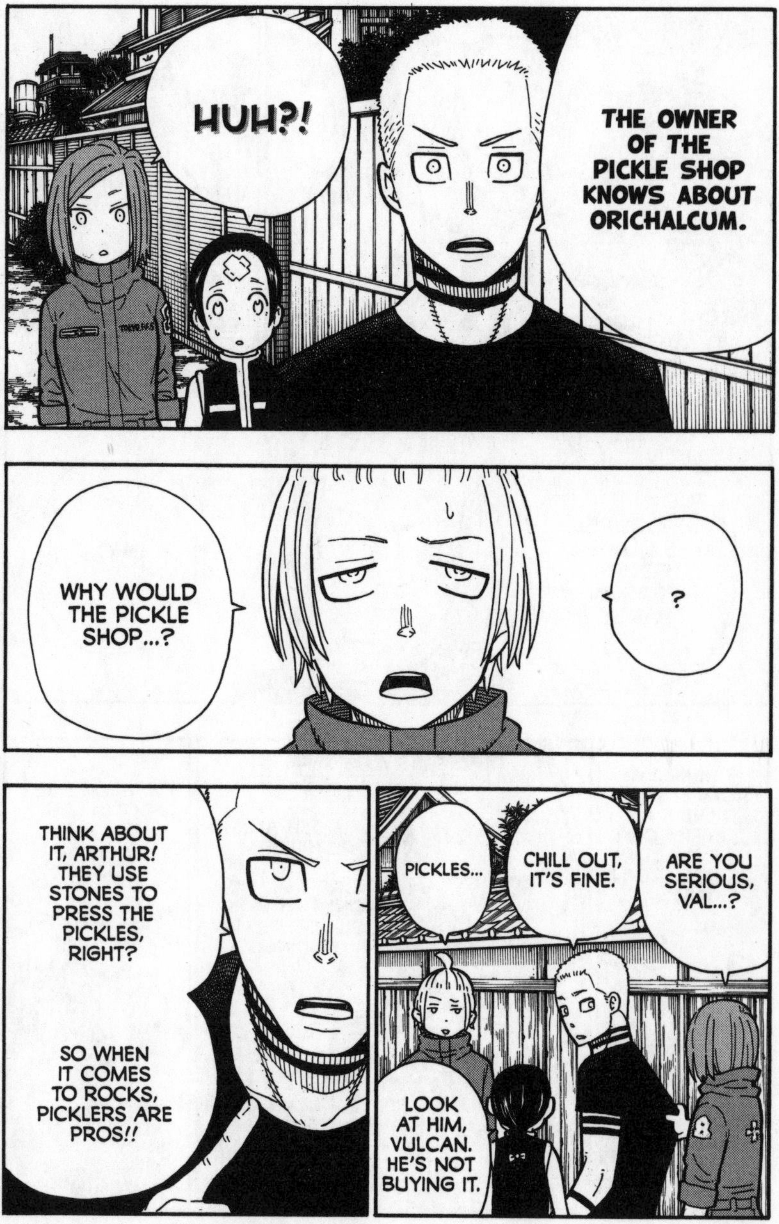
THE OWNER OF THE PICKLE SHOP KNOWS ABOUT ORICHALCUM.
HUH?!
?
WHY WOULD THE PICKLE SHOP...?
ARE YOU SERIOUS, VAL...?
CHILL OUT, IT'S FINE.
PICKLES...
LOOK AT HIM, VULCAN. HE'S NOT BUYING IT.
THINK ABOUT IT, ARTHUR! THEY USE STONES TO PRESS THE PICKLES, RIGHT?
SO WHEN IT COMES TO ROCKS, PICKLERS ARE PROS!!

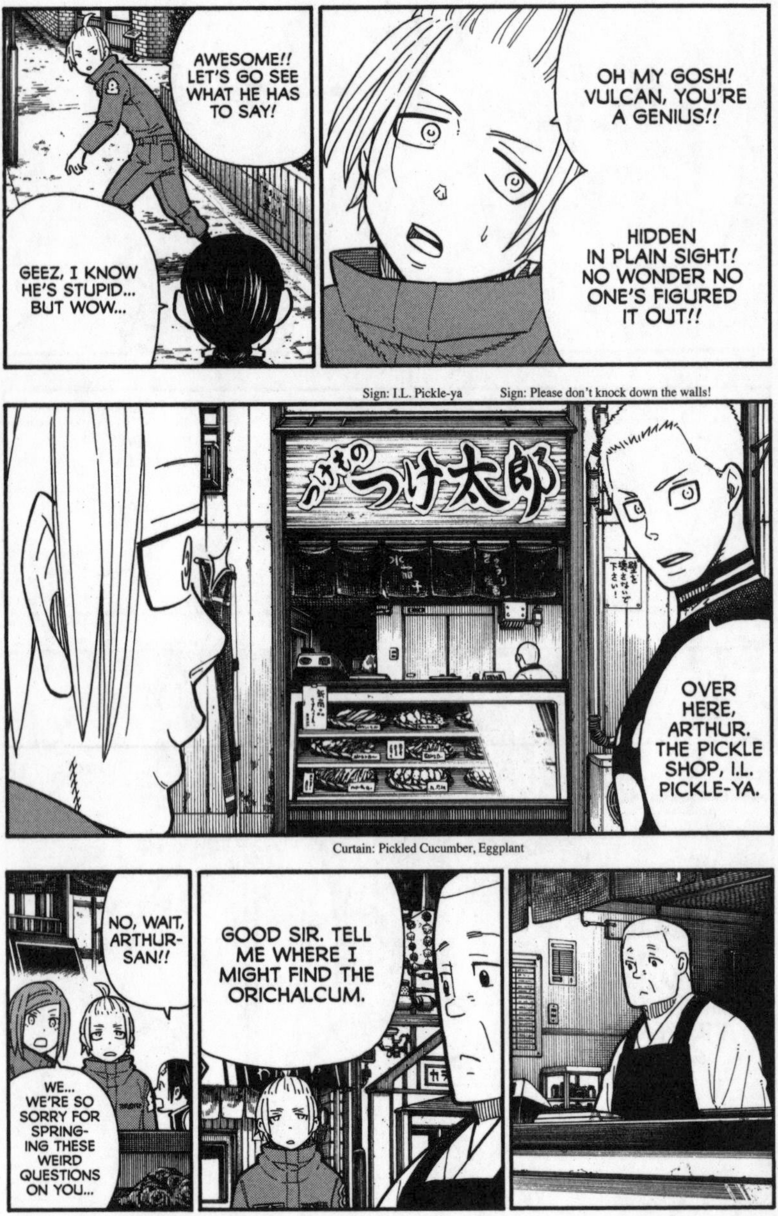
OH MY GOSH! VULCAN, YOU'RE A GENIUS!!
HIDDEN IN PLAIN SIGHT! NO WONDER NO ONE'S FIGURED IT OUT!!
AWESOME!! LET'S GO SEE WHAT HE HAS TO SAY!
GEEZ, I KNOW HE'S STUPID... BUT WOW...
OVER HERE, ARTHUR. THE PICKLE SHOP, I.L. PICKLE-YA.
つけもの
つけ太郎
GOOD SIR. TELL ME WHERE I MIGHT FIND THE ORICHALCUM.
NO, WAIT, ARTHUR-SAN!!
WE... WE'RE SO SORRY FOR SPRINGING THESE WEIRD QUESTIONS ON YOU...
Sign: I.L. Pickle-ya Sign: Please don't knock down the walls!

Curtain: Pickled Cucumber, Eggplant

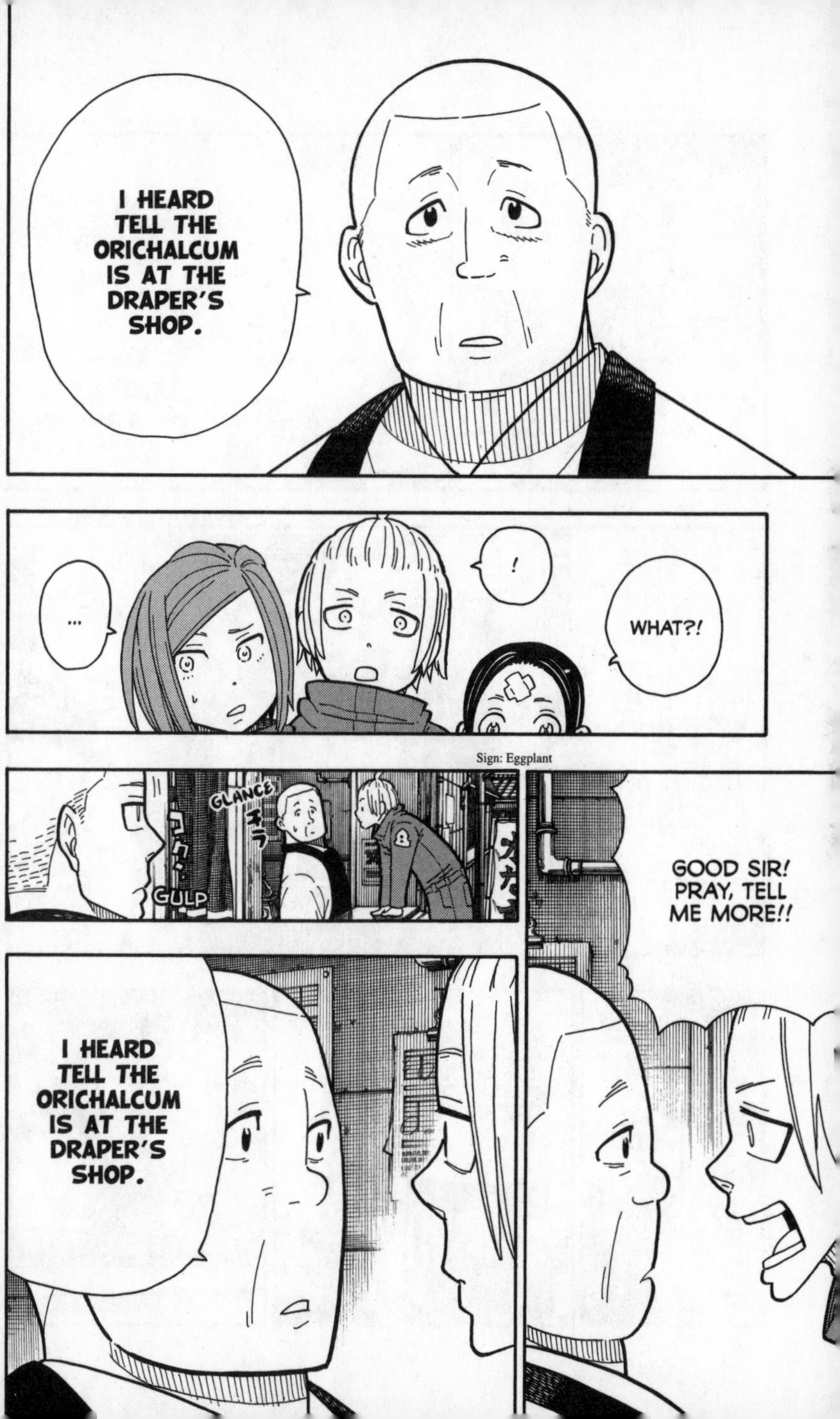
I HEARD TELL THE ORICHALCUM IS AT THE DRAPER'S SHOP.
WHAT?!
!
...
GOOD SIR! PRAY, TELL ME MORE!!
GLANCE
ギラ
ゴクッ
GULP
I HEARD TELL THE ORICHALCUM IS AT THE DRAPER'S SHOP.
Sign: Eggplant

Curtain: Pickled Cucumber
Curtain: Eggplant

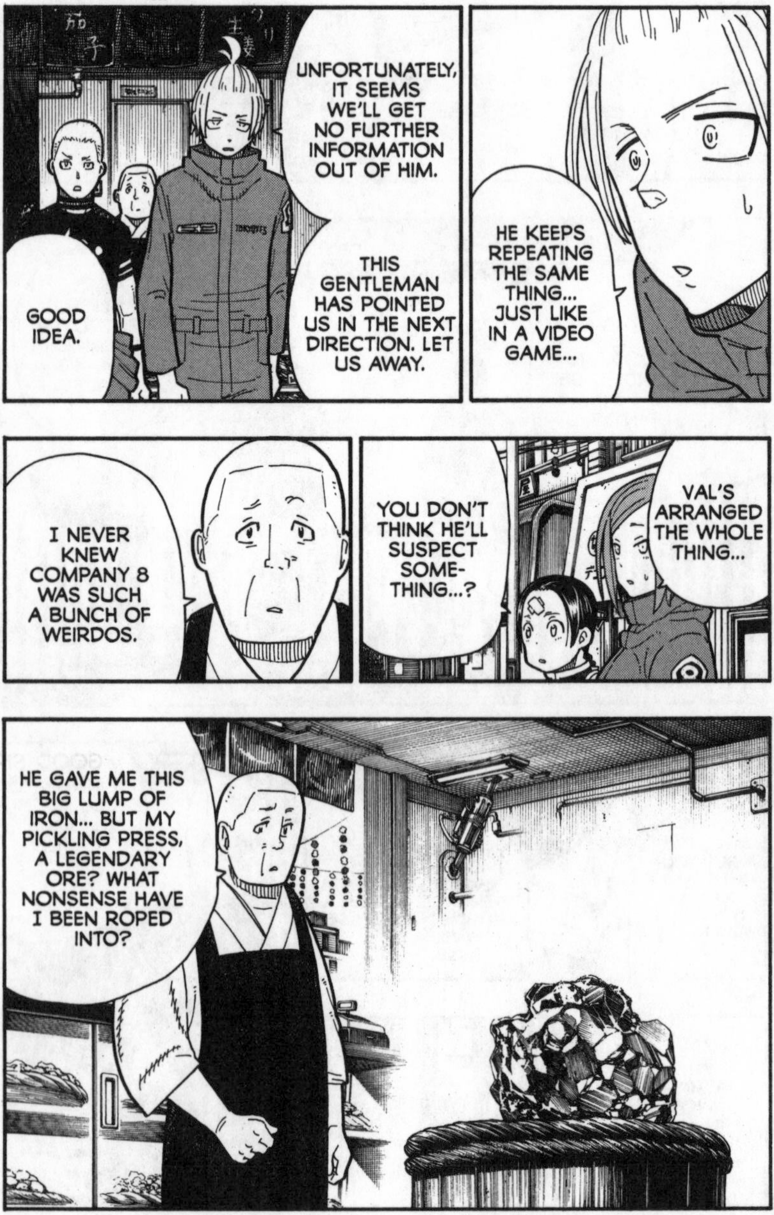
HE KEEPS REPEATING THE SAME THING... JUST LIKE IN A VIDEO GAME...
UNFORTUNATELY, IT SEEMS WE'LL GET NO FURTHER INFORMATION OUT OF HIM.
THIS GENTLEMAN HAS POINTED US IN THE NEXT DIRECTION. LET US AWAY.
GOOD IDEA.
VAL'S ARRANGED THE WHOLE THING...
YOU DON'T THINK HE'LL SUSPECT SOME-THING...?
I NEVER KNEW COMPANY 8 WAS SUCH A BUNCH OF WEIRDOS.
HE GAVE ME THIS BIG LUMP OF IRON... BUT MY PICKLING PRESS, A LEGENDARY ORE? WHAT NONSENSE HAVE I BEEN ROPED INTO?

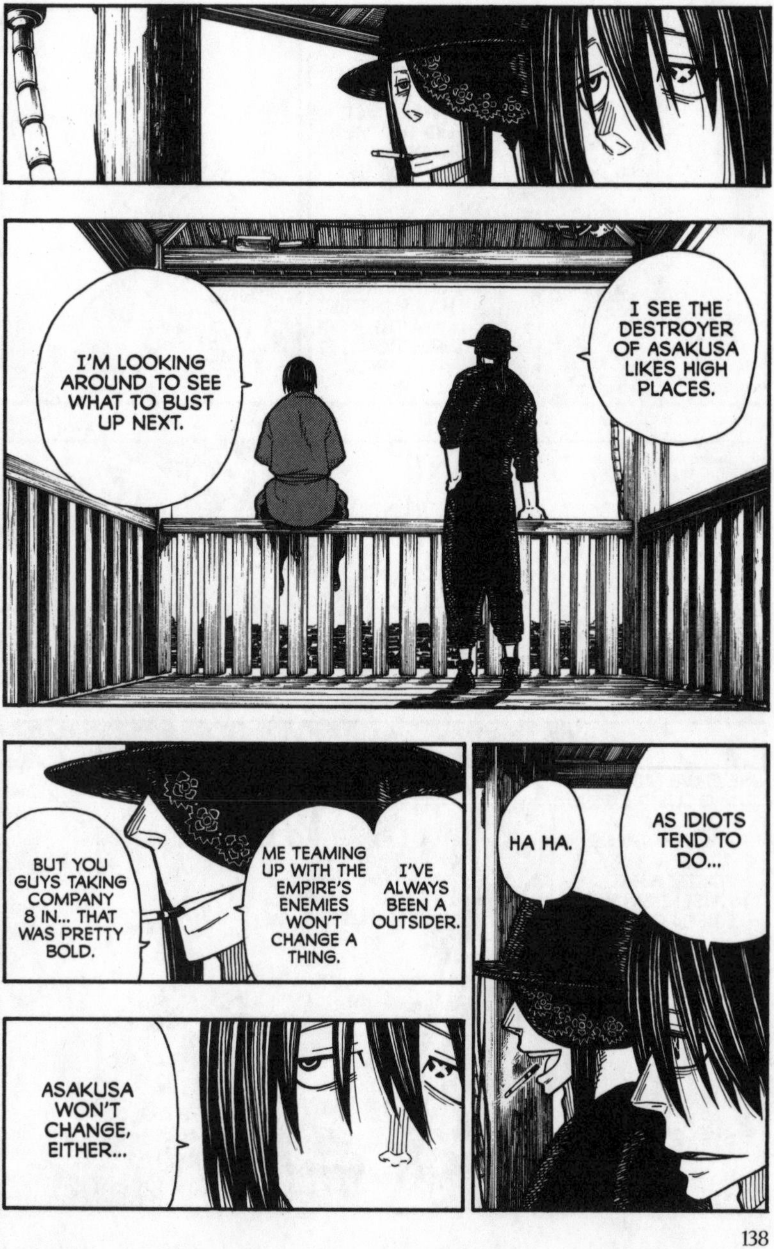
I SEE THE DESTROYER OF ASAKUSA LIKES HIGH PLACES.
I'M LOOKING AROUND TO SEE WHAT TO BUST UP NEXT.
AS IDIOTS TEND TO DO...
HA HA.
I'VE ALWAYS BEEN A OUTSIDER.
ME TEAMING UP WITH THE EMPIRE'S ENEMIES WON'T CHANGE A THING.
BUT YOU GUYS TAKING COMPANY 8 IN... THAT WAS PRETTY BOLD.
ASAKUSA WON'T CHANGE, EITHER...

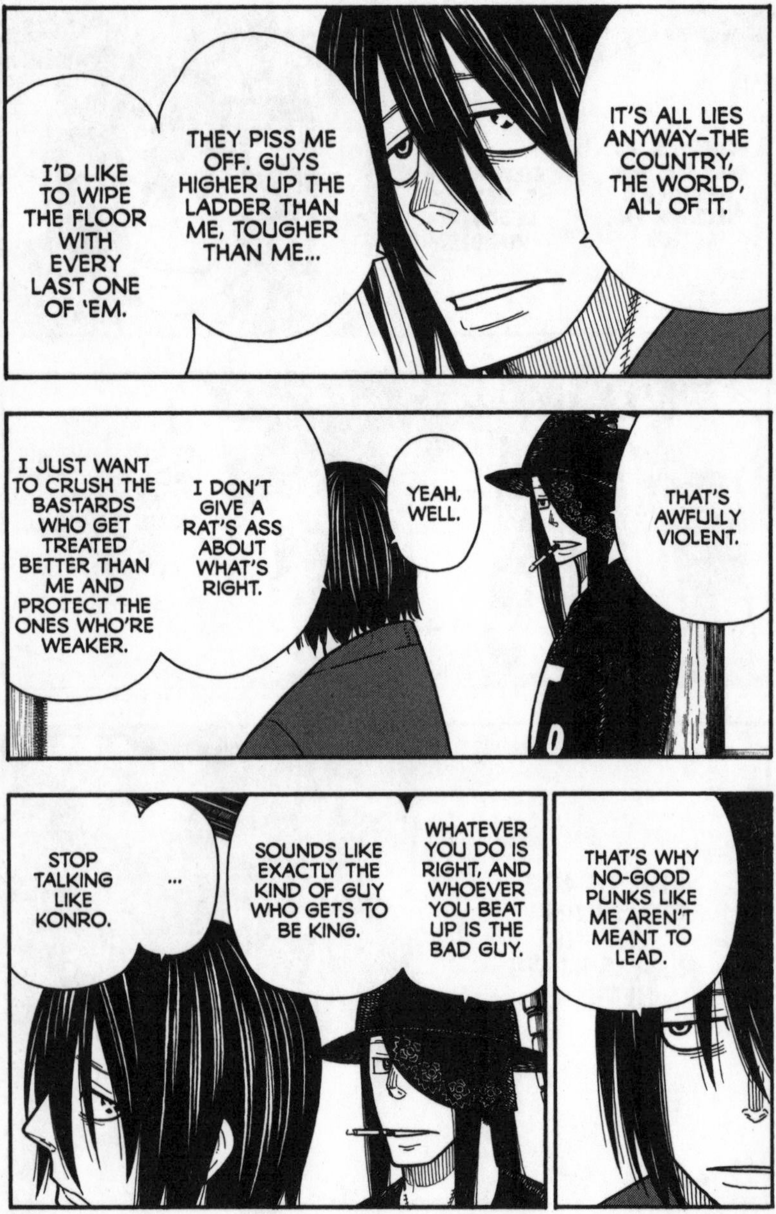
IT'S ALL LIES ANYWAY–THE COUNTRY, THE WORLD, ALL OF IT.
THEY PISS ME OFF. GUYS HIGHER UP THE LADDER THAN ME, TOUGHER THAN ME...
I'D LIKE TO WIPE THE FLOOR WITH EVERY LAST ONE OF 'EM.
THAT'S AWFULLY VIOLENT.
YEAH, WELL.
I DON'T GIVE A RAT'S ASS ABOUT WHAT'S RIGHT.
I JUST WANT TO CRUSH THE BASTARDS WHO GET TREATED BETTER THAN ME AND PROTECT THE ONES WHO'RE WEAKER.
THAT'S WHY NO-GOOD PUNKS LIKE ME AREN'T MEANT TO LEAD.
WHATEVER YOU DO IS RIGHT, AND WHOEVER YOU BEAT UP IS THE BAD GUY.
SOUNDS LIKE EXACTLY THE KIND OF GUY WHO GETS TO BE KING.
...
STOP TALKING LIKE KONRO.

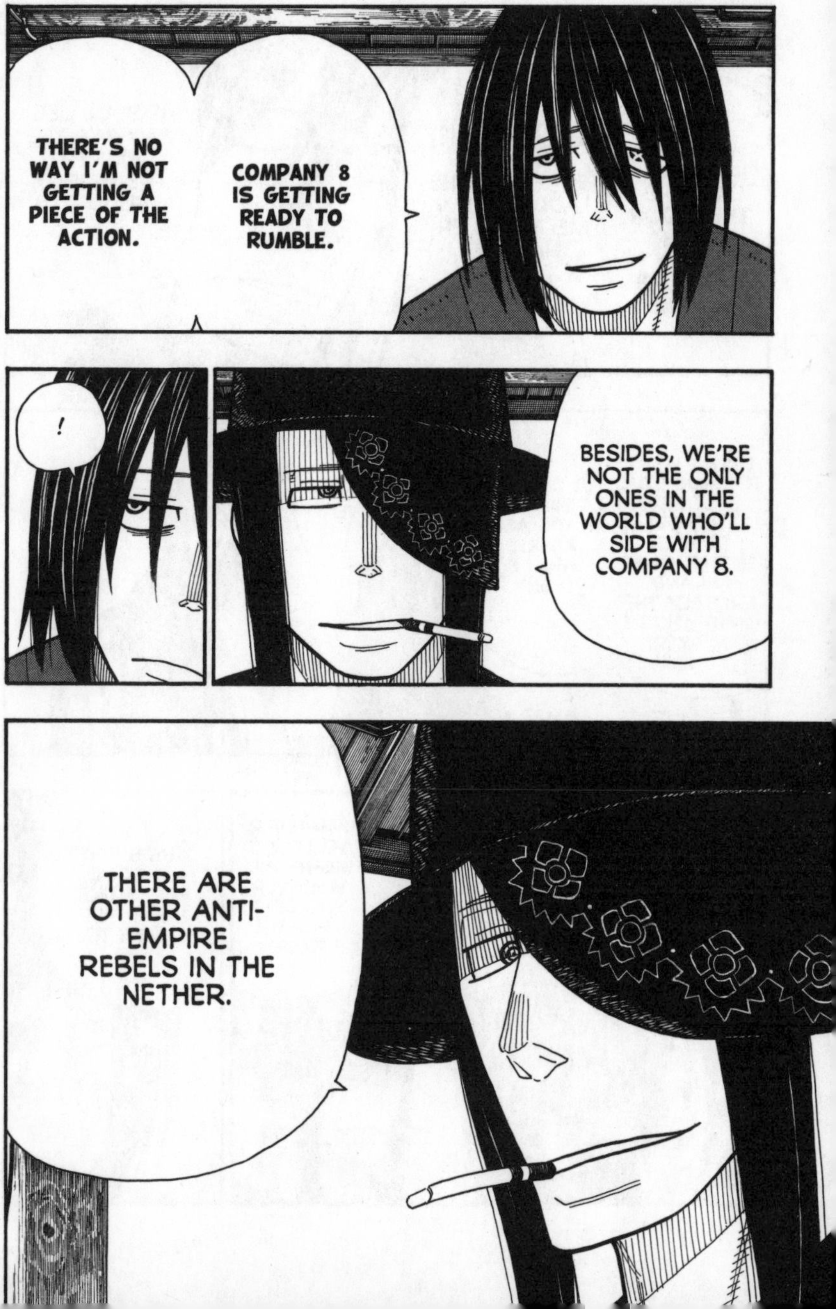
COMPANY 8 IS GETTING READY TO RUMBLE.
THERE'S NO WAY I'M NOT GETTING A PIECE OF THE ACTION.
BESIDES, WE'RE NOT THE ONLY ONES IN THE WORLD WHO'LL SIDE WITH COMPANY 8.
!
THERE ARE OTHER ANTI-EMPIRE REBELS IN THE NETHER.

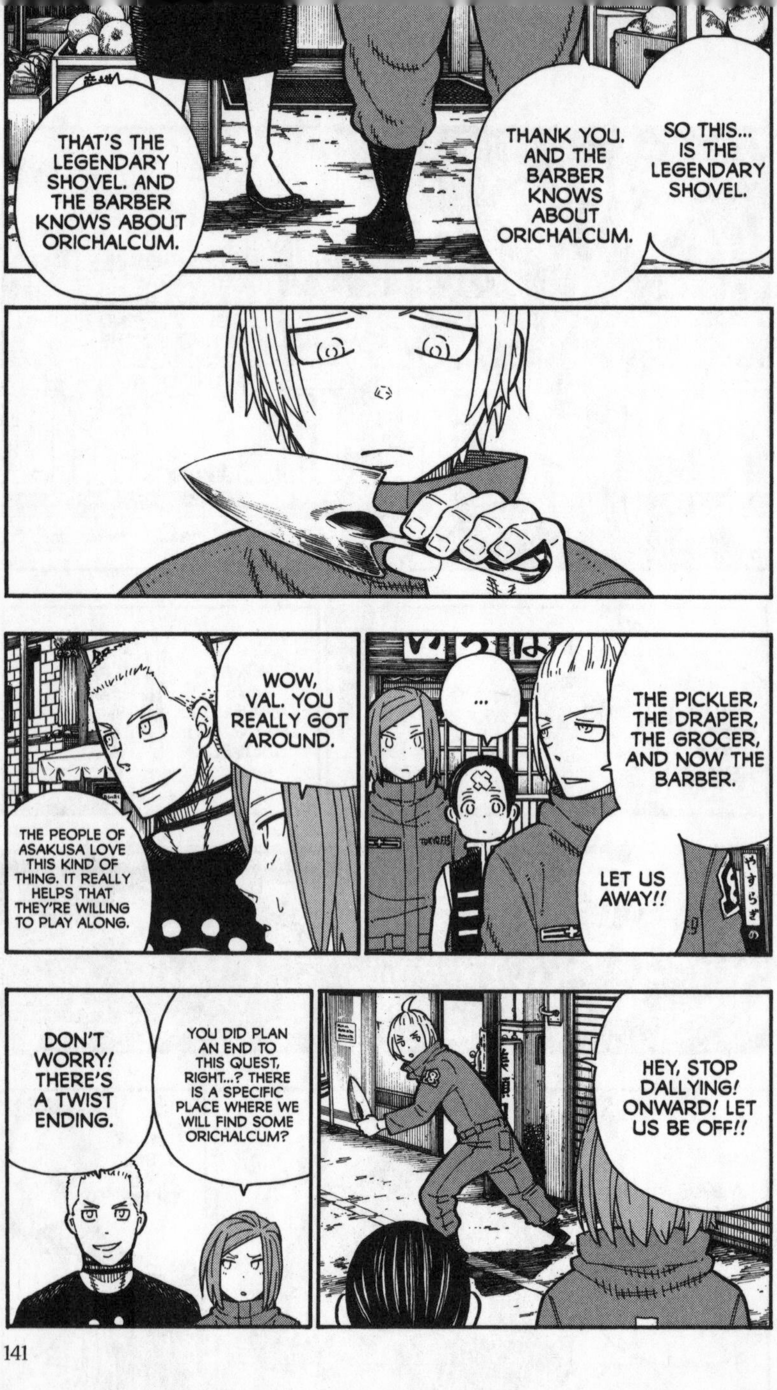
SO THIS... IS THE LEGENDARY SHOVEL.
THANK YOU. AND THE BARBER KNOWS ABOUT ORICHALCUM.
THAT'S THE LEGENDARY SHOVEL. AND THE BARBER KNOWS ABOUT ORICHALCUM.
THE PICKLER, THE DRAPER, THE GROCER, AND NOW THE BARBER.
...
LET US AWAY!!
WOW, VAL. YOU REALLY GOT AROUND.
THE PEOPLE OF ASAKUSA LOVE THIS KIND OF THING. IT REALLY HELPS THAT THEY'RE WILLING TO PLAY ALONG.
HEY, STOP DALLYING! ONWARD! LET US BE OFF!!
YOU DID PLAN AN END TO THIS QUEST, RIGHT...? THERE IS A SPECIFIC PLACE WHERE WE WILL FIND SOME ORICHALCUM?
DON'T WORRY! THERE'S A TWIST ENDING.

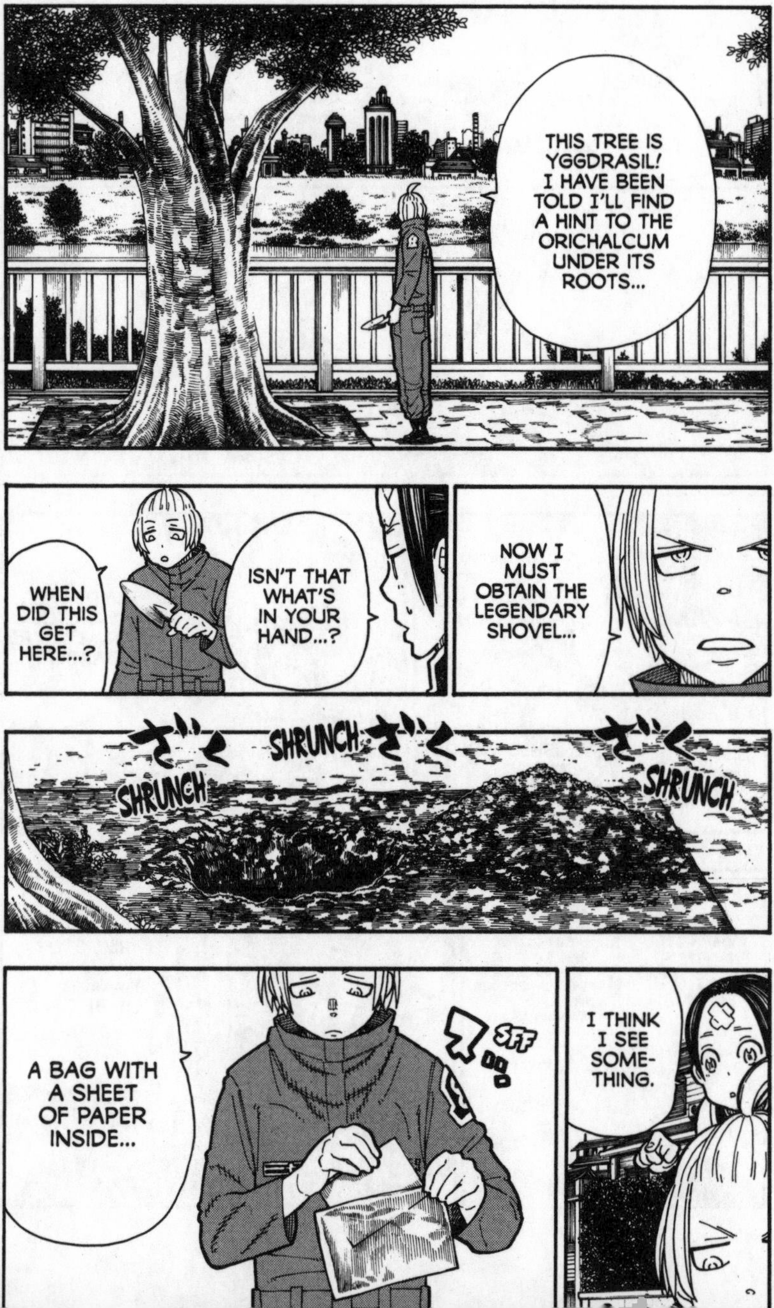
THIS TREE IS YGGDRASIL! I HAVE BEEN TOLD I'LL FIND A HINT TO THE ORICHALCUM UNDER ITS ROOTS...
NOW I MUST OBTAIN THE LEGENDARY SHOVEL...
ISN'T THAT WHAT'S IN YOUR HAND...?
WHEN DID THIS GET HERE...?
ざく
SHRUNCH
ざく
SHRUNCH
ざく
SHRUNCH
I THINK I SEE SOME-THING.
SFF
A BAG WITH A SHEET OF PAPER INSIDE...

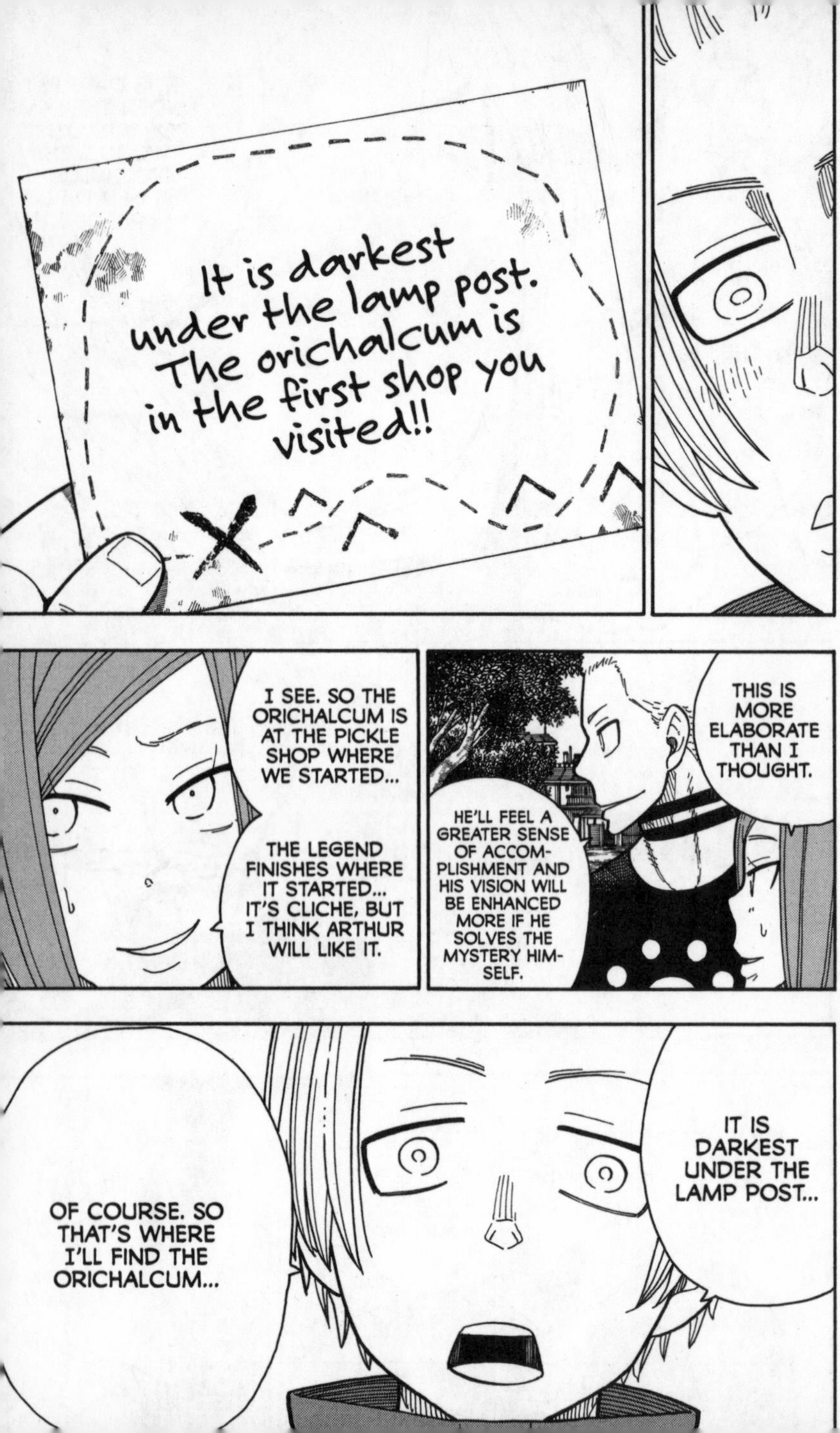
It is darkest under the lamp post. The orichalcum is in the first shop you visited!!
THIS IS MORE ELABORATE THAN I THOUGHT.
HE'LL FEEL A GREATER SENSE OF ACCOM-PLISHMENT AND HIS VISION WILL BE ENHANCED MORE IF HE SOLVES THE MYSTERY HIM-SELF.
I SEE. SO THE ORICHALCUM IS AT THE PICKLE SHOP WHERE WE STARTED...
THE LEGEND FINISHES WHERE IT STARTED... IT'S CLICHE, BUT I THINK ARTHUR WILL LIKE IT.
...
IT IS DARKEST UNDER THE LAMP POST...
OF COURSE. SO THAT'S WHERE I'LL FIND THE ORICHALCUM...

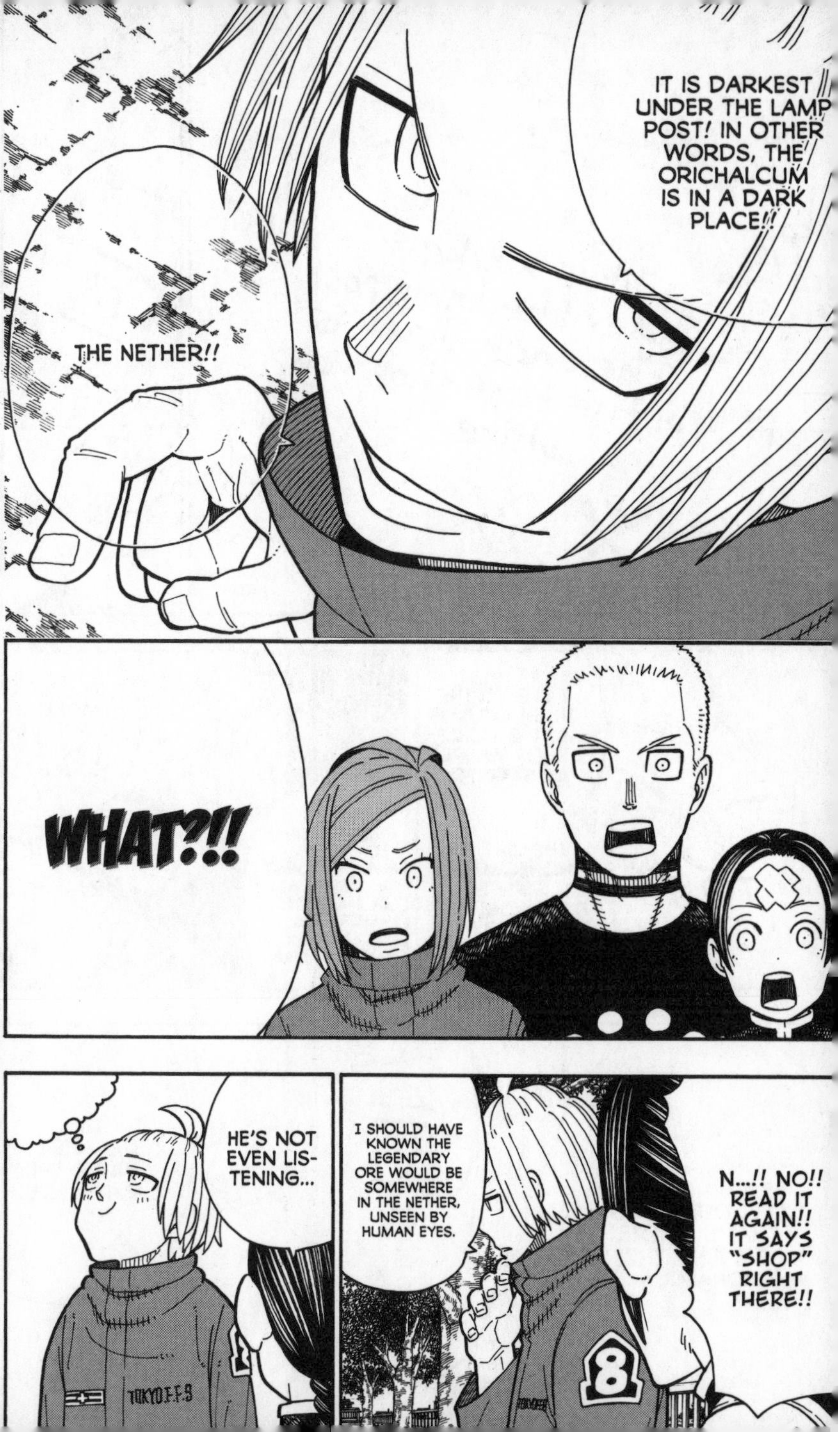
IT IS DARKEST UNDER THE LAMP POST! IN OTHER WORDS, THE ORICHALCUM IS IN A DARK PLACE!!
THE NETHER!!
WHAT?!!
N...!! NO!! READ IT AGAIN!! IT SAYS "SHOP" RIGHT THERE!!
I SHOULD HAVE KNOWN THE LEGENDARY ORE WOULD BE SOMEWHERE IN THE NETHER, UNSEEN BY HUMAN EYES.
HE'S NOT EVEN LIS-TENING...

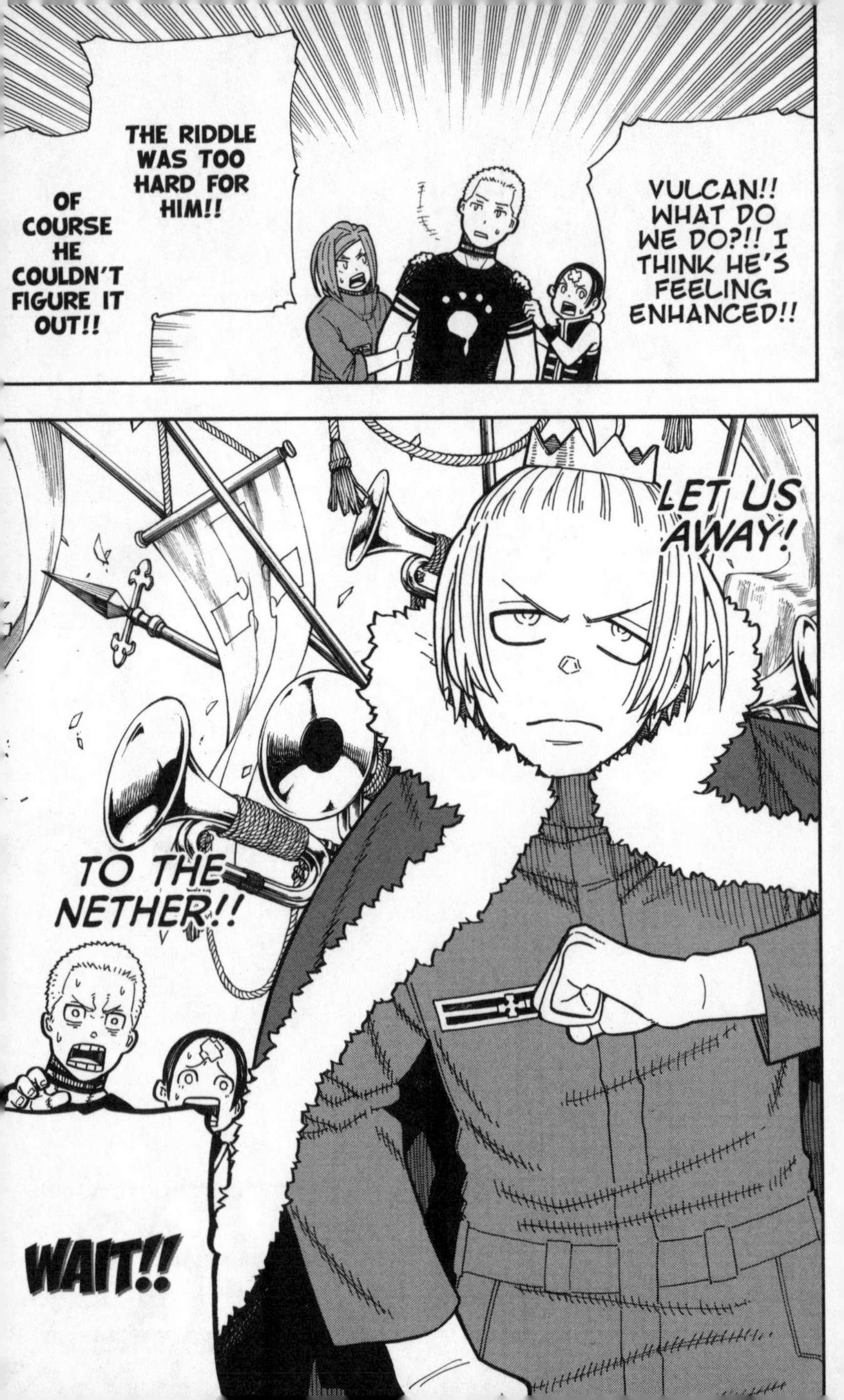
VULCAN!! WHAT DO WE DO?!! I THINK HE'S FEELING ENHANCED!!
THE RIDDLE WAS TOO HARD FOR HIM!!
OF COURSE HE COULDN'T FIGURE IT OUT!!
LET US AWAY!
TO THE NETHER!!
WAIT!!

FIRE FORCE

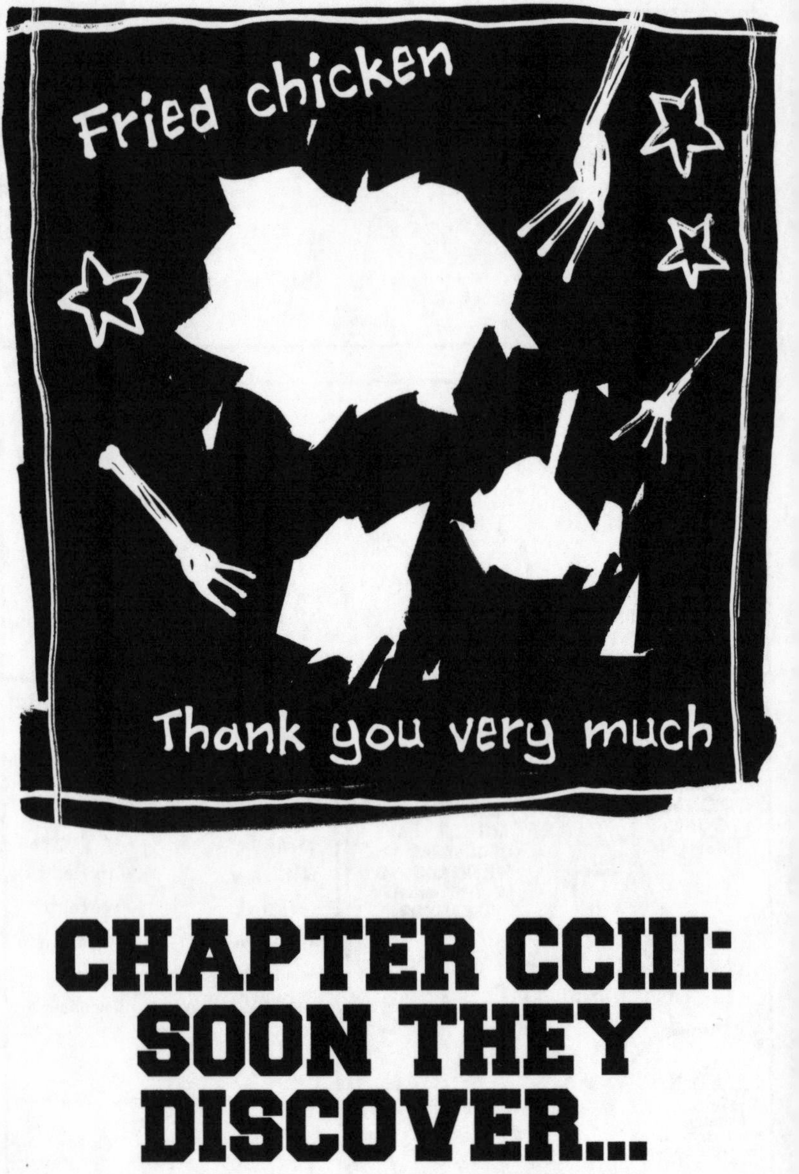
Fried chicken
Thank you very much

CHAPTER CCIII: SOON THEY DISCOVER...

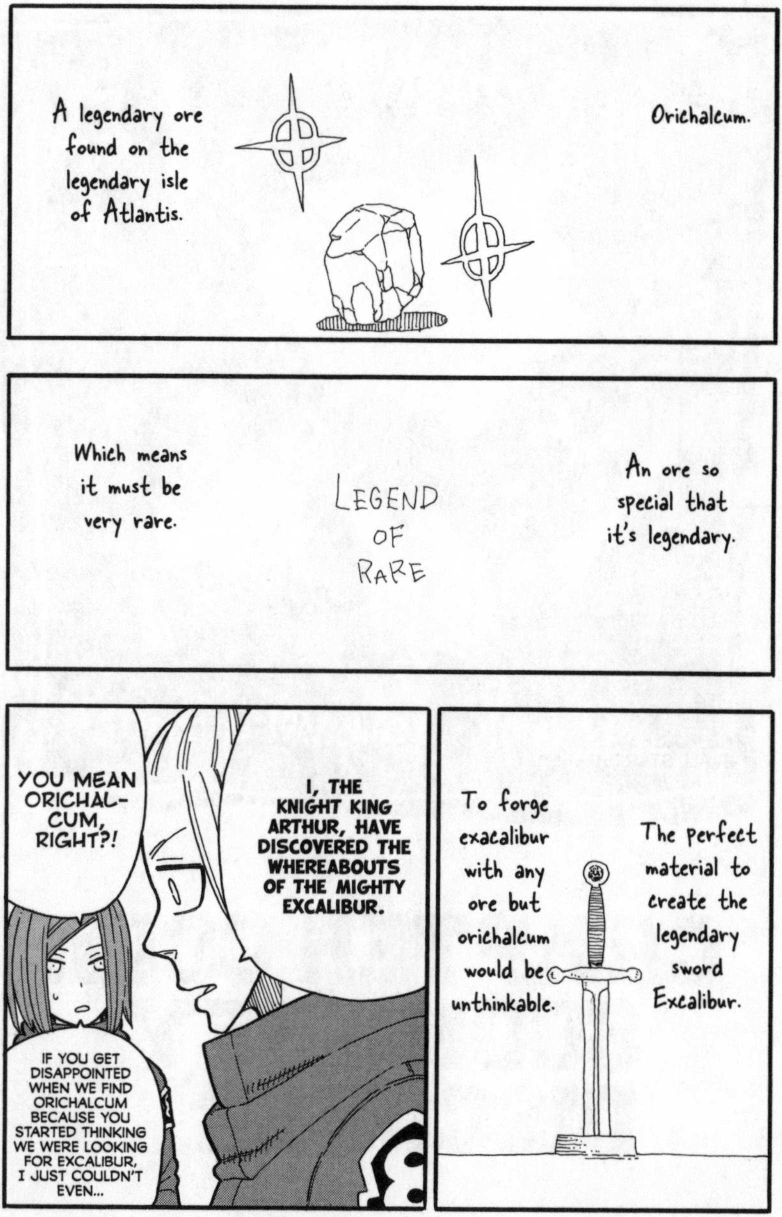
Orichalcum.
A legendary ore found on the legendary isle of Atlantis.
An ore so special that it's legendary.
LEGEND OF RARE
Which means it must be very rare.
The perfect material to create the legendary sword Excalibur.
To forge exacalibur with any ore but orichalcum would be unthinkable.
I, THE KNIGHT KING ARTHUR, HAVE DISCOVERED THE WHEREABOUTS OF THE MIGHTY EXCALIBUR.
YOU MEAN ORICHAL-CUM, RIGHT?!
IF YOU GET DISAPPOINTED WHEN WE FIND ORICHALCUM BECAUSE YOU STARTED THINKING WE WERE LOOKING FOR EXCALIBUR, I JUST COULDN'T EVEN...

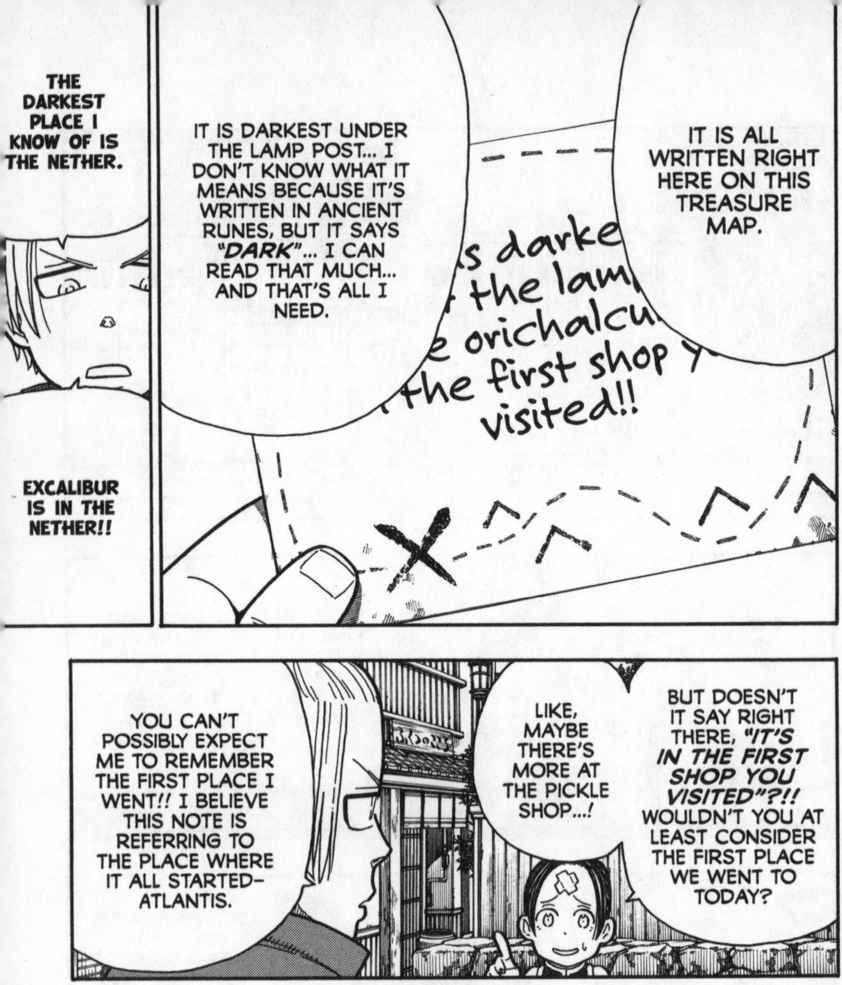
IT IS ALL WRITTEN RIGHT HERE ON THIS TREASURE MAP.
IT IS DARKEST UNDER THE LAMP POST... I DON'T KNOW WHAT IT MEANS BECAUSE IT'S WRITTEN IN ANCIENT RUNES, BUT IT SAYS *"DARK"*... I CAN READ THAT MUCH... AND THAT'S ALL I NEED.
s darke
the lam
e orichalcu
the first shop y
visited!!
THE DARKEST PLACE I KNOW OF IS THE NETHER.
EXCALIBUR IS IN THE NETHER!!
BUT DOESN'T IT SAY RIGHT THERE, *"IT'S IN THE FIRST SHOP YOU VISITED"?!!* WOULDN'T YOU AT LEAST CONSIDER THE FIRST PLACE WE WENT TO TODAY?
LIKE, MAYBE THERE'S MORE AT THE PICKLE SHOP...!
YOU CAN'T POSSIBLY EXPECT ME TO REMEMBER THE FIRST PLACE I WENT!! I BELIEVE THIS NOTE IS REFERRING TO THE PLACE WHERE IT ALL STARTED—ATLANTIS.

Sign: Steadfast

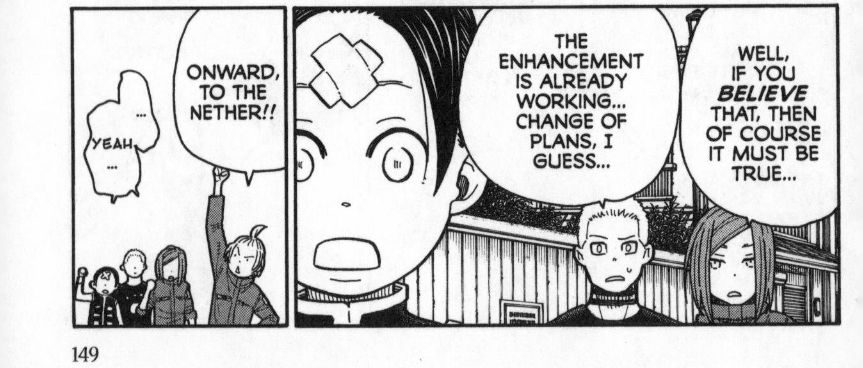
WELL, IF YOU *BELIEVE* THAT, THEN OF COURSE IT MUST BE TRUE...
THE ENHANCEMENT IS ALREADY WORKING... CHANGE OF PLANS, I GUESS...
ONWARD, TO THE NETHER!!
...YEAH...

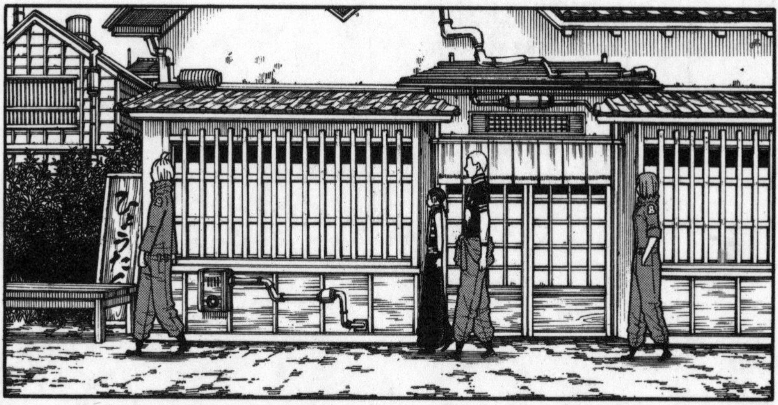

Sign: Gourd

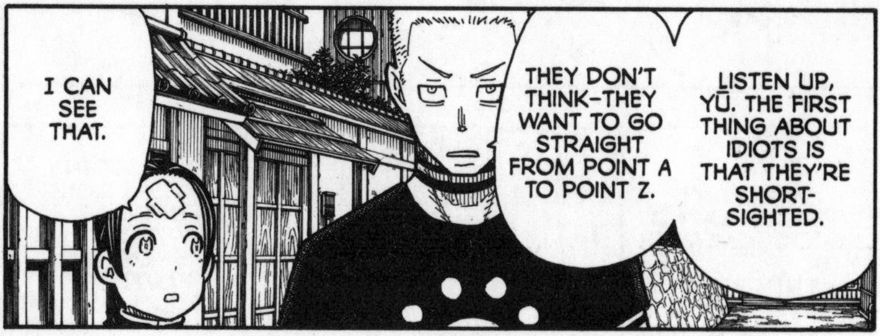
LISTEN UP, YŪ. THE FIRST THING ABOUT IDIOTS IS THAT THEY'RE SHORT-SIGHTED.
THEY DON'T THINK—THEY WANT TO GO STRAIGHT FROM POINT A TO POINT Z.
I CAN SEE THAT.

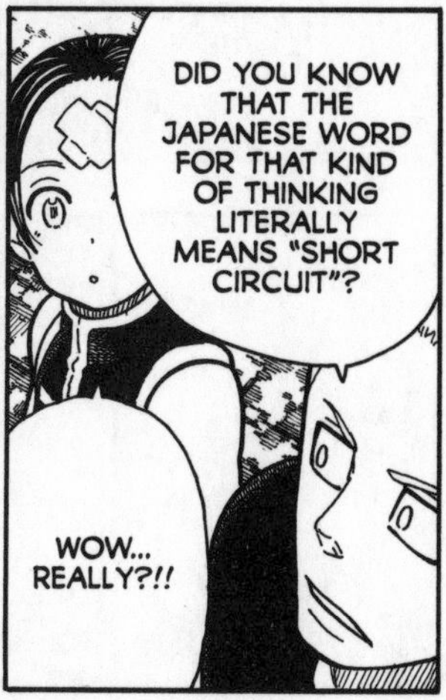
DID YOU KNOW THAT THE JAPANESE WORD FOR THAT KIND OF THINKING LITERALLY MEANS "SHORT CIRCUIT"?
WOW... REALLY?!!

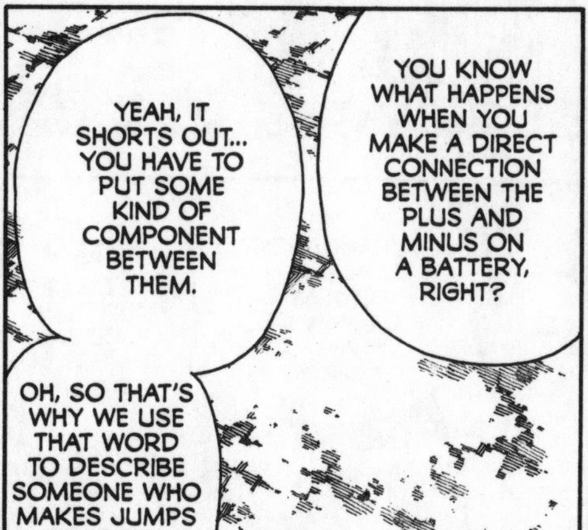
YOU KNOW WHAT HAPPENS WHEN YOU MAKE A DIRECT CONNECTION BETWEEN THE PLUS AND MINUS ON A BATTERY, RIGHT?
YEAH, IT SHORTS OUT... YOU HAVE TO PUT SOME KIND OF COMPONENT BETWEEN THEM.
OH, SO THAT'S WHY WE USE THAT WORD TO DESCRIBE SOMEONE WHO MAKES JUMPS IN LOGIC.

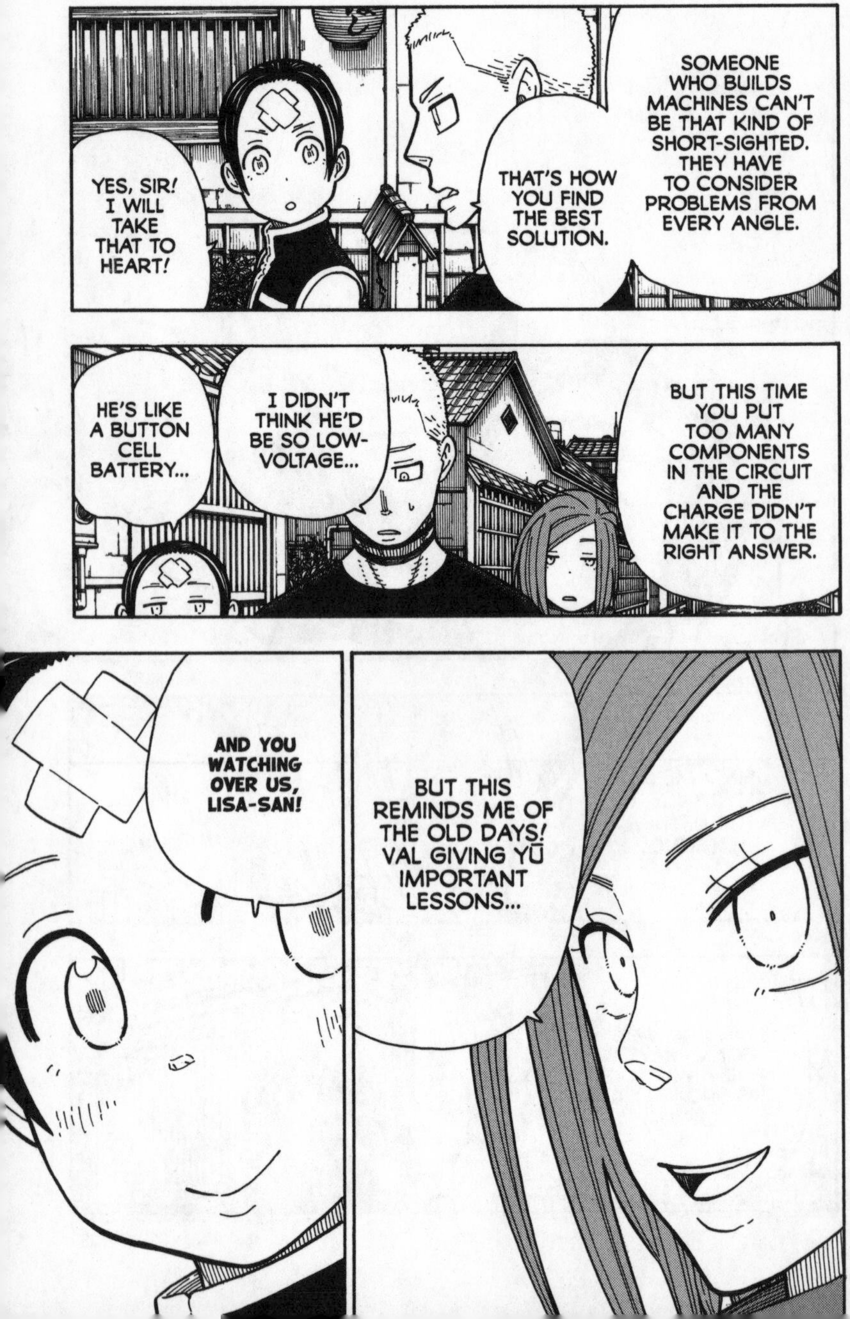
SOMEONE WHO BUILDS MACHINES CAN'T BE THAT KIND OF SHORT-SIGHTED. THEY HAVE TO CONSIDER PROBLEMS FROM EVERY ANGLE.
THAT'S HOW YOU FIND THE BEST SOLUTION.
YES, SIR! I WILL TAKE THAT TO HEART!
BUT THIS TIME YOU PUT TOO MANY COMPONENTS IN THE CIRCUIT AND THE CHARGE DIDN'T MAKE IT TO THE RIGHT ANSWER.
I DIDN'T THINK HE'D BE SO LOW-VOLTAGE...
HE'S LIKE A BUTTON CELL BATTERY...
BUT THIS REMINDS ME OF THE OLD DAYS! VAL GIVING YŪ IMPORTANT LESSONS...
AND YOU WATCHING OVER US, LISA-SAN!

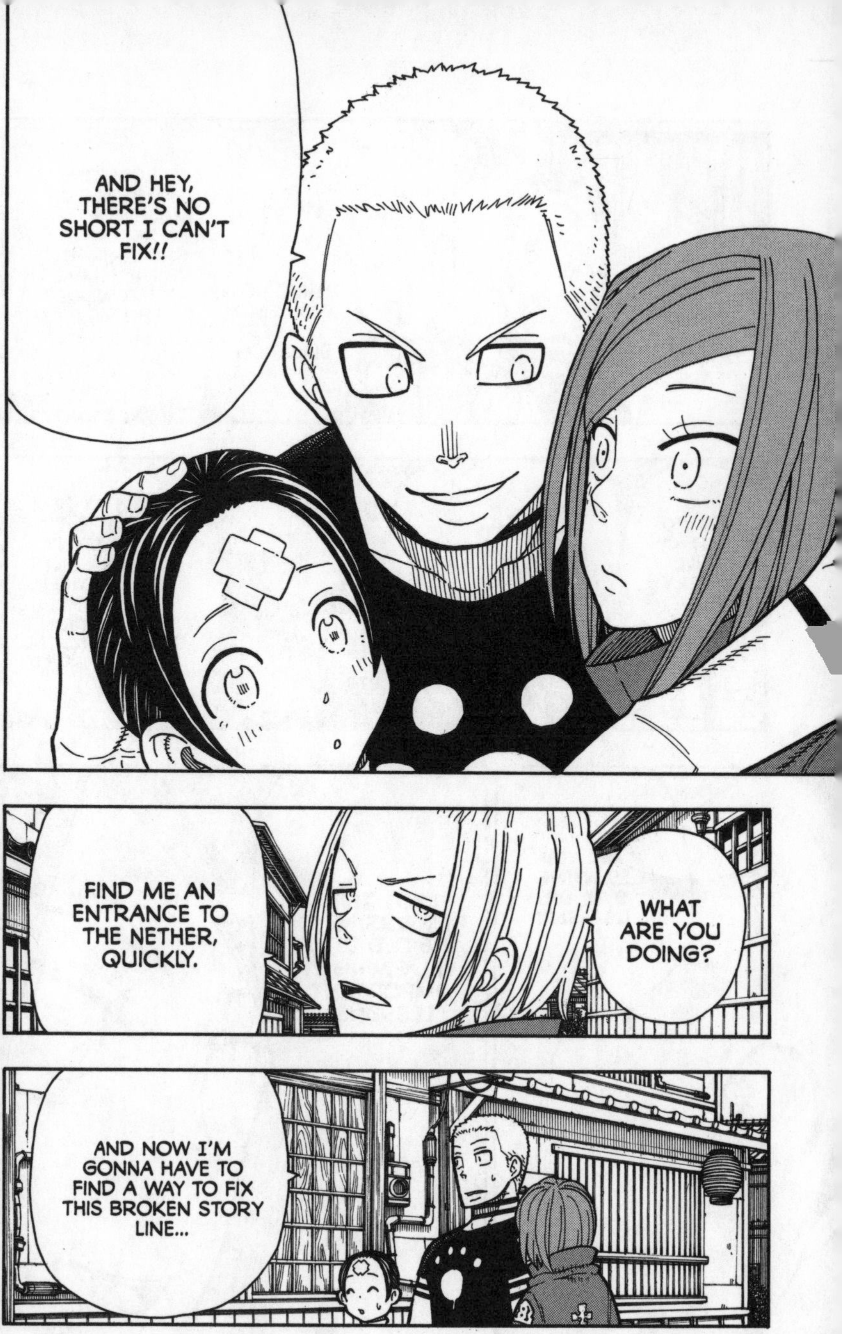
AND HEY, THERE'S NO SHORT I CAN'T FIX!!
WHAT ARE YOU DOING?
FIND ME AN ENTRANCE TO THE NETHER, QUICKLY.
AND NOW I'M GONNA HAVE TO FIND A WAY TO FIX THIS BROKEN STORY LINE...

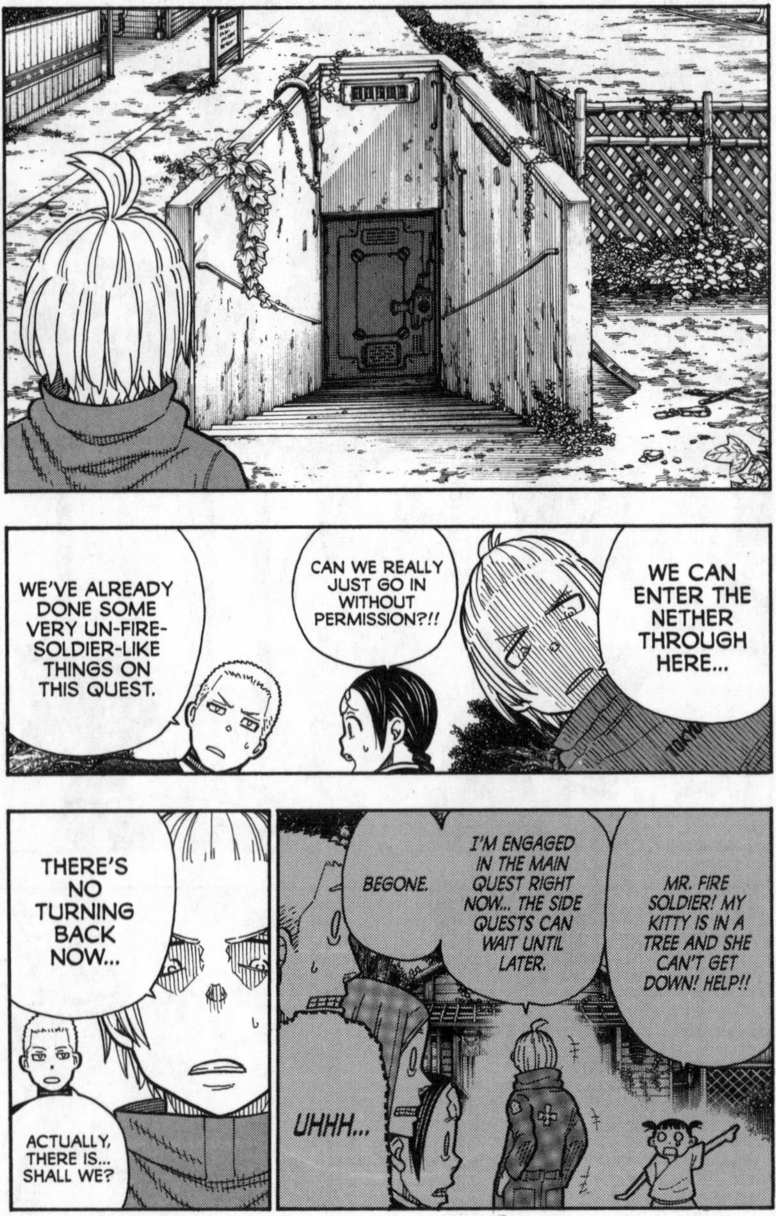
WE CAN ENTER THE NETHER THROUGH HERE...
CAN WE REALLY JUST GO IN WITHOUT PERMISSION?!!
WE'VE ALREADY DONE SOME VERY UN-FIRE-SOLDIER-LIKE THINGS ON THIS QUEST.
MR. FIRE SOLDIER! MY KITTY IS IN A TREE AND SHE CAN'T GET DOWN! HELP!!
I'M ENGAGED IN THE MAIN QUEST RIGHT NOW... THE SIDE QUESTS CAN WAIT UNTIL LATER.
BEGONE.
UHHH...
THERE'S NO TURNING BACK NOW...
ACTUALLY, THERE IS... SHALL WE?

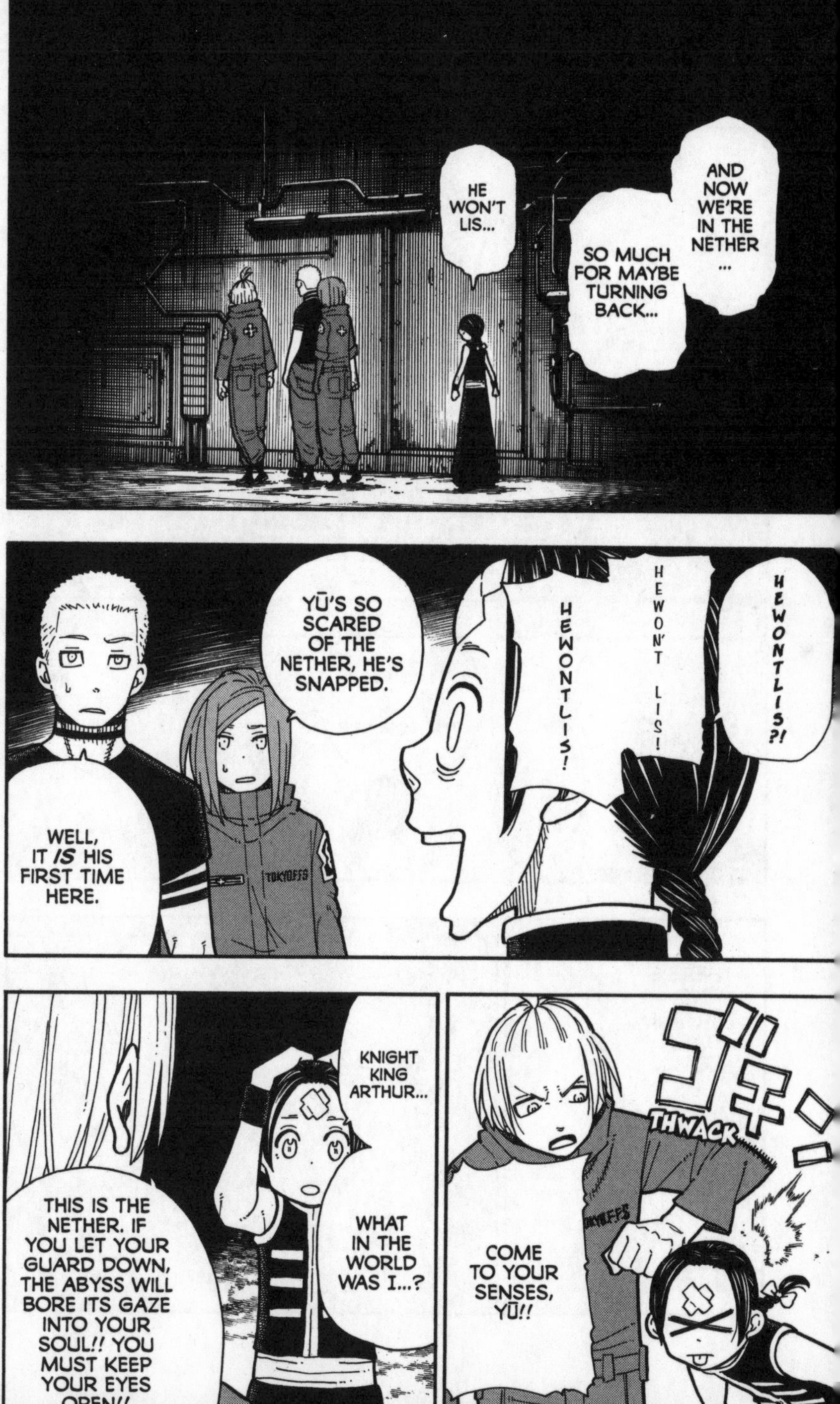
AND NOW WE'RE IN THE NETHER ...
SO MUCH FOR MAYBE TURNING BACK...
HE WON'T LIS...
HEWONTLIS?!
HE WON'T LIS!
HEWONTLIS!
YŪ'S SO SCARED OF THE NETHER, HE'S SNAPPED.
WELL, IT *IS* HIS FIRST TIME HERE.
THWACK
COME TO YOUR SENSES, YŪ!!
KNIGHT KING ARTHUR...
WHAT IN THE WORLD WAS I...?
THIS IS THE NETHER. IF YOU LET YOUR GUARD DOWN, THE ABYSS WILL BORE ITS GAZE INTO YOUR SOUL!! YOU MUST KEEP YOUR EYES OPEN!!

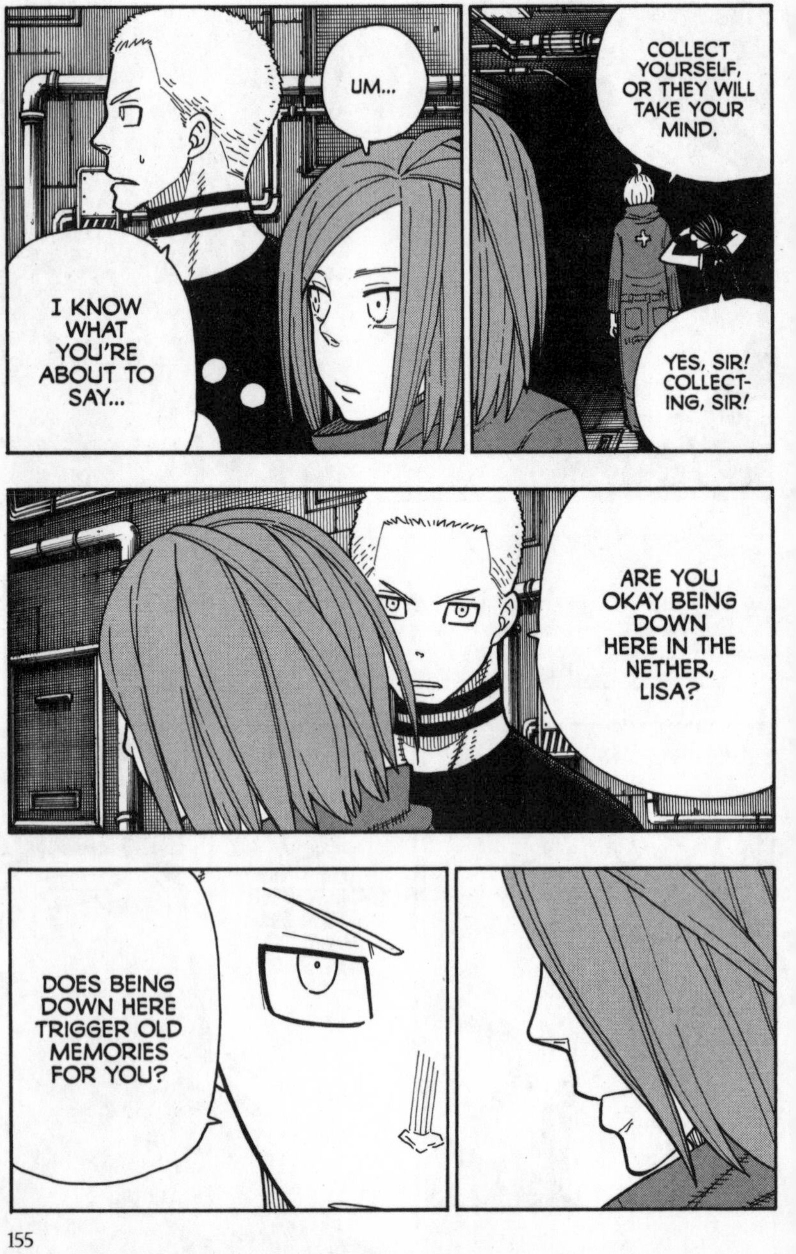
COLLECT YOURSELF, OR THEY WILL TAKE YOUR MIND.
YES, SIR! COLLECTING, SIR!
UM...
I KNOW WHAT YOU'RE ABOUT TO SAY...
ARE YOU OKAY BEING DOWN HERE IN THE NETHER, LISA?
DOES BEING DOWN HERE TRIGGER OLD MEMORIES FOR YOU?

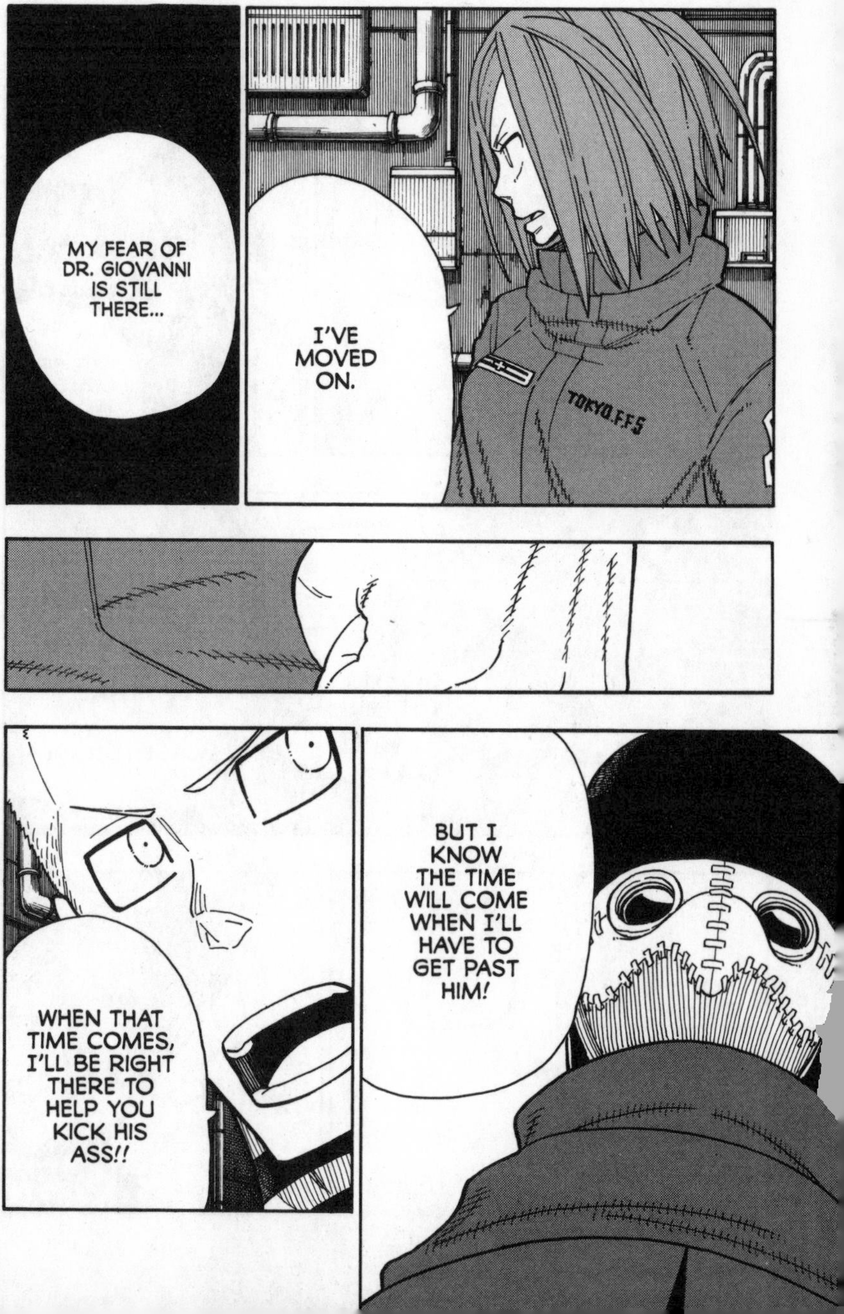
I'VE MOVED ON.
MY FEAR OF DR. GIOVANNI IS STILL THERE...
TOKYO.F.F.S
BUT I KNOW THE TIME WILL COME WHEN I'LL HAVE TO GET PAST HIM!
WHEN THAT TIME COMES, I'LL BE RIGHT THERE TO HELP YOU KICK HIS ASS!!

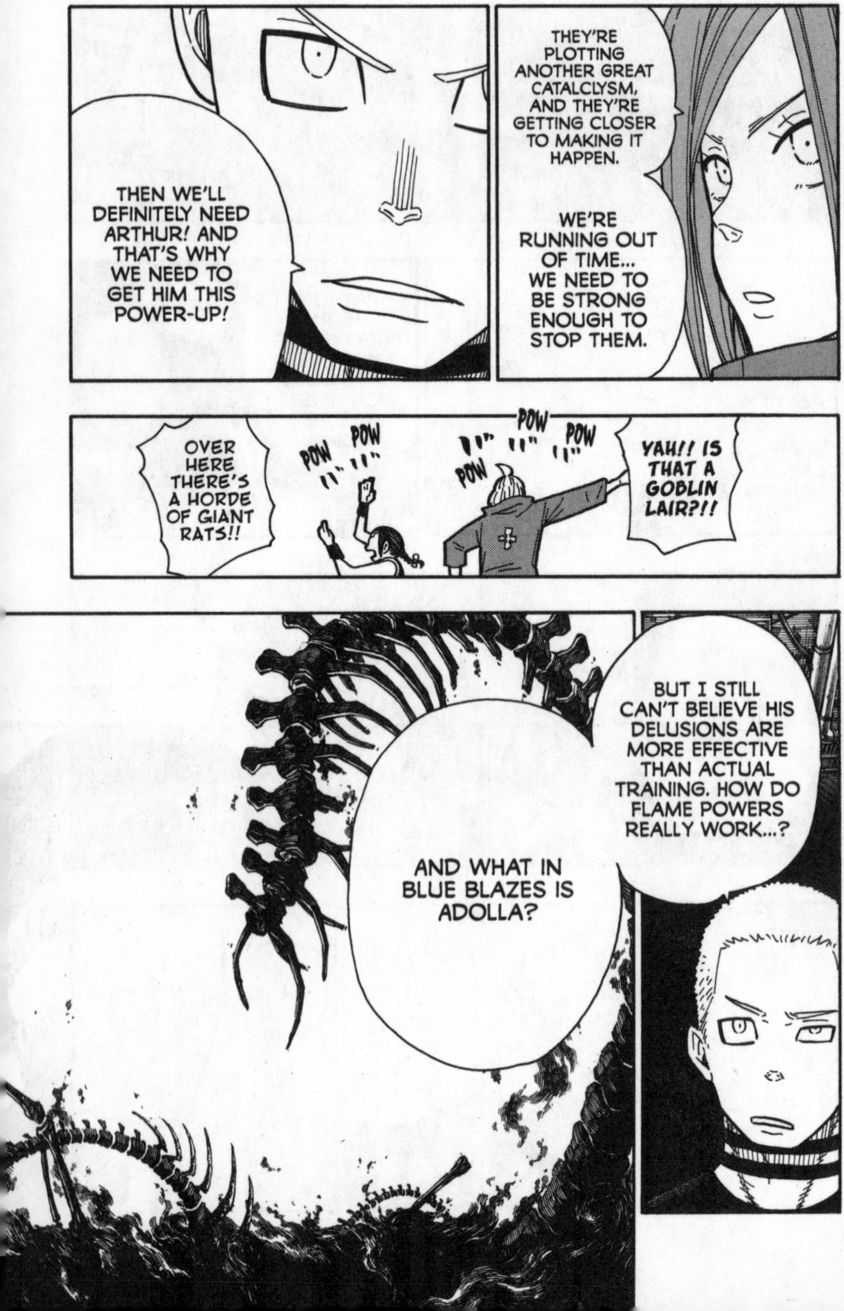
THEY'RE PLOTTING ANOTHER GREAT CATACLYSM, AND THEY'RE GETTING CLOSER TO MAKING IT HAPPEN.
WE'RE RUNNING OUT OF TIME... WE NEED TO BE STRONG ENOUGH TO STOP THEM.
THEN WE'LL DEFINITELY NEED ARTHUR! AND THAT'S WHY WE NEED TO GET HIM THIS POWER-UP!
YAH!! IS THAT A GOBLIN LAIR?!!
POW
POW
POW
POW
POW
OVER HERE THERE'S A HORDE OF GIANT RATS!!
BUT I STILL CAN'T BELIEVE HIS DELUSIONS ARE MORE EFFECTIVE THAN ACTUAL TRAINING. HOW DO FLAME POWERS REALLY WORK...?
AND WHAT IN BLUE BLAZES IS ADOLLA?

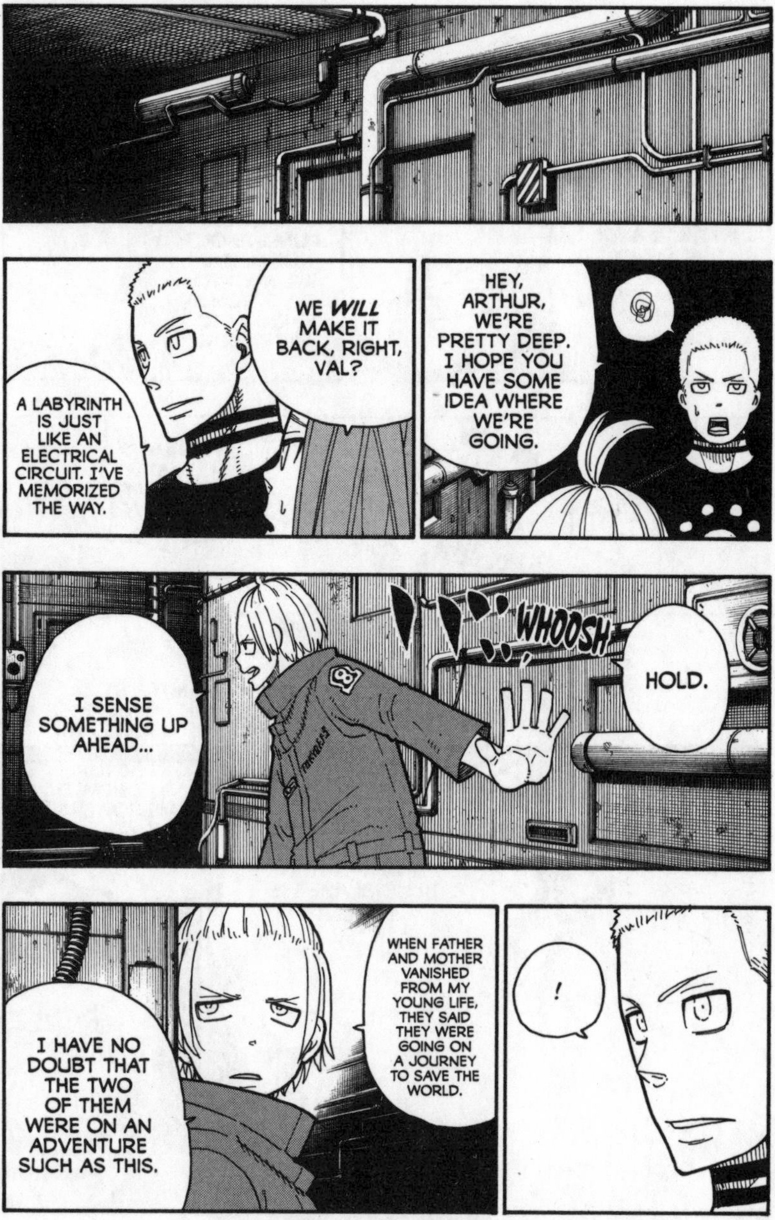
HEY, ARTHUR, WE'RE PRETTY DEEP. I HOPE YOU HAVE SOME IDEA WHERE WE'RE GOING.
WE *WILL* MAKE IT BACK, RIGHT, VAL?
A LABYRINTH IS JUST LIKE AN ELECTRICAL CIRCUIT. I'VE MEMORIZED THE WAY.
HOLD.
WHOOSH
I SENSE SOMETHING UP AHEAD...
!
WHEN FATHER AND MOTHER VANISHED FROM MY YOUNG LIFE, THEY SAID THEY WERE GOING ON A JOURNEY TO SAVE THE WORLD.
I HAVE NO DOUBT THAT THE TWO OF THEM WERE ON AN ADVENTURE SUCH AS THIS.

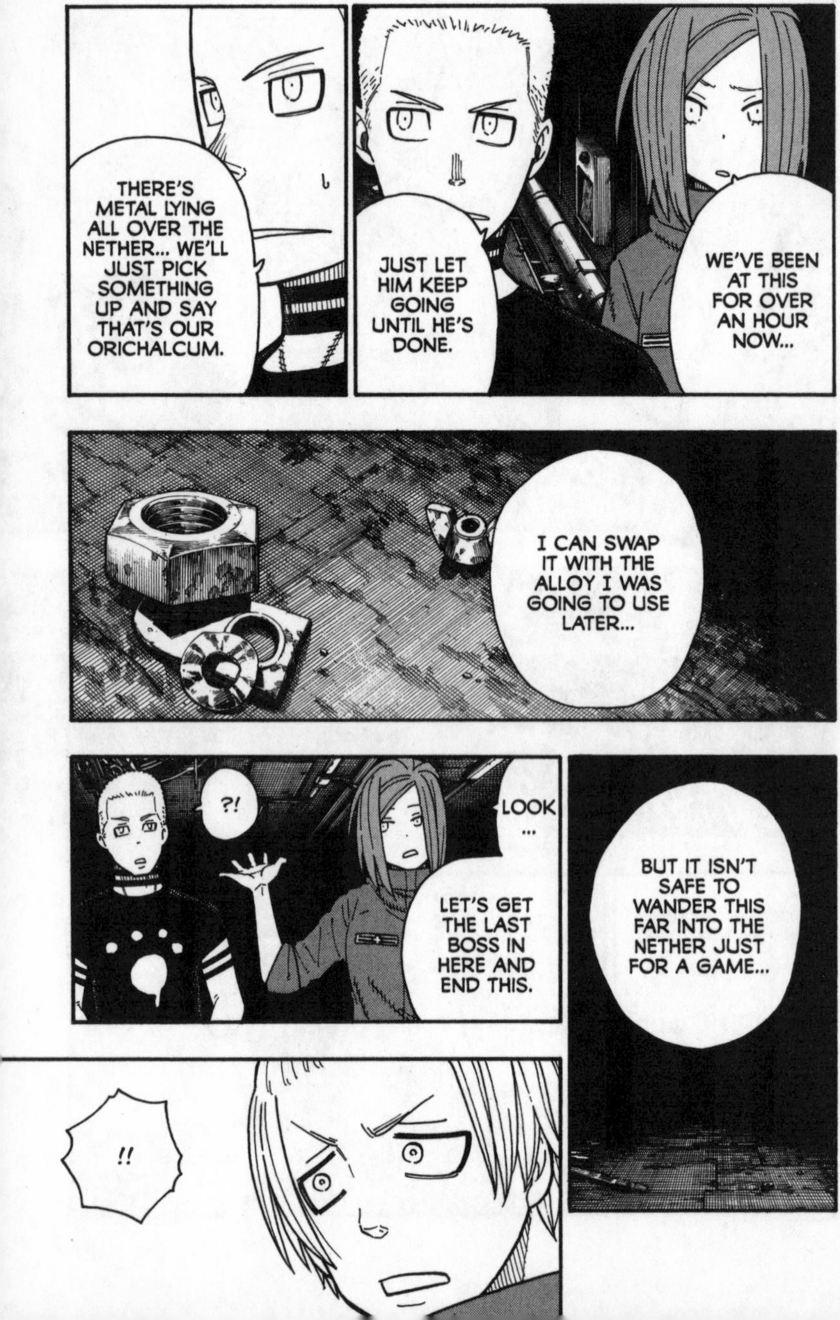
WE'VE BEEN AT THIS FOR OVER AN HOUR NOW...
JUST LET HIM KEEP GOING UNTIL HE'S DONE.
THERE'S METAL LYING ALL OVER THE NETHER... WE'LL JUST PICK SOMETHING UP AND SAY THAT'S OUR ORICHALCUM.
I CAN SWAP IT WITH THE ALLOY I WAS GOING TO USE LATER...
BUT IT ISN'T SAFE TO WANDER THIS FAR INTO THE NETHER JUST FOR A GAME...
LOOK...
LET'S GET THE LAST BOSS IN HERE AND END THIS.
?!
!!

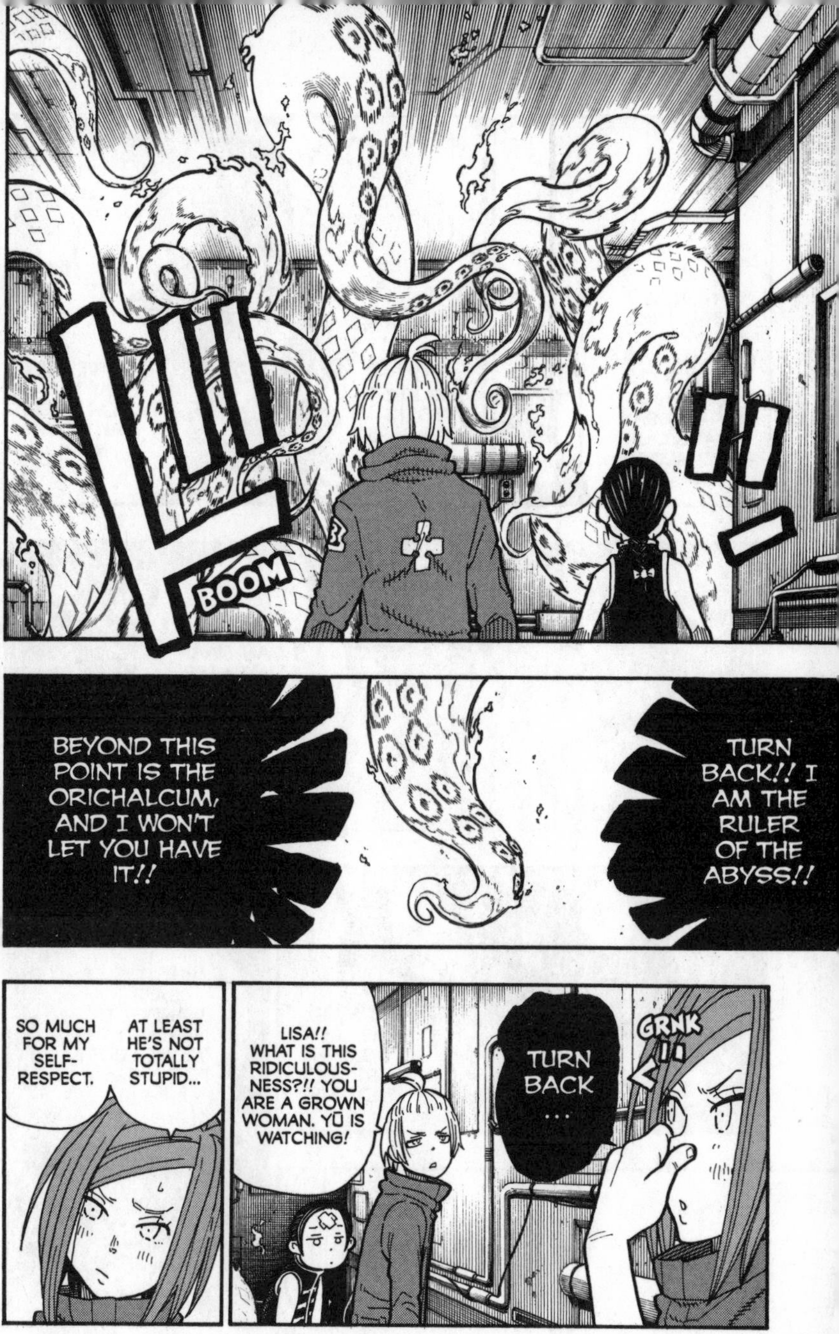
BOOM
TURN BACK!! I AM THE RULER OF THE ABYSS!!
BEYOND THIS POINT IS THE ORICHALCUM, AND I WON'T LET YOU HAVE IT!!
GRNK
TURN BACK...
LISA!! WHAT IS THIS RIDICULOUSNESS?!! YOU ARE A GROWN WOMAN. YŪ IS WATCHING!
AT LEAST HE'S NOT TOTALLY STUPID...
SO MUCH FOR MY SELF-RESPECT.

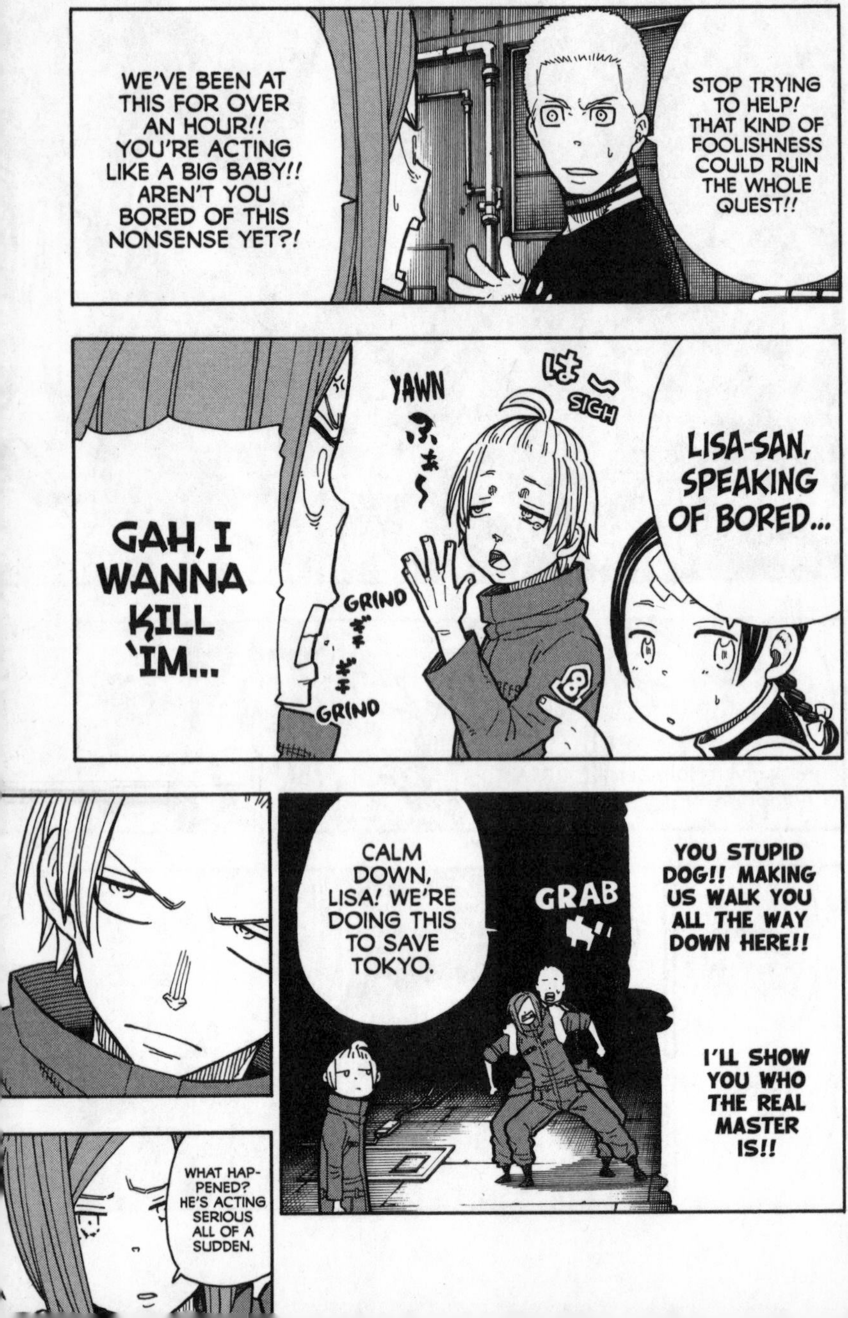
STOP TRYING TO HELP! THAT KIND OF FOOLISHNESS COULD RUIN THE WHOLE QUEST!!
WE'VE BEEN AT THIS FOR OVER AN HOUR!! YOU'RE ACTING LIKE A BIG BABY!! AREN'T YOU BORED OF THIS NONSENSE YET?!
LISA-SAN, SPEAKING OF BORED...
は〜
SIGH
YAWN
ふぁ〜
GRIND
ギギ
GRIND
GAH, I WANNA KILL 'IM...
YOU STUPID DOG!! MAKING US WALK YOU ALL THE WAY DOWN HERE!!
GRAB
CALM DOWN, LISA! WE'RE DOING THIS TO SAVE TOKYO.
I'LL SHOW YOU WHO THE REAL MASTER IS!!
WHAT HAPPENED? HE'S ACTING SERIOUS ALL OF A SUDDEN.

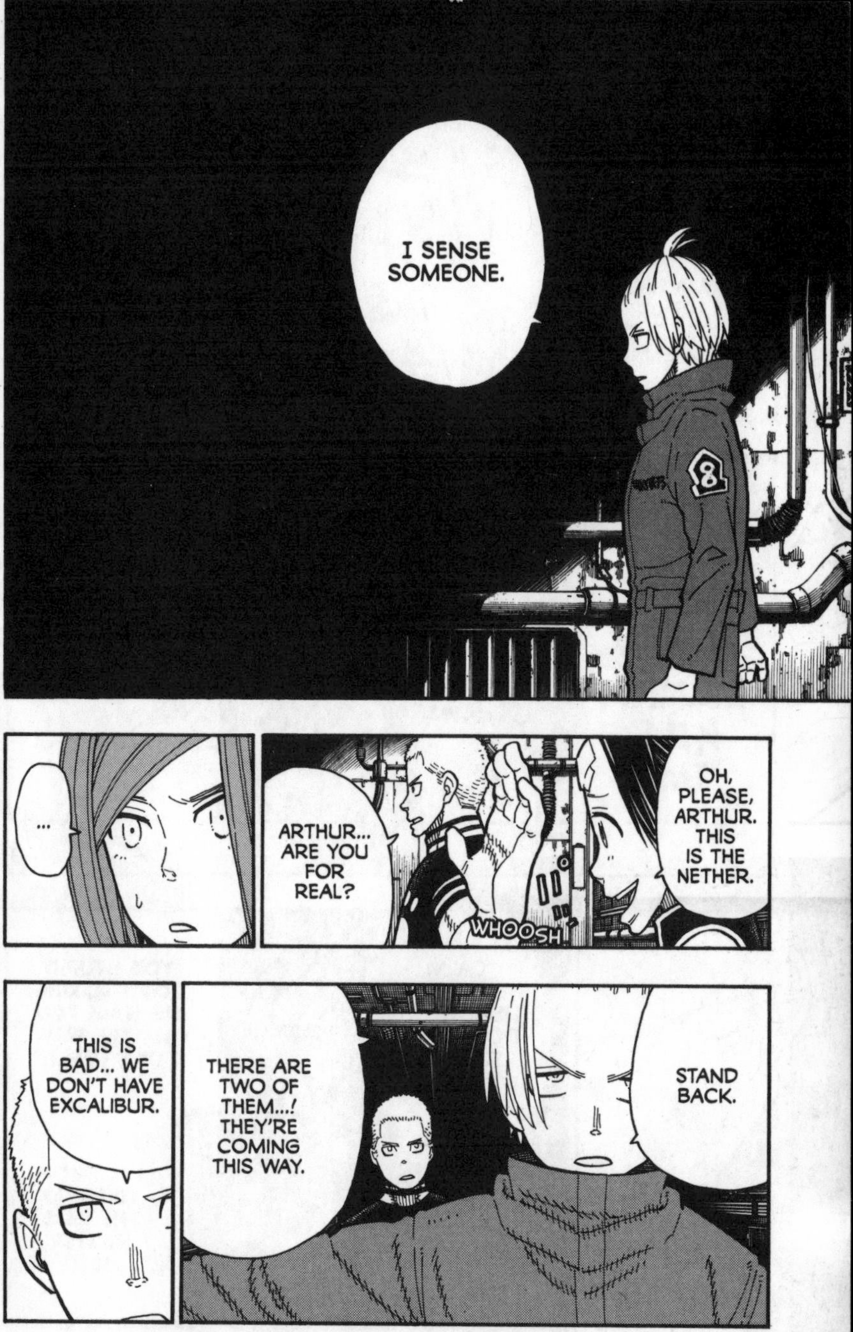
I SENSE SOMEONE.
OH, PLEASE, ARTHUR. THIS IS THE NETHER.
ARTHUR... ARE YOU FOR REAL?
WHOOSH
...
STAND BACK.
THERE ARE TWO OF THEM...! THEY'RE COMING THIS WAY.
THIS IS BAD... WE DON'T HAVE EXCALIBUR.

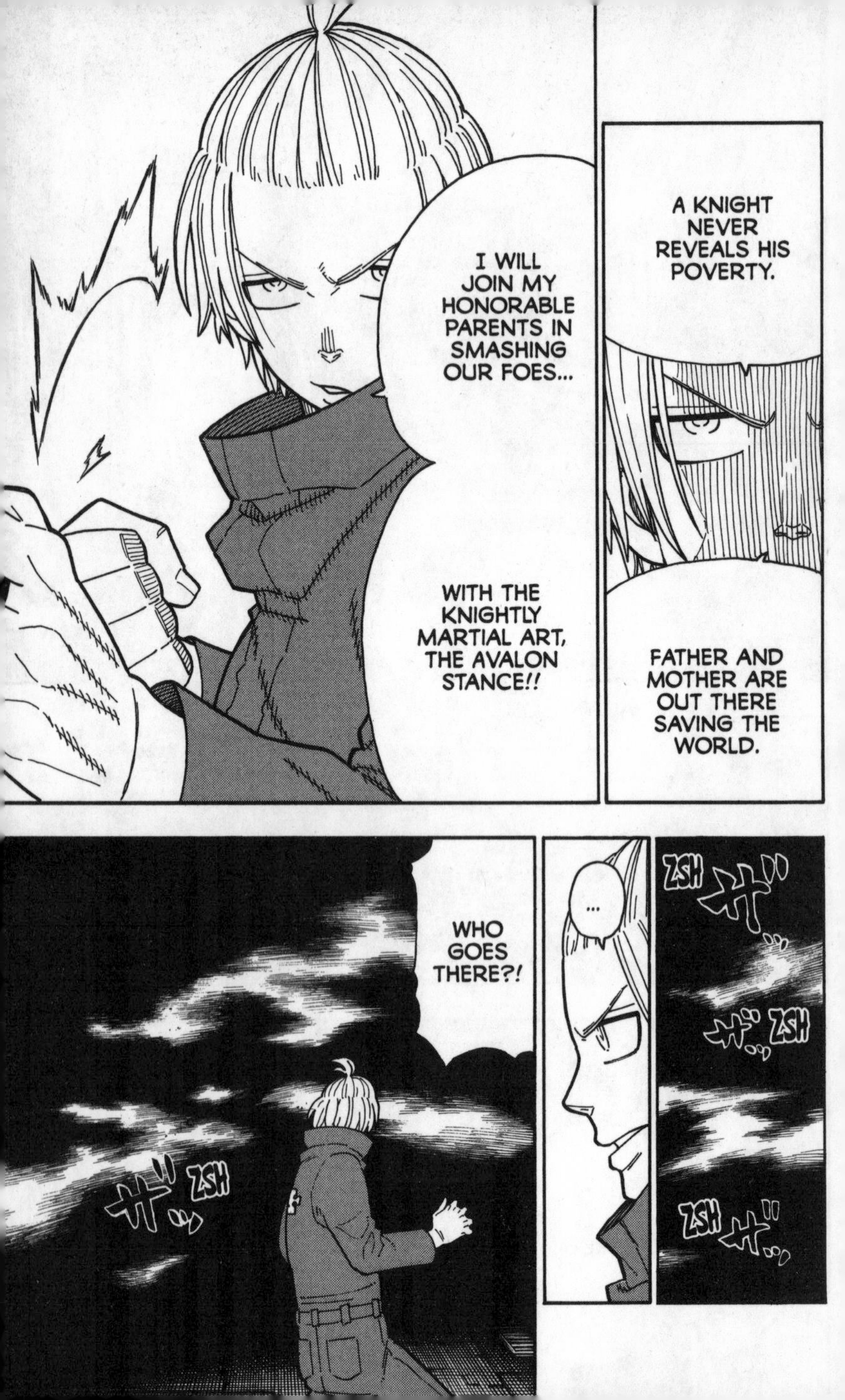
A KNIGHT NEVER REVEALS HIS POVERTY.
FATHER AND MOTHER ARE OUT THERE SAVING THE WORLD.
I WILL JOIN MY HONORABLE PARENTS IN SMASHING OUR FOES...
WITH THE KNIGHTLY MARTIAL ART, THE AVALON STANCE!!
ZSH
ZSH
ZSH
...
WHO GOES THERE?!
ZSH

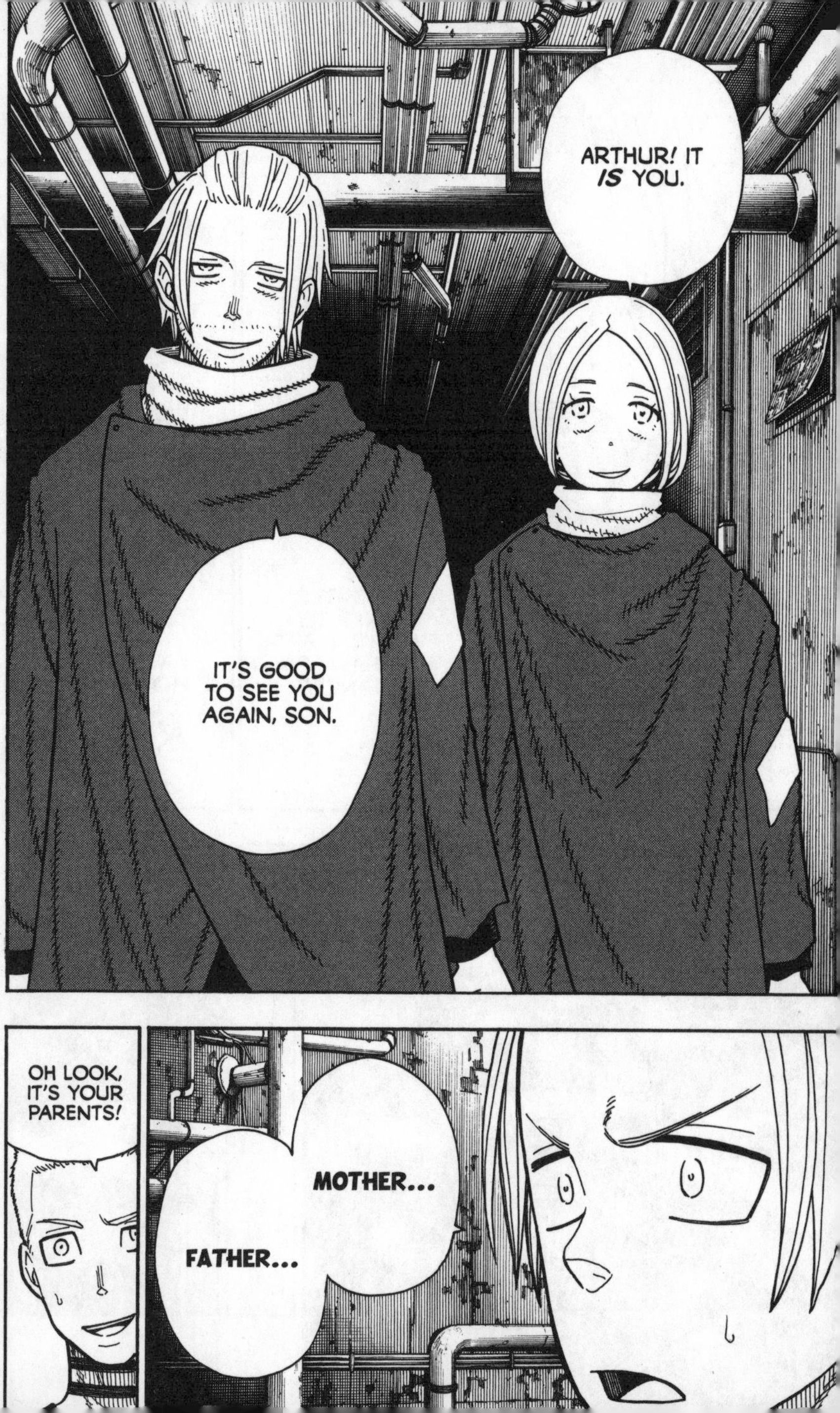
ARTHUR! IT *IS* YOU.
IT'S GOOD TO SEE YOU AGAIN, SON.
MOTHER...
FATHER...
OH LOOK, IT'S YOUR PARENTS!

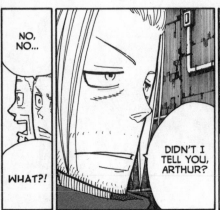

WAIT, WHAT?!
WHAT ARE YOU DOING HERE...?
DIDN'T I TELL YOU, ARTHUR?
NO, NO...
WHAT?!
To our beloved son Arthur,
Your mother and father have left on a journey to save the world!
The castle is now yours!! From this day onward, you are the king!!!
mother and father
ve left on a journey to
save the world!
FATHER, DOES THIS MEAN...?
NO... WAIT...
WHAT?!
YES.
IT DOES!!

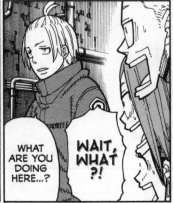

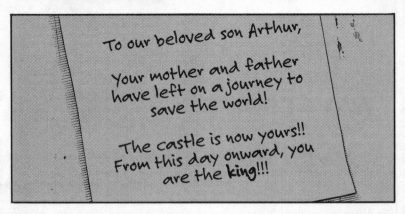

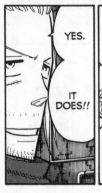

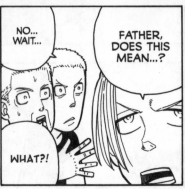

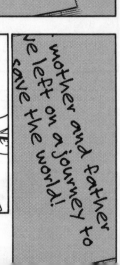

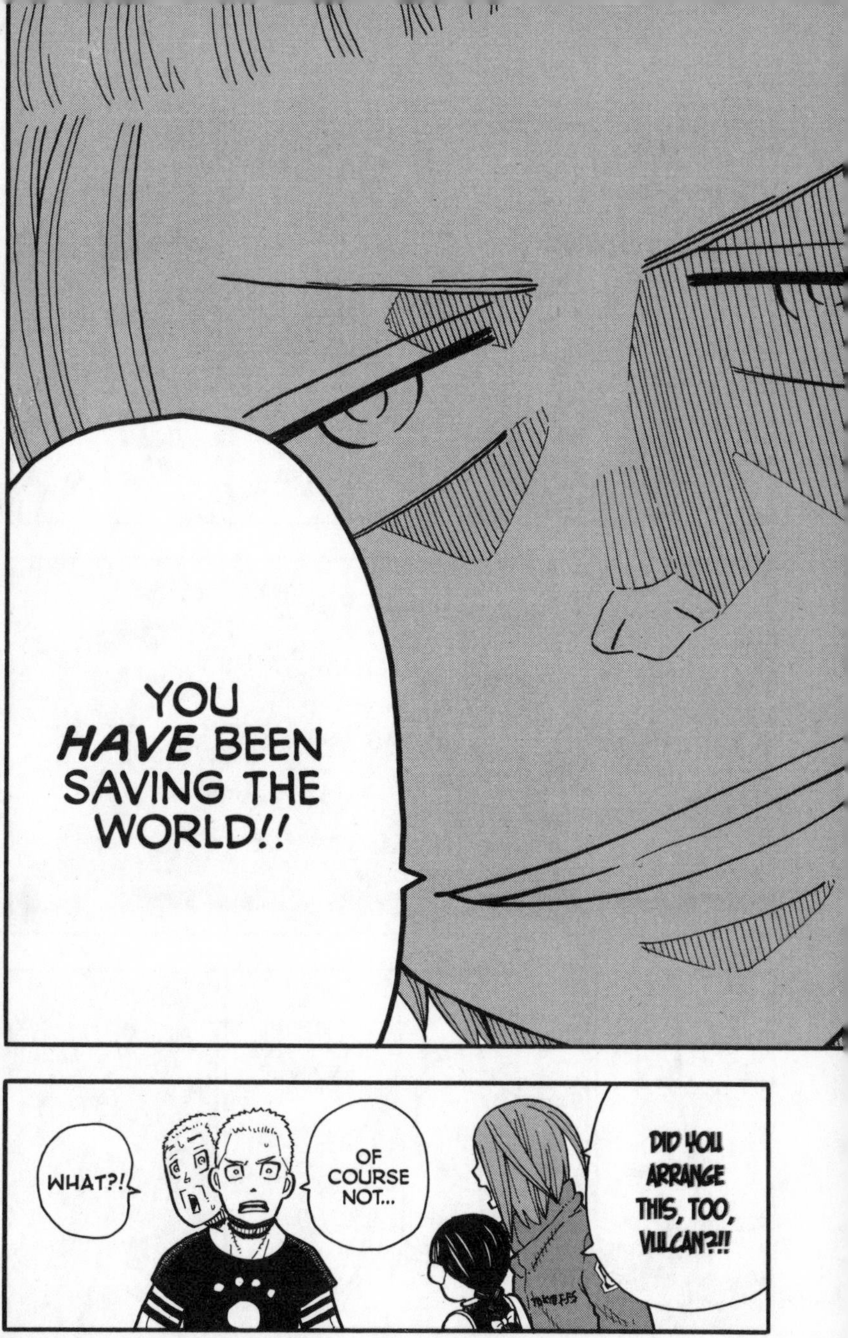
YOU *HAVE* BEEN SAVING THE WORLD!!
DID YOU ARRANGE THIS, TOO, VULCAN?!!
OF COURSE NOT...
WHAT?!

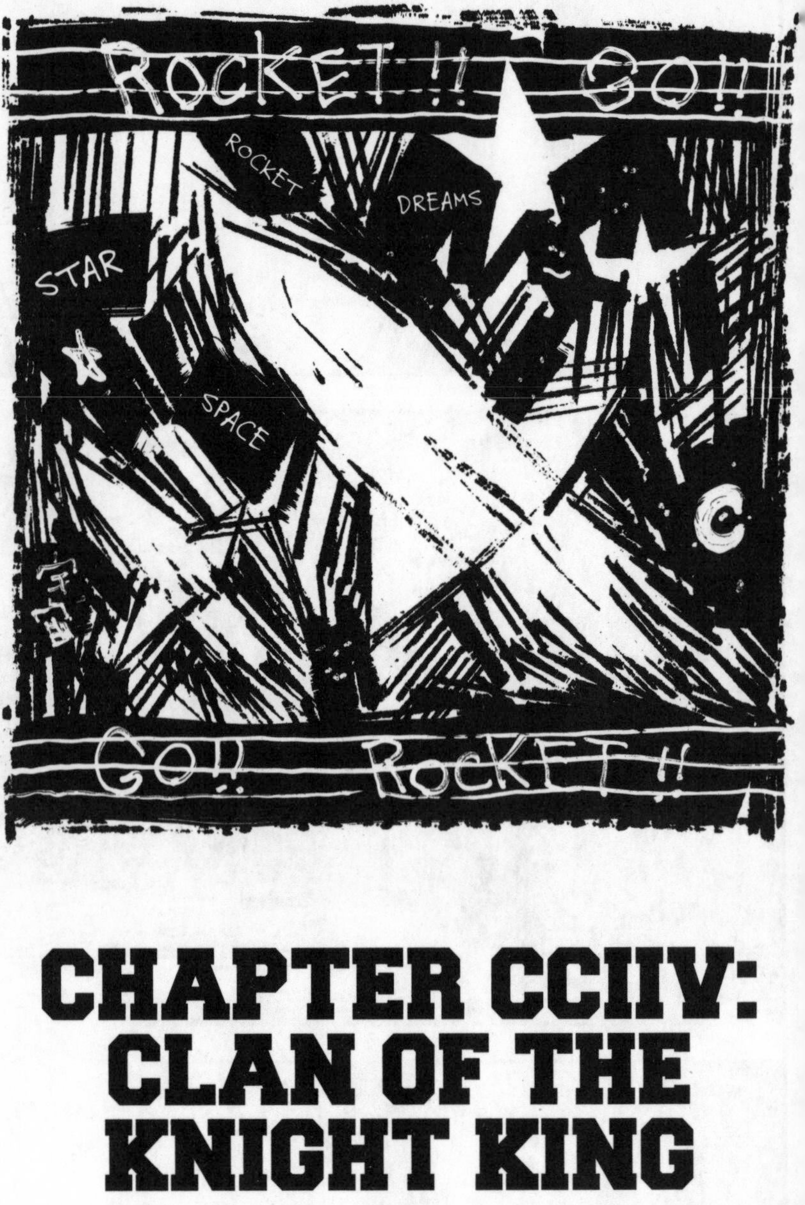
ROCKET!! GO!!
ROCKET
DREAMS
STAR
SPACE
GO!! ROCKET!!

CHAPTER CCIIV: CLAN OF THE KNIGHT KING

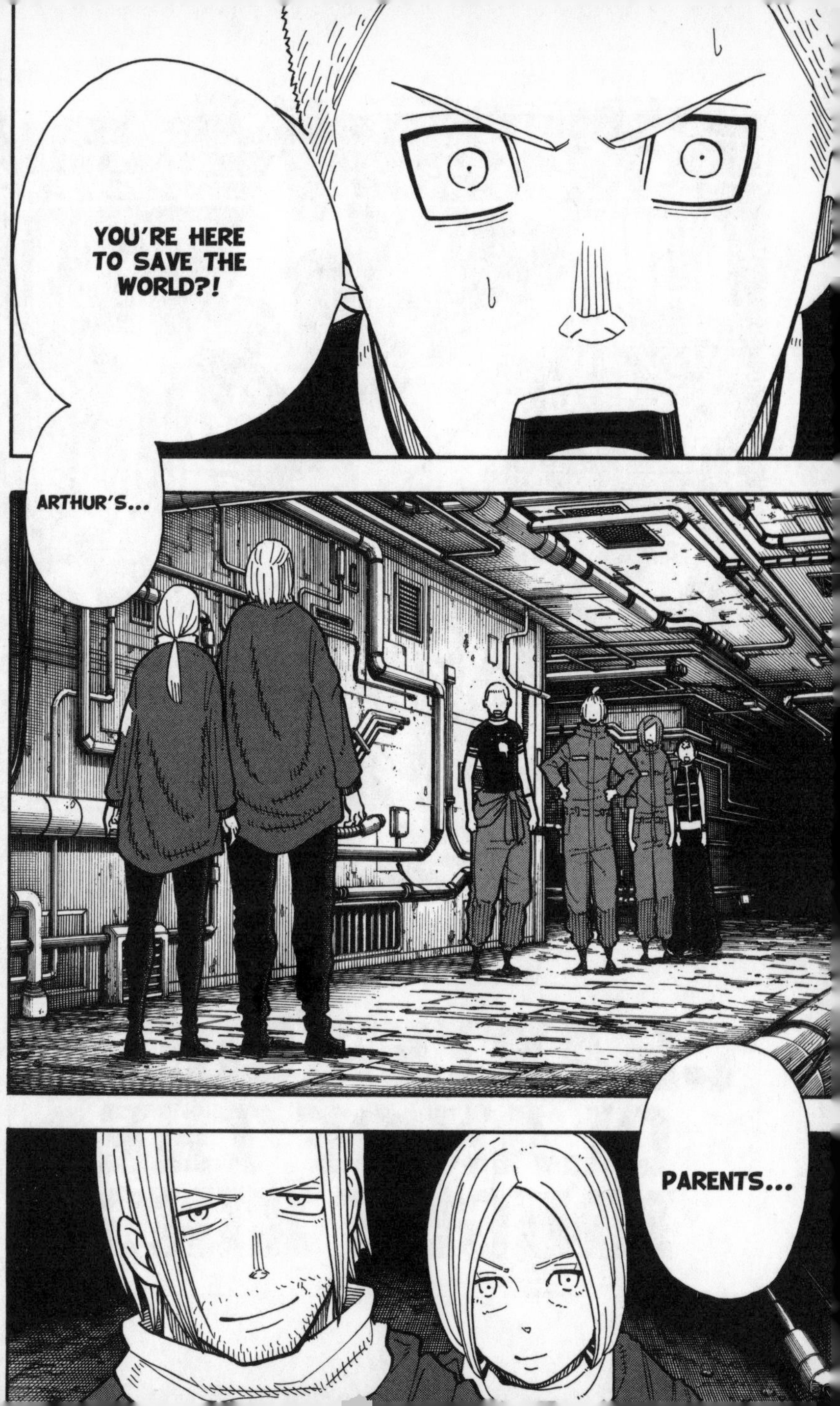
YOU'RE HERE TO SAVE THE WORLD?!
ARTHUR'S...
PARENTS...

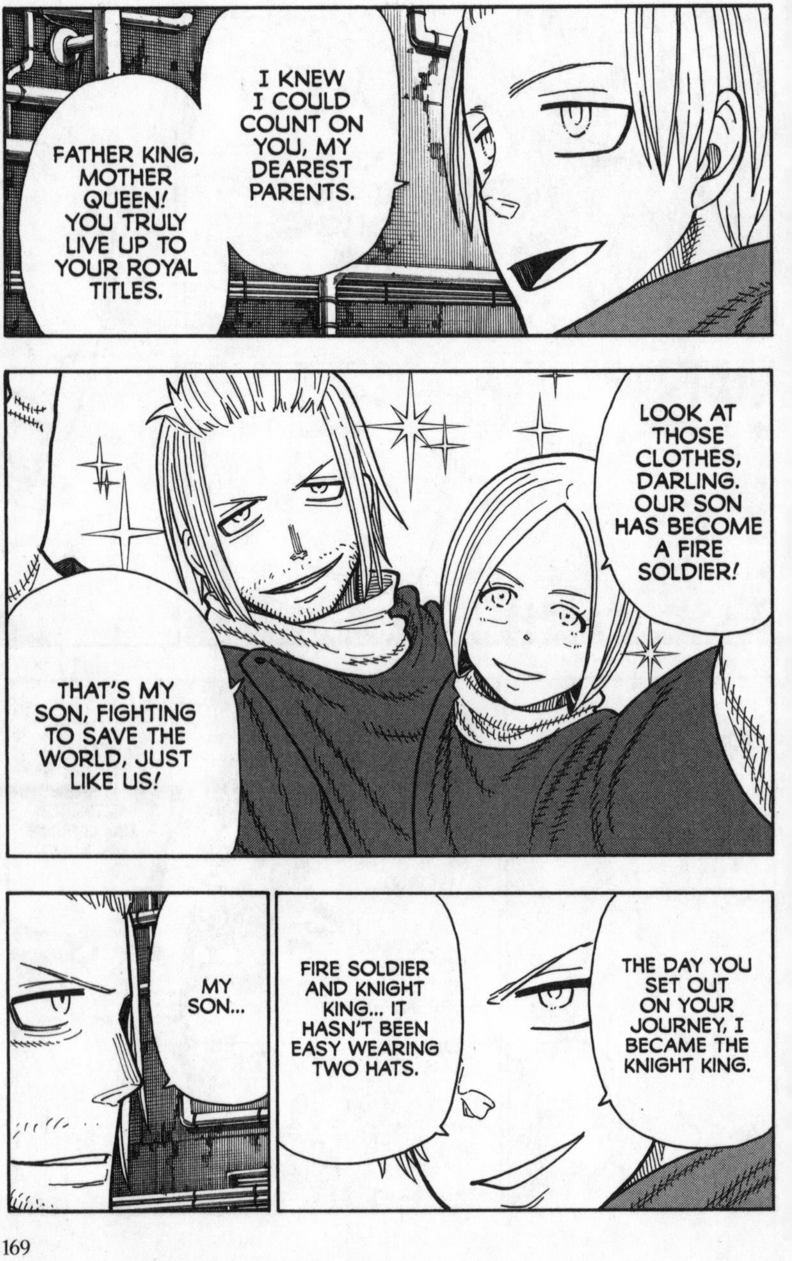
I KNEW I COULD COUNT ON YOU, MY DEAREST PARENTS.
FATHER KING, MOTHER QUEEN! YOU TRULY LIVE UP TO YOUR ROYAL TITLES.
LOOK AT THOSE CLOTHES, DARLING. OUR SON HAS BECOME A FIRE SOLDIER!
THAT'S MY SON, FIGHTING TO SAVE THE WORLD, JUST LIKE US!
THE DAY YOU SET OUT ON YOUR JOURNEY, I BECAME THE KNIGHT KING.
FIRE SOLDIER AND KNIGHT KING... IT HASN'T BEEN EASY WEARING TWO HATS.
MY SON...

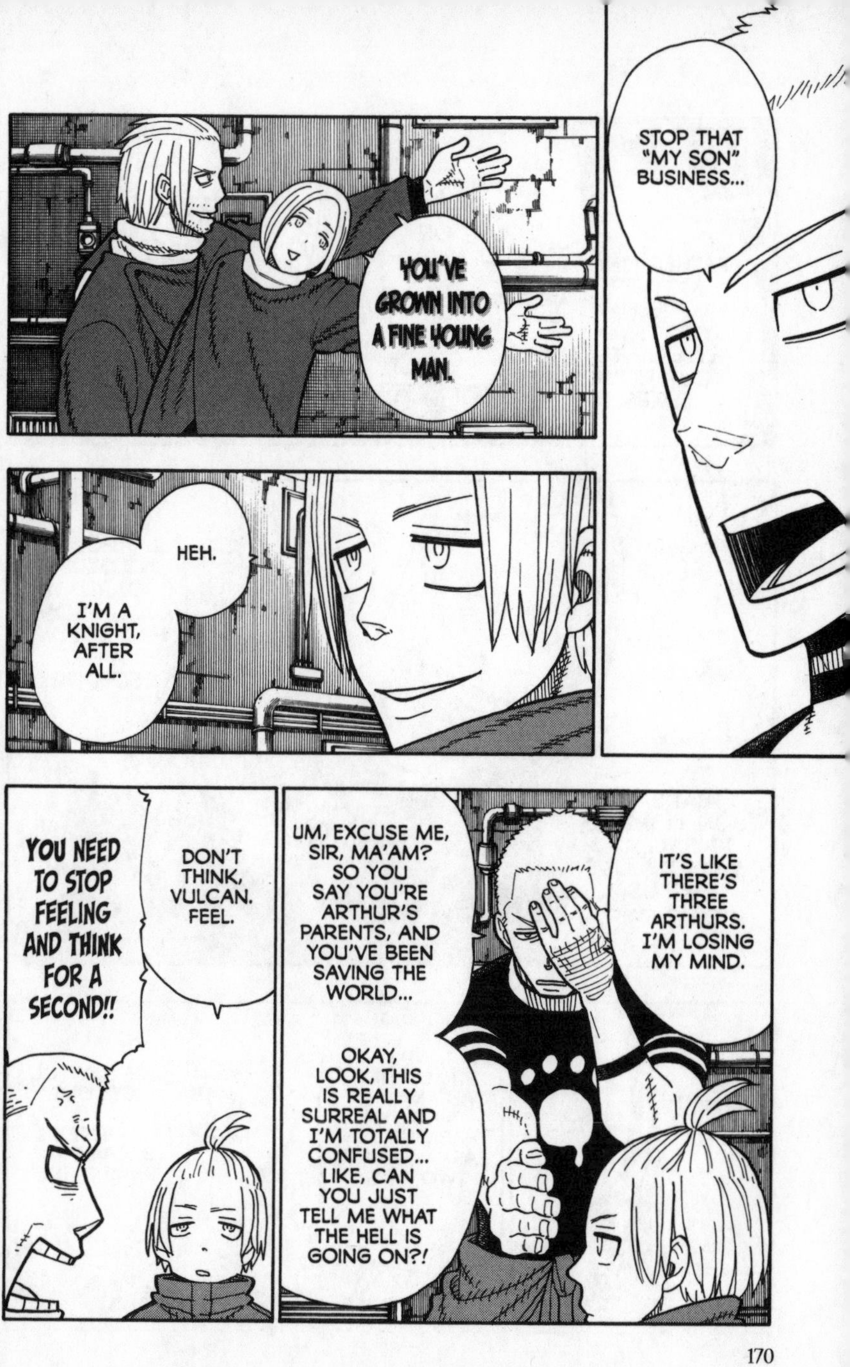
STOP THAT "MY SON" BUSINESS...
YOU'VE GROWN INTO A FINE YOUNG MAN.
HEH.
I'M A KNIGHT, AFTER ALL.
IT'S LIKE THERE'S THREE ARTHURS. I'M LOSING MY MIND.
UM, EXCUSE ME, SIR, MA'AM? SO YOU SAY YOU'RE ARTHUR'S PARENTS, AND YOU'VE BEEN SAVING THE WORLD...
OKAY, LOOK, THIS IS REALLY SURREAL AND I'M TOTALLY CONFUSED... LIKE, CAN YOU JUST TELL ME WHAT THE HELL IS GOING ON?!
DON'T THINK, VULCAN. FEEL.
YOU NEED TO STOP FEELING AND THINK FOR A SECOND!!

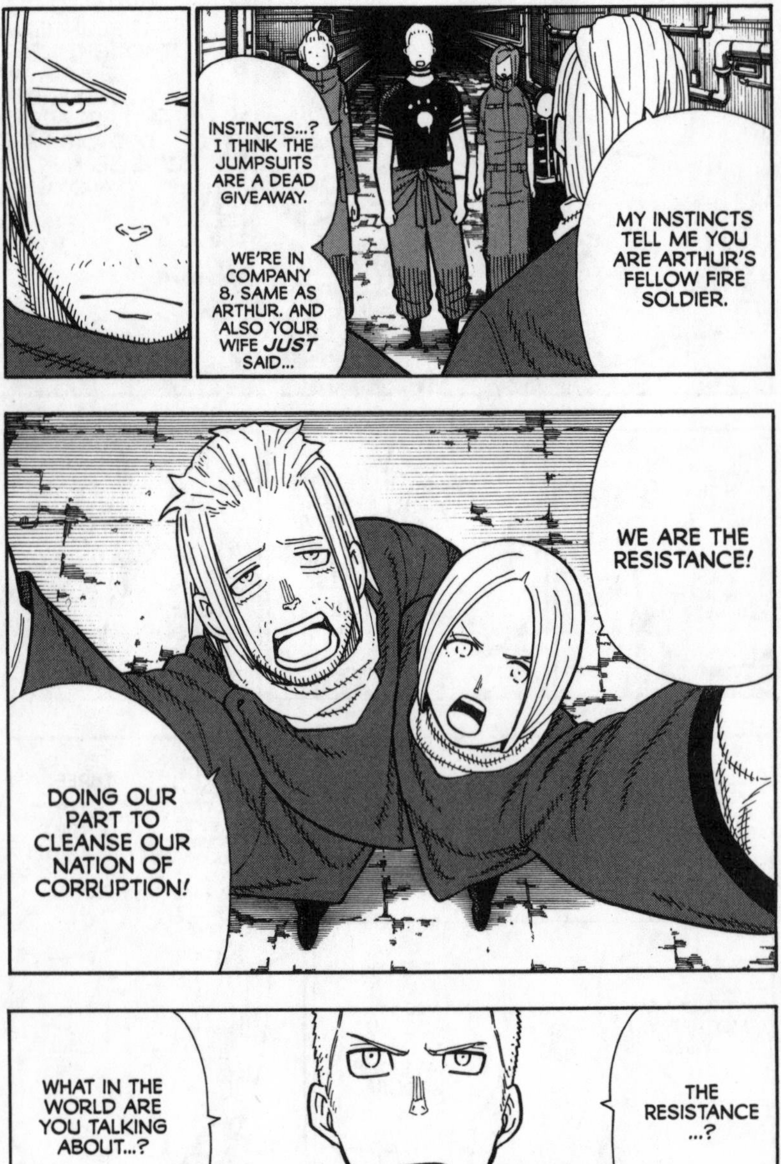
MY INSTINCTS TELL ME YOU ARE ARTHUR'S FELLOW FIRE SOLDIER.
INSTINCTS...? I THINK THE JUMPSUITS ARE A DEAD GIVEAWAY.
WE'RE IN COMPANY 8, SAME AS ARTHUR. AND ALSO YOUR WIFE *JUST* SAID...
WE ARE THE RESISTANCE!
DOING OUR PART TO CLEANSE OUR NATION OF CORRUPTION!
THE RESISTANCE ...?
WHAT IN THE WORLD ARE YOU TALKING ABOUT...?

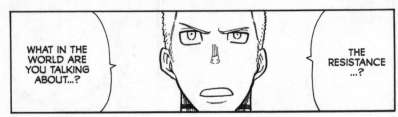

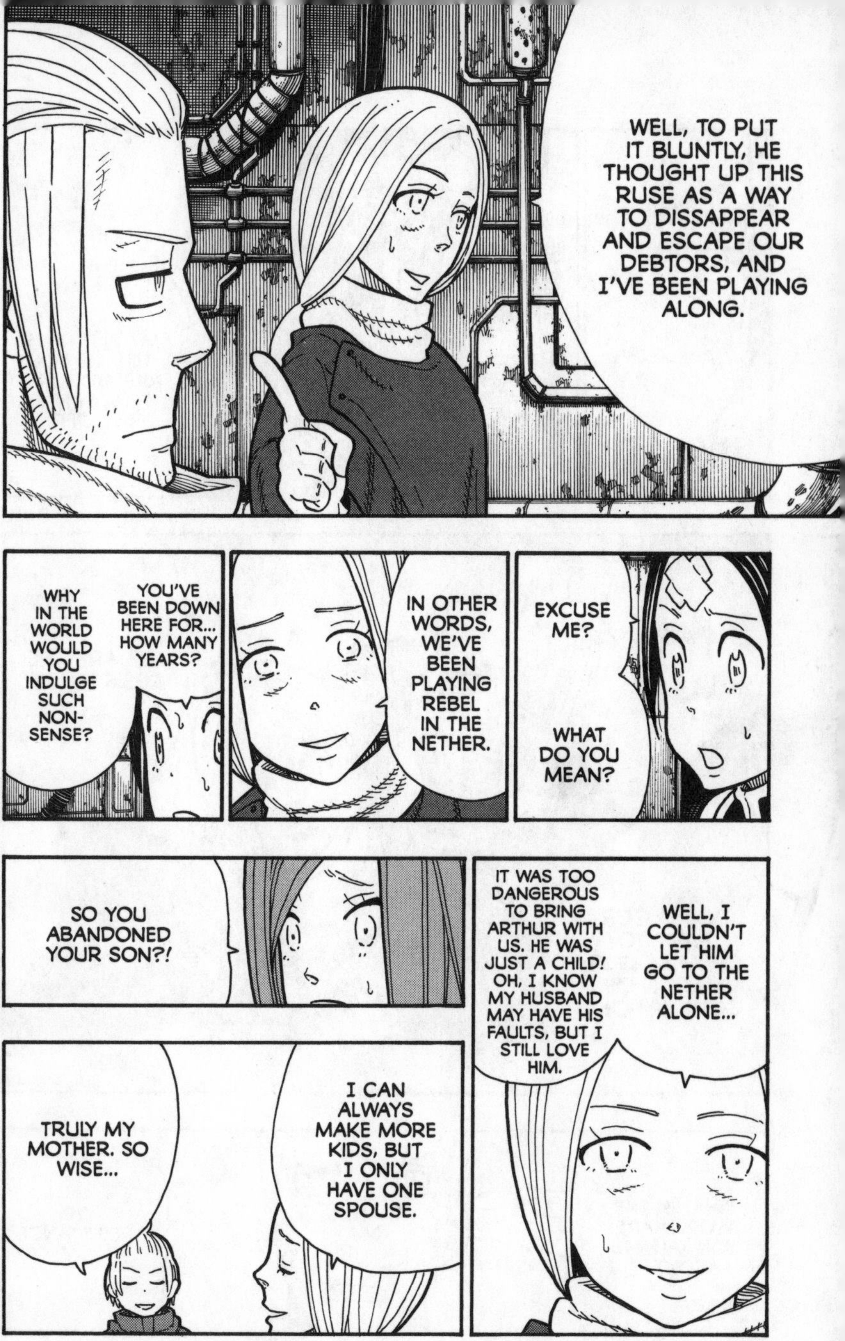
WELL, TO PUT IT BLUNTLY, HE THOUGHT UP THIS RUSE AS A WAY TO DISSAPPEAR AND ESCAPE OUR DEBTORS, AND I'VE BEEN PLAYING ALONG.
EXCUSE ME?
WHAT DO YOU MEAN?
IN OTHER WORDS, WE'VE BEEN PLAYING REBEL IN THE NETHER.
YOU'VE BEEN DOWN HERE FOR... HOW MANY YEARS?
WHY IN THE WORLD WOULD YOU INDULGE SUCH NON-SENSE?
WELL, I COULDN'T LET HIM GO TO THE NETHER ALONE...
IT WAS TOO DANGEROUS TO BRING ARTHUR WITH US. HE WAS JUST A CHILD! OH, I KNOW MY HUSBAND MAY HAVE HIS FAULTS, BUT I STILL LOVE HIM.
SO YOU ABANDONED YOUR SON?!
I CAN ALWAYS MAKE MORE KIDS, BUT I ONLY HAVE ONE SPOUSE.
TRULY MY MOTHER. SO WISE...

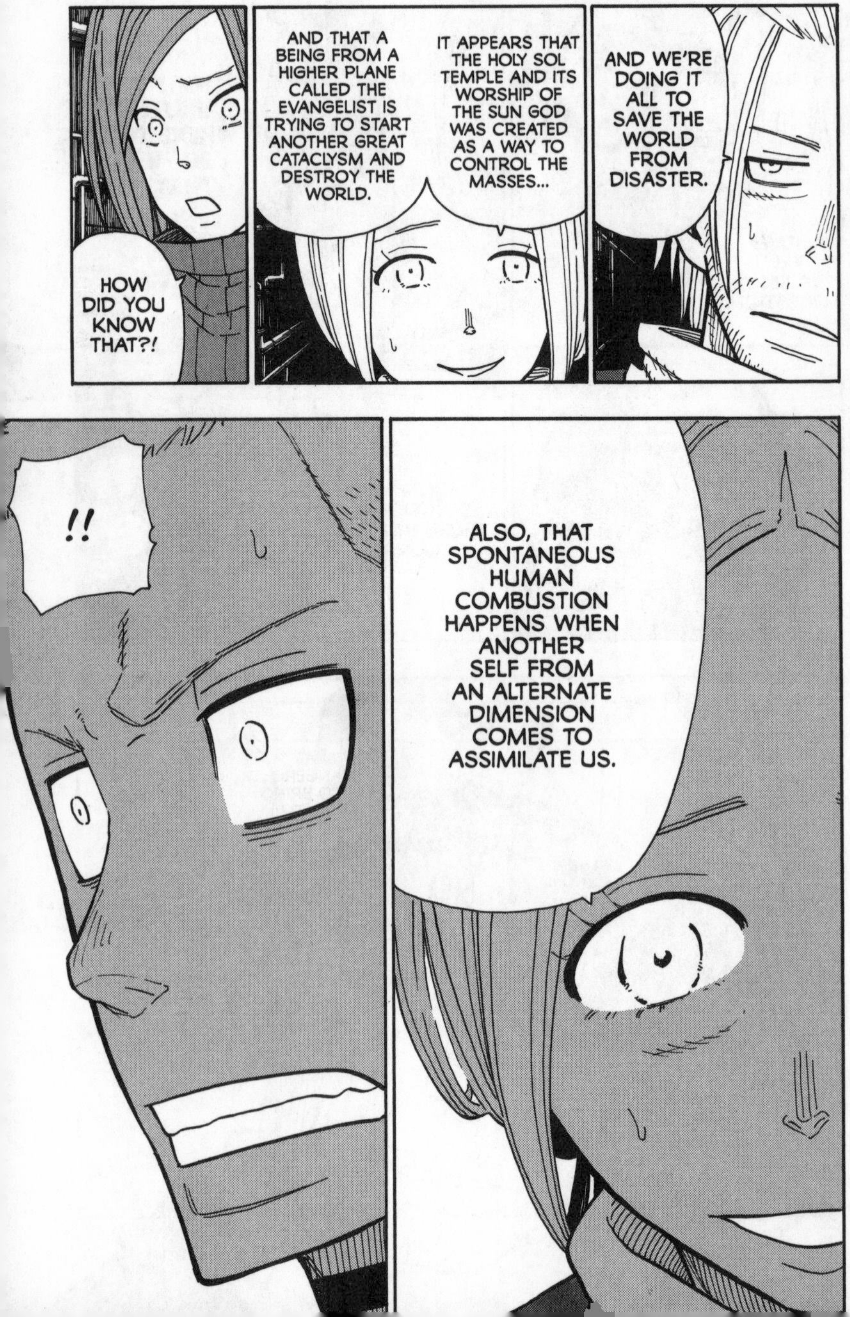
AND WE'RE DOING IT ALL TO SAVE THE WORLD FROM DISASTER.
IT APPEARS THAT THE HOLY SOL TEMPLE AND ITS WORSHIP OF THE SUN GOD WAS CREATED AS A WAY TO CONTROL THE MASSES...
AND THAT A BEING FROM A HIGHER PLANE CALLED THE EVANGELIST IS TRYING TO START ANOTHER GREAT CATACLYSM AND DESTROY THE WORLD.
HOW DID YOU KNOW THAT?!
ALSO, THAT SPONTANEOUS HUMAN COMBUSTION HAPPENS WHEN ANOTHER SELF FROM AN ALTERNATE DIMENSION COMES TO ASSIMILATE US.
!!

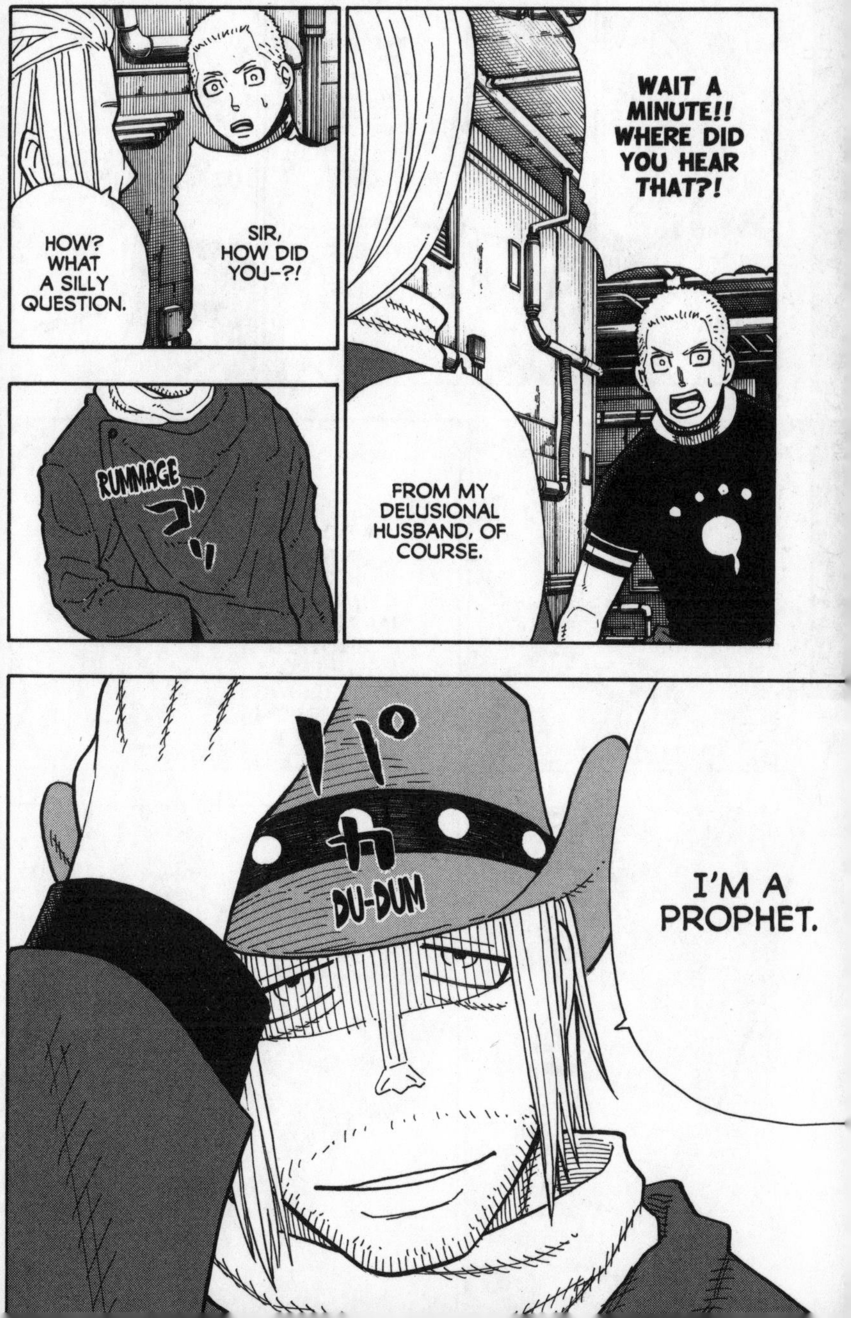
WAIT A MINUTE!! WHERE DID YOU HEAR THAT?!
FROM MY DELUSIONAL HUSBAND, OF COURSE.
SIR, HOW DID YOU-?!
HOW? WHAT A SILLY QUESTION.
RUMMAGE
I'M A PROPHET.
DU-DUM

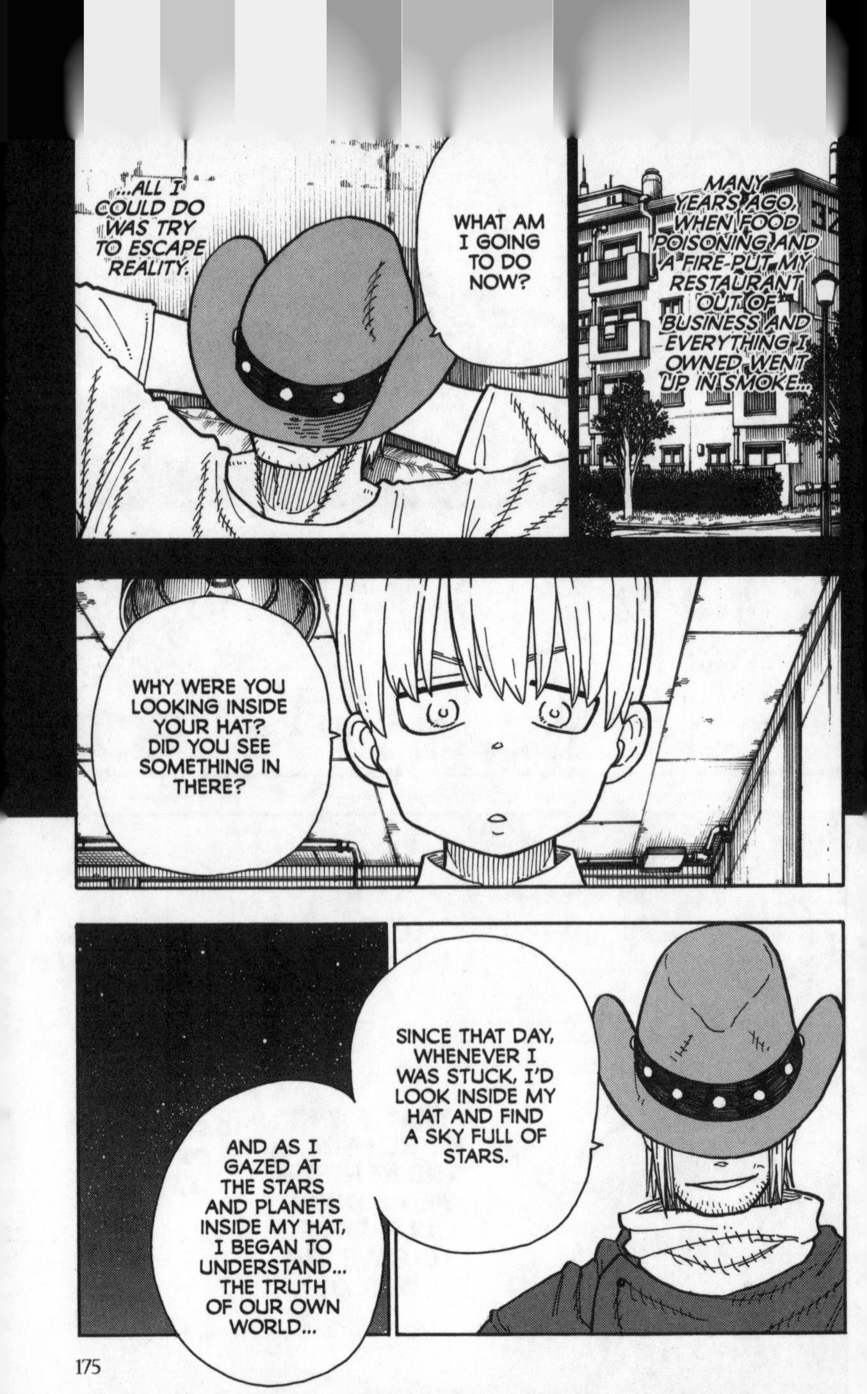
MANY YEARS AGO, WHEN FOOD POISONING AND A FIRE PUT MY RESTAURANT OUT OF BUSINESS AND EVERYTHING I OWNED WENT UP IN SMOKE...
WHAT AM I GOING TO DO NOW?
...ALL I COULD DO WAS TRY TO ESCAPE REALITY.
WHY WERE YOU LOOKING INSIDE YOUR HAT? DID YOU SEE SOMETHING IN THERE?
SINCE THAT DAY, WHENEVER I WAS STUCK, I'D LOOK INSIDE MY HAT AND FIND A SKY FULL OF STARS.
AND AS I GAZED AT THE STARS AND PLANETS INSIDE MY HAT, I BEGAN TO UNDERSTAND... THE TRUTH OF OUR OWN WORLD...

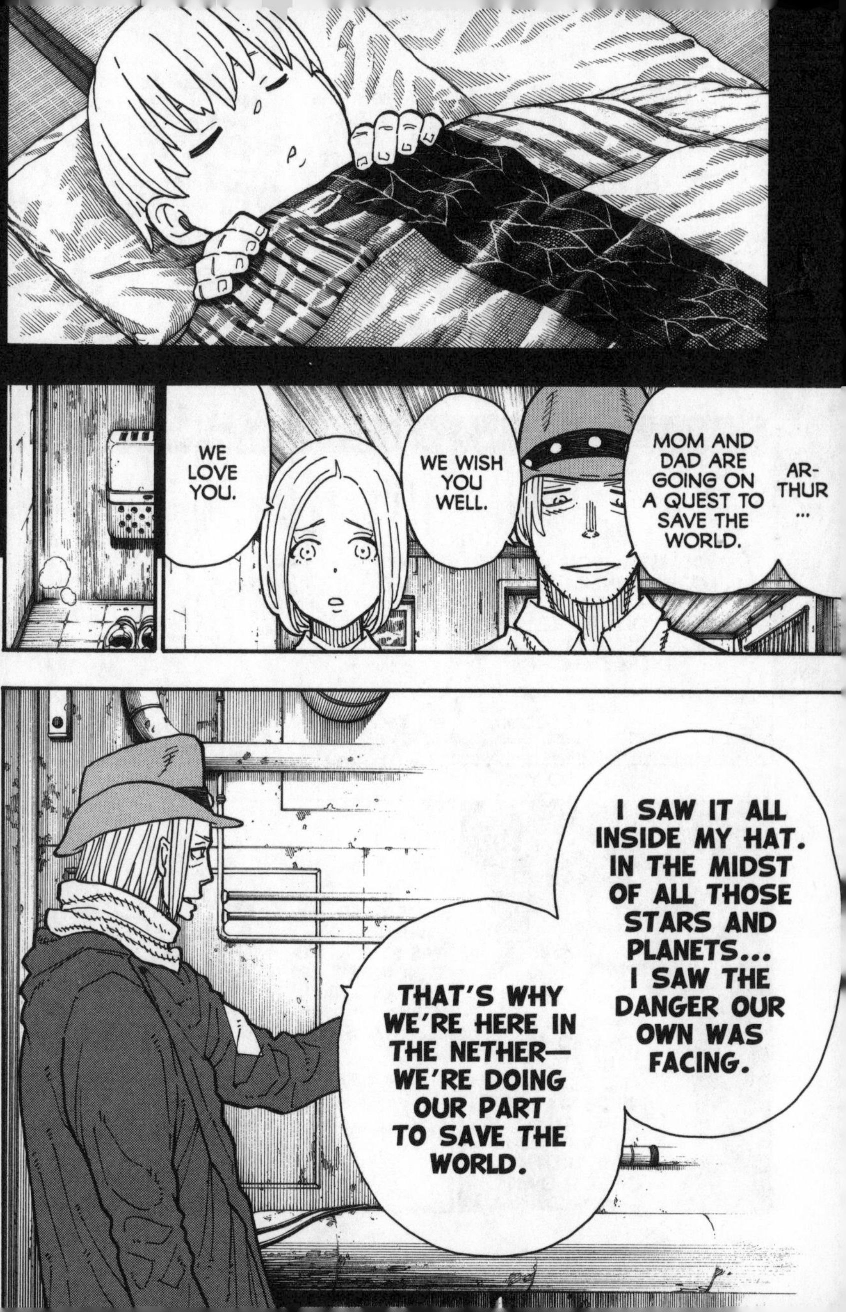
ARTHUR...
MOM AND DAD ARE GOING ON A QUEST TO SAVE THE WORLD.
WE WISH YOU WELL.
WE LOVE YOU.
I SAW IT ALL INSIDE MY HAT. IN THE MIDST OF ALL THOSE STARS AND PLANETS... I SAW THE DANGER OUR OWN WAS FACING.
THAT'S WHY WE'RE HERE IN THE NETHER— WE'RE DOING OUR PART TO SAVE THE WORLD.

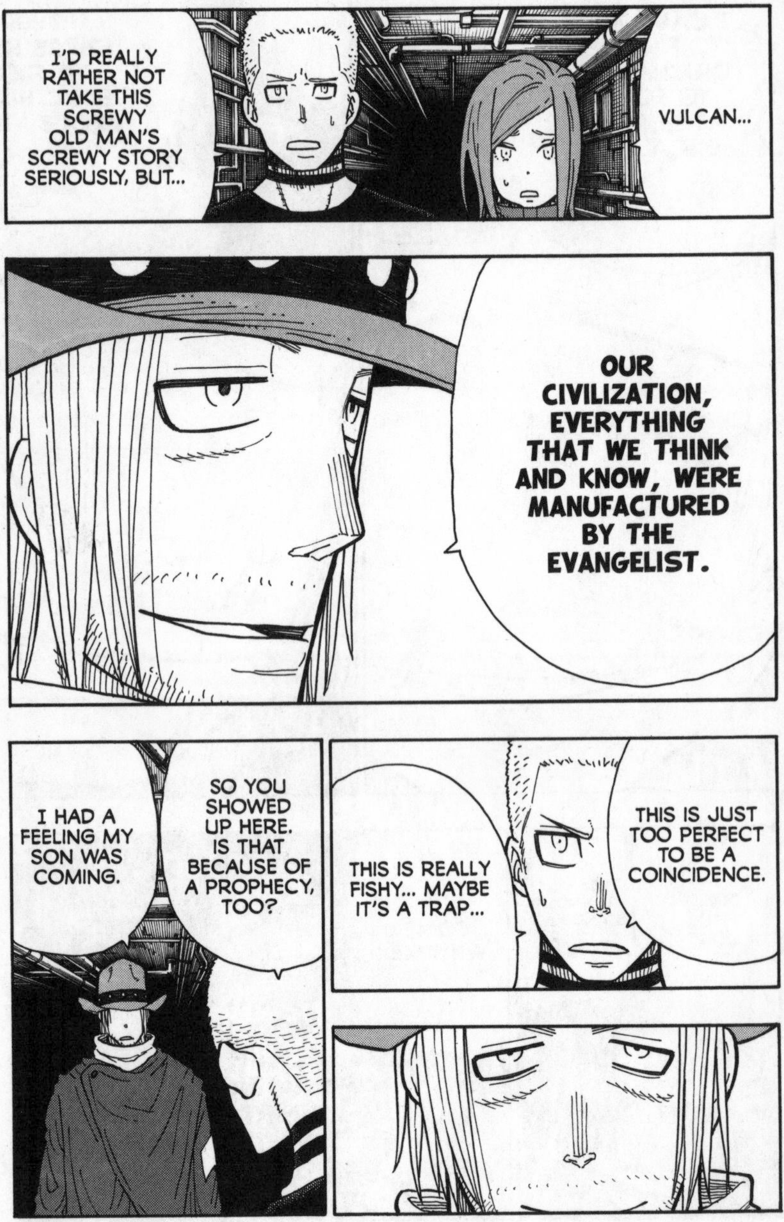
VULCAN...
I'D REALLY RATHER NOT TAKE THIS SCREWY OLD MAN'S SCREWY STORY SERIOUSLY, BUT...
OUR CIVILIZATION, EVERYTHING THAT WE THINK AND KNOW, WERE MANUFACTURED BY THE EVANGELIST.
THIS IS JUST TOO PERFECT TO BE A COINCIDENCE.
THIS IS REALLY FISHY... MAYBE IT'S A TRAP...
SO YOU SHOWED UP HERE. IS THAT BECAUSE OF A PROPHECY, TOO?
I HAD A FEELING MY SON WAS COMING.

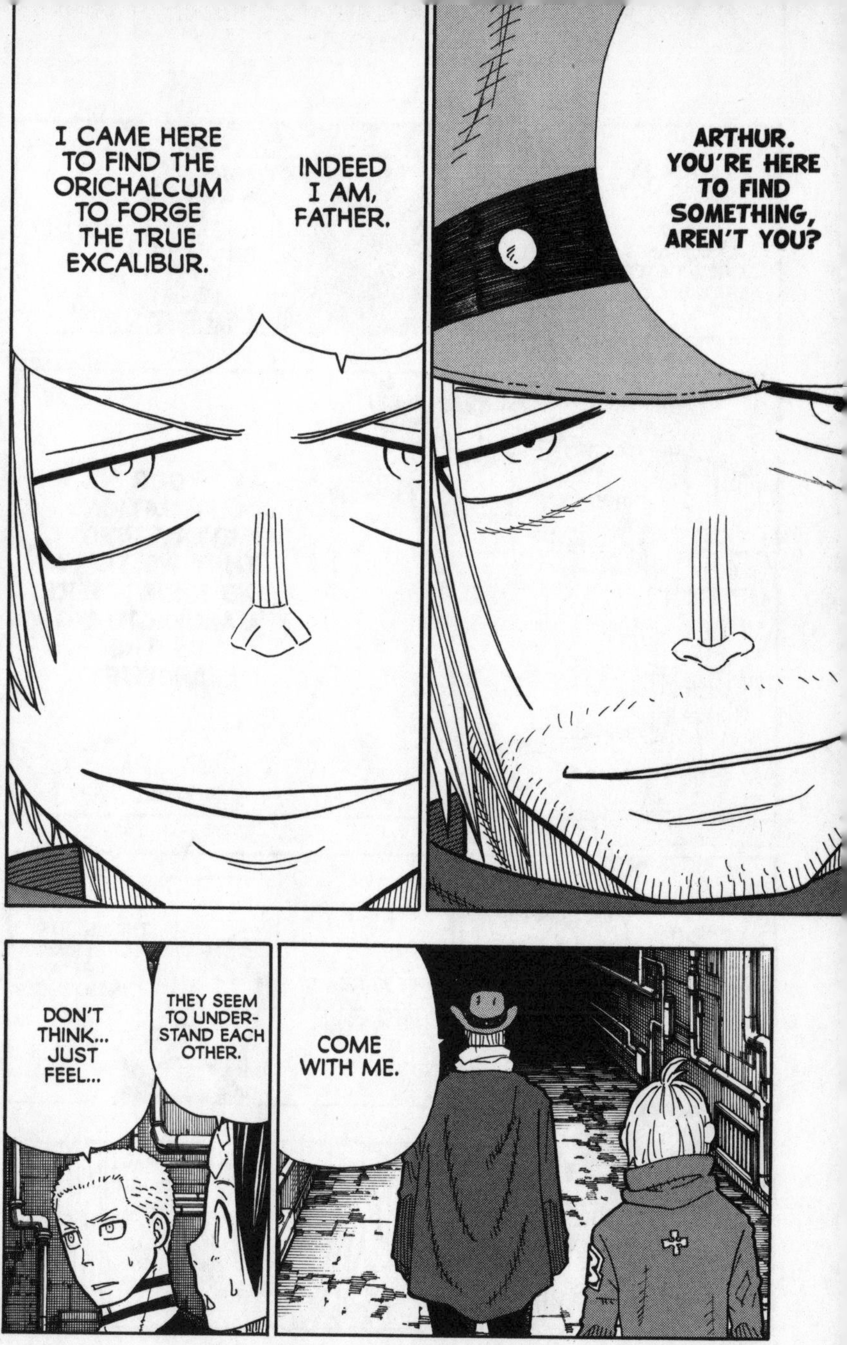
ARTHUR. YOU'RE HERE TO FIND SOMETHING, AREN'T YOU?
INDEED I AM, FATHER.
I CAME HERE TO FIND THE ORICHALCUM TO FORGE THE TRUE EXCALIBUR.
COME WITH ME.
THEY SEEM TO UNDER-STAND EACH OTHER.
DON'T THINK... JUST FEEL...

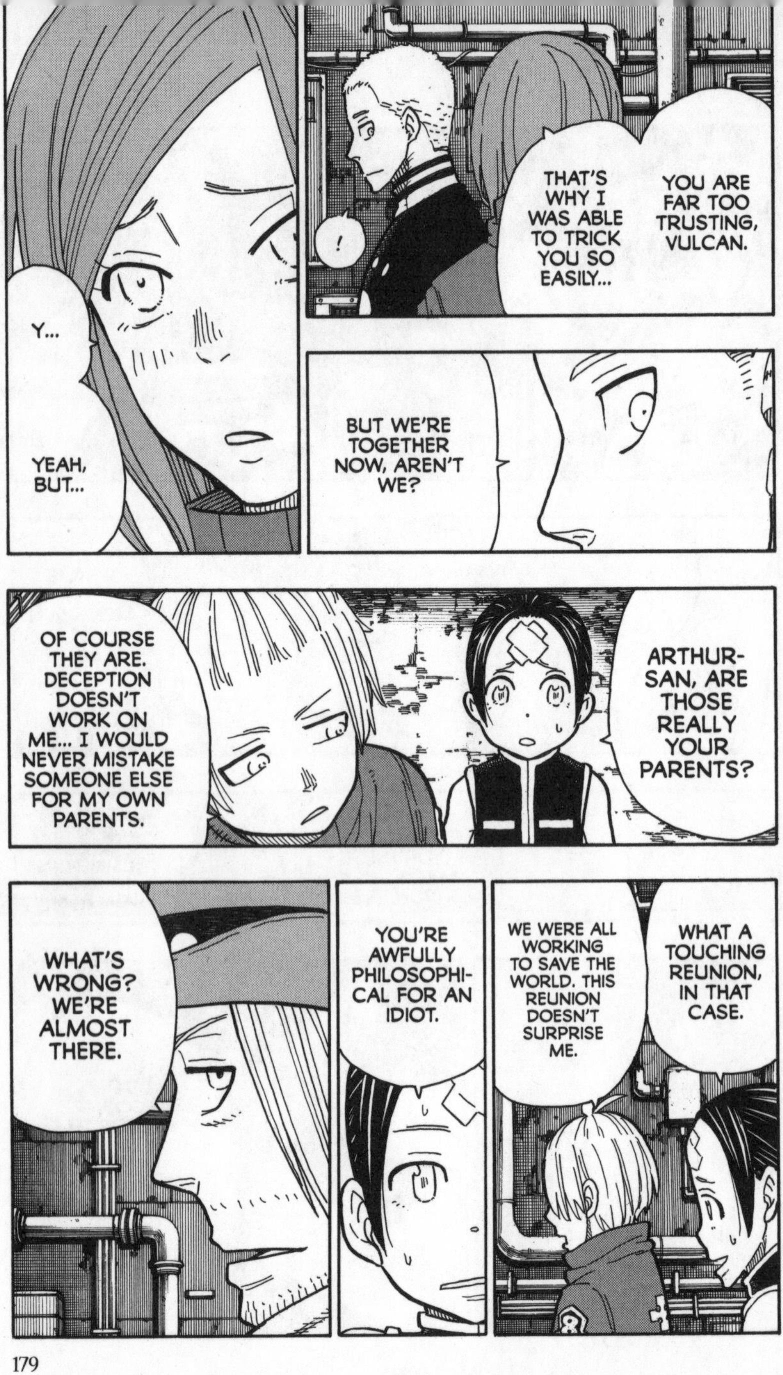
YOU ARE FAR TOO TRUSTING, VULCAN.
THAT'S WHY I WAS ABLE TO TRICK YOU SO EASILY...
!
BUT WE'RE TOGETHER NOW, AREN'T WE?
Y...
YEAH, BUT...
ARTHUR-SAN, ARE THOSE REALLY YOUR PARENTS?
OF COURSE THEY ARE. DECEPTION DOESN'T WORK ON ME... I WOULD NEVER MISTAKE SOMEONE ELSE FOR MY OWN PARENTS.
WHAT A TOUCHING REUNION, IN THAT CASE.
WE WERE ALL WORKING TO SAVE THE WORLD. THIS REUNION DOESN'T SURPRISE ME.
YOU'RE AWFULLY PHILOSOPHI-CAL FOR AN IDIOT.
WHAT'S WRONG? WE'RE ALMOST THERE.

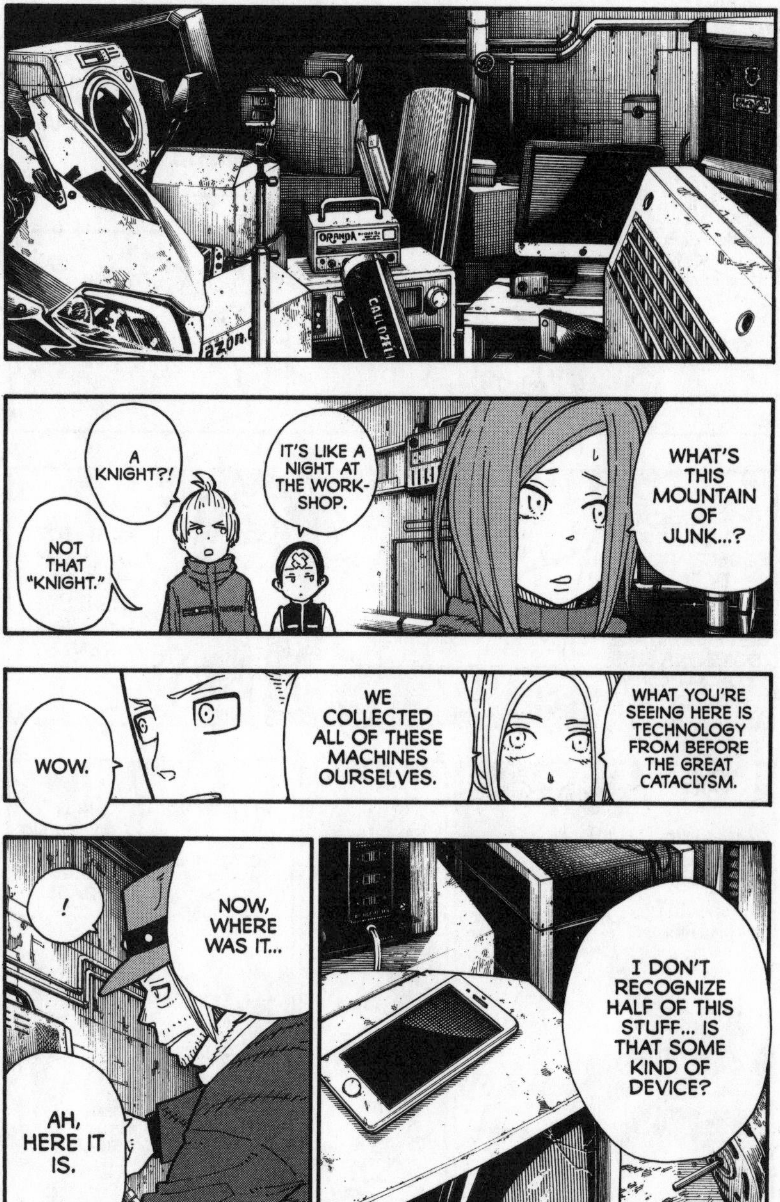
ORANDA
WHAT'S THIS MOUNTAIN OF JUNK...?
IT'S LIKE A NIGHT AT THE WORK-SHOP.
A KNIGHT?!
NOT THAT "KNIGHT."
WHAT YOU'RE SEEING HERE IS TECHNOLOGY FROM BEFORE THE GREAT CATACLYSM.
WE COLLECTED ALL OF THESE MACHINES OURSELVES.
WOW.
I DON'T RECOGNIZE HALF OF THIS STUFF... IS THAT SOME KIND OF DEVICE?
NOW, WHERE WAS IT...
!
AH, HERE IT IS.

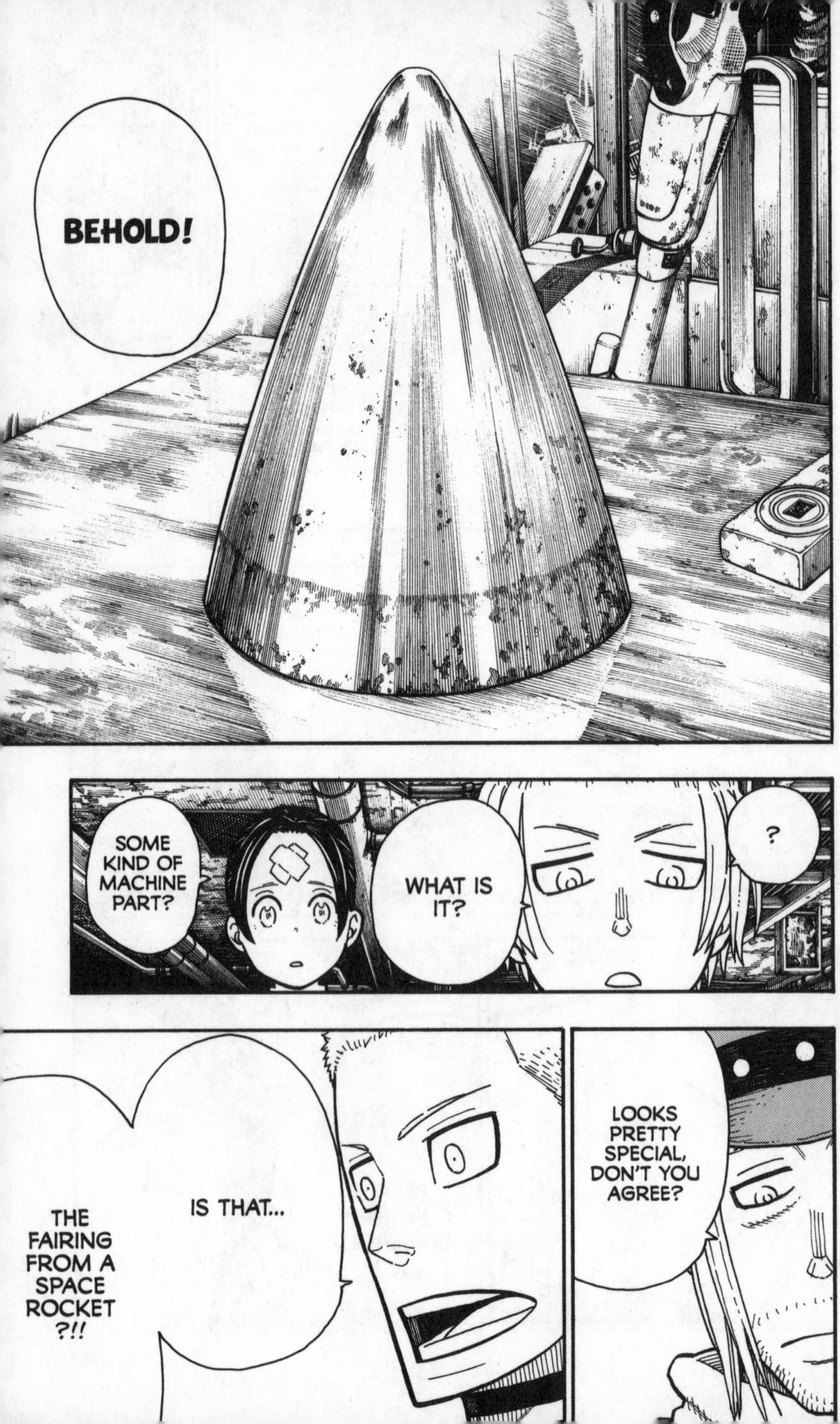
BEHOLD!
?
WHAT IS IT?
SOME KIND OF MACHINE PART?
LOOKS PRETTY SPECIAL, DON'T YOU AGREE?
IS THAT...
THE FAIRING FROM A SPACE ROCKET ?!!

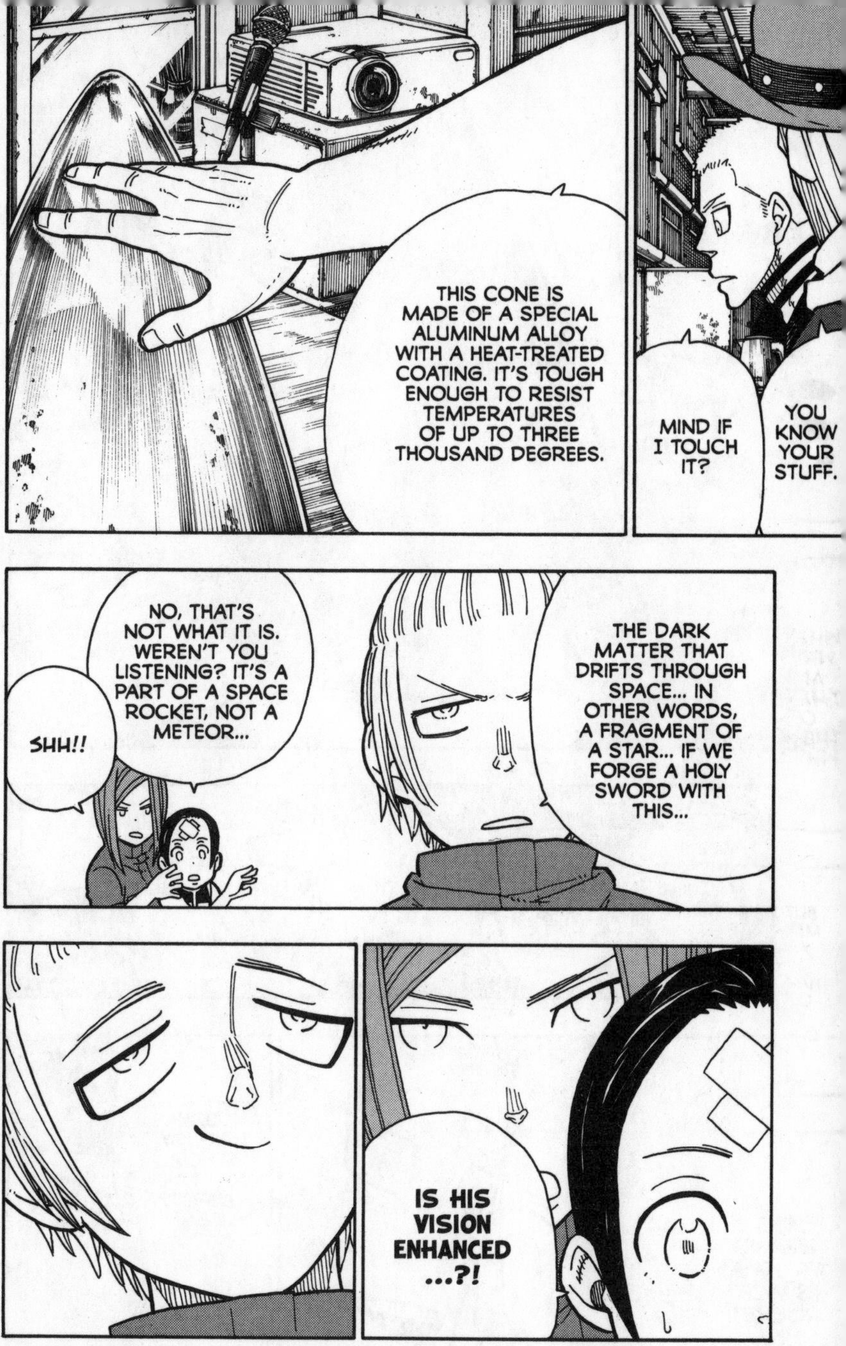
YOU KNOW YOUR STUFF.
MIND IF I TOUCH IT?
THIS CONE IS MADE OF A SPECIAL ALUMINUM ALLOY WITH A HEAT-TREATED COATING. IT'S TOUGH ENOUGH TO RESIST TEMPERATURES OF UP TO THREE THOUSAND DEGREES.
THE DARK MATTER THAT DRIFTS THROUGH SPACE... IN OTHER WORDS, A FRAGMENT OF A STAR... IF WE FORGE A HOLY SWORD WITH THIS...
NO, THAT'S NOT WHAT IT IS. WEREN'T YOU LISTENING? IT'S A PART OF A SPACE ROCKET, NOT A METEOR...
SHH!!
IS HIS VISION ENHANCED ...?!

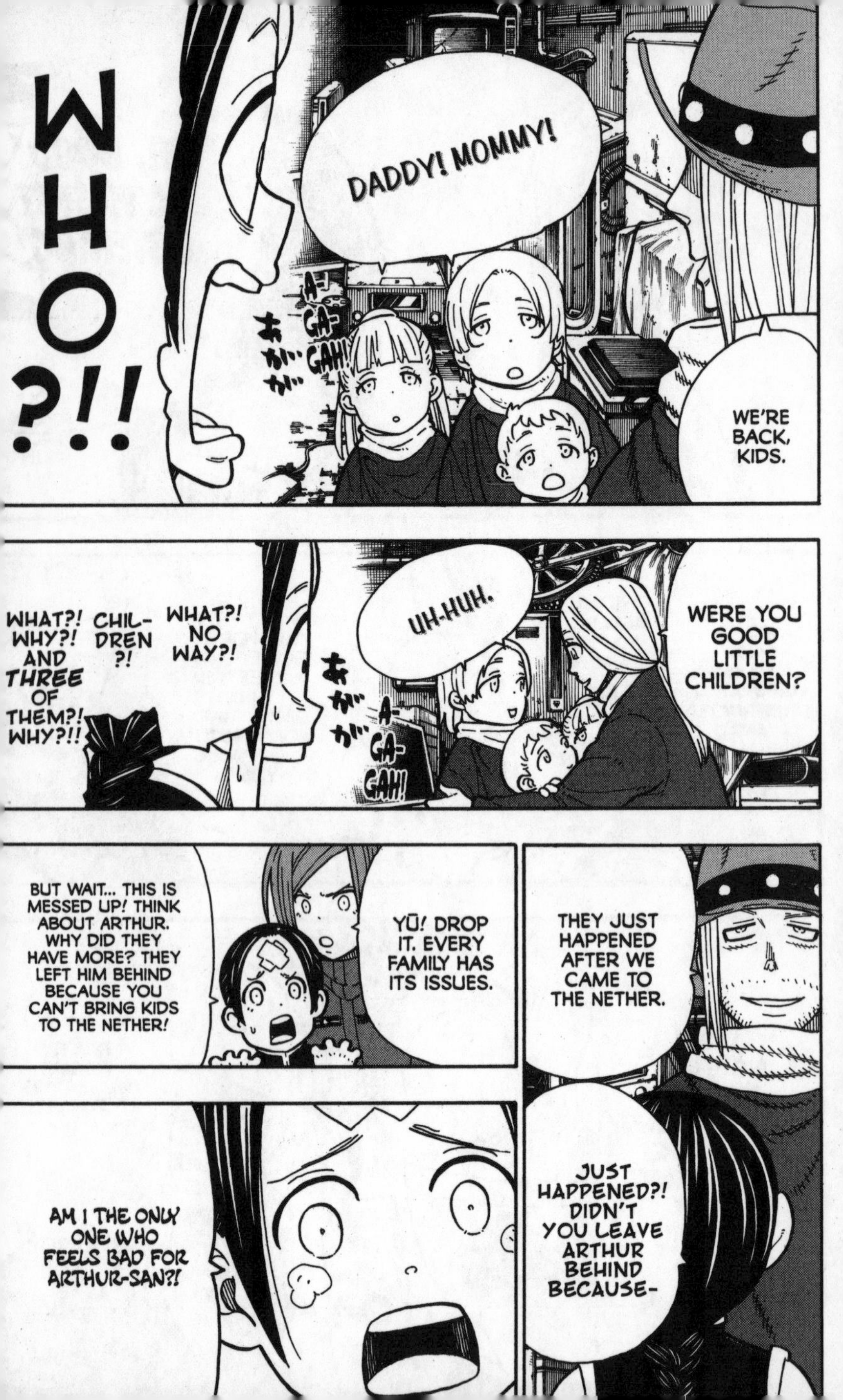
WE'RE BACK, KIDS.
DADDY! MOMMY!
あがが
A-GA-GAH!
WHO?!!
WERE YOU GOOD LITTLE CHILDREN?
UH-HUH.
あがが
A-GA-GAH!
WHAT?! NO WAY?!
CHIL-DREN?!
WHAT?! WHY?! AND THREE OF THEM?! WHY?!!
THEY JUST HAPPENED AFTER WE CAME TO THE NETHER.
JUST HAPPENED?! DIDN'T YOU LEAVE ARTHUR BEHIND BECAUSE-
YŪ! DROP IT. EVERY FAMILY HAS ITS ISSUES.
BUT WAIT... THIS IS MESSED UP! THINK ABOUT ARTHUR. WHY DID THEY HAVE MORE? THEY LEFT HIM BEHIND BECAUSE YOU CAN'T BRING KIDS TO THE NETHER!
AM I THE ONLY ONE WHO FEELS BAD FOR ARTHUR-SAN?!

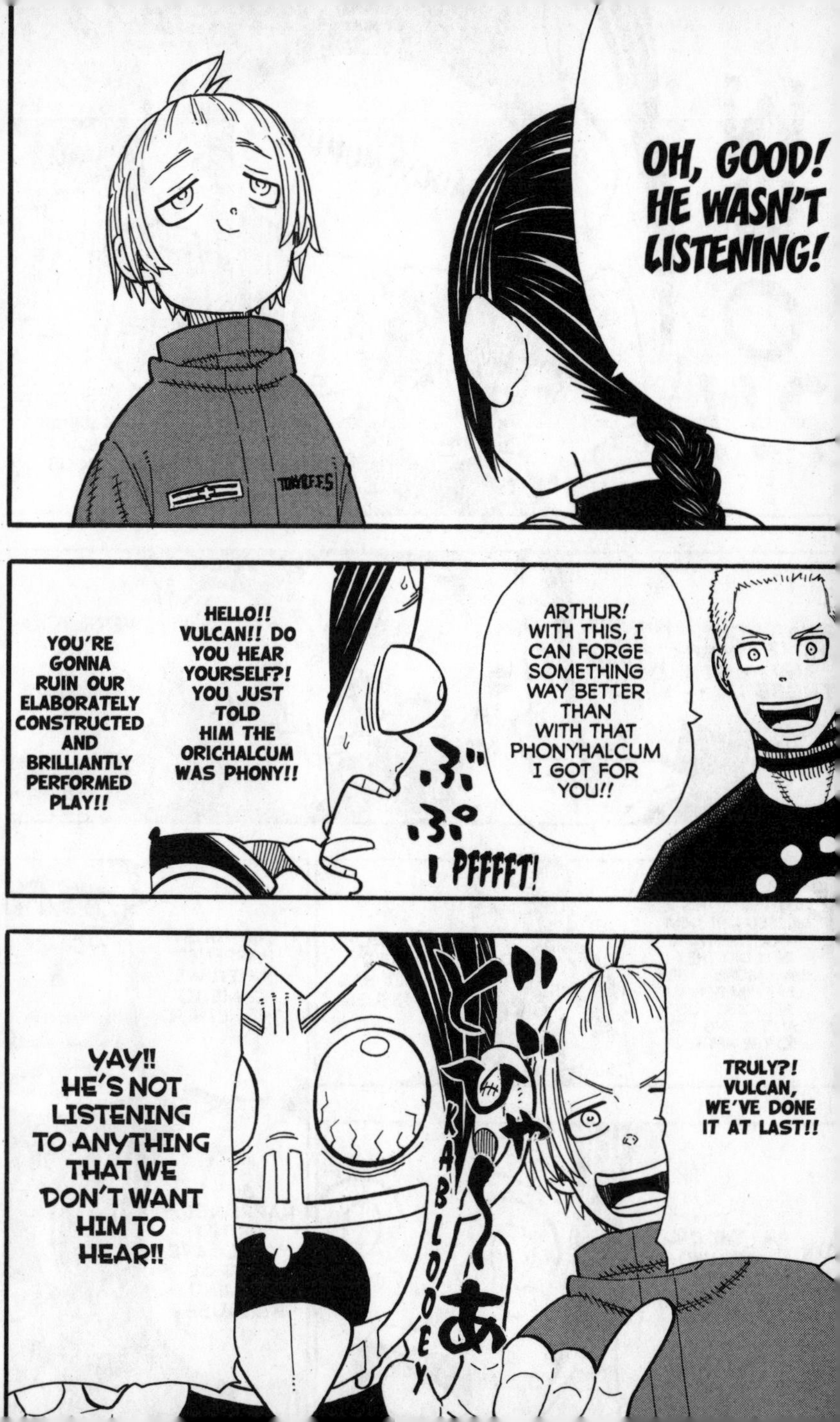
OH, GOOD! HE WASN'T LISTENING!
ARTHUR! WITH THIS, I CAN FORGE SOMETHING WAY BETTER THAN WITH THAT PHONYHALCUM I GOT FOR YOU!!
PFFFFT!
HELLO!! VULCAN!! DO YOU HEAR YOURSELF?! YOU JUST TOLD HIM THE ORICHALCUM WAS PHONY!!
YOU'RE GONNA RUIN OUR ELABORATELY CONSTRUCTED AND BRILLIANTLY PERFORMED PLAY!!
TRULY?! VULCAN, WE'VE DONE IT AT LAST!!
KABLOOEY
YAY!! HE'S NOT LISTENING TO ANYTHING THAT WE DON'T WANT HIM TO HEAR!!

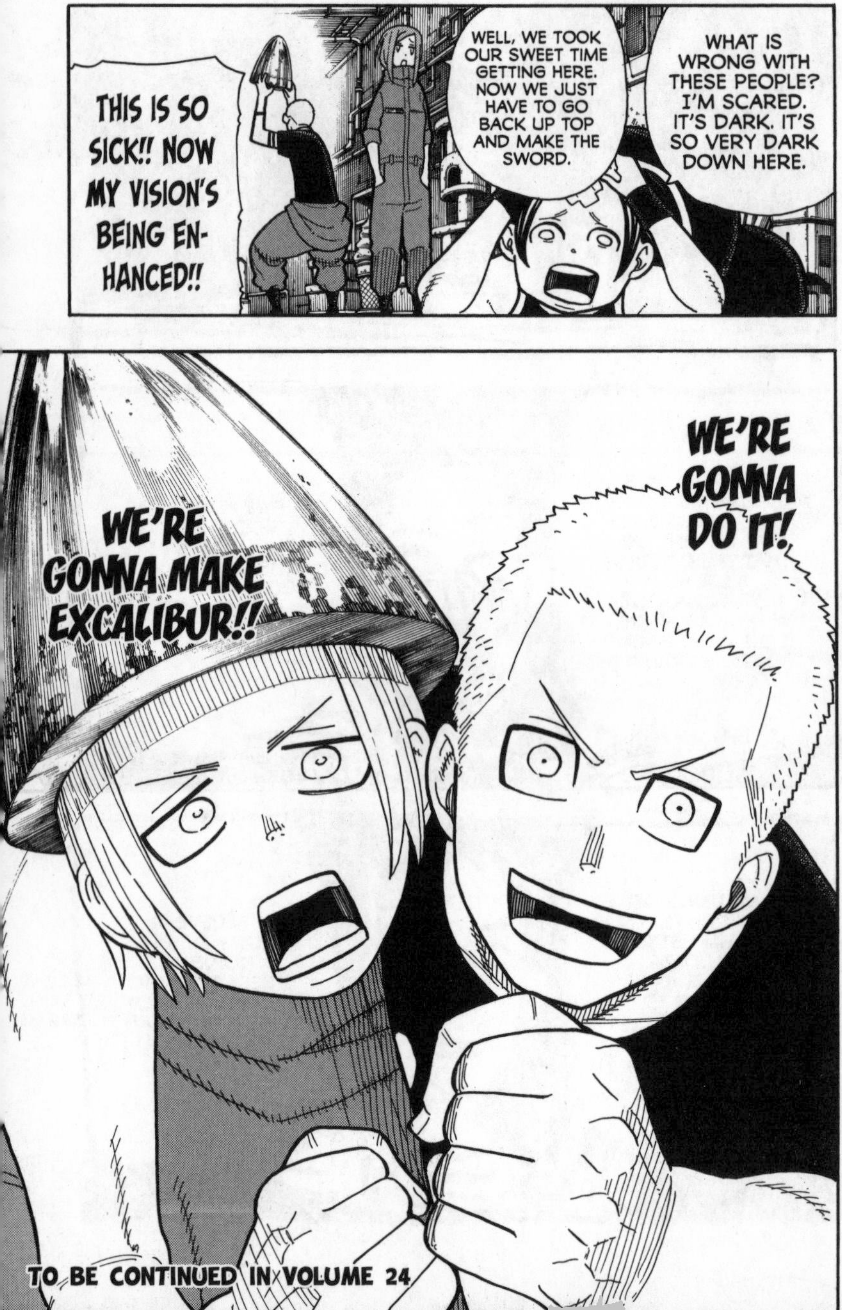
WHAT IS WRONG WITH THESE PEOPLE? I'M SCARED. IT'S DARK. IT'S SO VERY DARK DOWN HERE.
WELL, WE TOOK OUR SWEET TIME GETTING HERE. NOW WE JUST HAVE TO GO BACK UP TOP AND MAKE THE SWORD.
THIS IS SO SICK!! NOW MY VISION'S BEING EN-HANCED!!
WE'RE GONNA DO IT!
WE'RE GONNA MAKE EXCALIBUR!!
TO BE CONTINUED IN VOLUME 24

AFTERWORD MANGA: ATSUSHIYA

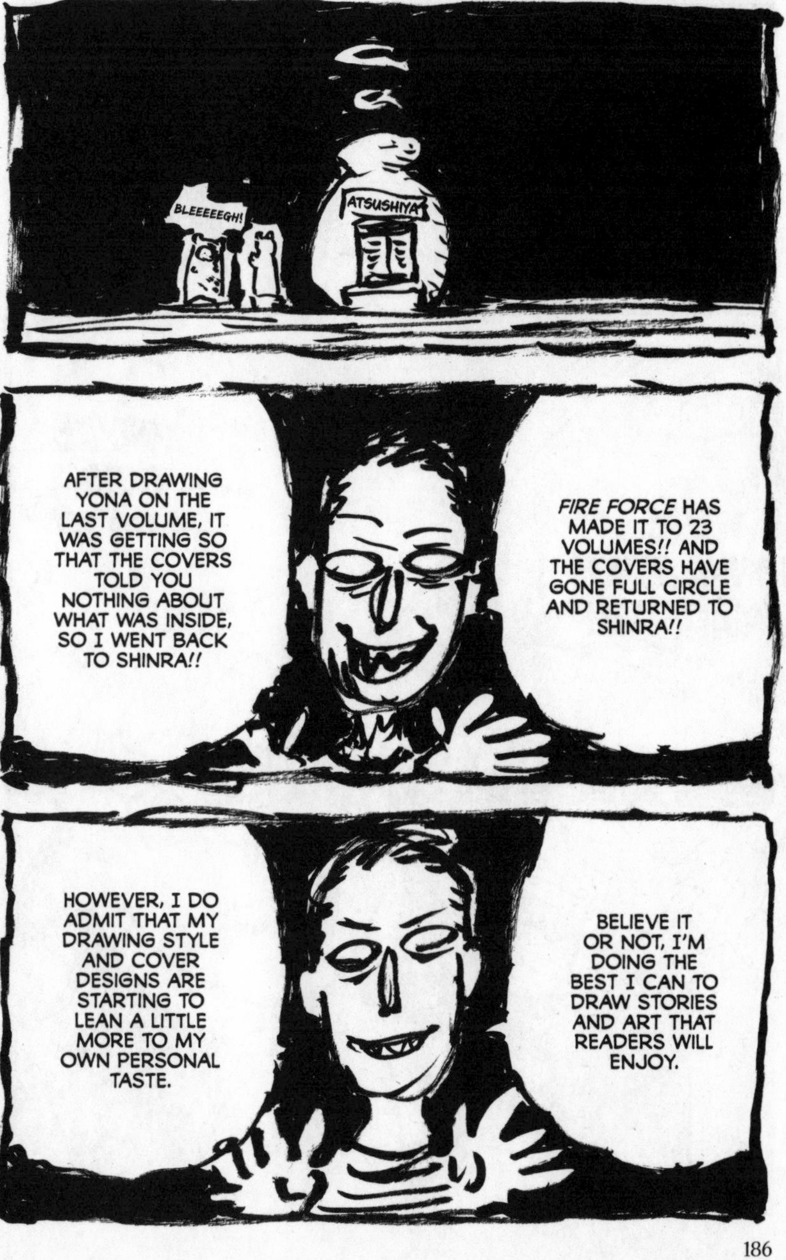
ATSUSHIYA
BLEEEEEGH!
FIRE FORCE HAS MADE IT TO 23 VOLUMES!! AND THE COVERS HAVE GONE FULL CIRCLE AND RETURNED TO SHINRA!!
AFTER DRAWING YONA ON THE LAST VOLUME, IT WAS GETTING SO THAT THE COVERS TOLD YOU NOTHING ABOUT WHAT WAS INSIDE, SO I WENT BACK TO SHINRA!!
BELIEVE IT OR NOT, I'M DOING THE BEST I CAN TO DRAW STORIES AND ART THAT READERS WILL ENJOY.
HOWEVER, I DO ADMIT THAT MY DRAWING STYLE AND COVER DESIGNS ARE STARTING TO LEAN A LITTLE MORE TO MY OWN PERSONAL TASTE.

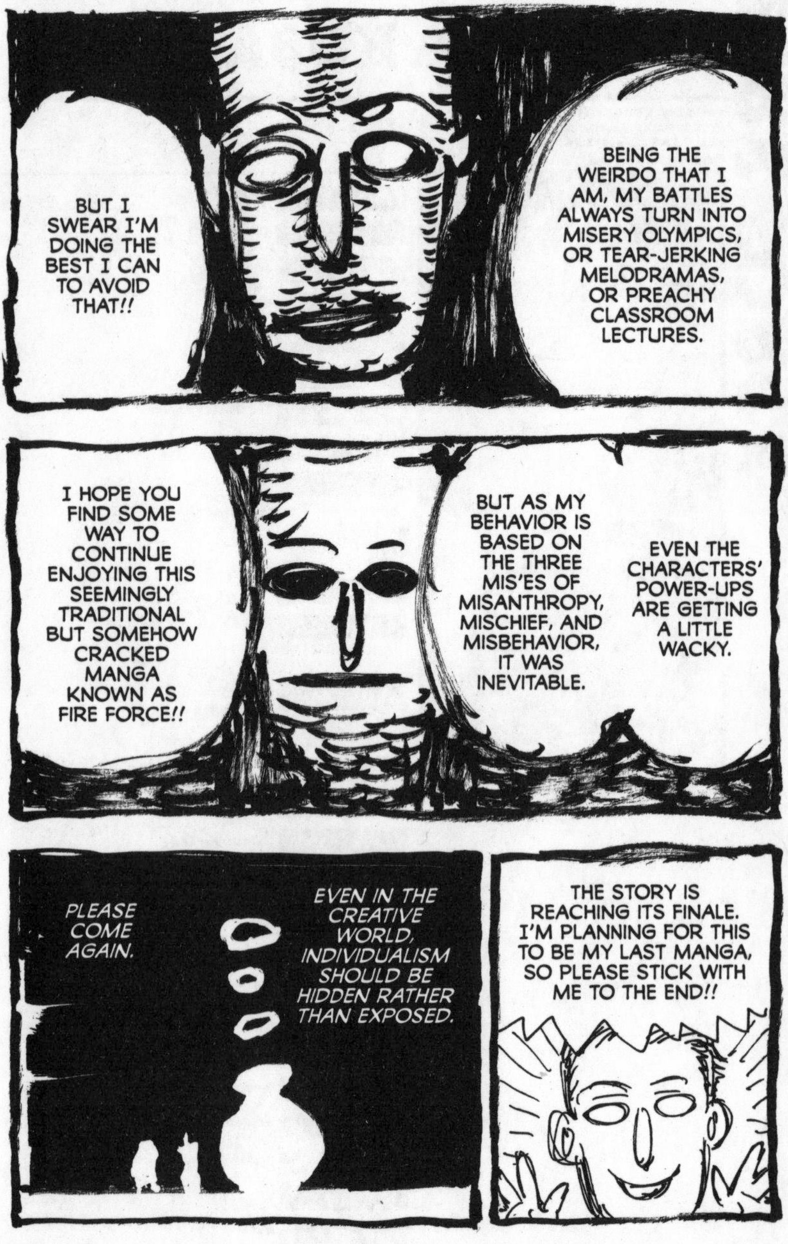
BEING THE WEIRDO THAT I AM, MY BATTLES ALWAYS TURN INTO MISERY OLYMPICS, OR TEAR-JERKING MELODRAMAS, OR PREACHY CLASSROOM LECTURES.
BUT I SWEAR I'M DOING THE BEST I CAN TO AVOID THAT!!
EVEN THE CHARACTERS' POWER-UPS ARE GETTING A LITTLE WACKY.
BUT AS MY BEHAVIOR IS BASED ON THE THREE MIS'ES OF MISANTHROPY, MISCHIEF, AND MISBEHAVIOR, IT WAS INEVITABLE.
I HOPE YOU FIND SOME WAY TO CONTINUE ENJOYING THIS SEEMINGLY TRADITIONAL BUT SOMEHOW CRACKED MANGA KNOWN AS FIRE FORCE!!
THE STORY IS REACHING ITS FINALE. I'M PLANNING FOR THIS TO BE MY LAST MANGA, SO PLEASE STICK WITH ME TO THE END!!
EVEN IN THE CREATIVE WORLD, INDIVIDUALISM SHOULD BE HIDDEN RATHER THAN EXPOSED.
PLEASE COME AGAIN.

FIRE FORCE

SHINRA KUSAKABE

AFFILIATION: SPECIAL FIRE FORCE COMPANY 8
RANK: SECOND CLASS OFFICER
ABILITY: THIRD GENERATION PYROKINETIC
Emits fire from his feet

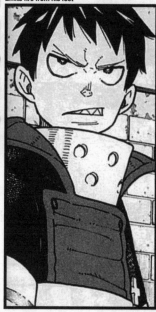

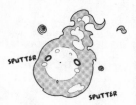

SPUTTER

SPUTTER

Height	173cm [5'8"]
Weight	67kg [148lbs.]
Age	17 years
Birthday	October 29
Sign	Scorpio
Bloodtype	AB
Nickname	The Devil's Footprints
Self-Proclaimed	Hero
Favorite Foods	Ramen Hamburgers Fried Chicken
Least Favorite Food	None
Favorite Music	Anything fast and awesome
Favorite Animal	Leopard Anything fast
Favorite Color	Red
Favorite Type of Girl	Pretty ones
Who He Respects	Commander Ōbi His mother
Who He Has Trouble Around	Pretty girls Arthur
Who He's Afraid Of	The Lieutenant
Hobbies	Soccer Futsal
Daily Routine	Breakdancing
Dream	To become a hero
Shoe Size	27cm [10]
Eyesight	2.0 [20/10]
Favorite Subject	Math
Least Favorite Subject	Language Arts

Translation Notes:

Wearing the *happi* backwards, page 10

The *happi* is the style of coat that Benimaru wears as part of his *hikeshi* firefighting uniform. In general, traditional Japanese clothing is worn with the left side (the wearer's left side) of the coat on top. It is considered bad luck to wear the right side on top, because that is how bodies are dressed for funerals. As such, wearing a *happi* backwards (with the right side on top) is a sign that you don't know how to properly wear traditional clothing and therefore could not possibly be a protonationalist like Benimaru, or anyone else from Asakusa.

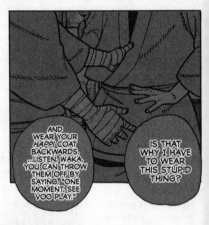

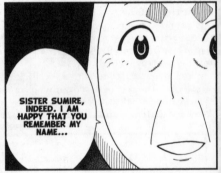

IS THAT WHY I HAVE TO WEAR THIS STUPID THING?
AND WEAR YOUR HAPPI COAT BACKWARDS. ...LISTEN, WAKA. YOU CAN THROW THEM OFF BY SAYING, "ONE MOMENT, SEE VOO PLAY."

Sister Sumire, page 85

Until now, when Sister Sumire was mentioned, her name was spelled with *katakana,* a set of characters based purely on sound, and it was easy to assume that she was named after the *sumire* flower—the violet. Now she introduces herself with *kanji* characters that give additional meaning to the sounds. *Sumi* means "charcoal," and *re* means "servant" or "slave."

SISTER SUMIRE, INDEED. I AM HAPPY THAT YOU REMEMBER MY NAME...

Stone to press pickles, page 134

To make Japanese pickles the old-fashioned way, vegetables of the desired variety are placed in a container with something heavy on top. This is to apply downward pressure and squeeze the moisture out of the vegetables.

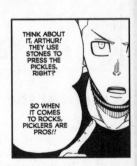

THINK ABOUT IT, ARTHUR! THEY USE STONES TO PRESS THE PICKLES, RIGHT?
SO WHEN IT COMES TO ROCKS, PICKLERS ARE PROS!!

I.L. Pickle-ya, page 135

Hopefully the proto-nationalist people of Asakusa will forgive the translators for localizing the name of this pickle shop for the sake of our English-speaking readers. in the old language, it is *Tsukemono Tsuketaro. Tsukemono* means "pickles," indicating what can be purchased at this establishment, and *tsuketaro* is a play on words. First, it's a given name for someone who pickles things—*tsuke* coming from the verb for "to pickle," and *taro* being a suffix for a male given name. it can also be a contraction of *tsukete-yaro,* which, depending on the context, can mean, "I'll pickle those for ya," or, "I'll pickle ***you.***"

The Destroyer of Asakusa vs. the Evangelist's Destroyers, page 138

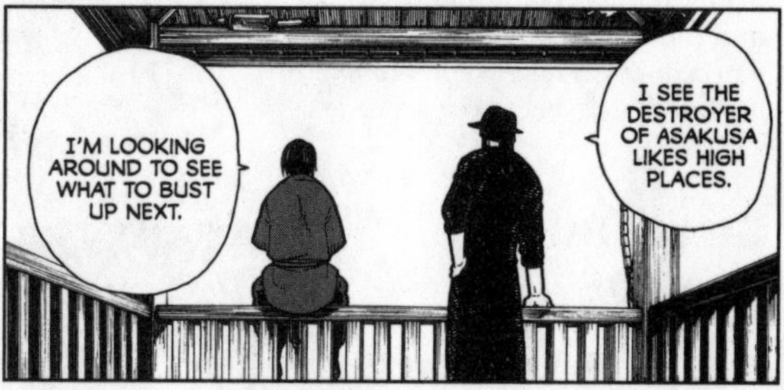
I SEE THE DESTROYER OF ASAKUSA LIKES HIGH PLACES.
I'M LOOKING AROUND TO SEE WHAT TO BUST UP NEXT.

Now that Captain Shinmon's nickname has returned, the translators feel it time to explain the difference between these two different types of destroyers. Benimaru is the *hakai-ō,* which literally means "destroyer king" or "king of destruction," with a specific connotation of breaking things. In other words, he's the sort of destroyer who goes around busting up people and things. The Evangelist's Destroyers are *hofuribito,* meaning literally "person(s) who destroy," with a connotation of defeat, death, and obliteration.

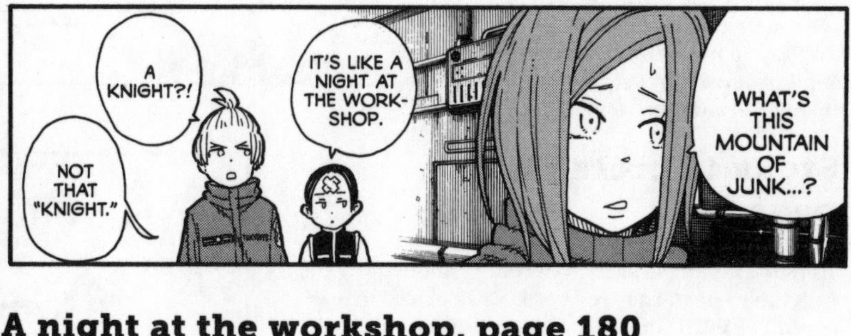
WHAT'S THIS MOUNTAIN OF JUNK...?
IT'S LIKE A NIGHT AT THE WORK-SHOP.
A KNIGHT?!
NOT THAT "KNIGHT."

A night at the workshop, page 180

In the original Japanese, Yū says he is feeling a sense of déjà vu, as if he's back at the workshop. The word for this sensation is *kishikan,* literally meaning "sense of having already seen." *Kishi* is also the Japanese word for "knight," so the whole term could mean "knight sense," or "feeling of knightliness."

FIRE FORCE

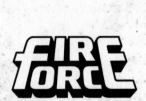

A Kodansha Comics Trade Paperback Original
Fire Force 23 copyright © 2020 Atsushi Ohkubo
English translation copyright © 2021 Atsushi Ohkubo

Published in the United States by Kodansha Comics, an imprint of
Kodansha USA Publishing, LLC, New York.

Publication rights for this English edition arranged through
Kodansha Ltd., Tokyo.

First published in Japan in 2020 by Kodansha Ltd., Tokyo.

ISBN 978-1-64651-209-6

Printed in the United States of America.

www.kodanshacomics.com

9 8 7 6 5 4 3 2 1
Translation: Alethea Nibley & Athena Nibley
Lettering: AndWorld Design
Editing: Ryan Holmberg
Kodansha Comics edition cover design by Phil Balsman

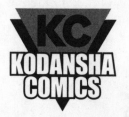

Publisher: Kiichiro Sugawara

Director of publishing services: Ben Applegate
Associate director of operations: Stephen Pakula
Publishing services associated managing editor: Madison Salters
Assistant production manager: Emi Lotto, Angela Zurlo